Key Concepts in Psychotherapy

Key Concepts in Psychotherapy

by ERWIN SINGER

With a Foreword by Edward S. Tauber

Second Edition

BASIC BOOKS, Inc., Publishers
New York

First Edition published by Random House in 1965
© 1965 by Random House, Inc.
© 1970 by Basic Books, Inc.
Library of Congress Catalog Card Number: 78–110104
ISBN: 0–465–03708–9 cloth
ISBN: 0–465–03709–7 paper
Printed in the United States of America
79 80   15 14 13 12 11 10 9

Grateful acknowledgment is made to the following for permission to quote material from the works listed:

Doubleday & Company, Inc. From Goethe's FAUST, translated by Walter Kaufmann. Copyright © 1961 by Walter Kaufmann.

Harvard University Press. From Susanne Langer, PHILOSOPHY IN A NEW KEY. Copyright, 1942, 1951, 1957 by the President and Fellows of Harvard College.

The Hogarth Press Ltd. From Sigmund Freud, THE STANDARD EDITION OF THE COMPLETE PSYCHOLOGICAL WORKS OF SIGMUND FREUD, revised and edited by James Strachey. And to Basic Books, Inc., publishers of THE COLLECTED PAPERS OF SIGMUND FREUD.

Houghton Mifflin Company. From C. R. Rogers, CLIENT-CENTERED THERAPY (1951), and COUNSELING AND PSYCHOTHERAPY (1942).

International Universities Press. From S. Tarachow, AN INTRODUCTION TO PSYCHOTHERAPY (1963).

Macmillan & Co., New York, and Routledge & Kegan Paul Ltd., London. From M. Buber, BETWEEN MAN AND MAN (1954).

W. W. Norton & Company, Inc. From Otto Fenichel, M.D., THE PSYCHOANALYTIC THEORY OF NEUROSIS. Copyright, 1945, by W. W. Norton and Company. From Harry Stack Sullivan, M.D., THE INTERPERSONAL THEORY OF PSYCHIATRY. Copyright, 1953, by The William Alanson White Psychiatric Foundation. And from THE PSYCHIATRIC INTERVIEW. Copyright, 1954, by The William Alanson White Psychiatric Foundation.

The Public Trustee and The Society of Authors, London. From Bernard Shaw, MAJOR BARBARA and SAINT JOAN.

The Ronald Press. From Franz Alexander and Thomas Morton French, PSYCHOANALYTIC THERAPY. Copyright, 1946, The Ronald Press Company.

The University of Chicago Press. From Frieda Fromm-Reichmann, PRINCIPLES OF INTENSIVE PSYCHOTHERAPY. Copyright © 1950, by The University of Chicago.

FOR HELENE

FOREWORD

To PRESENT AN INTRODUCTION TO PSYCHOTHERAPY IS NO EASY task. The contents of this type of book are addressed to students of psychology and psychiatry and cognate fields, who have had many years of background preparation behind them. They are electing a career in a field which is still young but has undergone significant development in roughly three quarters of a century, since it was set into motion by the giant contributions of Sigmund Freud. Freud tempered man's curious aversion to penetrating his inner life. Concern with mental health is now no longer suspect; in fact, the motivation to resolve psychological conflicts and to accept psychotherapy has become a widespread attitude in our present culture. Mental health programs are completely respectable and figure seriously in overall community planning in many parts of the Western world.

But what about the preparation of those who are going to assume the responsibility for the treatment of psychological and emotional problems? Instruction in the art and science of psychotherapy calls for constant reappraisal of its content and format. Historically its design has been mainly tutorial, partly because the practice of psychotherapy itself has been a person-to-person transaction. The patient has taught the psychotherapist much of what he has had to learn. Out of this integration the therapist has additionally learned to bring his own resources into play so that he could gradually come to be of increasing use to the patient's growth. The experienced therapist is now in a position to guide the student of psychotherapy more effectively in the inquiry into his patient's problems and can define more clearly what can improve the probability of a successful outcome of therapy.

Specifically, how has Dr. Singer set about accomplishing that mission? In my opinion, he has located a mode of presentation which is at once sensible and inspired, simply because it taps what is alive in all of us. He rejects oversimplification, talking down to the reader, or pontification. His approach brings to my mind the new math—the modern pedagogical paradigm for mathematical instruction. In the search for what might be usefully taught to the student embarking on the study of mathematics, our present generation has witnessed a startling discovery—namely, that instead of memorizing blindly arithmetic rules, the child could assimilate basic principles of the foundations of mathematics. As a consequence, the beginner could grasp what the subject was about: the parts began to fall into place; these pragmatic procedures were no longer tedious, meaningless rituals; an exciting landscape began to emerge. Courage to search further, to continue the adventure, has displaced the earlier more usual experience of drudgery, tacit bewilderment, and inadequacy feelings. The child's readiness to unfold and respond to this challenge is to the credit of those inspired and daring enough to test out the possibilities.

Just as are those teaching the new math, Dr. Singer, throughout his presentation, is always mindful of the basic qualities inhering in the human situation for valid problem solving. In psychotherapy a cardinal postulate is to be in touch with the roots of feeling, thought, and experience. Merely to teach the programming of procedures, although important, will lead nowhere since the technical understanding of the transaction is insufficient and will perpetuate illusory interchange. So much of the pathway of therapy consists in meeting up with the unexpected that flexibility in therapist and patient alike, fostering open-endedness, is crucial. The flexibility in therapy as in mathematics resides in or rests on grasping the fundamental assumptions. Perhaps the analogy between the teaching of mathematics and psychotherapy is strained because most of us are not concerned with developing into professional mathematicians; however, the best preparation for a potential future, whatever it be, is still a sound principle. In the case of the psychotherapist, his field is his profession and his patient will not show significant growth unless the therapist conveys the need for the patient's "professional" involvement in his own life.

I believe that somewhere in us there is a profound yearning to come close to the core of ourselves, to what is around us, to how we think, to our inner reflections. We begin with a ready responsiveness to what is authentic even if this characteristic or quality is not already in our own awareness. There is a sensed excitement or pleasure usually not accessible to verbalization when substantive ideas enter the immediacy of our experience.

I believe that Dr. Singer has captured in many ways what these core issues are for us who want to grasp the human situation. The essence of what troubles the therapist about himself, his patient, and the enterprise is thoughtfully and authentically presented. The student is not shielded from the minute he opens his mind to the study of psychotherapy. The central issues—indeed, the key concepts—are presented to encourage the student's urge to discovery. Dr. Singer cuts through controversial issues: he is not preoccupied with taking sides, expediency, or premature assurances of therapeutic outcome. Yet the spirit of the book is not an eclectic compilation of themes: Dr. Singer has his point of view, one which rests on deep respect for living itself as an art that requires constant reflection, engagement, and activation from within. The author has dexterously avoided the hazards associated with any profound inquiry into the human situation. Addressing oneself in depth to any topic draws one precariously to the brink of exhortation, moralizing, and propagandizing, but I believe the author has successfully transcended all these sins because he has a faith in man's drive to health.

—EDWARD S. TAUBER, M.D.
WILLIAM ALANSON WHITE INSTITUTE

New York City
March, 1965

PREFACE TO THE SECOND EDITION

THE REISSUE OF THIS SOMEWHAT EXPANDED EDITION OF MY BOOK first published about five years ago fills me with a sense of profound satisfaction. Of course my vanity is gratified—and what author even if he happens to be a psychoanalyst can deny that vanity is one of his human failings. But of more consequence is my joy occasioned by the evidence that this book dealing with issues and concepts vigorously attacked from several quarters was received with enough interest to warrant a second edition. Hopefully, my book has and now will continue to help keep alive concern with a discipline whose demise has been predicted for quite a while by many.

The main thrust of attack on intensive psychoanalytically (in the broadest sense of the term) oriented psychotherapy comes from two distinct groups of social scientists and mental health practitioners, though, clearly, the members of each of these groupings are not monolithically in agreement with each other.

The first large grouping sharply critical of psychoanalytic psychotherapy is made up of people advocating various types of community mental health programs. They are individuals who, motivated by sincere and urgent concern about the psychological well-being of large segments of American society, advocate new approaches to the solution of emotional difficulties as they manifest themselves in certain strata of our population. These critics believe that the intrapsychic and interpersonal conflicts traditionally examined and explored by psychotherapists are manifestations of disturbances in white middle- and upper-class society. Therefore, they maintain, traditional psychotherapeutic avenues are irrelevant for millions of impoverished whites and blacks whose social and cultural backgrounds vary significantly from those of middle-class America; the issues that they must resolve in their lives are, allegedly, different. In effect, these critics advocate that psychologists and psychiatrists concentrate on helping great numbers of people solve their social, educational, and economic reality problems. While some would let it go at that, leading to Professor Shatan's fear that community mental health programs may become the stretcher bearers of a bankrupt society, others go further and insist that this help can aid people in developing pride, resolution, and a readiness for political activism, eventuating in large-scale political and social reorganization.

This orientation, sparked by the ever more apparent crisis of the sixties, has led a good many theorists and practitioners to the advocacy and exercise of a professional socio-psychological activism whose results cannot yet be foretold, though there is some evidence that, despite temporary chaos, good will come from it. But this recognition also leads to the development of important questions: Are psychologists and psychiatrists the people best equipped to work in these areas, and, if they are not, should their training be reorganized so as to equip them for such activities? Social workers, especially those dealing with community organization work, political scientists, sociologists, and a host of other professionals have long been active in this area. Would not the demands of the critics of contemporary psychologists and psychiatrists require that these people change their professions? Perhaps they should, perhaps these professions are obsolete—but it also seems to many that there is room for both community activism and psychotherapeutic work. These functions may be carried out by different individuals or they may represent distinctly separate activities performed at different times by the same person. That is to say, a psychotherapist is not at all times a therapist and may function at times as a political activist, but he must not be a political activist when he listens to his patient and tries to help him understand himself even though this self-understanding may lead to the patient's increased social and political activity.

Hand in hand with these demands for socio-psychological activism one notices an air of contempt for the "old line" psychologists and psychiatrists who "just don't know where it is." This contempt comes mainly from younger members of the mental health professions and is so intense that it can lead to remarks like the comments made by a speaker at a recent conference of psychologists in which he suggested that present-day middle-aged psychotherapists cannot be trusted because, after all, most of them started their professional work during World War II, usually while in military service themselves, and at that time their basic mission was returning psychiatric casualties to action, to do more killing and to be killed. Similarly, the popular term "shrink" denotes a sense on the part of those who use this epithet that psychotherapists reduce the horizons of awareness and vision of those who consult them instead of helping them expand their minds, a feat presumably more effectively achieved by a plethora of "mind-expanding" drugs.

While there can be little doubt that many therapists have grown complacent, successful, and fat and identify themselves consciously or unconsciously with a moribund establishment, it is of course absurd—and most advocates of a more socially activist psychotherapy know this—to suggest that the majority of psychotherapists take a conservative and socially disinterested stance. Most practitioners of psychotherapy, even before Freud but certainly from Freud on, have been and still are fundamentally social critics even though their criticism of the hypocrisies and banalities of their times may not go far and deep enough. Even Freud, whose conservatism is so well known and led him to positions severely challenged in this book, was a social critic attacking a blind culture which refused to recognize biological truths. Jung, with all his short-comings, was most articulate in exposing the vulgarities and inanities of his place and time. And so did Adler, the Viennese socialist; so did Horney, Sullivan, and Rogers, and above all Fromm, the politically left pacifist and activist.

Why then all the uproar? Its force derives from several sources. First of all, it is the result of well-motivated impa-tience. Psychotherapy is a slow process, if by psychotherapy one means a procedure designed to promote growth into awareness and toward courage, wisdom, and strength, and the resolve to act upon these qualities. The scars of their past rob human beings of these essential qualities of maturity and are not easily eradicated—and who can blame people for wanting to see the reappearance of these qualities faster than most therapists are able to effect? And yet it is dangerous to let impatience, no matter how nobly motivated, destroy one's realization that personal growth is a solitary and painful and therefore slow process. It is dangerous to forget that speed-up procedures endanger the very heart of *personal* change, *in-dividually* nurtured and *privately* integrated into the fabric of one's being during agonizing hours of pain. The enormous danger of speed-up procedures is the horrifying possibility that personal growth will be more apparent than real, resting a good deal on suggestion effects, identification processes (the core of emotional pathology), and unexamined forces making one act in blindness—even when the acts performed may seem socially desirable. To illustrate: to quickly bring about the college drop-out's return to the university may do more harm than good if in the course of his return the development of personal identity is not furthered. Similarly, to help a de-pressed and hopeless resident of the black ghetto to become an active community organizer *may* merely indicate that he has found a diversion—valuable as it may be—instead of himself. The simple point is that the appearance of operational criteria associated with growth, while necessary (see Chapter 3), is not sufficient evidence that such personal growth has taken place.

Another and related factor making for discontent with

traditional psychotherapy is the undeniable fact that demands for psychological help far outdistance the manpower for this service. It was group therapy's original and lofty purpose to make psychological aid available to more people at fees they could afford *and* to facilitate emotional growth into awareness through group processes. The possibility of examining multiple transferences and the likelihood that members of a psychotherapy group would act as co-therapists for each other sparked the hope for more rapid progress. It was also hoped that the therapeutic process would be furthered and quickened by the group situation which would permit the patient to observe his behavior and reactions in a social—that is, group —setting. But the group therapy process also reduces the quiet solitude necessary for transformation and reintegration, and symptomatic results appearing relatively fast may merely indicate that the patient has reformed quickly. (That in many instances the outcome of individual psychoanalytic therapy is also reformation instead of transformation does not lessen the shortcomings of other procedures. It only highlights the fallibility of all human beings, including therapists who practice individual psychoanalytic therapy.) Therefore, as Professor Ben-Avi has shown so cogently, another force demanding "newer" procedures, such as group therapy, family therapy, and eventually community therapy, paradoxically must be found in the deeply engrained conservative ethos which equates more with better and fast with more desirable.

In addition it should be recognized that psychotherapeutic practices and pretensions have led many thoughtful people to disdain for psychotherapy in general. Obviously, the costs associated with it are staggering. This demands that therapists and others search for effective public underwriting of the costs involved instead of looking frantically for short cuts or more economical procedures—provided, of course, that the service psychotherapy renders is genuine, rather than illusory. If it is of no value, then we should not look for short cuts but heave it overboard altogether; if it is of value, we must find ways of making the service more widely available by methods that do not involve dilution by short cuts.

Unfortunately, there is a valid question concerning the genuine usefulness of psychotherapy. This question derives from the deplorably widespread though fallacious belief encountered even among therapists that a high educational level and the verbal facility associated with educational attainments are prerequisites for successful treatment. Since psychotherapy is essentially, though certainly not exclusively, a verbal process, insights and awareness are communicated verbally. But the intellectual understanding of one's behavior and the verbal expression of this intellectual understanding are not synonymous with genuine affective experience, authentic insight, and emotional growth (see Chapter 13). All too often this apparent insight is mistakenly accepted as the genuine article by the patient, who wants to feel that he has benefited and in his resistance tries to avoid true experience, and by the therapist, who wants to think that he has been of use while himself eager to avoid anxiety-arousing contacts with his client's experience. Such success-pretending shadow boxing is impossible with the less educated and the less verbally facile—hence the belief that they are not amenable to psychotherapy, when the truth is that they are not inclined to go along with the unfortunate pretenses of some therapists. The implications of the statement that the poor and the uneducated neither desire nor are capable of benefiting from psychotherapy merely indicate the pretentiousness of he who makes the statement and his preference for the detachment of explanation over sharing of experience during therapeutic sessions. It appears, at least to this observer, that it is the height of pretentiousness to assume that members of "lower classes" are not interested in coming close to the nature of their experience or that the capacity to develop emotional insight is dependent on economic or educational status.

This slowly growing recognition that verbal formulations do not necessarily denote or in any way facilitate genuine experience has given rise to the development of therapeutic procedures practiced in encounter groups or in similar situations. While there can be little doubt that physical contact between people *can* facilitate awareness of experience and the insight implied in such awareness—this observation actually represents one of the more durable and important contributions of Reich and his followers—the cultism and the mystique which often surround encounter groups tend to mitigate their genuine effectiveness. Furthermore, the often frenzied emotional pitch and turbulence associated with such group experiences inevitably reduce the quietude necessary for meaningful integration of insight and the contemplative relaxation which full grasp of experience demands.

In a similar vein, the increasingly popular practice of marathon therapy—also motivated by the belief that intensification of therapeutic exposure to the point of exhausion will reduce resistance and therefore will lead to change more quickly—has drawbacks comparable to those discussed earlier: it avoids the sad recognition that change itself is painful and therefore slow, especially when one is convinced that one's way of life represents the only road to survival; it makes painstaking exploration and grasp of experiential detail difficult if not impossible altogether; and above all in its very conception it tends to disregard the natural pace of individual emotional growth.

All the procedures discussed so far represent innovative efforts advocated by people primarily concerned with the welfare of individuals who, they believe, have suffered too long either from self-imposed lack of awareness or from oppressive social forces. But another group of presumably innovative procedures is advocated by people primarily concerned with the perpetuation of existing social norms and conventions and the individual's adjustment to them. Behavior therapists, behavior modifiers, and social engineers, as they sometimes call themselves, make up the second large group of detractors of intensive analytically oriented psychotherapy. Their motto is: All that matters are results and results are measured in terms of adjustment to—read "fitting in with"—social demands. There is nothing innovative about this position or, as shall be seen, the procedures these people employ.

Indeed, they are as old as authoritarianism and oppression, and employing the appellation "shrink" with them seems truly justified.

Under the cover of scientific objectivity, i.e., guided by the maxims of logical positivism and especially by its particular definition of "meaning," behavior therapists by and large seem unconcerned with the inner life of their clients and concentrate almost exclusively upon the patient's public behavior. As long as the individual acts in accordance with presumably agreed upon standards, he is deemed emotionally well; deviation from these norms is considered pathological. In addition, behavior therapists or modifiers seem convinced that the refinements of the S-R model of learning, as they were developed by a chain of American behaviorists, culminating in Professor B. F. Skinner's formulations, are adequate for understanding the development and the conditions necessary for bringing about changed behavior. Employing behaviorism's highly mechanistic model of man, i.e., a model in which man appears rather passively and helplessly determined by situations external to him and their effects upon his basic and essentially visceral needs, behavior therapists have developed an array of gadgets and conditioning (and deconditioning) procedures in which these gadgets are employed. They range from relatively simple and innocuous noise makers and similar startle-producing instruments to complex apparatuses and procedures in which electric shocks are administered in association with the exposure of pictures presumably pleasurable to the patient. In the latter instance the obvious hope is that the displeasure associated with the shock will carry over to a growing displeasure with the situations depicted, even though they were originally pleasurable to the patient.

Let it be admitted that this work is likely to bring about "results" more frequently and faster than traditional psychotherapy if one accepts the behavior therapist's definition of results. Man is all too prone to search for external guidelines and conditioners because freedom of choice and action, and the awareness of such freedom and the responsibility associated with this awareness, are frequently unbearable. But this very search for external motivators and this very abandoning of freedom are the essential expressions of psychopathology itself. (See Chapters 1–3.) "Escape from freedom," as Fromm among others has shown so well, is giving up one's humanness, represents self-oblivion, leads to willing submission to totalitarian domination, and is therefore pathological, even when the immediate behavioral results of this escape from freedom seem desirable. After all, as Professor Davis has pointed out, Mussolini did make the trains run on time—no mean and indeed a desirable feat—but as he rightfully suggests the cure was and all too frequently still is worse than the disease. Professor Skinner's taking pride in the fact that difficult psychiatric patients could be induced to go to the hospital dining room in orderly fashion subsequent to the employment of conditioning methods when they had refused to do so earlier seems justified only if one assumes that ends justify the means employed. If the disturbing and certainly at least at times self-destructive acts of patients represent unfortunate and highly idiosyncratic methods of communication (see Chapter 4), then the reduction of symptomatology without the patient and the therapist grasping its message merely represents a suppression of potentially useful, though socially undesirable, channels of communication. Viewed from this vantage point, behavior therapy is fundamentally fascistic brainwashing, scientifically presented and obscured enough to make it socially palatable. It is a procedure which induces the person by rewards and punishments to give up his admittedly misguided and ineffectual search for identity and to abandon for the sake of acceptability all hope for individuality. It tries to reduce him to the level of Esau. It is a procedure which disregards man's heart as long as "law and order" are maintained. In Germany they used to say: *Ordnung muss sein.*

These harsh comments are not designed to accuse behavior therapists of being heartless totalitarian beasts—far from it, most of them seem very concerned people. These comments are merely designed to show that our impatience and our "scientific" traditionalism frequently lead us to actions whose implications were not examined and are potentially detrimental to man.

Clearly, my position is that of an author and practitioner committed to the belief that only genuine self-understanding will make for meaningful change; indeed, that the move from self-oblivion to self-understanding in itself represents the most meaningful change that can occur. This does not mean, as some authors have suggested, that all who share this conviction are merchants of friendship and love. It merely means that we do not care to play God by conditioning or modifying people's behavior.

Yes, it seems to me that a good deal of psychotherapy and its underlying conceptions deserve searching and critical examination—but such an examination first of all demands knowledge of that which is to be examined critically. It was my original aim in writing this book to expand familiarity with the underlying notions, beliefs, assumptions, and constructs of modern psychotherapy. I hope that the new edition of this book will continue to expand knowledge about psychotherapy's propositions, making meaningful dialogues more readily possible.

ERWIN SINGER

Provincetown
July, 1969

PREFACE TO THE FIRST EDITION

THIS BOOK WAS WRITTEN IN THE HOPE THAT IT WILL REDUCE some of the confusion and ambiguities which engulf the beginning student of human behavior as he approaches the literature of psychotherapy. In his reading he encounters a variety of authors who use the same or similar terminology to denote different phenomena and processes. Not only are their constructs different; so are their underlying frames of reference, assumptions, and philosophical orientations. Their conflicting vantage points inevitably lead to differing interpretations of observable clinical manifestations—even though the descriptive terms used are the same. Mindful of the confusion that can result if the same term is used for different constructs, theory-builders have occasionally coined new terms. Unfortunately, the properties of these newly developed terms are all too often not spelled out succinctly and so some students are left with the incorrect impression: "Oh, I see, he simply means by this term what So-and-So meant by this or that word." Even some rather sophisticated and knowledgeable authors have interchangeably used terms derived from different systems and hence based on different assumptions. Thus the incorrect notion has arisen, for instance, that *transference* and *parataxis* "really mean the same thing—it's just a question of semantics";

that *insight* has the same meaning for Rogers as it does for Jung; or that *counter-transference* means to all authors the therapist's hostile attitudes toward his patient.

To some extent, then, this book can be thought of as a dictionary and an attempt to clarify the terminology of various authors. But this alone would have been a feeble excuse for writing a book. In addition, I set myself the task of showing how specific frames of reference logically lead to particular conceptual definitions and how a given vantage point underlying a theory of psychotherapy represents a series of assumptions concerning the nature of man. I have also tried to delineate the particular value systems implicit in a theory, whether clearly avowed or merely hinted at. Finally, I hoped to add a bit to the existing conceptual frameworks by suggesting certain redefinitions and reconceptualizations.

Many people have contributed to this book. The teachers who influenced my thinking most will become apparent, for this volume does present a point of view and makes no pretense at being fully nonpartisan. I am indebted to those teachers for the stimulation they have offered and the insights they have helped me gain. I owe a special debt of gratitude to my students who insisted that I clarify my own views and who challenged me mercilessly whenever I seemed to try to slide over some difficult issue. Above all, I am grateful to a number of human beings who permitted me to gain glimpses of their innermost states and allowed me to share their most private experiences.

Many colleagues have helped me by listening patiently, but I would be remiss were I not to mention specifically several friends who have encouraged me, read all or parts of the manuscript at various stages of completion, and offered valuable advice. Although final responsibility for the contents of this book must rest with me, I am pleased and proud to acknowledge helpful comments offered by Dr. Edward S. Tauber of New York University and the William Alanson White Institute, Drs. Avrum H. Ben-Avi and Herbert Turkel of New York University, Dr. Edgar Levenson of the William Alanson

White Institute, Drs. Herbert Nechin, Gladys Natchez, and Jerome Singer of The City University of New York, Dr. Manuel Zane and Mr. Jack Feder of New York City, and Dr. L. Joseph Stone of Vassar College. Miss Susan Shiller of the University of Denver was very helpful in preparing the typescript.

Without the help and encouragement offered by my wife and children this book could not have been written.

ERWIN SINGER

CONTENTS

Key Concepts in Psychotherapy

C H A P T E R   O N E

The Historical and Philosophical Roots of Psychotherapy

When James Bryant Conant contributed a booklet to the Harvard Case Histories in Experimental Science he remarked in the foreword:

> Science we shall define as a series of concepts or conceptual schemes arising out of experiments and observations. From the experimental work and careful observations of nature came the scientific facts that are tied together by the concepts and conceptual schemes of modern science. The rather sudden burst of interest in the new "experimental philosophy" in the seventeenth century is historically related to a new interest on the part of thoughtful men in *practical matters* ranging from medicine through mining to the ballistics of cannon balls. But while the problems were often suggested by the interest of the learned men in the *practical arts*, the development of science involved something more than the type of experimentation by which the practical arts had been developing for centuries. The method of reasoning employed in mathematics (for example, in geometry), commonly called deductive reasoning, had to be combined with the method of experimentation that came from the practical arts before science could progress

rapidly. The interaction of these two streams of human activity was largely responsible for the development of physics and chemistry; the focus of attention was shifted from an immediate task of improving a machine or a process to a curiosity about the phenomena in question. New ideas and concepts began to be as important as new inventions, and their interweaving began to produce conceptual fabrics whose various threads gained support from one another as well as from the direct results of experiment and observation [1950, p. 4; emphasis supplied—E.S.].

The new interest on the part of thoughtful men in practical matters to which Conant refers is, of course, the reflection of the spirit of Enlightenment, a trend of thought which swept through Europe sparked by the discoveries of Newton, a spirit which had as its mottoes freedom, reason, and humanitarianism and as its prophets such men as Voltaire, Rousseau, Hume, Pope, Mendelssohn, and Kant.

Thus modern physics and chemistry were fathered by the desire to improve man's lot and could not have come about had it not been that thoughtful men harbored values which caused them concern for the welfare of all. This interest in human betterment moved them to develop new methodologies and new conceptual schemes describing physical and chemical events.

Contemporary psychology had similar origins. Increasing attention to the betterment of man's well-being (however defined) gave rise to new modes of investigation and new conceptualizations of man's behavior, its mainsprings and dynamics. The history of psychoanalysis is a clear illustration of this general proposition. Freud's concern with what he deemed human difficulties, notably the hysterias, and his desire to ameliorate such conditions became the starting point for the development of a theory as well as a method of inquiry into human behavior. No matter how faulty some may think his formulations were, they have become respectable enough to enter significantly into present-day theories of learning and motivation.

Obviously, man's betterment is by no means of only recent concern, nor are his nature and the workings of his behavior. In this respect psychology and its application in psychotherapy parallel the history of all other disciplines. Physics, biology, chemistry, and the like are also ancient concerns, as are their applications. Yet the physical and biological laws which presumably describe the workings of the universe are constantly changing; in parallel fashion one observes constant change of the models of the nature of man which various theorists propose. But interest in man's betterment and resultant changes in conceptual schemes and subsequent methods of exploration cannot take place unless there exists a particular, essential psychological precondition in innovators. This psychological foundation is the inner freedom to be dissatisfied with the *status quo* and a self-image that includes a strong sense of independence. So long as man thought of himself as an essentially helpless creature dominated by forces outside his control, precise understanding of himself and his universe was precluded. Conversely, only when man experienced himself as capable of mastery and control could he address himself to the task of greater exploration and understanding; only then could he actually conceive of himself as capable of understanding and modifying what is. Heralded by the Age of Reason, the Era of Enlightenment took most significantly this psychological stance.

It is therefore by no means surprising that one notices during the period of Enlightenment not only profound changes in political thought and scientific approach to the physical universe but also increasing attention to psychological problems. Rousseau's *Discours sur l'origine de l'inégalité parmi les hommes* was published in 1754, his pedagogical novel *Émile* in 1762. Barely eighty years later Herbert Spencer wrote most eloquently on sociological and psychological questions, the nature of man and his inherent freedom. In the meantime Thomas Jefferson had addressed himself pointedly to similar questions:

> I am among those who think well of the human character generally. I consider man as formed for society, and endowed by nature with those dispositions which fit him for

society. I believe also, with Condorcet, as mentioned in your letter that his mind is perfectable to a degree of which we cannot as yet form any conception.

After surveying advances made in many areas of human endeavor and sketching the tasks ahead, Jefferson concludes:

> I join you therefore in branding as cowardly the idea that the human mind is incapable of further advances. This is precisely the doctrine which the present despots of the earth are inculcating . . . [Oppenheimer, 1953, pp. 108–9. From a letter of June 1799].

Or a different example from Herbert Spencer:

> . . . while in individual bodies the welfare of all other parts is rightly subservient to the welfare of the nervous system, whose pleasurable or painful activities make up the good and evil of life; in bodies politic the same thing does not hold good, or holds good to but a very slight extent. It is well that the lives of all parts of an animal should be merged in the life of the whole, because the whole has a corporate consciousness capable of happiness or misery. But it is not so with a society; since its living units do not and cannot lose individual consciousness; and since the community as an whole has no general or corporate consciousness distinct from its components. And this is an everlasting reason why the welfare of the citizens cannot rightly be sacrificed to some supposed benefit of the State; but why on the other hand, the State must be regarded as existing solely for the benefit of citizens [1860, pp. 98–99].

While Spencer referred to contemporary political and economic problems, his remarks point up clearly the philosophical mood of the era, a mood concerned with the advancement, improvement, and betterment of man's lot. Passive acceptance had given place to resolute determination. It is not that previous epochs had not witnessed remarkable statements concerning human potential and possibilities—the cultural history of man is ample testimony to the ability of some men to transcend their times—but that a remarkable upsurge of interest in man and his nature and position in the universe took place around the mid-eighteenth century. This upsurge makes it easily understandable that a systematic attempt to study man and his potential was in the offing. While it is always difficult to fix a precise date or event as the starting point of scientific epochs, one might place the onset of the systematic attempt to study and understand man in the year 1879 when Wundt opened the doors of the first psychological laboratory at the University of Leipzig.

Concern with man's betterment, however, immediately runs into certain philosophical difficulties. Scientific interests proceed relatively unhampered when the investigator is occupied with *description* of events, their mechanics and dynamics. But the *application* of descriptive findings has far less to do with the actual findings than with independent moral and ethical principles. The application, the art, that utilizes findings is determined by one's definition of what constitutes "betterment," of what one means by "salvation." The debate over such a definition rages among contemporary scientists, between men such as Pauling and Teller. While the debate on one level is concerned with such factual questions as the actual destructive potential of modern weapons, on another level it centers around the question of whether the use of such instruments would advance or retard human betterment. In the biological disciplines one meets a similar problem when research findings and therapeutics are juxtaposed. Judgment of the need for therapeutic intervention is relatively independent of scientific considerations and much more the outgrowth of moral propositions.

The point is best illustrated by using surgery as an example. Surgical procedures are multidetermined. The findings of anatomy, physiology, biochemistry, and similar disciplines make it possible to predict what is likely to happen to the organism if the surgeon were to engage in a particular intervention or if he were to abstain from it. The desirability of such outcomes, however, is independent of these scientific considerations. If one predicts that under conditions X a patient will die but that under conditions Y he will live, the decision to institute conditions Y is a function of the desire to see the patient live. What the physician has come to consider "good" or "evil"—his ethical position—will determine what he considers pathological. Thus the definition of health and illness in physical medicine is not a simple scientific proposition but the reflection of a particular orientation to life. In practicing his art, the physician insists implicitly that all that which prolongs life and contributes to the maximal exercise of the potentials of an organ is "good" (and he equates this "good" with "healthy"), all that detracts from life and maximal exercise of organ potential he considers "evil" (equated in his particular vocabulary with "unhealthy"). He says that a lung is healthy to the extent to which it is capable of discharging what may be considered the "inherent," "God-given," or "nature-given" function of the lung. He posits an "essence" which characterizes the lung and develops such an essence on the basis of what he believes the ultimate function of this organ to be: the perpetuation of life. He proceeds on the basis of this belief and ethical conviction. How deeply concerned with and aware of this problem of values the medical profession is can readily be seen when one examines the particular terms employed in the Hippocratic Oath, administered to all graduates of medical schools. It reads:

> You do solemnly swear, each man by whatever he holds most sacred . . . that into whatsoever house you shall enter, it shall be for the good of the sick to the utmost of your power, you holding yourself far aloof from wrong . . . that you will exercise your art solely for the cure of your patients and give no drugs, perform no operation, for a criminal purpose . . . [Bridgewater & Sherwood, 1950, p. 898].

Obviously the terms employed in the oath demand constant personal evaluation, based on a conception of what is "good" for the sick and what is "bad." The destructive applications of scientific knowledge by certain German physicians during the Hitler era was morally correct within the Nazi system of values; it was adjudged immoral within other systems of values. The term *criminal* as employed in the Hippocratic Oath also requires definition, such definitions being developed either individually or consensually in laws which reflect the values of a culture. Certain operations such as abortions are deemed "immoral" and hence "bad" in certain cultures and not "immoral" and hence not "bad" in others, at least under certain circumstances. So-called mercy killing, while collectively considered "bad" and hence illegal in our culture, is often tacitly and occasionally openly subscribed to by some physicians on the basis of the particular practitioner's definition of "good" and "evil."

Even more pointedly, the problem of moral values in medicine is posed in a document reputed to be the morning prayer of Maimonides (1931) before he visited his patients. In it Maimonides simply states that he considers it "good to guard the life and health of God's creations." He therefore implored God to help him to be moved by one guideline only—the desire to protect and prolong life.

The practitioner of physical medicine is obviously in a better position than his colleague in the area of emotional healing: he has some guidelines in the development of operational definitions of "health," "life," and "well-being" and consequently what is "good," for it is relatively easy for him to point to an "essence" for each organ or an essence for physical life itself—its protection and prolongation. As one turns to mental or psychological life one finds no such guidelines, no ready operational definitions concerning what constitutes psychological "life" and certainly not what constitutes "emotional health." Unavoidably this becomes almost exclusively a problem area of ethics—and what one deems ethically lofty another may deem reprehensible and wicked. The recognition of this fact has made for increasing dissatisfaction with the concept of "mental health" and has led to lively discussion of avenues towards a definition of emotional well-being. Smith addressed himself to the problem in an article entitled " 'Mental Health' Reconsidered: A Special Case of the Problem of Values in Psychology." He concluded:

> In the study of optimal human functioning, I have argued, behavioral and social scientists can put their special qualifications to work towards the clarification of

values among which people must choose and the causal relations that are relevant to value choice. From it we should not only increase our knowledge about ways and means of attaining the values we agree on; we should also bring to light factual relationships that have a bearing on our choice of what values we pursue individually and socially. To the extent that the behavioral sciences develop in this direction, they contribute to providing a badly needed bridge between what C. P. Snow has called "the two cultures" of the scientists and the humanistic intellectuals [1961, p. 306].

Smith's position is quite clear: he is willing to abandon the old notions of "mental health" or "mental illness," is willing to heave these vague concepts overboard in favor of the study of value systems, their genesis and consequences.

Smith's article appeared only a month after the journal in which it had appeared had published an equally important contribution by Littman (1961) under the somewhat misleading title "Psychology: The Socially Indifferent Science." Littman argued that it is imperative that psychologists "transcend" their observations of cultural and social differences and consider common underlying denominators; explore human universals, even though such human universals might reflect themselves in different ways in different cultures and different social groups. By implication he looks to psychology to provide a description of a "human essence," for only then could one be in a position to decide between the merits of competing values; only then could one decide that a particular value is superior to another value, one person "healthier" than another.

Perhaps the most vocal contributor to the rising insistence that psychotherapy must be concerned with the study of human values, morals and ethics—aside from Fromm (1941, 1947, 1950, 1955, 1956, 1959, 1962)—is Szasz (1957, 1958, 1960, 1961). A prolific writer, Szasz has made his point over and over again—there is no such thing as "mental illness." Thus he insists in "The Myth of Mental Illness" that:

My argument was limited to the proposition that mental illness is a myth, whose function it is to disguise and thus render more palatable the bitter pill of moral conflicts in human relations [1960, p. 118].

A year later, in "The Use of Naming and the Origin of the Myth of Mental Illness," he further developed his theme that what is usually referred to as "mental illness" cannot be called "disease," for one is dealing not with a biological phenomenon but with a specifically human phenomenon, the problem of values and value choices:

> In order to secure the scientific advances that have been made in our field, I believe we could do no better than to recast our knowledge in a psychosocial, linguistic, and ethical framework. This would entail a re-emphasis of the difference, rather than the similarities, between man the social being and man the mammal. It would also result in abandoning the persistent attempts to convert psychologists and sociologists to biologists (physicians) or physicists, and they themselves would no longer need to aspire to these roles [1961, p. 65].

An even more articulate position is pursued by Mowrer (1960) who, in his paper " 'Sin,' the Lesser of Two Evils," suggests that "mental symptoms" are the reflection of unacknowledged, unavowed, and unexpiated sin and resultant guilt. He insists that human beings are responsible organisms and that their problems have to do with avoidance of their inescapable human responsibility. In many ways Mowrer's thought runs quite parallel to the thesis developed by Buber (1957) in his William Alanson White Memorial Lectures, in which he took psychologists and psychiatrists to task for generally talking about the "feeling" of guilt and hardly ever about "guilt" as such.

In the following pages the discussion will return to what apparently seems to so many the crucial issue in psychological well-being, the problem of personal responsibility, but it should also be remembered that such a position has its critics. Ausubel, for example, in a paper titled "Personality Disorder *Is* Disease," while applauding the profession for abandoning its ethically neutral stance, maintains:

... the view that personality disorder is less a manifestation of illness than of sin, i.e., of culpable inadequacy in
meeting problems of ethical choice and responsibility,
and that victims of behavior disorder are therefore
morally accountable for their symptoms, is neither logically nor empirically tenable. Guilt is only a secondary
etiological factor in anxiety and depression, and in other
personality disorders is either not prominent or conspic-
uously absent [1961, p. 74].

Many clinical workers vigorously insist that guilt is a primary
factor in psychological manifestations, but Ausubel supports
his position:

It is quite true, as Szasz points out, that "human relations
are inherently fraught with difficulties," and that most
people manage to cope with such difficulties without becoming mentally ill. But conceding this fact hardly precludes the possibility that some individuals, either
because of genically or environmentally induced sus-
ceptibility to ordinary degrees of stress, respond to the
problems of living with behavior that is either seriously
distorted or sufficiently unadaptive to prevent normal interpersonal relations and vocational functioning [p. 72].

Ausubel finds the escape hatches from ultimate personal responsibility: genetics and environment. These are the time-
honored roads to rationalization, roads clearly quite at variance with the thinking of those who insist that human beings
can transcend their biological heritage and environmental setting and therefore suggest that what ails them is their attempt
to avoid responsibility, that what makes them well is helping
them assume such personal responsibility.

It might be asked why so much space has been devoted here
to the view that the focus of inquiry must be the values human
beings harbor and the choices they make. The reason lies in
the consequences of the proposition. If one accepts the position that the focus of inquiry must be the person's system of
values, one is confronted with two difficult yet relatively well-
defined issues: (1) what, if anything, may then be deemed the
"essential" nature of man; what constitutes the aggregate of

what Littman (1961) calls "human universals"; and (2) should this aggregate, once determined, be the guide in deciding whether a person's system of values is "healthy" or "ill"; should one consider a system of values in harmony with such "human universals" as reflecting well-being or is a system of values which rejects "human universals" reflective of the good life? These considerations lead to the conclusion that the definition of psychopathology depends upon the psychotherapist's conception of the nature of man (including as an ingredient his belief as to whether it is possible for human nature to accept or reject itself) and upon the psychotherapist's philosophical position in relation to this conception—whether he considers it "good" to accept or reject "human universals." A therapist then deems nonpathological all those aspects of behavior which are in accordance with his idealized image of man; all that is at variance with this image is pathological.

The history of personality theory and psychotherapy bears testimony to the truth of this assertion. Freud (1922a) maintained that psychopathology requiring treatment was a manifestation of inadequate sublimation, for his ideal image of man was man sublimating. He held definite ideas concerning the nature of the "human universals" and was convinced that certain aspects of these had to be "sublimated"; he was convinced that it was desirable as well as within man's capacities to engage in this process of self-rejection via sublimation. Jung (1956a) saw another image; therefore his definition of pathology and his therapeutic interests and aims were different. Adler (1939), Horney (1945), Rank (1945), Fromm (1947), Sullivan (1953), Rogers (1951) have all had their own visions of man and developed definitions of pathology and therapeutic goals accordingly.

These observations should make clear why one finds so many definitions of what is healthy and what is sick. When a psychotherapist believes that a particular person is in need of help he means that this person deviates significantly from what the therapist values as the essence of man; this deviation causes the individual harm because it interferes with the fulfillment of this essence. Similarly, an individual may experience feelings or engage in private behavior which he considers pathological because they seem to him at variance with his image of man. Here the basic meaning of psychological conflict becomes clear: the patient says "There is a gap between the image of man I cherish and the image I have of myself." This formulation has validity for almost any condition for which human beings seek the help of therapists. If a person seeks psychotherapeutic aid for his obsessions he says, in effect: "I believe such obsessions to be contrary to the nature of man." Or if he seeks to rid himself of the discomfort of anxiety or boredom, he implies that he believes that anxiety and boredom are *not* essential features of human existence. But it should be noted that a person can be aware of an experience as disturbing only to the extent to which he has previously—be it ever so long ago or ever so fleetingly— experienced freedom from such distress, only to the extent to which he is in a position to compare varying states of his own personal experience. (Chapter 11 contains further discussion of this issue.) Or if the court refers a juvenile for "antisocial" behavior, the court implies that in its opinion such behavior is not in accordance with the essence of man. Whatever the reasons for referral, images and values are implicit and often explicit. Of course, various personal definitions of pathology are developed not only in terms of acts committed but also of acts omitted and of essential qualities felt to be lacking. Often patients express the hope that psychotherapy will bring about "self-confidence," make them "more aggressive," "cultured," and so forth, whatever these terms may mean. In doing so they imply that their image of man includes these attributes, which they believe are now missing.

If the definition of emotional well-being and illness is a function of the value system maintained by the definer, it would follow that the breadth of his system and the ideal of man as it emerges from this system will determine how much or how little he deems pathological. The narrower the ideal, the more one will view as pathological; the wider one's vision of what constitutes humanness, the smaller the area of activities and behavior which can be defined as pathological. By width and narrowness is meant, of course, degree of specificity rather than anything else. To illustrate: if one views fulfillment of human destiny as reflected in the pursuit of only a limited range of occupations or interests, then all who are not so occupied or interested are seen as deviant, pathological. Conventionality and narrowness in their real sense (emphasis upon specifically approved behavior) result in a markedly constricted image of man leading to a significant extension of what is considered pathological and a consequent restriction of the realm of health. It is important to note that such rigid specification of what constitutes health may be found in all kinds of groups, pseudo-liberal as well as conservative. Many a bohemian denizen of Greenwich Village has notions concerning man's essence as definitely circumscribed and narrow as those of the Park Avenue matron. The color and the location of the circles they draw may differ, but the radii may be equally small.

The systematic pursuit of this line of thought leads to a definition of well-being relatively divorced from specific norms and deviations from norms, a conceptualization which centers on the extent to which a human being fulfills his individuality, regardless of cultural norms or group standards or another person's values. Thus well-being may be defined as self-actualization, in Goldstein's terms (1951), or the realization of a human being's unique and individual potentialities and the employment of his energies in accordance with his individuality. Such a point of view seemingly rejects the notion of an essential and universal striving, seemingly insists that there is no inherent universal human essence, but simply individual potentials which are or are not fulfilled. But if one examines this proposition carefully one will notice that it, too, postulates some universal essence, though perhaps in rather uncommon terms; such a point of view, like any other, is deeply anchored in a system of values.

Such a view maintains that man's essence is his capacity to define himself; he fulfills this to the extent to which he strives toward the development of a personal center. This position does not define man's central meaning in any fashion other than as his capacity to find his way of life. Once again one is confronted with a definition of well-being which is the reflection of values held by the definer, for this point of view clearly considers "good" all that is in accord with the unfolding of self-defining potential, with the development of one's own individual style and temperament. Conversely, this view considers "evil" all that blocks such a development. It is a point of view which, in effect, emphasizes the norm of the individual rather than the norm of the group, a point of view which insists that there is no right way save the way the individual finds for himself; that there is no right way and yet paradoxically only one right way—the road of individuality. All that is in harmony with this search is "health," all that hinders it is "illness." This is, of course the psychological foundation of the liberal democratic tradition, the legacy to psychotherapy of the Era of Enlightenment. And if one recalls for a moment the quotations from Jefferson and Spencer cited earlier it will become obvious how closely developments in political thought and certain developments in psychological thinking have paralleled each other.

This parallel becomes even more obvious when one examines the single proposition which underlies all forms of psychotherapy: the proposition that *man is capable of change and capable of bringing this change about himself,* provided he is aided in his search for such change. Were it not for this inherent optimism, this fundamental confidence in man's ultimate capacity to find his way, psychotherapy as a discipline could not exist, salvation could come about only through divine grace. Interestingly enough, this is a position existential thinkers have maintained for a long time. This rather old movement in thought—existentialism is by no means a recent development and has its roots in such diverse systems as that of the Stoics and the writings of St. Thomas, among others—finds its culmination in some of the writings of Heidegger (1953) and, somewhat later, Sartre (1957). Greatly influenced by Husserl's (1928) emphasis upon phenomenology, Heidegger developed conceptions which put man's "resolute decisions" in the center of all psychological considerations. From this emphasis upon such personal decision it was but a short step to Sartre's dictum "Existence precedes essence," his insistence that man has no essence in the usual sense of the word. A table, Sartre pointed out, has an "essence" which precedes its existence, for it is man-made, is conceived before it is developed, is constructed for a certain purpose by man and consequently is good or bad depending upon how well or how inadequately it fulfills the essence of "tableness" which one may define in advance. Not so, however, the argument runs, with man—he exists before he has an essence, unless we conceive of a God- or nature-given essence, for it is man himself who eventually defines himself.

Man is therefore a subject and not an object in the grammatical sense, for subjects define themselves through their own activities while objects are defined by the activities of subjects; subjects modify, objects are modified. The understanding of the psychological aspects of freedom and responsibility, writers within this framework insist, hinges on one's appreciation of the fact that this is the inescapable situation in which man finds himself. Value systems become the reflections of how men either shoulder or reject the burden of freedom to struggle toward self-definition.

The argument might be offered that norms based on certain predetermined absolutes and assumed essences cannot be abandoned in the search for a definition of the "good life." One might argue that ethical standards must exist for the mere survival of each person, that an ultimate insistence upon respect for the uniqueness and individuality of everyone may lead to chaos and to condoning activities which are destructive; that unless absolutes are posited before man exists no meaningful definition of emotional health (and consequently of therapeutic aims) is possible. To some extent, this is a position with which nobody can argue—not even Sartre. If one examines Sartre's proposition (1957) one notices that he does posit the essence referred to before, an essence which he presents in a way that might make one overlook the fact that it has been stated. Furthermore, the essence Sartre suggests does not precede existence but is considered by him as part and parcel of existence: the essential and inherent capacity and freedom to engage in agonizing acts of self-determination. The freedom to define oneself and the capacity to exercise this personal freedom become the essentially human. And if this capacity for self-definition be man's essence, all those aspects of man which interfere with his capacity to engage in such a self-definitional pursuit are viewed as pathological, all aspects which further this undertaking are his healthy facets.

If one posits such an essence, health becomes defined by the degree to which a person is free to perceive himself as an independently acting and reacting unit, experiences consciously the choices at his disposal, and makes choices with a conscious sense of responsibility for them. In a way, one winds up where Freud (1937) was when he insisted that the reduction of the unconscious, the heightening of awareness and consciousness were the hallmarks of health. Of course, Freud is far from Sartre or Goldstein or others in explaining why consciousness and awareness are so difficult to achieve or how consciousness is reduced or enhanced in individuals, but the conception that consciousness (and consequently responsibility) are at the center of a definition of health—that the freedom to be conscious, aware, and responsible defines the concept of health—is where most theoretical writers meet.

It appears that Breuer and Freud (1957) had such thoughts in mind when they described hysterias as reductions in freedom to move, for conversion symptoms clearly restrict the freedom to engage in specific physical activities. In addition the hysteric refuses to assume responsibility for this self-imposed reduction of freedom and ascribes it to physical ailments for which he feels he cannot possibly be held responsible. Similarly, the person moved by obsessions or compulsions seems to state his predicament concisely when he insists "I don't know what makes me do it, but I feel forced to, compelled." In the psychoses this reduction of freedom and responsibility is even more obvious and marked. If a man says that he is moved by radar waves he says that he is not free to move according to his own will; when he says that he must be constantly on the lookout for vicious impulses in people, he suggests that his behavior is inevitably governed by the schemes of others; when he insists that he is Napoleon, he states that he must act in accordance with the way Napoleon acted. When a person insists that somebody is transmitting lewd ideas into his head with some devilishly clever device he thereby refuses responsibility for the obvious fact that *he* has such ideas. When somebody reports that he experiences moments of depersonalization, moments in which he does not know that he exists, he speaks of moments during which he does not feel free to experience whatever he does experience. When one says that a person does not have much insight, one simply means that he is not free to know and to feel, that he has restricted his capacity for knowledge of his experiences; yet, simultaneously, one implies that such a capacity is his.

Once again we return to the fundamental and optimistic notion concerning human nature upon which the idea of psychotherapy is based: the image of man as capable of being (or at least becoming) free to know and able to make responsible choices on the basis of his knowledge. Only a system of values which places this freedom at the top of its hierarchy has any use for the idea of psychotherapy. Freedom as a psychological phenomenon will require discussion and elaboration in subsequent chapters, but it may be stated here that the ultimate aim of psychotherapy is the enhancement of this freedom to know and the reduction of irrational and self-imposed limitations of knowledge. It is therefore clear why those who do not conceive of man as potentially free, who do not value freedom, or indeed who deny its existence (such as those who insist that man's destiny is dominated by his blood or the soil from which he comes, or those misinterpreters of Marx who insist that man's behavior is simply a function of some material laws) have nothing but scorn and contempt for psychotherapy.

Aside from the obvious implications for economic and political thought pointed out by Fromm (1961), the notion that man is free has had a singular significance for changes in educational practices. So long as educators think of human beings as essentially dominated by some "conservative" instincts which render them incapable of choices, so long do we see educational practices which imply that the aims and goals of education are "indoctrination," resembling the slow and painful process of taming a wild animal or teaching a dog new tricks. Under such circumstances the learning process is essentially a passive process of conditioning in which information is provided by one individual and soaked up mechanically by another, various conditioning procedures being employed by the teacher.

The development of the theory of psychotherapy follows a similar road. If man is seen as requiring normative standards of conduct because he is really incapable of free choice then psychopathology is defined as a failure to acquire such standards, and the acquisition of such normative behavior becomes the psychotherapeutic goal—giving rise to psychotherapies which are essentially of the information-giving, advice-offering, or hypnotic-suggestion varieties. Underlying such conceptions of psychotherapy and parallel educational practices is, of course, a mechanistic-association theory of learning. It should be recalled in this connection that Freud and early American behaviorists were, despite all their quarrels, greatly impressed with each other, for both cherished the notion of learning by association. But the differences between Freud and essentially behavioristic learning theorists were greater than the convictions they shared. They differed markedly on motivation and determinism, Freud being basically interested in understanding the motivational bases for learning while his contemporaries in behaviorism (imbued with the spirit of logical positivism) were primarily interested in the mechanics of learning. Therefore Freud (1905b) became greatly concerned with the problem of instinctive, inherent directional properties in man, reflecting themselves in man's desires and the choices and compromises made in the ultimate pursuit of his instinctual goals. Freud was significantly influenced on this issue by Schopenhauer and fully admitted his admiration for him (1933).

As Freud searched for the motivational roots of behavior there developed, first in Germany and later in the United States, a school of thought which also placed motivation in the center of learning theory: classical Gestalt theory and later

Lewinian field theory. Starting with Wertheimer's (1959) writings through the contributions of Köhler (1925) and Koffka (1924) on to the later theories of Lewin (1936, 1942), one notices an insistence upon dynamic motivating factors in man's formal and social learning. Here one notes a significant historical parallel. Freud, while greatly impressed by Pavlov and his work, became increasingly concerned with motivation for he saw man as capable of making some (though in many ways limited) choices and studiously examined conditions which led to particular choices; the new field theorists, employing different terms such as "valence," also saw man as a choice-making organism and their interest therefore also focused upon inner determinants for man's decisions. Thus Freud and his contemporaries in Gestalt and field theory de-emphasized the concept of "conditioned habit" and in so doing expressed their belief in a certain degree of human autonomy, abandoning the model of man which envisioned him as essentially a driven creature of habits. To be sure, Freud came to a position in which he saw the motivational foundations for man's choices in the somewhat mechanical terms of the "pleasure principle" in terms of instinctual need systems which must be satisfied somehow, a position remarkably similar to that of more recent behaviorists such as Hull and his followers, who in considering motivation also see "need reduction" as its foundation (Hilgard, 1956). (The fact that these theorists define "need reduction" as an intervening variable, while Freud's analogous "pleasure principle" is clearly a hypothetical construct, does not detract from the essential similarity in position.) In any case one observes two simultaneous developments: (1) a shift of emphasis in learning theory (at least in some quarters) from "conditioned" man to man as a motivated being who is capable of choices in accordance with his motivations; and at the same time (2) the emergence of a psychotherapy which also envisions a motivated man free to choose, even though the number of choices available to him and their foundations are seen as rather limited.

With the gradual emergence of a vision of man endowed with at least limited freedom to choose, the emphasis in attempts to modify behavior shifts from conditioning, advice-giving, coaxing, coercing, and blatant suggestion-offering (hypnotic or otherwise) to reeducation—to helping man develop insight so that he may choose freely, appropriately, and meaningfully. On the importance of helping man to make choices freely and with insight all schools of what is loosely referred to as "dynamic psychotherapy" agree. Freud (1951) saw this freedom as somewhat limited: while man was dominated by his instincts he was free to know that they had to be curbed, to choose among various methods of curbing them, and then hopefully to sublimate them even if this sublimation entailed "discontent." Others, such as Fromm (1962), rejecting Freud's instinct theories, see man's potential freedom as less limited, and there is hardly a psychotherapist today who does not claim adherence to a position somewhere along this general continuum. At the same time, unwillingness to exercise this freedom, expressed in various symptoms and behavioral manifestations, is essentially what is seen as psychopathology: the refusal of the freedom to know, to experience, to act—to be. The acceptance of one's inherent freedom to be, with all that such acceptance entails, is emotional well-being; self-enslavement by refusing to accept this freedom is psychopathology.

While most schools of thought agree upon this basic proposition, they differ in their conceptions of precisely what man would know if he only exercised this freedom. Consequently they differ as to why knowledge is often so fearsome a thing as to make man avoid self-knowledge and, in avoiding it, become neurotic. That man tries to evade freedom in order to avoid noxious knowledge the theorists agree; concerning the nature of this noxious knowledge they disagree. They further agree that such knowledge may entail a good deal of anxiety and that it is because the feeling of anxiety is so noxious that knowledge will often be evaded. In a way they agree that the neurotic is a coward insofar as he tries to avoid the anxiety potentially brought about by certain insights—but they disagree in delineating those potentially anxiety-arousing awarenesses. This is not the place to engage in a detailed examination of the various schools of thought concerning the sources of anxiety; there exists a body of scholarly literature on the topic (May, 1950;

Munroe, 1955). What is needed is a rough recapitulation of two polar positions, since they go far in determining how one understands particular concepts of psychotherapy or what meaning one attaches to typical phenomena observable during psychotherapy.

Broadly, the two positions may be referred to as a "tension reduction" or "regression" hypothesis on the one hand and a "self-actualization" or "activity-seeking" hypothesis on the other. The former postulates that the inherent tendency of all living matter is its own self-elimination, that "the child is born in anger" and that human beings under the best of circumstances spend their lives in the pursuit of pleasure which is simply the elimination of pain. Stimuli are said to arise in human beings from within and impinge upon them from without, and life's enterprise is seen as focused upon reducing the impact of such inner and outer stimulation. Man is said to be inherently conservative and his instincts have this conservative quality; there is an inherent longing for the *status quo ante*—the elimination of stimulation.

Freud's (1900) idea of the Oedipus complex exemplifies this position. The child desires union, more precisely reunion, with the mother (or eventually, mother-substitutes) who will reduce his tensions, excitations, and disequilibrium—this representing (an, alas, only partial) return whence one came, to the womb. Life is viewed as a constant struggle between this inherently regressive and conservative striving and a world which unreasonably forbids these fundamental promptings to self-elimination. The best one may do is become aware of this inevitable human dilemma, reckon with it, and find roundabout, sublimated, socially approved avenues which will afford at least partial and symbolic gratification of this striving. To Freud, pathology was the reflection of a person's refusal to recognize this fact. Instead, the neurotic engages in all kinds of maneuvers to avoid what is unavoidable; this constitutes his illness. In the last analysis, human beings do not care to know their basic nature and the specifically regressive character of this nature, for such knowledge has implications and ramifications which are unbearably noxious.

Implicit in this orientation is the deep conviction that

Thanatos is a much older force in man than Eros, and even though many contemporary adherents of Freud have abandoned this view (Hartman, 1939; Erikson, 1950; Rapaport, 1951) at least by implication, Freud (whose capacity to see the logical consequences of his position was uncanny) outlined it clearly and stated it precisely in one of his last formulations (1933). He saw that the theory of regression, of fixation, of the repetition compulsion, stood or fell with the acceptance or rejection of the idea of an inherent regressive pull in human nature reflecting itself either in natural masochism or, if educationally redirected, in sadism (1933, pp. 142–48): in self-destruction or in aggression. Masochism or sadism could be sublimated, Freud believed, but such sublimation did violence to the natural tendency of man even though it was essential for human survival. Every cultural development was understood as the reflection of a chain: from masochism to sadism and their expression in sexuality to that renunciation of instincts which results in cultural progress (Freud, 1951). This gloomy outlook Freud tried to support scientifically by observations and data drawn from animal behavior and investigations in comparative embryology as well as certain historical and early anthropological findings (1920, 1933, 1942), and he was able to amass a good deal of data which lend themselves to such interpretations. But they were interpretations of rather inconclusive evidence examined by a gloomy and pessimistic and rather biased observer, an observer greatly influenced by unfortunate events in his life and by what he thought Darwin had found.

There is no doubt that acquaintance with Darwin's writings had already determined Freud's choice of profession and he apparently thought that Darwin had made observations which supported his own ideas about the nature of man's instincts (Jones, 1955). His interpretation of Darwin's thinking and findings has been challenged, notably by Montagu (1951), who suggests that this particular understanding became popular because it fitted into the social and economic ethos of the times; it seemed to lend "nature's" support to an unbridled and exploitive laissez-faire capitalism. Even though Darwin's writings lend themselves to different interpretations, Freud accepted the idea that they offered such support to his notions of innate hostility and pursued the search for its true origins to the eventual postulation of hostility directed against oneself as the foundation of all outside-directed violence.

The second polar position is also clearly prevalent in Western thought. Certainly since the publication of *Contrat Social*, men—including, at one time, Freud (1894) himself—have seen aggression as a resultant rather than as an original force. Within the psychoanalytic community Jung (1933) saw the organism as constantly striving with an eye to future unfolding, understanding, and growth; Adler's (1927, 1939) concept of "social feelings" is devoid of hostile and regressive origins. Goldstein's (1951) position is even more clear-cut; he simply proposed an inherent "self-actualizing" tendency in man, a tendency which is the exact antithesis of the regression and the tension-reduction hypotheses. He too observed behavior which might make one think that man's natural tendency is to go back, to be dominated by the repetition compulsion, to "linger on" in the terms of Goethe's *Faust*—but he viewed these behavioral bits quite differently, seeing them as attempts to fulfill oneself despite almost insurmountable difficulties. Rogers' (1951) writings show thinking akin to Goldstein's on this point. And Sullivan (1953) presented interpretations of behavior which posit the basic presence of a power motive, a desire to progress and expand rather than to regress and shrink. Schachtel's (1959) discussion of "focal awareness" and the "activity affect" also implies an inherent tendency toward expansion rather than restriction, even though Schachtel also posits the existence of what he calls the "embeddedness affect." Fromm's (1955) position is quite unequivocal: he says that hostility is unlived life; he proposes that man's basic aim, far from being regressive, is indeed progressive—man cannot bear standing still, experiences the need to transcend himself and to leave the *status quo.*

These theorists consequently propose that psychopathology represents man's attempt to avoid the knowledge of his finiteness, his helplessness, and his dependence upon the world around him. They furthermore propose that psychopathology is failure to confront those forces which interfere with self-actualization, whether biological or social. Mental illness is seen as a refusal to acknowledge one's reactions in the face of such restricting and limiting circumstances. These latter theorists see man horrified by his awareness that fulfillment is so difficult and so limited, while Freud proposed that man is horrified by the awareness that living in harmony with one's regressive and destructive instincts is dangerous and can never be complete. While both groups assert "You have the capacity to do what you must do" and "It's better to know than not to know, for to hear and see and know is health," they differ—and this difference is crucial—on what is to be seen, heard, and known. One group exclaims "Be aware of your inherent regressive tendencies but renounce them." The other group insists "Be aware of your inherent power and constructive potentials and accept them—with the satisfactions they can bring and the pain and burdens they impose."

These two contrasting conceptions concerning the basic nature of man must bring in their wake differing therapeutic aims, differing knowledge and awareness toward which therapists will try to help their patients. It is also quite clear that their differences in viewing man's basic purposes will lead them to different ways of understanding behavior or "symptoms." Which interpretation is correct depends essentially upon which conception of man's fundamental striving is more adequate and in closer accord with verifiable constructs. It is here that one must turn to the science of psychology to find meaningful guidelines for the practice of the art. The following chapter will therefore be devoted to a discussion of research data which shed some light upon the crucial question as to what constitutes the basic tendency in man, regressive tension-reduction or self-actualization.

► Summary ◄

1. The definition of emotional well-being is not a scientific matter but a reflection of ethical values maintained by the

definer. This is true not only in psychotherapy but also in medicine and in any other area of human endeavor where scientific data are applied in order to bring about "desirable" ends.

2. All schools of psychotherapy which claim allegiance to what is called "dynamic psychology" fundamentally maintain that lack and avoidance of self-knowledge are the core of psychopathology. Emotional conflicts in a person reflect the discrepancies between the values he professes and the values he genuinely harbors, albeit in unconscious or dissociated fashion. The dynamic psychologies propose that it is possible and imperative for man to be in touch with his attitudes (based on values) even though such knowledge entails discomfort. They maintain that the development of such self-knowledge represents the basis for personal fulfillment. In assuming this position dynamic psychologies take an ethical stand which insists that it is better to know than to live in ignorance.

3. But various schools of thought differ on the basic aims and conditions of human existence, and therefore on the question of what human beings try to evade. Freud's excitation-reduction hypothesis (pleasure principle) is markedly at variance with what may be referred to as the self-actualization hypothesis.

4. The therapeutic process will depend on what the therapist deems the ultimate aim of human beings. There exist empirical data which must be examined in order to arrive at a relatively valid conception concerning these two polar positions. Only then may one engage in a meaningful definition of emotional well-being—or the "good life"—and only then may one attempt to outline the aims and goals of psychotherapy.

The Aims and Goals of Psychotherapy: Theoretical and Empirical Foundations

WHAT SUPPORT DOES THE EXPERIMENTAL AND NONCLINICAL RE-search literature provide for either of the polar positions outlined in Chapter 1? *Does the available evidence support an excitation-reduction or a stimulus- and activity-seeking tendency as the basic drive in the phylum?* It must be admitted at once that evidence from investigations in various realms is still sketchy and much work will have to be done before definitive statements can be made. Nevertheless there are enough data available to make certain outlines and trends discernible.

Evidence comes from two quarters: animal experimentation and studies of the behavior of human beings.

Since the earliest days when psychoanalytic theory began to make an impact upon psychological and psychiatric thinking, research workers using animal subjects have addressed themselves to the investigation of the psychoanalytic constructs advanced by Freud and his students. Many of these early studies were summarized by Sears (1943); his presentation and interpretation of material caused a good deal of discussion even in those psychological circles not previously much concerned with Freudian thinking. One of the best known "early" investigations was a study by Levy (1934). Examining the behavior of litter-mate puppies raised by three different feeding procedures—bottles with slow-flowing nipples, bottles with fast-flowing nipples, and nursing at the bitch—Levy found a definite progression in the animals' "oral" activities between meals. Puppies raised on fast-flowing nipples sucked more than puppies raised on slow-flowing nipples, while those raised by the mother engaged in even less oral activity between meals (on their bodies, rubber balls, and the finger offered by the investigator). While the study's results have important bearing upon certain aspects of psychoanalytic theory not under discussion here, they also offer some (although relatively little) evidence concerning the central question posed earlier. If a simple excitation-reduction tendency were operating, it would be reasonable to expect that the puppies whose visceral deficit was reduced most rapidly (those raised on fast-flowing nipples) should show the least interim oral activity. Simple homeostatic principles suggest that behavior initiated by internal stimulation (visceral deficit) should subside once the previous balance is re-established. But exactly the reverse was the case. It seems that the deprivation experienced by the fast feeders was of oral activity as such. The striving toward activity without excitation-reduction as a consequence appears suggested by this early experimental finding.

That the problem must be more complex is of course suggested by the fact that the puppies raised on slow-flowing nipples also engaged in much between-meal orality. This observation could be explained by drawing upon a long-established psychoanalytic postulate concerning the peculiar nature of instincts and its relation to the development of fixations, for obviously the behavior of both groups of non-mother-fed puppies reflected what theorists call fixation. It has long been proposed by psychoanalytically orthodox authors that both "excessive satisfactions" and "excessive frustrations" at a particular level of development will result in the organism's fixation at that state, although the emphasis is clearly upon excessive satisfactions. In this connection Fenichel commented:

> What are the factors responsible for evoking fixations? . . .
> 1. The consequence of experiencing excessive satisfactions at a given level is that this level is renounced only with reluctance; if, later, misfortunes occur, there is always a yearning for the satisfaction formerly enjoyed.
> 2. A similar effect is wrought by excessive *frustrations* at a given level. One gets the impression that at developmental levels that do not afford enough satisfaction, the organism refuses to go further, demanding the withheld satisfactions. . . .
> 5. Most frequently, however, fixations are rooted in experiences of instinctual satisfaction which simultaneously gave reassurance in the face of some anxiety or aided in repressing some other feared impulse [1945, pp. 65–66].

If one were to accept this formulation, one could say that some of the puppies experienced "excessive satisfactions" and others "excessive frustrations." But there is little evidence to suggest that a "later misfortune" explains the persistence of orality. It seems therefore more reasonable to explain the data by postulating that in either instance of nipple-raising, frustrations were experienced by the puppies: those raised on slow-flowing nipples experienced frustration in their attempts to reduce hunger pains, those raised on fast-flowing nipples experienced frustration in their search for oral activity, one of the few activities puppies of this age are capable of. But if this is so, stimulation and excitation as such cannot be deemed inherently noxious.

This observation is of course in direct opposition to thoughts developed in 1920 by Freud (1942), thoughts foreshadowed earlier in his *Three Contributions to the Theory of Sex:*

> Despite all divergence of opinion regarding it in psychology, I must firmly maintain that a feeling of tension must carry with it the character of displeasure. I consider it as conclusive that such a feeling carries with it the impulse to alter the psychic situation and thus act incitingly,

which is quite contrary to the nature of the perceived pleasure [1905b, p. 605].

Freud apparently saw at one point the dangers associated with his growing insistence that excitation as such was noxious, and he tried to call a halt to this line of thinking:

> It seems that in the series of feelings and tensions we have a direct sense of increase and decrease of amounts of stimulus, and it cannot be doubted that there are pleasurable tensions and unpleasurable relaxations of tension. The state of sexual excitation is the most striking example of a pleasurable increase of stimulus of this sort, but it is certainly not the only one [1924a, p. 160].

That Freud (1933) nonetheless wound up suggesting that Thanatos was an older and more potent force than Eros and therefore the more powerful instinctual component moving living matter toward destruction, including self-destruction, toward the coming to rest once again in an inorganic stimulus-free state was discussed in Chapter 1. Though the road his thinking took had many turns, it led inevitably to the assumption that seeking a stimulus-free existence was the inherent object of man's instinctual life. Levy's (1934) study and its implications do not offer any support for this basic position, nor do they support Schachtel's (1959) assertion that "only the hungry infant will . . . be eager to suck" (p. 29).

Even more convincing are some data reported by Hunt. In an experiment designed to study the relationship between early feeding frustration and adult hoarding behavior of rats Hunt made some startling, though incidental, observations. He described his experimental procedures in these terms:

> To determine whether feeding-frustration in infancy alters the hoarding behavior of adult rats, we have compared the number of pellets stored, both before and after 5 days of relative hunger in adulthood, by animals which had been submitted to 15 days of feeding frustration during late infancy with the number of pellets stored by their litter-mates which had been allowed unlimited food continuously. Both experimental animals and controls were otherwise allowed unlimited food [1941, p. 341].

Most of Hunt's findings are not relevant here. What is pertinent is his observation that the control animals—which had never before been frustrated—although fully sated during the adult prefrustration period, hoarded at least as many if not more pellets than the experimental animals:

> In this pre-frustration hoarding the means for the control groups are even very slightly, although not significantly, larger than the means for the experimental groups. . . . It is quite evident from these results that the infantile feeding-frustration to which these experimental animals were submitted did not make them as adults hoard while satiated [p. 349].

Again one is confronted with apparently self-initiated behavior unexplained by visceral deficit as a motivating force, behavior not accounted for by "judiciously" applied frustrations.

Trends suggesting some inherent directional properties of behavior were merely incidental byproducts of these and similar early studies. Indeed, the question of primary instinctual direction did not become a prominent and focused research area until the 1950s, so it is by no means surprising that so careful a review of the experimental literature on psychoanalytic theory as the one offered by Hilgard (1952) contains no references to it. But relevant data finally started to come in.

Sporadically in earlier decades but with increasing frequency through the 1950s there were reported in the literature animal experiments which drastically undermined the notion that the acquisition of behavioral patterns could be understood in excitation-reduction terms. Considerable work has suggested that organisms, far from avoiding the novel just because it is new, seem to seek and tend to explore it unless this tendency is interfered with. Most pointedly these studies suggested that there operates within animals a tendency to engage in unrewarded exploration, locomotion, and activity in general. Crucial experiments have been reported which make it difficult to continue explaining animal activities as derivates of tension-reduction tendencies. Excellent summaries of these studies exist (Butler, 1958; Cofer, 1959; White, R. W., 1959). These reviews are so thorough and so incisive that all that will be offered in the following paragraphs is a synopsis of the main findings and conclusions of these reviewers, notably White's summation.

Experimental work by Butler (1953), Butler and Harlow (1954), and Berlyne (1955) indicates that animals explore their environs even though they are totally sated and do so in the absence of any discernible visceral deficit. As a matter of fact, there are data available supporting the notion that actual need reduction, of hunger for example, is not as rewarding as the opportunity to engage in eating *per se*. On this point Wolfe and Kaplon (1941) report that the learning process in chickens was furthered when food intake was accomplished by a lot of pecking of small pellets rather than by a small amount of pecking when large pellets were offered. These findings tend to agree with Levy's observations that nursing as such was important for the puppies he studied. There are available even more pointed reports from Harlow and some of his co-workers (1950) indicating that the opportunity to engage in activity for activity's sake motivated animals to learn complicated tasks.

A summary of his own work by Berlyne (1960) suggests that animals exhibit remarkable curiosity when confronted with novel situations and stimuli, even though his interpretation of this phenomenon (to be dealt with later) need not be accepted. Berlyne's data supply strong evidence for the position that organisms, far from avoiding stimulation and sensory excitation, tend to search for such excitation, exploring new objects by employing all sensory modalities available to them. Similar behavioral preferences for an increase rather than a decrease of excitation are also reported by Montgomery (1954), but perhaps most revealing are data published by Harlow (1958).

On the basis of his extensive studies and observations, Harlow concluded that one can observe in young animals a decided affinity for the dummy "mother-substitutes" which offer the infant animal maximal opportunities for sensory stimulation. In his provocative discussion Harlow posits that this stimulation and excitation attract the infant animals. In addition he reports specific experimentation highly relevant to the question whether stimulus-reduction can be thought of as an instinctive tendency:

> In our initial experiment, the dual-mother surrogate condition, a cloth mother and a wire mother[1] were placed in different cubicles attached to the infant's living cage. . . . For four newborn monkeys the cloth mother lactated and the wire mother did not; and for the other four, this condition was reversed. In either condition the infant received all its milk through the mother surrogate as soon as it was able to maintain itself in this way. . . . The infants were always free . . . to contact either mother, and the time spent on the surrogate mothers was automatically recorded. . . . Data [obtained] make it obvious that contact comfort is a variable of overwhelming importance . . . , whereas lactation is a variable of negligible importance. With age and opportunity to learn, subjects with the lactating wire mother showed decreasing responsiveness to her and increasing responsiveness to the nonlactating cloth mother, a finding completely contrary to any interpretation of derived drive in which the mother-form becomes conditioned to hunger-thirst reduction. The persistence of these differential responses throughout 165 consecutive days of testing is evident . . . [1958, p. 676].

Harlow's results seem unequivocal: search for more contact and more sensory stimulation rather than less contact and less excitation was the inherent instinctual tendency of the experimental animals.

It is well to reiterate the relevance of these findings for the concerns of psychotherapy. If the search for contact and activity is counter-nature and merely a reluctantly acquired behavior facet, then the diagnostic procedure becomes an effort to understand what events and circumstances interfered with this process of reluctant acquisition and submission to cultural

[1] Each "surrogate" is built of wire mesh, but the cloth mother is covered with terry cloth, affording the opportunity to snuggle.—E.S.

demands for active participation in life's affairs. The corresponding therapeutic aim will be aiding the patient to redirect his energy from homeostatic contact and activity avoidance to enforced sufferance of activity and contact with others. If, on the other hand, the search for contact and activity is indeed the inherent tendency, the individual's withdrawal and inactivity will be viewed as reactive deviations from nature's course. Then the psychologist's efforts will be directed toward grasping what events moved the patient to abandon his natural course and helping him therapeutically to overcome those inner and outer obstacles which led to his particular reactions.

Within the area of observations and study of humans, data bearing on the question of any inherent direction of strivings are more plentiful—and more subject to influence by uncontrollable and unknown environmental variables. Common observation of an almost insatiable curiosity on the part of infants and children and their ability to drive even the most well-meaning adults to distraction with their incessant explorations and inquiries may be taken by some as evidence for the basic existence of what Schachtel (1959) has called the "activity affect" or what Murphy (1958a) has referred to as "The Yen to Discovery." Others insist that these observations must not be interpreted in this manner. They claim that the infant engages in such behavior because it has been associated with tension reductions. One may even find in the literature suggestions that the desire to read is associated with voyeuristic infantile tendencies (Fenichel, 1945) and that one is dealing with adequately sublimated voyeuristic (and ultimately excitation-reducing) tendencies when he observes a youngster or adult engrossed in the perusal of literature.

In addition to obvious motor exploratory activities, other observable phenomena also seem to testify to an expansion-seeking potential in the human makeup. These phenomena, too, can be explained by those so inclined in tension-reduction terms or, as is more frequently the case, they may be disregarded altogether. Reference is made to the highly controversial area of extrasensory perception. Regardless of what one may think about the existence of extrasensory perception, there is a persistent theme running through the literature on this subject which is relevant to the present discussion and must be considered seriously. This is the theme of "novelty." Such investigators as Pratt and Woodruff (1939) and Scherer (1948) have observed that experimental subjects by and large tend to do better at the beginning of a series of trials than later on. They report that this decline can be reversed by changing the character of the stimuli employed, i.e., by substituting new test stimuli for old ones. These findings are of course quite in harmony with Berlyne's (1950, 1955) reports that new stimuli increased activity, specifically the exploratory activity of experimental animals.

Another highly interesting theme to be found in the literature on extrasensory perception is the observation that individuals who are convinced that extrasensory perception is fact rather than fiction also tend to show higher amounts of trial-series "hits" than those who are quite skeptical about such phenomena. But this kind of "faith" may be taken as nothing more than an index of openness to possibilities no matter how fantastic they may seem and a readiness to make oneself available to experience no matter what its nature. Murphy has stressed this point in his review of findings in extrasensory perception:

> In the case of the other high scoring subject, the excitable and at times grandiose attitudes, the naive belief in the impossibility of being wrong, are brought clearly into relation to a problem very widely considered in parapsychology, namely, the relation of subjects' attitude to success in the task, experimental conditions being otherwise held constant [1958b, p. 70].

Schmeidler (1960), while acknowledging and finding supportive data for the assertion that "believers" ("sheep") do better than "nonbelievers" ("goats"), adds significantly that one must also differentiate between sheep who exhibit an uncritical and somewhat absurd faith and those whose readiness to believe seems governed more by curiosity and eagerness to learn about seemingly strange phenomena. In other studies Schmeidler (1961, 1962) has explored further facets and factors which seem to influence the appearance of extrasensory-perception phenomena. The details of these studies need not be reviewed here, but the findings bespeak a factor, operant more in some and less in others, which contributes to the ability to establish contact with stimuli. According to Schmeidler's reports this factor seems highly correlated with personality variables usually associated with what is broadly referred to as "good adjustment."

Schmeidler's data are unequivocal. The Rorschach characteristics of her subjects who are highly successful on extrasensory perception tasks are replete with indices usually thought of as denoting spontaneity, a readiness and willingness to experience inner stimuli undefensively and to become and remain aware of the nuances of inner and outer stimulation. Whether this is an inherent capacity perpetuated in the lives of some and lost in the course of development by others is of course hard to say. Schmeidler's findings seem more consonant with the assumption that one is dealing with an inherent quality rather than with sublimatory processes, for her "unsuccessful" subjects produce Rorschach protocols replete with indications that these individuals are actively struggling to delimit the horizons of their awareness. On the other hand, her highly extrasensorily perceptive subjects do not show indications of strong stimulus-avoidance tendencies.

What makes Schmeidler's data even more significant is the degree to which several features of her findings dovetail with observations reported in other areas of investigation. Research in "subliminal perception" has indicated the fact that many individuals exhibit a remarkable capacity to perceive material without being aware of the fact that such perception has taken place. There are reports on the perception of stimuli flashed on a screen for such a short duration or with such low intensity of illumination that no conscious knowledge of the stimuli flashed in this fashion occurs (Bach & Klein, 1957; Klein, Spence, Holt, & Gourevitch, 1958; Eagle, 1959). Holt has indicated the scope of this type of investigation:

> We have turned to the study of the kinds of influences marginally presented stimuli can have: effects on learning, on association, on imagery reported by drawings or

verbally, on hypnotic dreams, on judgements of concurrently but supraliminal stimuli, and on reaction-times. We have also been interested in finding the factors in the situation, in response modality, in state of consciousness, and in the subject's defenses and controls, that maximize the impact of incidental stimuli [1963, p. 5].

While the concept of "subliminal stimulation," like its predecessor "perceptual defense," has had its severe critics (Eriksen, 1960), there is little doubt that phenomena such as those reported by McGinnies (1950), who worked in the latter area, and phenomena described by Spence and Holland (1962), working on subliminal perception, are observable. If these are valid observations, even though some methodological criticisms (Turkel, 1955) may also be valid, it seems likely that individuals do not simply avoid stimuli, but that some individuals (for whatever reasons) do not become aware of them. Furthermore, it becomes apparent that there are individual differences in this preferential way of being inattentive and that this inattentiveness is more pronounced in some than in others. Judging from data supplied by another tangentially related area of research, that of "incidental learning," it seems likely that this inattentiveness is a secondary development and not the reflection of a primary force. It can repeatedly be demonstrated that some human beings, asked to focus upon and learn a particular body of information, will simultaneously learn other material presented in an incidental manner with the data to be focused upon (Pine, 1960) and that remarkable individual differences are observable. The expansive properties of human beings seem to be much more prominent than tension-reduction theorists like to think, even though they may explain findings in these areas in simple associative terms: what is associated with stimulus reduction is learned even though the material is not stimulus-reducing itself.

This potentially expansive quality of humans appears in research in extrasensory perception and in studies dealing with subliminal perception and incidental learning. A further important parallel is to be noted in the observation that personality characteristics of individuals showing high ability in subliminal perception correspond closely to the specific personality variables Schmeidler (1960) reports as characterizing her "well-adjusted sheep." Eagle (1962), who has done pioneer work in extracting factors associated with high scores in subliminal sensitivity, reports that this quality correlates extremely well with such dimensions (among others) as gregarious and social interests in other people, receptivity to inner clues, an introspective orientation, active fantasy life and vivid imagery, a confident outlook, cognitive openness, and a diffuse (changeable) rather than rigidly crystallized sense of identity. While the language employed and the instruments used by Eagle are different from those utilized by Schmeidler, their findings match closely.[2]

These qualities are also precisely the dimensions reported by Goldberger and Holt (1958) as significantly associated with superior ability to endure and even enjoy sensory deprivation in isolation chambers; it is as if this inner strength and sensitivity to inner stimuli made one less dependent upon outer stimulation. Finally it is to be noted that Singer (1951) and Singer and Berkowitz (1958), working in the area of empathic capacity, and Kaplan and Singer (1963) and Eimer (1964), studying variables associated with alienation, have reported data highly compatible and theoretically consistent with these. Again and again the suggestion is made that rather than shrinking from stimulation human beings tend to search for stimuli—inner or outer, sensory or extrasensory, subliminal or supraliminal. Obviously, this stimulus-seeking tendency is not uniform in quantity and varies in intensity from individual to individual. While the data reported on human subjects do not afford the opportunity to decide whether this stimulus-seeking quality is inherent or acquired, information reported by students of human behavior combined with that provided by animal experimenters makes it appear most likely that it reflects a "progressive" nature of instincts rather than a "conservative" nature of instinctual energy.

One more area of investigation that provides additional evi-

[2] This view was supported in a personal communication of Professor Schmeidler to the author.

dence on this basic issue deserves mention. Since the early 1950's increasing attention has been focused upon reactions of individuals to sensory isolation (Solomon, Kubzansky, Leiderman, Mendelson, Trumbull, & Wexler, 1961). The fact that investigators refer to this isolation as "deprivation" signifies their belief that isolation is synonymous with deprivation, a belief which is by no means new. Tyrants and jailers have long known that man cannot survive psychologically or physically when isolated, even though so-called basic needs may be satisfied. The findings are highly suggestive of the view that the developmental progression is grossly interfered with when organisms are deprived of various stimulations. Studies have shown how subjects resist and/or compensate for minimization of sensory input and discuss circumstances under which "regressive" phenomena follow deprivation. While the investigations cannot shed light upon an inherent directional tendency in energy utilization, and while the resolution of the question of inherent versus acquired tendency is missing, it is of importance to note that these studies are highly compatible with experimentation discussed earlier. They are also in striking harmony with Hebb's (1955) often-cited suggestion that a reticular-activation system operates within organisms making for a generalized drive state, a position which, in the words of R. W. White, would commit one:

> to the novel idea of a neuro-genic motive, one in which the state of the nervous system and the patterns of external stimulation conspire to produce motivated behavior [1959, p. 301].

Summarizing the implications of findings produced by studies in sensory deprivation, Kubzansky and Leiderman conclude:

> Thus, one of the major implications of this work may lie in providing a demonstration of the functional utility of a drive or drives which serve to bring the individual into more diversified contact with his environment. Behavior theory has at various times postulated such drives and called them "exploratory," "curiosity," and "manipulative," and Hebb has pointed out their implications for

theories of animal motivations. These concepts have sometimes been linked to such conceptions of human motivation as "mastery" and "competence" in an attempt to show their relevance to the maintainance of the organism. The present studies suggest a biological basis for these drives which ties them more intimately to a functional view of behavior. They also provide a conceptual basis for a closer link between theories of animal and human motivation [1961, p. 237].

This drive toward contact has important consequences for the whole concept of "drive," as R. W. White points out:

If we admit exploration to the category of drive we are thus committing ourselves to believe that drives need have no extraneural sources in tissue deficits or visceral tensions, that they are not necessarily activated by strong or persistent stimuli, that they do not require consummatory responses, and that drive increase can sometimes be a mechanism of reinforcement [1959, p. 302].

At another point he comments:

The simple mechanics of need reduction cannot possibly serve as the basis for a theory of learning. Twenty years of research have thus pretty much destroyed the orthodox drive model [p. 305].

The observations on which White based these conclusions have had reverberating effects throughout the psychological world and psychotherapeutic circles. For instance, they led Berlyne to develop a theory of behavior which saw what he called "conceptual conflict" rather than visceral disturbances as the mainspring of motivation:

The drive states that are fomented by disequilibrium arise not out of visceral disturbances or aversive external stimuli, but out of unsatisfactory relations between the subject's own responses. Changes in behavior that remove disequilibrium are ones that avert surprise and uncertainty. Ability to recognize and respond to invariants amid the shifting appearances of objects must diminish complexity and moderate the impact of change. So, once more, we find testimony to the importance of conceptual conflict [1960, p. 302].

It is of course by no means necessary to accept Berlyne's assumption that the organism is eager to avert surprise and uncertainty; as a matter of fact a good case could be made for the assumption that this is precisely what the organism in its evolution is constantly striving for, but one does see the emergence of a theory of behavior capable of explaining activities without postulating visceral deficits and attempts to reduce them. That Berlyne's theory employs the idea of some deficit as a motivating force and avoids postulating an activity drive in its own right and with activity as its own aim is self-evident.

White's comments and the data on which they are based have significant consequences for the understanding of processes commonly observed in psychotherapeutic work. Since these consequences will be dealt with extensively in Chapters 9, 10, and 13, it will suffice merely to illustrate them here. If, for instance, the "orthodox drive model" held any validity, it would indeed be reasonable to understand transference behavior as an expression of the repetition compulsion, of an inherent tendency to return to familiar ground, of the desire to remain in the embedded and undifferentiated state which the Oedipus complex represents, and of hostility toward those who are experienced as interfering with a desire for excitation-reduction. Were this the case, the therapeutic goal would be that of helping the patient give up those "natural" longings; in the process of divesting himself of these impulses the transference would be resolved. But if no evidence for the orthodox drive model can be found, transference reactions must be understood in totally different terms. Then it may become reasonable to postulate that the distortions which characterize transference are operations in the service of salvaging some limited possibilities for survival, expansion, and contact with the world. If so, the therapeutic aim evolves into helping the patient experience the premises by which he lives as invalid (although they may have been valid in the past).

These research findings have also led to a reawakening of interest in Allport's (1937a, 1937b) concept of "functional autonomy." In one of his later books Allport reasserted his previous well-known position that motivation cannot be explained satisfactorily in the tension-reduction terms proposed by both Freud and the S–R theorists. He insisted:

> The S–R psychologist or psychoanalyst may *claim* that adult interests can be traced to his chosen unchanging energies, but he cannot *prove* that they are [1961, p. 211]. . . .
>
> Much motivation, we repeat, is unconscious, infantile, and hidden from oneself. The important point, however, is that *some* motivation is functionally autonomous, especially in personalities that we consider normal, mature, sound [p. 217].

Allport was somewhat reluctant to posit an inherent tendency toward contact, expansion, and activity *qua* activity. He cautiously refrained from such a step, though he came close to it:

> It would be wrong to say that the "need for competence" is the simple and sovereign motive of life. It does, however, come as close as any need (closer than the sexual) to summing up the whole biological story of development. We survive through competence, we grow through competence, we become "self-actualizing" through competence [p. 214].

Unfortunately the term *need* confuses the issue. This term is so thoroughly associated with the concept of deficit and a context of "relief *from*" that one often overlooks the possibility that "need" can also take the preposition *to*. It is this need *to* be in contact and *to* use oneself and one's given apparatuses that Allport stressed:

> Up to now the "behavioral sciences," including psychology, have not provided us with a picture of man capable of creating or living in a democracy. These sciences in large part have imitated the billiard ball model of physics, now of course outmoded. They have delivered into our hands a psychology of an "empty organism," pushed by drives and molded by environmental circumstances. What is small and partial, what is external and mechanical, what is early, what is peripheral and opportunistic— have received the chief attention of psychological system builders. . . .

Curiously enough, many of the ardent adherents of the "empty organism" theory of human nature are among the most zealous fighters for democracy. No paradox is more striking than that of the scientist who as a citizen makes one set of psychological assumptions and in his laboratory and writings makes opposite assumptions respecting the nature of man.

Given time it seems probable that psychology will ripen in the direction of democracy's basic assumptions. Some of the considerations we have reviewed indicate that the evolution is well under way. The emerging figure of man appears endowed with a sufficient margin of reason, autonomy, and choice to profit from living in a free society. The portrait, however, does not discard the darker portion of truth discovered by the youthful psychology of the recent past. This truth stands, and it will ever remain the duty of psychology to correct idealistic exuberance [1955, pp. 100–1].

Allport's warning against naïve insistence upon man's goodness is well taken, his warning against forgetting that the primary tendency toward contact can easily become a tendency toward destruction by contact must be heeded, but his vision of man as capable of *direct* construction and not simply sublimating destructiveness into constructiveness is supported by solid research data available today.[3] Other authors have also reaffirmed their conviction, now based on evidence, that human potentialities are wider and more multifaceted than previously assumed. After acknowledging the undeniable fact that human beings are eager to deal with their primary drives, such as hunger, thirst, sex, and so forth, Murphy remarked:

The *capacity* to deal with a complex world of here and there, and with past, present, and future, the *capacity* to deal with abstractions which give general laws cutting across the maze of particulars has entailed the *urge to do*

[3] This renewed confidence in man's capacities and potentialities for active cooperation as primary tendencies has also brought in its wake a renewed interest in some of Adler's (1939) thinking, for it must not be forgotten that Adler was among the first to emphasize this "social" and contact-seeking quality in man as an inherent quality rather than simply as a characteristic acquired by sublimation.

all of this. The impulse to perceive, to understand, to imagine is just as much part of human nature as are the specific adjustment processes which we describe in terms of visceral drives [1958a, p. 32].

Murphy was quite ready to postulate an activity drive similar to the one advanced by Schachtel (1959) when he commented at a later point:

> *The very processes of learning and thinking may in themselves become satisfying.* There may be a movement from the initial satisfaction in color to the delight in manipulating the colors to produce a picture [p. 35].

No suggestion here of civilization, culture, and human cooperation being only reflections of adequately sublimated regressive tendencies. This renewed confidence in the human capacity to expand, to cooperate, to love, and to create rests not simply on hope and faith but also on relatively incontestible evidence that a striving in this direction operates within man. Chein expressed a similar position:

> Let me, however, note some special aspects of this enterprise which flatly contradict the notion that the absence of excitation is a rewarding state. A person who loses his desire for food does not typically rest content in his blessed state, but finds this an occasion to seek medical or psychotherapeutic assistance; and I suspect that even a dyed-in-the-wool S–R operationalist would, *horribile dictu,* seriously contemplate going to a psychoanalyst if he finds himself without sexual libido or given to quick discharge of sexual tension by virtue of premature ejaculation [1962, pp. 31–33].

With the destruction of the "orthodox drive model" and the inevitable rejection of need-reduction as a basis for learning and motivation to learn, and with the increasing evidence for a "drive" toward contact with the environment and search for stimulation, the foundation for the psychoanalytic model of human development and psychopathology disappears. If the nature of the id—the instinctual forces in general—is not fundamentally regressive, seeking contact only for discharge, the re-establishment of homeostasis, and subsequent withdrawal into ultimately inorganic states, then the original psychoanalytic foundations for the development of the ego are lacking. Presumably the ego was born out of the necessity to mediate between the regressive strivings of the pleasure principle operating within the id on the one hand and the demands of reality and the reality principle on the other. If the assumed conflict is illusory, if the id is shown as not regressive in nature, then at least two alternative conceptualizations emerge.

First, the concept of an ego born out of necessity, derived from the id, taming impulses into social acceptability (sublimation), could be replaced by the notion of an ego coming into existence independently and autonomously, deriving its energy from sources other than the id and subject to different laws. One is then confronted with an ego which is not, so to speak, just the moderate wing of an extremist party but is a party in its own right. Stripped of all its fancy jargon this is, of course, the position taken by contemporary ego-psychologists. But when Hartmann (1939), Rapaport (1951), and others talk of an "autonomous ego" and its apparatuses, when the concept of a "conflict-free ego sphere" appears, orthodox psychoanalytic theory is destroyed—not just broken with, as Hall and Lindzey (1957) would have it. Such a revolution also demands a radical rewriting of the theory of fixation, of the psychosexual stages of development, the concept of defense, and a new conceptualization of the Oedipus complex—for the conservative nature of instincts and the search for stimulus avoidance are fundamental to all these constructs as they appear in the psychoanalytic literature.

If human expansion is possible without man being spurred on by threat; if activity is not merely a reflection of sad resignation that "this is the way of the world and there is nothing one can do about it"; if, instead, it is postulated that human activity can be the reflection of *Funktionslust* (Bühler, 1922), what is the utility of the concept of the conservativism of the id? There is little realistic value in maintaining that regressive hostility and destructiveness are inherent instinctual tendencies (especially if the idea of such an instinctive pull lacks any substantive empirical bases). Yet this is precisely what Rapaport does when he comments in one of his discussions on ego autonomy:

> Suppose that twenty of us should land on a desert island. At first we would all try to do all the jobs, mutual assistance and good will running rampant. But *since the nature of man is what it is, quarrels would start and some people would begin to stake out their claims* [1951, pp. 250–51; emphasis supplied—E.S.]

Rapaport prefers to invoke this view of "human nature" rather than the restricting forces of nature which specifically threaten expansive efforts of each member of this imaginary community.

Insisting that human nature is necessarily characterized by such a regressive noncooperative streak has inevitable consequences. It allows one to persist in viewing pathology as the outcome of inadequate sublimation. It helps one overlook the possibility that climatic and other natural threats have often given rise to social organizations which make personal expansion difficult if not impossible. Furthermore, this position allows one to forget the fact that social and economic organizations originally designed to help man survive develop a dynamism of their own, making for their perpetuation even when the conditions they were to deal with originally do not prevail any longer. This point of view allows one to ignore the very real possibility that "regressive" tendencies stem from limiting social and economic organizations and their multitude of institutions rather than from "inherent instinctual promptings." That one is dealing with such an attempt to overlook this possibility is pointedly suggested by Freud's (1937) comment that not only the id but also the outlines of the future ego are probably laid down hereditarily. This remark has actually been a point of departure for contemporary psychoanalytic "ego-psychologists."

As we have seen, there is another way of viewing behavior— and hence psychopathology—without assuming such inherent regressive tendencies. Such a conceptual reorientation suggests that pathology, far from being an inadequate reconciliation of inherent regressive strivings with reality demands, represents an unfortunate compromise between inherently expansive strivings and crippling reality constrictions resulting in the development of distortions of what one might have been. From this vantage point, pathology represents adaptation to oppression and acceptance of crippling demands in the hope of salvaging some life, some shred of dignity or at least the illusion of dignity. This surrender results in self-negation, abandoning the basic human capacity to be free and to make responsible choices.

Kaiser (1955) has discussed this issue masterfully in addressing himself to conceptual problems in the development of a theory of cure. May (1953) has sketched a moving parable: he tells of a man who was put into a cage in which he lacked nothing but his sense of active self-utilization and of how, after initial anger and resistance, the poor devil, in apparent eagerness to avoid facing his indignity any longer, grew to like his caged existence. Fromm's (1955) definition of mental health is also consonant with the idea suggested here: that the fulfillment of an inherent human striving toward stimulation and contact with inner and outer experience represents the essence of well-being. Fromm said specifically:

> *Mental health is characterized by the ability to love and to create, by the emergence from incestuous ties to clan and soil, by a sense of identity based on one's experience of self as a subject and agent of one's powers, by a grasp of reality inside and outside of ourselves, that is, by the development of objectivity and reason* [1955, p. 69].

By "objectivity and reason" Fromm of course does not mean detached indifference or rationalization but rather the fulfillment of a primary potentiality for learning to know oneself and others in a basic, thorough, and profound way. On the basis of this knowledge, Fromm proposes, man becomes capable of using himself to the fullest of his biological and physiological potentials. That there exists such a primary potentiality that can be utilized if circumstances are advantageous seems supported by contemporary research findings. The fact that circumstances are not always advantageous for fulfillment is also all too obvious. To help the individual maintain his willingness to fulfill this primary potentiality, or to regain such willingness if it has been stifled, will become the objectives of preventive and reconstructive psychotherapy respectively. A more specific and operational delineation of these goals will be offered in Chapter 3.

► *Summary* ◄

1. Data supplied by animal research concerning the nature and direction of inherent behavior tendencies lead to the conclusion that motivation toward activity cannot be understood in tension-reduction terms; there is overwhelming evidence that organisms strive toward stimulation, excitation, and contact.

2. Data culled from a variety of research endeavors with human beings, while lacking the definitiveness of some of the animal experimentation, are in harmony with this view of motivation.

3. The influence of these findings upon the thinking of theory-builders in psychology has been sketched and some implications for a definition of psychological well-being and for the sources of pathology were drawn.

The Aims and Goals of Psychotherapy: Some Operational Criteria and Definitions

THE DISCUSSION OF EMPIRICAL DATA HAS SUGGESTED THAT THE primary inherent direction of the organism is toward activity and that fulfillment of this tendency represents psychological aliveness and emotional well-being. This is by no means a new thought; indeed, it is deeply rooted in the history of ideas. What is required at this point is a development of the operational definitions and characteristics of "activity."

Throughout man's recorded history one encounters the idea that meaningful activity is based on the desire for continuous *effort* in its own right, not on mere concern with the outcome of actions. Personal definition reflects itself primarily in strenuous attempts to labor creatively rather than in the tangible results. This idea is so deeply ingrained in the history of human thought that it is by no means surprising to find reference to it in the Old Testament. When Moses (Exodus III:2ff.) was ordered by the Voice from the Burning Bush to lead the Israelites out of Egypt and he asked for the name of Him who gave the command, the answer is said to have been the riddle: "I am who I am." Ancient Hebrew had two tenses, the imperfect

and the perfect, and the fact that the answer is in the imperfect—the form denoting lack of completion—has certain implications. The response may be interpreted to characterize the
God of Moses as multifaceted and unceasing in His efforts. It
becomes clear why Judaism forbids either the utterance of the
name of Deity or the painting of His image: both would sig-
nify a limitation totally at variance with a conception of God
who reveals Himself in ongoing and limitless activity. The extension to man becomes obvious with the reminder that man is
said to be made in His image (Genesis, I:26). In many reli-
gions murder and suicide are among the cardinal sins, the
latter not only because it reflects despair—inability to conceive
of change and consequently a denial of actively changing conditions, including grace—but also because both suicide and
murder make the active continuity of life an impossibility,
deny the essence of existence (Cohn, 1930; Fagothey, 1963).

Equating life with active striving has also been the central
theme of many literary works. Only one example will be examined here, partly because it represents such a widely known
landmark in the history of thought and literature, partly because the work addresses itself succinctly to the issue at hand.
In Goethe's (Kaufmann, 1962) treatment of the Faust myth,
God and Mephistopheles meet, at the beginning of the play, in
Heaven. God is holding court and since He does not really
mind Mephistopheles (indeed, is rather fond of him) the
fallen angel of light is invited to be present. Goethe's God
refers to Mephistopheles as *Schelm*, a rogue or knavish jester.
In the *Prologue in Heaven* God puts it this way:

> Of all the spirits that negate,
> The knavish jester gives me least to do [p. 89].

He goes on to explain why He is so fond of Mephistopheles:

> Appear quite free on that day, too;
> I never hated those who were like you: . . .
> For man's activity can easily abate,
> He soon prefers uninterrupted rest;
> To give him this companion hence seems best
> Who roils and must as Devil help create [p. 89].

Shortly before these complimentary remarks by God, Mephistopheles has referred to his "distinguished and famous cousin," the snake who had whispered to Adam and Eve that to eat the apple of the Tree of Knowledge would make them Godlike, for then they would know right from wrong—and they wanted to know. Mephistopheles is thereby clearly aligned with inquiring disobedience and the quest for knowledge, on the side of man's striving and capacity for self-perfection. Goethe's thoughts are obvious: stimulation and alertness (activity as such) are essential and the devil by being stimulator becomes creator too. To Goethe's God the object of man's activity is of secondary interest; what is of primary importance is that man be active. He recognizes that there can be no meaningful search without the possibility of failure, that man's attempt to rise has dignity only if it carries within it the possibility of falling. Only when he "prefers uninterrupted rest" is man lost.

This theme controls the rest of the drama; for Goethe it is the universal human drama. God and the devil engage in a wager. God bets Mephistopheles that he will be incapable of deterring Faust—even given a free hand and no matter how he may try—from man's chosen road of search, inquiry, and rejection of lethargy. God fully expects that Faust will make wrong choices; this is inevitable, God insists—"Man errs as long as he will strive" (p. 87)—but this erring will not lead to Faust's damnation. Faust will not be the devil's unless and until he becomes satisfied with the wares of complacency and lethargy Mephistopheles has to offer. Goethe forcefully presents the idea that perpetual striving for expansion rather than achievement represents meaningful action.

Mephistopheles sets out to meet Faust and enters with him into an agreement which parallels the wager he had concluded with God:

FAUST:
If ever I recline, calmed, on a bed of sloth,
You may destroy me then and there.
If ever flattering you should wile me
That in myself I find delight,

If with enjoyment you beguile me,
Then break on me, eternal night!
This bet I offer.
MEPHISTOPHELES:
I accept it.
FAUST:
Right.
If to the moment I should say:
Abide, you are so fair—
Put me in fetters on that day,
I *wish* to perish then, I swear.
Then let the death bell ever toll,
Your service done, you shall be free,
The clock may stop, the hand may fall,
As time comes to an end for me [pp. 183, 185].

Faust is depicted as a character certainly not conventionally virtuous. The *affaire* Margarete is not very pretty—and yet in the end Faust is saved. (Margarete is saved, too, even though she is executed for the murder of her child. Her salvation is brought about by her refusal to abandon personal responsibility for her behavior; she refuses simply to shift responsibility to Faust—and in so doing she also saves Faust.) Faust is eventually saved because he was never satisfied to "recline, calmed, on a bed of sloth," because he did not commit the one unpardonable sin, did not cry out "Abide, you are so fair—" As the drama closes, Faust, now a very old man, states his psychological credo:

This is the highest wisdom that I own,
The best that mankind ever knew;
Freedom and life are earned by those alone
Who conquer them each day anew [p. 469].

This is clearly Goethe's own definition of sanity, of how well-being reflects itself in continuous effort expended in work and love—in more generic terms, in unceasing productivity valued for its own sake rather than for its rewards.[1] Goethe had often

[1] In one of his most profound discussions, Kaufmann (1960) came to somewhat different and also similar conclusions. He argued that "Faust's wager with Mephistopheles had been based on the false assumption that one could not appreciate the present without becoming a Philistine"

been accused of being a dilettante, of spreading himself too thin; he did not mind this at all. Effort expended was of value to him even if such effort were not to bear significant fruit. His was neither grim Calvinism nor despair, but a recognition of the human situation. Pulsating activity was the essence and the aim of living and of sanity for this man who exhibited a "kind of magnificent Narcissism," as Mann called it. Mann's description is singularly important for an operational definition of psychological well-being:

> . . . a self-repleteness, much too serious, and striving too constantly for self-perfection, intensification and re-distillation of its ingredients, to merit so trivial a word as vanity—a profound joy in the ego and its evolution [1948, pp. xiii–xiv].

Other writers have also placed active, absorbed striving in the center of their considerations of emotional well-being. Shakespeare, Ibsen, Kafka, Camus are only a few who have been involved with elaboration of the theme that the most striking characteristic of life is the exertion of physical, intellectual, or emotional effort. This is of course what prominent thinkers on psychotherapy have also maintained. When Freud remarked that a psychologically healthy person is characterized by his ability to derive satisfaction from *"lieben und*

(p. 76). He supported his conviction that Goethe deemed this a "false assumption" by citing a famous passage from Faust's last speech in which the old man exclaimed:

Then, to the moment I might say:
Abide, you are so fair!
The traces of my earthly day
No aeons can impair [Kaufmann, 1962, p. 469].

An explanation for Faust's eventual redemption despite his seeming repudiation of the contract's terms can be found in the varying affective connotations with which man may cry out "Abide!" Such a wish may be expressed with fear of the future and regressive nostalgia in one's heart or with the urgent desire for more time to savor fully one's experience before passing on to further involvements. In the end Faust could cry out "Abide!" without debilitating horror and nostalgia and much more with intense longing for pulsating experience. For a penetrating discussion of the relationships among nostalgia, living in the future, and pathological impoverishment of affective experience, see Levenson (1961).

arbeiten" (Erikson, 1950) he referred to the ability to derive pleasure from active efforts in self-utilization. This was for Freud an ability developed only reluctantly; for Adler (1939), Fromm (1955), and Sullivan (1953) it was an inherent characteristic of human beings.

If one accepts these premises, the question of the need for psychotherapeutic help (or the evaluation of improvement) hinges on how active the individual is or has grown to be. But because meaningful activity is not defined simply by the outcome of actions, it is necessary to outline indicators which reveal the degree to which creative effort brings satisfaction to a person so that genuine activity may be distinguished from what may be called pseudo-activity—behavior which only masquerades as effort. Neurotic behavior may readily be viewed as pseudo-activity far removed from the sort of activity Mann spoke of. Studies of youngsters with severe discipline problems (Hirsch & Singer, 1961), rigid persons (Eimer, 1962), and highly opinionated and dogmatic individuals (Kaplan & Singer, 1963) have offered evidence that their activity is only seeming activity, that they are intellectually lethargic, emotionally inactive, and often even physically slothful. The neurotic does not avail himself of his potentialities (including his sensory capacities), his intellectual armamentarium, and his emotional reactivity; when he does use these capacities he does so in an uninvolved and detached fashion, mechanically and without interest. The classic fugue state, the shallowness of the hysteric's outbursts, the trivia with which the obsessive preoccupies himself, and the detachment and emotional flatness which characterize many psychotics amply illustrate this point. The activities in which such individuals often engage, even with a flavor of furious tension, have a somnambulistic quality and fail to meet the criteria for activity advanced here; their behavior lacks the qualities of involvement, interest, and the desire to transcend the given. They are thus pseudo-activities rather than activities.

The amount of interest a person invests in his actions is, then, an outstanding criterion of genuine activity and consequently of emotional well-being. Activity is defined by involvement, not by merely going through the motions while telling oneself that one labors. Some rather disturbed individuals in moments of insight put their problem in precisely those terms; they say that they have the sense of doing nothing, of wasting their time, and of being totally uninterested. They often report that they cannot get themselves to do anything unless they feel forced. At times they even go through elaborate rituals to create the illusion of being pushed into action. This need for external force runs the gamut from young students' avoidance of intense engagement with subject matter until the cram sessions under the external threat of failure to the ability of some individuals to engage in sexual activity only when rape fantasies or similar illusions accompany the act. It is as if such persons feel compelled to renounce the activity which is the hallmark of their aliveness—and therefore can engage in the necessary functions of living only when their independence and responsibility for action can be denied.

Pursuit of this line of thinking leads to a related question: Is the person engaged in activity with others involved; is he interested enough to be aware of the nature of his interaction and of the way in which he affects those around him? Of course, one must consider the real effect the person has upon others—not what he tells himself about his impact—an awareness usually referred to as sensitivity. Such sensitivity demands personal attentiveness, and attention is a most intense activity itself. For example, genuine listening represents a highly active process; it requires concentrated attention to stimuli and to the inner reactions prompted by them; an absorbed awareness both of the speaker and of oneself as listener. One encounters the pretense of sensitivity in pseudo-listening with its simulated attention, simulated concentration, and simulated activity. It occurs when an individual seems to listen but does so neither to hear the message nor to hear his own reaction, but rather to use what he hears as a springboard for his own preconceived notions, or pseudo-notions. The pseudo-listener reveals a profound lack of interest in the other person or idea; all he cares about is making noise. At the same time he exposes his lack of interest in himself, even though one might easily be misled into thinking of him as "egocentric." Thus pseudo-listeners may often appear rather active, but their argumentativeness merely masks frantic attempts to remain inactive. The other person becomes just a tool for self-aggrandizement.

Genuine activity is by definition absent because pseudo-listening cannot contribute to change. This absence denotes the lack of "a profound joy in the ego and its evolution"—as if the person's basic motivation is to minimize the possibility of evolution. The pseudo-listener is also utterly inactive in the sense of being totally unreceptive, for receptivity is itself an activity. Indeed, receptivity to one's own thoughts and feelings and the thoughts and feelings of others is the essential activity which makes meaningful learning (and thus personal change) possible. Usually the pseudo-listener focuses upon a word or a phrase used by the speaker and tries to engage him in intellectualized and sterile argumentation—in a *pseudo-exchange.* While this pseudo-exchange occasionally takes the road of a meaningless pseudo-agreeing, most frequently the road is that of equally meaningless *pseudo-debate.* The argument and the desire to win become all-important. This struggle to win for winning's sake constitutes the nadir of inactivity.

Avoidance of activity is even more pointedly encountered in a symptom picture which recently roused much concern, the widely reported inability of a significant percentage of youngsters of school age to learn to read (Roswell & Natchez, 1964). The situation here is somewhat analogous to nonlistening, except that what is not listened or attended to is the written rather than the spoken word. It is as if the child remained static. A comparable nonresponsiveness occurs in very subtle and highly disguised fashion in avid readers who report that they must reread and reread and still do not have a ghost of an idea of what they have read. At times such people state their problem succinctly and correctly by saying that they are incapable of paying attention or concentrating. What they hear goes in one ear and out the other; when they read they don't grasp or remember. An even more subtly disguised but even more pathological frozenness is seen in those with the apparent ability to pay attention to what is presented in any other fashion, but who do so without being in any way moved. They read many books, engage in many conversations, listen to music, view paintings—yet none of these stimulations affects them. The stimuli register on a sensory level, yet the person fails to go beyond where he was before. Such a person does not react, hears no inner voices, and remains inactive.

The third ear Reik (1949) has written about so eloquently, the inner ear attuned to the subtleties of one's own personal reactions, capable of aiding the listener in his quest to grasp the full nature of what is communicated, seems to be deaf in such individuals. Attention—the sensitivity to oneself which represents the foundation for the full grasp of the stimulus—is missing. Such inattention (such fundamental inactivity) was known to the ancient Hebrews. When in their most holy prayer the people of Israel are exhorted to *hear* what they are being told, the term employed is not the available synonym derived from the Hebrew word for "ear." Hearing is not to proceed by listening with the ear; a much more profound listening or hearing is called for, a hearing with the third or inner ear, with one's viscera, with one's full being: an attending to one's inner voices. This lack of intensive hearing is referred to here as inactivity; it is total involvement in one's reactions to stimuli which is deemed activity.

Such activity requires utmost effort. Schachtel (1959) points out that such "focal attention" represents an extremely difficult task and is therefore of relatively short duration He has suggested that this difficulty may well be responsible for the child's often-exasperating demands to have a story read over and over again. The child seems to have caught the content of the story; he seems fully aware of such slight dishonesties as attempts to skip a line or a short passage and immediately objects, demanding that everything be read. This type of behavior may be taken as evidence for the repetition compulsion —or as evidence for the child's simple desire to remain with a given stimulus in accordance with the presumed conservatism of his nature. Schachtel, however, suggests the possibility that one really encounters here the child's inability fully to grasp all his own reactions to the material in one or two readings, that he is capable of such intense attention for only short periods of time and consequently requires numerous readings. Schachtel suggests that such behavior may be akin to that of adults eager to reread a book, revisit an exhibition, or rehear a symphony lest they miss nuances in the communication and the subtleties of their own experience. It may reflect the hope that the next time one will discover something new in the encounter, or will discover a new intellectual, emotional, or esthetic reaction in oneself.

Quickness and activity are therefore *not* synonymous. Too often quickness is the exact opposite of activity, representing glibness rather than action. For this reason many psychotherapists are suspicious when a person claims too quickly to have grasped the nature of his own experience. Such an "ability" frequently stands for a capacity to exchange quickly one form of schema of oneself for another without the genuine activity implied in serious search. Quickness is therefore the hallmark of pseudo-activity and pseudo-aliveness. An illustration will point up the futility of "quick" understanding.

☐ An apparently highly gifted and in formal terms very intelligent twenty-year-old college student sought help for his inability to study and do written assignments. He claimed to be greatly distressed by his wasting time and opportunities, but no matter how he tried he could not mobilize himself to productive effort.

His finally seeking therapeutic help was precipitated by his procrastination in writing a term paper for one of his courses. The young man had written a short essay which had greatly impressed his professor, who then called him to his office to give him additional references and to offer the student help in developing his paper. The first draft was long overdue and the patient had not even started on it.

The therapist casually mused that he wondered what the patient thought about the instructor's feelings on this matter. With the flicker of a smile and no hesitation whatsoever, the young man replied: "Oh, I can catch it quite distinctly. This must be my hostility toward authority figures."

No signs of effort really to "catch" anything but instead the urgency to find quick, presumably impressive, but (alas) also glib formulations came to the fore. □

This does not mean that ponderous belaboring of trivia necessarily reflects activity and life; such dissipation also suggests an attempt to waste time and in so doing to avoid genuine activity while gravely wearing the mask of active involvement. Nonetheless a variety of contemporary educational and psychological measuring devices do try to assess the "quickness" with which certain associational bonds are established or the number of minutiae with which a person is capable of busying himself. One may conclude that this reflects the test-developers' expression of a culture which in many ways rewards both glibness and "busy work," a culture in which image rather than substance assumes paramount importance, as Boorstin (1962) and other contemporary critics (Whyte, 1956; Barzun, 1959) have pointed out so excellently.

The discussion so far may be summarized by saying that psychological well-being is synonymous with psychological aliveness; that this aliveness shows itself most potently in effortful activity; and that activity, paradoxically, both requires and reflects itself in openness to stimulation—internal or external, intellectual, physical, or emotional. Evaluating a person's psychological well-being therefore revolves around the assessment of his availability and openness to experience. Such openness cannot exist unless the person is ready to experience the unforeseen, the odd, the new, even the fantastic, shows the willingness to be surprised. Inability to stand surprise thus becomes one of the common denominators of emotional illness. In the course of active engagement individuals are bound to stumble upon surprising elements around them and within them; if this is disturbing, the best guarantee against surprise is utter inactivity or the disguised inactivities described above.

Why do some human beings studiously avoid surprise? Traditionally, the explanations take some variation of the homeostatic principle as their point of departure. It is contended that the unfamiliar is inherently frightening, that the organism innately shies away from the new, that the conservative nature of nature militates against the awareness of the surprisingly novel within and outside the individual. Writers who do not accept this theory of inherent conservativism (Rogers, 1951; Sullivan, 1953) propose that the new and unforeseen is avoided only when it has noxious implications—when it is anxiety-arousing either directly or by association, or when such awareness has damaging consequences for a cherished self-image. In a similar vein, Freud (1925b) suggested that resistance to the psychoanalytic theory of behavior had its origins in the fact that the insights psychoanalysis offers to man reflect unfavorably upon him. In a different context Freud (1904a) called attention to phenomena such as slips of the tongue which bring to the fore unknown and hence surprising elements in the person. Since these facets had been pushed out of awareness because of their original anxiety-arousing potential, people are prone to deny the significance of such phenomena just as they try their best not to be surprised and to rationalize away these potentially surprise-evoking events.

Fromm's (1951) thinking runs along similar lines; he suggests that many dreams reveal startling insights on the part of the dreamer, unpleasant insights which are rejected in waking life in order to avoid anxiety. He illustrates his point by citing a dream in which a trusted business associate is seen as a mean crook, certainly a surprising and potentially anxiety-arousing idea. As it turned out, the dreamer was correct; shortly after the dream it became known that his partner had falsified the books. Fromm suggests that the dreamer had noticed something about his partner he would rather not have seen and relegated this disturbing awareness to the realm of unawareness, only to be startled by the dream.

In addition to anxiety, there is another important factor which may be held responsible for man's avoidance of surprise. The occurrence of something surprising is a potent reminder to a person that he is neither complete nor omniscient, and that life is full of uncertainties. The new or surprising, whether the explicit implications are pleasant or unpleasant, is disturbing if the individual is loath to think of himself as unfinished or uncertain. A person who must think of himself as complete and omniscient cannot possibly bear the new and surprising. To think this way is important to people who have experienced situations in which lack of perfection was anxiety-producing or was frowned upon by significant persons in their past, or where it implied the danger of all kinds of attacks and destruction. The person who has never had the opportunity to develop a sense of basic trust, and who from distrust must always be ahead of the game, must know all there is to know lest he perish. It is highly characteristic of the individual who dare not be surprised that he is pervasively suspicious; he views life as a jungle inhabited by wild and ferocious beasts.

The person without the capacity to experience surprise virtually denies his existence by surrendering the possibility of developing himself in any expansive fashion. Living under the belief that genuine growth and development are dangerous, he abandons what is both the instrument and the symptom of growth: the ability to be startled. Since the awareness of this surrender is unbearable (Fromm, 1955), pseudo-activity is employed to mask the devastating insight of psychological death. The person in this dilemma organizes his world in mechanical or magical terms, full of rules and regulations he has learned but does not understand. He reacts often like a well-functioning computer, producing responses and answers as they were programmed into the machine without the creative ability to develop new insights. Under such circumstances activity is simply mechanical responding; pseudo-activity takes the place of genuine activity. Uncertainty is reduced to a minimum lest he become aware of the independent and responsible existence he dare not face. The tragedy of the person incapable of surprise is that to maintain some semblance of life he has secretly committed psychological suicide and then cloaked this suicide with illusory life. A clinical excerpt will illustrate.

☐ A highly obsessional young man was in the habit of describing any conflict between him and another person in endless though irrelevant detail. He would ruminate about the exact location, time, and other external aspects of the event. Asked why he spent so much time on these matters, he would reply indignantly that these details might lead to valuable associations clarifying the psychological meaning of the occurrence. Eventually it became clear that in the overwhelming majority of these instances, far from being wronged, he—a man who prided himself on his considered concern for humanity—had grossly humiliated somebody else. It could be seen, however, that while expressing marked chagrin at this revelation, a faint smile crossed his lips. When this was called to his attention, he denied it vehemently but after this had occurred several times and the therapist had asked him to pay close attention to the nature of his experience, he finally remarked with obvious surprise and some genuine concern that he did feel some pleasure about having humiliated somebody. He had suddenly learned something genuinely new about himself and, although it was nothing he felt he could be proud of, he mentioned that he experienced a sense of satisfaction, less depression, and less hopelessness. □

What had happened? The patient's frozenness and inability to grasp his experience had momentarily lifted and he was therefore capable of making a surprising discovery, revealing to him at least fleetingly his ability to become genuinely active as a self-observer instead of being forced to engage in verbal busy work.

An intricate relationship exists between the capacity for surprise and the capacity to listen, for whenever one truly listens one exposes oneself to the possibility of surprise. If one does not want to be surprised his best bet is not to listen, either to others or to himself. The capacity for surprise is synonymous with the capacity to stand uncertainty, yet every genuine activity by initiating change implies uncertainty of outcome. Active listening, too, entails uncertainty, change, surprise, and ultimately self-awareness. The person who cannot bear the sense of his changing because it requires his independent and responsible existence, the man for whom *embeddedness* (Schachtel, 1959) is of paramount importance, is incapable of active listening lest he expose himself to the inevitable surprise which activity and its implicit personal change bring about. Therefore, Hutchinson (1941) concluded that he who actively produces something new after having listened to himself and others simultaneously also "becomes something as well" (p. 43). He who dares not become something new dares not listen and dares not be surprised.

Yet, the capacity to experience surprise joyfully is basic to the organism, albeit a capacity all too often lost. It is clearly observed in the infant who diligently tries to master a new skill or gain new insight. The quest for novelty and the pleasure he takes in his development are strikingly evident on the face of the toddler when he performs a most surprising and startling feat, a feat fraught with uncertainty: when he rotates the image of the world ninety degrees, leaves the prone position and struggles to sit and then to stand upright. This quest for uncertainty, not certainty; for surprise, not tranquillity; for the new, not the familiar is the prototype of each achievement and scientific or artistic advance in the history of mankind. Avoidance of surprise seems more adult than childlike; more the reflection of neurotic inactivity than of the restlessness which characterizes well-being.

Another facet of psychological well-being requires more detailed discussion. Competitiveness, though often thought of as a hallmark of activity and vigor, in fact implies the exact opposite. People engaged in competitive activity—one even hesitates to use the term *activity* in this connection—violently engage in behavior which focuses not primarily upon the task at hand but upon the reduction or destruction of somebody else. To win supremacy is all-important; concern with expansion of self, with surprise, or with genuine experience is secondary or totally lacking. Material that has been mastered for essentially competitive purposes can be readily discarded once the competition has stopped, for at that moment it is no longer useful. The competitive orientation denies the value of interest for interest's sake, denies the value of activity *qua* activity. Indeed, it is likely that the competitive individual is in search of the ultimate inactivity made possible by supremacy; unless, of course, he then fears being dislodged. The head that wears the crown rests uneasy only if it is the crown and not the joy of actively using one's abilities that is important, if maintaining status is cherished over evolving.[2]

Just as speed cannot be taken as an index of activity, neither is competitiveness a characteristic of genuine activity. It is rather a denigration of competence. The competitive orientation is not of commitment but of *pseudo-commitment* and *pseudo-declaration,* for commitment clearly means a stand *for* or on behalf of something or somebody, not simply one against something or somebody. Of course, human beings are capable of deluding themselves into believing that they are truly devoted to something while they are in fact merely against something. Under such circumstances the pseudo-commitment becomes an empty gesture, designed to avoid awareness of the lack of commitment and to camouflage destructive hostility. Thus hostility, being simply against without simultaneously being for something, is the ultimate antithesis of genuine activity. Consider this excerpt from the author's clinical material:

☐ During a heated Presidential election campaign, a twenty-four-year-old male patient seemed thoroughly committed to the candidacy of one of the contenders. The young man considered him by far the more desirable candidate because he seemed to the patient much more "liberal," and the patient had always thought of himself as politically left of center. His parents, on the other hand, were clearly and outspokenly in support of the other candidate. The patient lived away from home but visited his parents about once a week. While he did not wear the campaign button of his candidate during the week, feeling that this kind of campaigning was silly, when he went home to visit he would sprout the largest campaign button he could find and flaunt it before his parents. (One of his biggest

---

[2] Looked at this way, *all* competitiveness is a move against somebody rather than an effort to grow, learn, and develop. Undoubtedly, those social and economic systems which take as their point of departure the law of the jungle and the perversion of Darwinian thought will foster competition and thereby promote psychological illness and psychological death. For these reasons Fromm (1955, 1962) maintains that psychological well-being requires ultimately a total economic and social reorientation and reorganization, a position thoroughly supported by this author.

complaints had always been the conformist attitude of his parents. He had often expressed keen disappointment with his father's gross dependence upon his [the patient's] mother, the father's inability to do anything without the wife's approval, his readiness to change his own position in order to please his wife. But not the patient; he felt he was free and committed to what he felt was right, he was truly independent, although his troublesome symptoms existed despite such freedom of the spirit.)

He could not understand at all why his domineering mother, who openly supported the other candidate, would smile benignly and happily when the patient appeared at her house with his enormous, defiant campaign button. Clearly mama knew better. She knew that her son was not really committed to his candidate but was only against hers. To this extent, of course, his behavior was only apparently independent. It was actually governed, in a roundabout way, by the position she took. He was not really for, he only pretended to be for, somebody; she was still calling the tune. □

An additional important aspect characterizing activity deserves mention. Genuine activity cannot take place unless the individual is prepared to forget convenient schematizations learned on previous occasions and is capable of doing so. While many schematizations are undoubtedly useful in man's effort to bring order into his personal universe and enable him to deal efficiently with a multitude of life's problems, such schematizations also diminish the degree of his involvement and experience. The quest for order (often a reflection of the desire to avoid surprise) leads not infrequently to rigid and premature attempts at categorizing and schematizing and therefore culminates in a type of abstracting which all too often precludes activity and reactivity altogether. In other instances, this makes for diminished refinement of intellectual understanding. To illustrate: human beings learn rather quickly that an organism of given shape, size, and other characteristics may be abstractly classified and referred to as a dog. They learn to employ concepts which facilitate communication and through categorization bring about order. But, as Rapaport and his associates (1945) pointed out so well, any concept embraces both more than any one given instance and also at the same time minimizes the specifics subsumed under the concept. The concept of dog embraces many more dogs than any given dog and at the same time any given dog is more than just a dog—it may be short-haired or long-haired, small or big, friendly or mean.

In every act of categorizing one loses as much as one gains. Genuine activity is therefore characterized by a peculiar readiness not to categorize or abstractify in a once-and-for-all fashion; by a readiness to see the varying realms to which a particular object may belong simultaneously; by a willingness to forget convenient classification procedures so as to make possible the development of new methods of categorization. Psychologists are fond of referring to this willingness and readiness as "ability to shift." This term is quite appropriate, provided it is clearly understood that underlying this ability to shift is a readiness to leave things unsettled, to stand uncertainty, to leave things open, a readiness which makes further exploratory activity possible.[3] If things are settled, categorized, and once-and-for-all-time decided, further activity is clearly precluded. Genuine activity therefore requires—paradoxical as this may seem—the capacity to abandon what has been learned to make new learning and understanding possible. This capacity, though usually associated with strictly intellectual pursuits, is of course also essential in other areas of living. Obviously, only when men were ready to abandon the "knowledge" that the earth was flat could they learn that it was round. Similarly, only when one can abandon certain learned ways of looking at emotional experiences can he go on and learn to see more sharply and correctly the nature of his emotional reactions. Only a person who can forget that he has learned to look upon himself as one who is never angry can learn that he is angry when anger is indeed what he experiences.

This capacity to shift one's perceptual approach, a capacity

[3] The concept of "intolerance of ambiguity" originally introduced by Frenkel-Brunswik (1949) is closely related to the thoughts suggested here.

necessary for genuine activity, can be observed most strikingly in the play activities of children. What is frequently referred to as imaginativeness reflects this flexibility. Any object with box-like characteristics can become a car that is pulled along the ground, any stick can become a shovel, any enclosure can become a house. Careful observation will reveal that the child does not really confuse a little matchbox with a car, a stick with a shovel, or an enclosure with a house. However, the child seems willing to acknowledge some similarities when such similarities are useful in the pursuit of activity and will abandon them when they are no longer useful in his quest for action. Creative imagination, a characteristic feature of the active individual, is found most prominently in the child; absence of such creative imagination characterizes the adult neurotic and the psychotic. Exercise of childlike creative imagination, implying flexibility and activity, also reflects adult sanity —as Trilling and others have so often pointed out, although all too frequently in vain. Trilling wrote:

> . . . in the early nineteenth century, with the development of a more elaborate psychology and a stricter and more literal view of mental and emotional normality, the statement [that the poet was "mad"] was more strictly and literally intended. So much so, indeed, that Charles Lamb, who knew something about madness at close quarters and a great deal about art, undertook to refute in his brilliant essay, "On the Sanity of True Genius," the idea that the exercise of the imagination was a kind of insanity. And some eighty years later, the idea having yet further entrenched itself, Bernard Shaw felt called upon to argue the sanity of art, but his cogency was of no more avail than Lamb's [1957, p. 155].

He goes on to point out that active utilization of imagination in the creative endeavor, the artistic expression of what is grasped, denotes sanity rather than insanity and concludes that:

> Nothing is so characteristic of the artist as his power of shaping his work, of subjugating his raw material. . . . What marks the artist is his power to shape the material of pain we all have [p. 170].

The emphasis is clearly upon the activity in artistic creation which differentiates the artist from the essentially inactive neurotic, even though the latter may try to imitate the active involvement of the creative person. But his imitation is sham and pretense rather than activity.[4]

The criteria here proposed for the evaluation of emotional well-being can be summed up in one word: *childlikeness*. Not childishness (which seems a development of later life) but childlikeness characterized by activity and reflected in attentive involvement, openness to experience, readiness for surprise, willingness to stand uncertainty, and the capacity to shift flexibly the focus of perception and inquiry. It seems childlike to be able to listen—consider the rapt attention of which children seem capable—adults are too eager to make points of their own; it seems childlike to be able to go over something time and again, to be able to be thorough—there is ample evidence of this type of behavior in children, while the adult (especially the neurotic adult) is all too eager to "get on with it quickly and get it over with," even if this means reading a condensation of a novel or the digest of the news; it seems childlike to be inquisitive, to explore, to give a shriek of glee when a surprising discovery is made—boredom seems an adult and neurotic phenomenon; it seems childlike to be adventurous—the neurotic is inactive in his cowardice.

His own body and his own emotions as well as the universe around him serve the child as fields for exploration, and the courage required to stand up reflects courageous activity rarely equaled in so-called maturity. Bettelheim (1950) once suggested that these explorations are interfered with from the earliest days of life. He made the telling point that the very way in which appliances are designed is in total disregard of the inquisitive nature of the child. Finally, it must be noted that the devotion and solidarity of which children are capable are of an order hardly ever surpassed in adulthood. The sensitive adult is indeed touched when he observes a toddler on the playground discovering an old dirty Dixie cup cover, picking it

---

[4] For a fuller presentation of the problem of creativity and empirical data related to the present discussion, see Getzels and Jackson (1962).

up, and then with the greatest glee running over to somebody and offering it gladly, handing over such a treasure with a grunt designed to communicate "Here, have it. . . ." Children are notorious for their readiness to give away toys—somehow naïvely expecting to be handed toys by others with equal willingness, of course—until they become educated that one ought not to be such a "stupid sucker." Only then does one notice a presumably inherent selfishness in youngsters. And the readiness of the child to defend his friend, to protect him, and to further his welfare is something poets write about; psychologists with rare exceptions such as Sullivan (1963) are much too busy with "grave and serious" matters to take note.

Equating psychological well-being with childlike qualities is by no means a recent development. The thought that "a little child shall lead them" to salvation reflects ancient recognition that the child in man represents his hold on sanity. The same idea is also expressed poetically by Nietzsche (Kaufmann, 1954) in *Thus Spoke Zarathustra*. This well-known story is of a man who at thirty abandons life as he knows it, seeks the solitude of the mountains, and remains there for ten years. At the age of forty he decides to leave his place of meditation and rejoin his fellow men. On the way back he meets an old man he had apparently passed on his way into the mountains ten years earlier. This is what the old man has to say to Zarathustra in the Prologue:

> No stranger to me is this wanderer: many years ago he passed this way. Zarathustra he was called, but he has changed. At that time you carried your ashes to the mountains; would you now carry your fire into the valleys? Do you not fear to be punished as an arsonist?
>
> Yes, I recognize Zarathustra. His eyes are pure, and around his mouth there hides no disgust. Does he not walk like a dancer?
>
> Zarathustra has changed, Zarathustra has become a child, Zarathustra is an awakened one; what do you now want among the sleepers? You lived in your solitude as in the sea, and the sea carried you. Alas, would you now climb ashore? Alas, would you again drag your own body? [Pp. 122–23].

This reawakening to childhood constitutes the goal of the psychotherapeutic process. The lifting of the childhood amnesia which Freud (1904c) saw so clearly as the aim of psychoanalytic investigation has much wider ramifications than the simple, factual recall of events past and has as its aim the reorganization of experience into essentially childlike human terms. The operational reflections of emotional well-being and/or psychotherapeutic success are those qualities which reflect and make possible active growth and enable a person to bear the inevitable anxiety associated with the uncertainties of change. Only when the individual is capable of facing this anxiety can he use his vision fully and experience himself and the world around him in realistic and rational rather than fictitious terms. The specific aspects of the psychotherapeutic aim as sketched here contribute to this single goal of emotional re-education—the reawakening of fearless awareness.

If these are the qualities the therapeutic encounter is to rekindle, it is reasonable to hope that they also be qualities of the therapist. Freud (1912b) insisted that the "basic rule" for the patient to say all that comes to his mind without censoring has a significant counterpart for the therapist. He recommended to the therapist that he maintain an "evenly suspended attention" (p. 111) to the patient's communications and his own reactions and associations to the material produced, not to censor or reject his own experience vis-à-vis the patient. He did not suggest that the analyst simply verbalize his thoughts, feelings, and reactions, he merely insisted that the analyst not dismiss them as meaningless. (When Groddeck [1951] referred to himself as a "wild analyst," what he meant was that he was not afraid of seemingly wild associations, hunches, reactions, and intuitive voices within him.) Freud's admonition has bearing upon the specifics of emotional well-being outlined here. The therapist must be capable of genuinely listening to others. He must be prepared for and even cherish the experience of surprise, must eagerly strive to reduce as much as possible his own needs to schematize experience, and must be capable of declaring and committing himself. In brief, he must himself be prepared to struggle toward achieving the maturity of the child.

The therapist must possess these characteristics so that he may lead a fruitful life of his own devoid of the temptation to exploit his profession and his patients for his own neurotic ends, such as the obscuring of his own inactivity or the dissembling of his own lack of aliveness. Only when the therapist can bear truths about himself, when he has reached a level of psychological well-being characterized by genuine love for knowledge of himself, will he be capable of hearing the patient and grasping how he remains inactive. Then he will also be able to understand the patient's premises which make him prefer this state of semiconsciousness—only then will the therapist be in a position to help his patient toward greater activity and productive living. Freud (1937) recognized the importance of these qualities for the practitioner of psychological healing in an important paper written in the last years of his life:

> . . . the special conditions of analytic work do actually cause the analyst's own defects to interfere with his making a correct assessment of the state of things in his patient and reacting to them in a useful way. It is therefore reasonable to expect of the analyst, as a part of his qualifications, a considerable degree of normality and correctness. In addition he must possess some kind of superiority, so that in certain analytic situations he can act as a model for his patient and in others as a teacher. And finally we must not forget that the analytic relationship is based on a love of truth—that is, on a recognition of reality—and that it precludes any kind of sham or deceit [1937, p. 248].

Possession of the characteristics of emotional well-being outlined in this chapter is of importance not only for the therapist; it is equally valuable for the work of the teacher and the guidance counselor. Not only psychotherapists but also teachers and counselors labor to help others grow toward a full sense of freedom. The nurturing and development of the inner freedom to hear oneself fully frees one to hear others; and the freedom to use one's powers actively brings in its wake the readiness to let others use their powers equally productively.

Because the origins of contemporary psychotherapy and modern education are deeply rooted in man's struggle for personal growth, dedicated teachers and therapists are committed to aid human beings in this process of emerging.

But it must be remembered that as this struggle has intensified during the nineteenth and twentieth centuries, opposing forces outside as well as within man have also increased. In addition to the cultural, economic, political, and social forces opposed to this growth (see p. 19), equally powerful and restrictive forces operate within man. They are the fears every human being feels when he becomes aware of his inevitable personal responsibilities, fears which facilitate denial of his potentialities. And only the most unobservant would deny that such forces of fear reside in every man. They reside in the teacher as well as in the psychotherapist, they reside in the student as well as in the patient. And teachers as well as therapists are responsible for helping their charges to deal with these forces of fear. They can only do so to the extent to which they have effectively dealt with them themselves. Once again one cannot help being awed by the depth of Freud's insight:

> Here let us pause for a moment to assure the analyst that he has our sincere sympathy in the very exacting demands he is expected to fulfil in carrying out his activities. It almost looks as if analysis were the third of those 'impossible' professions in which one can be sure beforehand of achieving unsatisfying results. The other two, which have been known much longer, are education and government [1937, p. 248].

Freud recognized, though with undue pessimism, how difficult it is to grow toward what he had called the "love of truth" and how "impossible" and yet essential it was to help individuals grow toward such love. When Sullivan (1947) defined "psychiatric cure" unequivocally as a progressively expanding evolution of the self and self-awareness, he too placed the accent on a love of truth concerning one's own being. And Fromm's (1955) definition of emotional well-being: "The mentally healthy person is . . . [he] who is in the process of being born as long as he is alive . . ." (p. 275) certainly echoes an insistence and emphasis upon a striving for continuous unfolding as the hallmark of psychological maturity and vitality. Both Sullivan and Fromm could do so, happily, with more optimism than Freud because both saw the nature and the roots of man's conflict in terms quite different from those Freud proposed, because neither of them saw this conflict in the essentially biological terms Freud had advanced. Neither denied the conflict *in* man but each in his own way conceived of it as an extension of conflicts *around* man rather than inherently caused by the presence of Eros and Thanatos. More will have to be said on this point in subsequent chapters.

But Freud was the first to call attention to this conflict in man, and therein lies his monumental contribution, even though he saw its origins in terms unsupported by present-day findings. The significance of his contribution lay neither in his defining the opposing forces as he saw them nor in the intricate theories he spun concerning their origins and manifestations, but in his fearless insistence that there was a conflict in man, that the effects of this conflict may make him appear less than a saint, and the recognition that man could move closer to saintliness by acknowledging his humanness and the visions and vistas that self-awareness opens.

Bruner summed up the case for Freud in precisely those terms when he wrote:

> Can Freud's contribution to the common understanding of man in the twentieth century be likened to the impact of such great physical and biological theories as Newtonian physics and Darwin's conception of evolution? The question is not an empty one. Freud's mode of thought is not a theory in the conventional sense, it is a metaphor, it is an analogy, a way of conceiving man, a drama. I would propose that Anaximander is the proper parallel: his view of the connectedness of physical nature was also an analogy—and a powerful one. Freud is the ground from which theory will grow, and he has prepared the twentieth century to nurture the growth. But far more important, he has provided an image of man that has made him comprehensible without at the same time making him contemptible [1957, p. 285].

Psychotherapy is dedicated precisely to this aim: to make man comprehensible to himself, to help man fearlessly see himself, and to help him learn that this process of self-recognition, far from producing contempt, implies and brings about the achievement of dignity and self-fulfillment.

► *Summary* ◄

1. Genuine activity is synonymous with emotional well-being. This equating of activity with psychological health is deeply rooted in the religious and literary heritage of civilized man.

2. Such self-transcending activity has certain reflections which may be defined and described. Among them one finds most prominently the capacities to be attentive, to be surprised, and to bear uncertainty courageously. A variety of factors and forces make difficult the achievement of such maturity —maturity which incorporates a childlike quality.

3. Genuine, functional activity implies and brings about self-awareness and the recognition of one's essential incompleteness. At the same time the development of such knowledge and the striving toward heightened levels of awareness—even though awareness may never be complete—is in itself the hallmark of emotional well-being.

4. Various authors employing different basic assumptions agree that the struggle toward awareness and the physical, intellectual, and emotional activities accompanying this effort constitute operational definitions of psychic health.

Communication, Symbolization, and Symptomatology

A new step is taken with the development of man. First of all the emotions become more specified. They are no longer dim and vague feelings; they refer to special classes of objects. But there is still another feature that we find nowhere except in the human world, though, there are to be sure innumerable human reactions which do not differ in principle from animal reactions. If a man answers an insult by knitting his brows or clenching his fist, he acts precisely in the same way an animal does when it shows its teeth in the presence of an enemy. But generally speaking human *responses* belong to quite a different type. What distinguishes them from animal reactions is their *symbolic* character. In the rise and growth of human culture we can follow step by step this change of meaning. Man has discovered a new mode of expression: symbolic expression. This is the common denominator in all his cultural activities: in myth and poetry, in language, in art, in religion, and in science [Cassirer, 1955, p. 54].

CASSIRER'S THOUGHTS, DEVELOPED FURTHER IN ANOTHER BOOK (1956), are quite clear and raise an important question: Why this expression of feelings and emotions? Some authors insist that such metapsychological questioning is meaningless; others argue that an adequate answer to this question sharpens the understanding of man's nature, needs, pathology, and health. As was pointed out in Chapter 2, numerous investigators have proposed that behavior in general and expressive behavior in particular occurs when visceral imbalances force the individual to turn to others for help in re-establishing homeostasis, and that those symbolic communications which cannot be ascribed directly to excitation-reduction tendencies are explainable in terms of associated reinforcement (Dollard & Miller, 1950). The position that tissue deficits are responsible for all, including communicative, behavior culminates in Feigl's (1959) hope for an ultimately strictly operational neuro-physiological approach to behavior sequences. Within this framework symbolizations and communications are conditioned intervening variables, means to an end (positivists may even frown at that much teleology) but certainly not ends in themselves.

Others have thought about the problem in different terms and therefore developed different conceptions. Some observers suggest that only a relatively small amount of behavior communicates physiological imbalances and that therefore the origins of communicative behavior must be found in other than strictly excitation-reducing tendencies. Other psychological motives, they insist, must enter (White, R. W., 1959). As a philosopher Langer has concerned herself with this issue extensively. She remarked in one of her contributions:

That man is an animal I certainly believe; and also that he has no supernatural essence, "soul" or "entelechy" or "mind stuff," enclosed in his skin. He is an organism, his substance is chemical, and what he does, suffers, or knows is just what this sort of chemical structure may do, suffer, or know. When the structure goes to pieces, it never does, suffers, or knows anything again. If we ask how physical objects, chemically analyzable, can be conscious, how ideas can occur to them, we are talking ambiguously; for the concept of "physical object" is a conception of chemical substance *not* biologically organized. What causes this tremendous organization of substance, is one of the things the tremendous organisms do not know; but with their organization, suffering and impulse and awareness arise. It is really no harder to imagine that a chemically active body wills, knows, thinks, and feels, than that an invisible intangible something does so, "animates" the body without physical agency, and "inhabits" it without being in any *place* [1948, pp. 31–32]. . . .

Now this is a mere declaration of faith, preliminary to a confession of heresy. The heresy is this: that I believe there is a primary need in man, which other creatures probably do not have, and which actuated all his apparently unzoölogical aims, his wistful fancies, his consciousness of value, his utterly impractical enthusiasms, and his awareness of a "Beyond" filled with holiness. Despite the fact that his need gives rise to almost everything that we commonly assign to the "higher" life, it is not itself a "higher" form of some "lower" need: it is quite essential, imperious, and general, and may be called "high" only in the sense that it belongs exclusively (I think) to a very complex and perhaps recent genus. It may be satisfied in crude primitive ways or in conscious refined ways, so it has its own hierarchy of "higher" and "lower," elementary and derivative forms. . . .

This basic need, which certainly is obvious only in man, is the need for symbolization [p. 32].

Here is a point of view which considers symbolizations and communications not merely means to an end but ends in themselves, expressions of a basic tendency—and certainly not a stimulus-reducing tendency. To Langer's mind the urge to depict inner states and thereby to transcend the narrow confines of one's being is an inherent and independent human striving. She made this quite clear in another passage:

There is a widespread and familiar fallacy, known as the "genetic fallacy," which arises from the historical method in philosophy and criticism: the error of confusing the *origin* of a thing with its *import,* of tracing the thing to its most primitive form and then calling it "merely" this archaic phenomenon. In a philosophy of symbolism this mistake is particularly fatal, since *all elementary symbolic forms have their origin in something else than symbolic interest*. Significance is always an adventitious value. Words were probably ritualistic sounds before they were communicative devices: but this does not mean that language is now not "really" a means of communication, but is "really" a mere residue of tribal excitement. Musical materials, likewise, presumably had other uses before they served music; that does not imply that music is "really" not an intellectual achievement, and expression of musical ideas, at all, but is in reality a mere invocation of rain or game, or a rhythmic aid to dancers or what not [pp. 201–2].

In assigning the urge to communicate to the realm of basic human strivings, Langer parallels Sullivan's (1953) thinking notably his idea that direct and immediate physical contact and communication between organisms is a prerequisite for life; that the child's development will suffer significantly if such opportunities for contact are absent or minimal. Spitz's (1945, 1946, 1955) clinical studies of infants suffering from hospitalism led him to a similar conclusion, even if one makes allowances for the inaccuracies in his data suggested by Pinneau (1955a, 1955b). And Harlow's (1958) previously cited research supports Spitz's findings, Sullivan's theoretic conceptions, and Langer's "heresy." Few psychological or psychiatric investigators go so far as openly to suggest that the urge to communicate in symbolic form is an inherent tendency, but their data certainly lend themselves easily to such interpretation.

Acceptance of the need for communication as a basic tendency of the human being has certain implications for the theory of pathology and the theory of psychotherapy as outlined in the preceding chapters. It leads to the emphasis upon communicative activity as a hallmark of emotional well-being; to the insistence that human beings are psychologically healthy when their activities are intelligible and validifiable symbols of their inner experiences, and that they are pathological when their pseudo-activities disrupt adequate communicative exchange. This point of view posits that all activity is communicative and is either an adequate or inadequate expression of inner states; that even obscure symbolizations (inevitably associated with inactivity or pseudo-activity) are paradoxically also expressive and thereby communicative. Through his confusing symbolizations the patient expresses his desire neither to know nor to experience himself. It is as if he said: "I must tell you that I feel detached and eager to remain removed." But to some extent he apparently also wants to overcome this detachment. Were he unalterably opposed to activity and the aliveness embodied in revealing himself, he would not express his inner states even in his idiosyncratic manner.

An individual's symbolic expressions become unintelligible when he feels that active attention to himself (as a separate entity) and the activity implied in emotional and intellectual living are frowned upon and he therefore experiences them as dangerous. When out of defensiveness and his desire to survive at least marginally he feels forced to be inactive by being inattentive the clarity of his communication must suffer. If the therapeutic process is designed to bring about a diminution of such alienation and concomitantly a greater awareness of self, it is incumbent upon the therapist to help the patient become aware of his experiences by grasping them as they come through in the patient's distorted messages. In grasping the meaning of the patient's expressions and sensing the experiences from which he has shut himself off, the therapist helps the patient see himself as a member of the human race, as a person who can be understood and who can understand himself. And in this process of communicative understanding the therapist joins his patient as a fellow man. The significance of this meeting will be discussed later, notably when the meaning of interpretations and the theory of cure will be considered, in Chapters 9 and 13. All that needs to be noted here is that in understanding the patient's symbolizations the therapist encounters the patient's humanness and in so doing reduces his isolation, which is tantamount to nonbeing. Once again the insights of Freud are significant, no matter how often unnecessary constructs detracted from their potency. In an age which had pinned its hopes upon an artificial rationalism, his was the voice which insisted that man was constantly engaged in a

process of communicative symbolization and that these messages more often than not expressed human voices other than
the voice of pure intellectual reason. Freud insisted that the
study of a person's symbolizations was the study of this individual; that the only way he could be understood was through
the understanding of his symbols, that this was the road to
grasping who he was and what his purposes were.

Despite this profound recognition, Freud and many of his
students unfortunately looked upon symbolization as a process
designed to obscure rather than to communicate. This peculiar
contradiction was a direct consequence of their general theory
of man. So long as the image of man was a vision of him as
both inherently regressive in nature and simultaneously eager
to hide this tendency, symbols had to be understood as methods of dissembling rather than tools in expression. The position
is clearly revealed in a critical comment by Ferenczi:

> I should like to raise here an objection. . . . Only such
> things (and ideas) are symbols in the sense of psycho-
> analysis as are invested in consciousness with a logically
> inexplicable and unfounded affect, and of which it may
> be analytically established that they owe this affective
> over-emphasis to *unconscious* identification with another
> thing (or idea) to which the surplus of affect really be-
> longs. Not all similes therefore, are symbols, but only
> those in which the one member of the equation is re-
> pressed into unconsciousness [1913, pp. 277–78].

Here is a point of view diametrically opposed to ideas advanced by Langer and Cassirer and also at variance with the
deep insight revealed in the suggestion that every move is at
the same time a gesture. Symbolism is here in the service of
*re*pression rather than in the service of *ex*pression. To be sure,
people frequently employ *seemingly* obscuring substitutions
when they try to banish from consciousness material experienced as too anxiety-producing. But even such instances are
basically important expressions of crucial significant inner
states. They are statements saying: "I am afraid to know and
expand through self-knowledge."

Lest it be thought that orthodox psychoanalytic thinking

on this issue has changed very much since those early days of Ferenczi, quotations from Fenichel's writings on the same issue many years later will show differently:

> Another strange characteristic of archaic thinking is represented by symbolism. In adults a conscious idea may be used as a symbol for the purpose of hiding an objectionable unconscious idea; the idea of a penis may be represented by a snake, an ape, a hat, an airplane, if the idea of penis is objectionable. The symbol is conscious, the symbolized idea is unconscious. The distinct idea of a penis has been grasped but rejected. However, symbolic thinking is vague, directed by the primary process. It is not only a method of distortion; it is also part of the primal prelogical thinking. Again the censoring ego uses regressive methods. Again, when distorting through symbolism, the ego in its defensive activities makes use of mechanisms that previously operated automatically without any intent. The use of symbols is a falling back into an earlier primary stage of thinking, by means of which intended distortions are brought about. In dreams, symbols appear in both aspects, as a tool of the dream censorship and also characteristic of archaic pictorial thinking, as part of visualizing abstract thought. . . .
>
> The regressive nature of symbolic distortions explains two facts: (a) that the symbols, being a residual of an archaic way of perceiving the world, are common to all human beings, like affective syndromes; (b) that symbolic thinking occurs not only where distortions have to be made but also in states of fatigue, sleep, psychosis, and generally in early childhood, that is, in all states where archaic ego characteristics are in the foreground [1945, p. 48].

More recently Rubinfine (1961) has also dealt with symbol formation as if it were an obscuring mechanism. Apparently little has changed within classical psychoanalytic theory on this issue over the years.

Strikingly different is the discussion of symbols and their function by those who adopt a different image of man. Sullivan, for instance, unencumbered by the notion that man is inherently regressive and actually assuming an inherently expansive tendency in human nature (power motif), viewed symbols as essentially expressive:

> I am afraid, that for practical purposes, all human behavior so purely and unquestionably manifests the organization of experience into what are in effect signs—whether symbols or signals—that an attempt to discriminate intelligibly in human behavior between what is symbolic and what is nonsymbolic is far more misleading than it is helpful [1953, pp. 186–87].

Sullivan's position, so unlike that of Fenichel, may of course be taken by some as unwarranted reductionism. But reductionism can be less dangerous than classification along misleading lines.

The consequences of the position that all behavior is symbolic expression are unmistakably illustrated by Fromm's thinking. If all human expression inevitably proceeds through symbolization, then the focus of inquiry must shift away from the "whys" of symbolization to the particular connections between inner states and expressive forms. Fromm remarks:

> What are symbols? A symbol is often defined as "something that stands for something else." This definition is rather disappointing. It becomes more interesting, however, if we concern ourselves with those symbols which are sensory expressions of seeing, hearing, smelling, touching, standing for a "something else" which is an inner experience, a feeling or thought. A symbol of this kind is something outside ourselves; that which it symbolizes is something inside ourselves. Symbolic language is language in which we express inner experience as if it were a sensory experience, as if it were something we were doing or something that was done to us in the world of things. Symbolic language is language in which the world outside is a symbol of the world inside.
>
> If we define a symbol as "something which stands for something else" the crucial question is: *What is the specific connection between the symbol and that which it symbolizes?* [1951, pp. 12–13].

Fromm's thought led him to further conclusions. Symbolizations are not only employed in the process of communication with others—the outside world at large—but also aid the individual in communing with himself, in gaining sharply focused insight. His symbolizations may help him bring into bold relief dissociated aspects of himself. This recognition demands detailed treatment in its own right (see Chapter 13). At this point the artistic treatment of this idea in a dream sequence of Bergman's film *Wild Strawberries* will suffice as an illustration. His dream symbols help the hero to a heightened awareness of his own inner situation.

□ He dreams of a barren and deserted village; the windows are shuttered, the stores are empty. Clocks have no hands, time has stopped, there is only an eye, the trade sign of an optician, watching. Suddenly a hearse races down the street, crashes into a lamp post; the coffin slips out, breaks open, and the dreamer sees himself in it: he realizes that he is dead. □

Obviously this is expression, communication with self, not repression.

The understanding of symbols as expressive rather than repressive has important practical consequences. It allows for the insight that symptoms are the patient's representations of his inner state. The symptom a patient exhibits is then an expression, symbolic as any expression must be, of his inner situation. Of course, it may be a relatively simple or extremely complex statement. It may be concerned with only one or it may compress several facets of experience.

Freud (1915b, 1922a, 1933) discussed the "double-edged" meaning of the symptom. As he saw it, each symptom symbolized an impulse and at the same time an effort to oppose it. This understanding of the neurotic symptom has undergone little change within psychoanalytic circles (Fenichel, 1945; Tarachow, 1963). A similar point of view can be found also in the writings of non-Freudian psychoanalysts (Arieti, 1955; Fromm-Reichmann, 1946; Sullivan, 1947). The differences between the latter authors and Freud center around the nature of the impulse and the powers held responsible for its denial. While Freud, in line with his general thinking about man, saw the symptom as a compromise between primitive regressive impulses and forbidding outer and eventually inner-reality agencies, other theorists see the symptom as a compromise between the desire to survive and progress and originally outer (eventually internalized) forces opposing this growth. Fromm-Reichmann (1946), for instance, maintained that any symptom contains not only forces pushing toward defensive self-denial, oblivion, and avoidance of self-actualization, but also energies fighting for life and psychological survival—no matter how feeble. One group views the symptom as an outgrowth of inadequate sublimation, unsuccessful renunciation, and insufficient resignation to the inevitable discontents of civilization; other groups view symptomatology as the consequence of inadequate self-assertion, or a lack of courage to follow one's individual lifeline, or an attempted evasion of anxiety and disapproval.

There are varying views about the internal structure of symptom-formation, but Freud's general proposition that neurotic behavior and symptoms reflect ambivalence, in the sense that they depict conflictual facets within the individual, remains by and large unchallenged. This complication is the basic theme in Freud's understanding of the symbolic value of symptoms and runs like a Wagnerian *Leitmotiv* through the clinical material he presented. His case of little Hans shows this clearly (1909). Hans' particular symptom, a phobic avoidance of horses leading to his refusal to leave the house lest he meet one in the street, was taken by Freud to symbolize at once a hostile wish, the inner experience of this hostility, and Hans' fear of its consequences making for its denial. Several circumstances combined to concretize "horse" as an excellent symbolization of "father." One might ask why Hans was hostile to the father and then felt forced to displace his hostility. It would be difficult to engage in analytic work twice removed; Freud's analysis of Hans was already once removed, a kind of mail-order analysis. But it is possible that, contrary to Freud's suggestion, Hans' hostility was directed less against the father as the inevitable Oedipal rival than against him as a reminder of Hans' own sexual, animalistic (horselike) nature. In view of his cultured home with its high intellectual and artistic interests, the question seems not how much the boy was afraid of his hostile impulses toward the father but to what extent Hans rejected his own biological destiny. The Epilogue (Freud, 1922) to the case report leaves the distinct impression that the marital adjustment of the parents left much to be desired, that there was probably a good deal of discord resulting in divorce. Just how much of this discord was noticed by Hans, making for anxiety and eventually anger with the man he held responsible for causing such discomfort? Whatever the final answer, Freud made it abundantly clear that he considered the symptom a statement of Hans' inner situation, even though exception can be taken with his insistence upon its inevitably instinctual Oedipal nature.

The understanding of symptoms as expressions of conflicts is the foundation on which the work of the psychological investigator rests, be he diagnostician or therapist. (This is a somewhat artificial differentiation, because both are concerned with essentially the same problem: grasping the meaning of behavior and the inner human situation underlying behavioral manifestations.) The ultimate working base of both therapist and diagnostician is their conviction that human beings will inevitably express their inner states symbolically and must do so as long as they live. The work of the psychological practitioner rests on his belief that human beings are capable of understanding the symbolizations employed by their fellow men—are capable of "consensually validating" the personal significance of symbols.

All authors feel free to make this assertion, implicitly or explicitly, because each in his own way maintains that certain crucial experiences are universal and therefore potentially known and capable of being understood by others. Freud (1900, 1936) posited the universality of the Oedipus complex and its attendant castration anxiety. His conviction that each human being must deal with this inevitable experience differs from Adler's (1927) assertion that some other but also inevitable and therefore universal experience (organ inferiority) must be dealt with by each individual in the course of his life.

Rank (1945, 1959) posited experiences he assumed every human being is bound to encounter in his development (separation) and so did each personality theorist whose thinking gave rise to psychotherapeutic approaches. What these systems have in common is that each advances a particular *condition humaine*. Of course authors differ significantly in their definition of the universal human situation, and they differ when they discuss the consequences of these inevitable encounters in living. Most theorists nevertheless agree at least implicitly with Sullivan's (1947) comment that ". . . we are all much more simply human than otherwise . . ." (p. 7), even though what being "simply human" means is defined in various ways.

This generally assumed communality enables one human being to grasp another's experience through understanding his symbolizations. Were such understanding of another person's symbols impossible, psychotherapy as a curative procedure could not exist, for then nobody could develop knowledge of another individual's experience and motivation; patients would remain ununderstood and incomprehensible even to themselves. Belief in the universality of crucial human experiences (no matter how defined) and belief that these experiences and the potential conflicts attending them will inevitably be expressed in symbolic forms capable of being understood by others is the point of no return for contemporary dynamic psychotherapy. It is therefore suggested that consensual validation of the inner state of one person depends upon the other's freedom to be aware of similar states within himself, and to conceive of himself as symbolizing them in similar terms.

This immediately raises a difficult issue: the danger that in his attempts to grasp the inner meaning of symbols used by the patient, and in his effort to get in touch with his patient's experience, the therapist will project his own feelings, ascribing to the patient what goes on within him. Such a projecting process and the dangers surrounding it are unavoidable. Projection is ever-present in the effort to understand another individual because such an effort always requires placing oneself in his position and therefore projection plays a prominent and inevitable role in the empathic process. Unfortunately, since Freud (1911) described the mechanism of projection in his discussion of paranoia, projection has been closely associated with pathology. The term has become associated with the particular defensive operation of ascribing one's own inner tendencies to another person. This is presumably done to avoid acknowledgment that these tendencies are part of oneself.

Where self-avoidance is the intent, a pathological process is undoubtedly present because it represents attempts to reduce self-knowledge. But it would be nonsensical to talk of a pathological process when nondefensive awareness of inner experience is utilized in an effort to understand more fully the meaning of behavior observed in others. A full understanding of others can in fact take place only when nondefensive projection is brought into play. A man stands on a crowded subway platform, for example, and observes how one person with bundles under his arms struggles out of a car, hindered in his attempts by a forward-surging crowd. The passenger fighting his way out shakes his head vehemently and the observer infers that the man is angry. He makes this assumption on the basis of his knowledge that were he in such a situation he would be angered by the rudeness. It seems to him reasonable to surmise the man's anger although his hunch lacks validation. He may therefore approach the stranger and inquire if he was indeed angry. The man may acknowledge that he was annoyed, that he shook his head in angry disapproval. If so, the meaning of the symbolic expression and the experience behind it had been grasped correctly and thus the hunch based on nondefensive projection was validated. Or the man may deny any anger, saying that he more or less expects this type of behavior on the subway and that shaking his head had been occasioned by some irritant on his forehead such as a bead of sweat or a strand of hair he had tried to shake off. The inquirer may assume that the man is telling the truth if he is at all capable of envisioning himself responding good-humoredly in similar circumstances. He may, however, be inclined to believe that the man is "repressing" his anger and that the observer was able to know more than the subject because he is less defensive, more readily in touch with the experience of anger.

If he is at all reasonable he has to admit that this is at best a possibility and that further investigation would be necessary to determine exactly what went on in the man fighting his way out of the subway.[1] None of the possibilities cited could be construed as reflecting pathological projection. One could speak of pathological projection only if the observer was unaware of his own anger in such situations and ascribed anger to the other person to remain unaware of such tendencies within himself.

Similarly, pathological projection by the therapist in his work with patients occurs when he rejects self-knowledge and wishes to remain unaware of personal attributes and qualities. This is a constant danger, and the therapist must always guard against it; this danger is also one of the reasons a personal analysis is an essential prerequisite for the practice of psycho-analytic therapy (Freud, 1937; Fromm-Reichmann, 1949b). Nevertheless the therapist must not avoid utilizing knowledge of himself in his quest to grasp the meaning of his patient's symbolizations. Tauber (1952, 1954) has pointed out how the therapist's reactions to the patient, especially reactions which might make the therapist defensive, can lead to enhanced un-

---

[1] In this connection Royce's distinction between signs and symbols is significant:

> The essence of this distinction is that the sign reveals a one-to-one correspondence, whereas the symbol provides a one-to-many relationship. Although it is true that the sign and the symbol are alike in that they both point beyond themselves to "something else," it is also true that the "something else" they point to is quite different. The "something else" which the sign points to or stands for is definite and specific—such as the conditioned stimulus standing for shock, or the red light on the highway meaning "stop." The "something else" the symbol stands for is also definite and specific; however, it can stand for a wide variety of things at different times and places. . . . The literal, or one-to-one, relationship of the sign must be clearly differentiated from the surplus meaning, or one-to-many relationships, of the symbol [1965, p. 16].

Thus, in Royce's terms, our man's shaking his head is a sign denoting some inner state but, lacking direct and immediately understandable meaning, it is a symbolic statement of some inner state. Since all individual human expressions inevitably have some surplus meaning, human behavior or individual "signs" must always be understood as "symbols."

derstanding of the patient—provided the doctor is ready to examine his reactions carefully, is ready to learn from them about himself and the patient. (Also see Chapter 13.)

A final comment about the use of projection in understanding communicative symbols. Were the subway rider swinging wildly at the crowd, cursing and screaming, little doubt would exist about his inner state. Merely shaking his head made the development of insight more difficult, though it did reflect some inner state, whether anger toward the crowd or eagerness to remove an irritant from his forehead. One may conclude that difficulty in grasping the meaning of symbols increases when they can represent a wide range of divergent and even contradictory feeling tones. Laughter, for instance, can express various experiences. Human beings may laugh at others, with others, out of malice or out of joy, when they feel relieved, and when they are anxious and wish to deny their discomfort. Only when the observer is familiar with this wide range of laughter-producing possibilities within himself can he understand its meaning when he sees somebody else laughing. Were a therapist incapable of experiencing laughter under any one of these circumstances, were he to reject the possibility of a particular circumstance making him laugh, he would be incapable of grasping the meaning of laughter in a patient when it was occasioned by such a personally rejected dynamism. A clinical illustration demonstrates the importance of the therapist's capacity to project himself nondefensively:

☐ A male patient, a social worker by profession, reports an intense anxiety attack during the preceding day. He had attended a psychiatric staff conference at the hospital in which he worked. In the course of the conference there was discussed a young man who had recently been admitted with obvious symptoms of paranoia. The patient to be presented was plagued by the constant sense that people were uttering a phrase which seemed to him highly derogatory. He had frantically moved from one section of the country to another in the hope of escaping his tormentors, but no sooner did he get off the bus in a distant strange town then he thought he heard somebody shout this phrase at him.

The presenting psychiatrist had elicited this information and the nature of the phrase after overcoming the patient's intense reluctance to reveal it and only after he had promised complete confidence. The chief psychiatrist had agreed to conduct his interview with the patient (in front of the staff) in such a fashion as to give the patient the impression that nobody but the treating psychiatrist was aware of his delusion.

Suddenly during the presentation of the patient the social worker felt himself gripped by a strong desire to call out the phrase and became so terrified by this urge that he left the conference abruptly; upon returning to his office he broke into laughter that seemed absurd to him. He was panic-stricken for the rest of the day.

In his therapeutic session he ruminated about the possibility of being grossly self-destructive, for he clearly felt that had he done what he almost did he would have been discharged, would have had to leave his profession, and would be in disgrace. He also wondered about the extent of his hostility to patients if he could be tempted to engage in such insults and assaults.

The therapist listening to the incident also experienced the urge to laugh and envisioned how the presenting psychiatrist would feel and look had his patient been overcome by this impulse. What had been treated as a delusional symptom would suddenly represent a correct perception by the paranoid patient: he could not trust anybody—betrayal was all around. He pondered the possibility that the social worker had identified with the hospitalized patient and had his feeling of intense hostility not so much against the presented patient as toward the presenter who could be viewed as an authority—an unreliable, untrustworthy authority who betrayed confidences. And the presenting psychiatrist could also have been made to look quite foolish in the eyes of the paranoid patient had the social worker acted out his impulse. □

This understanding of the situation was made possible by the therapist's ability to experience anger with irrational authority and his capacity to conceive of expressing it through ridicule.

If symptoms are concrete representations, a person's symptom choice symbolizes succinctly important aspects of his inner state. Full understanding of the symptom is synonymous with understanding the patient and the more profoundly the symptom is understood, the more meaningful has been the communication between patient and therapist. The reason symptomatic cures are deemed undesirable lies in the fact that the disappearance of the symptom, no matter how immediately pleasing to all parties concerned, is ultimately a sign that the communicative process has become somewhat reduced, making further explorations more difficult, unless, of course, the disappearance of the symptom is based upon thorough insight and subsequent resolution of the communicated conflict.

☐ A young man in his early twenties seeks help with what he thinks is his problem in very specific and simple terms. The problem, as the patient sees it, is almost complete impotence and, what is equally disturbing to him, sexual arousal only when some strange woman in a place highly inappropriate for sexual expression, such as the subway or the street, happens to be gripped by a coughing spell.

Careful investigation revealed the various personal meanings of this symptom and symbolization. The patient said through his symptoms: (1) I reject women, want to tell them that they are meaningless to me, and cannot move me; indeed, I do not want them to be of any significance to me (impotence); (2) I can allow myself to feel any interest in them only when I see them in what seems to me a helpless and ridiculous position; they are worthy of my attention only when I see them in what I deem a pitiful situation, then I can magnanimously feel moved by them (arousal through coughing spell); (3) my contempt and hostility are somewhat diminished if and when the person is distant and inaccessible; then I am somewhat moved by the woman, for then there is also little chance for me to express my hostility (arousal in subways, etc.).

The patient's all-pervasive fury and sense of destructiveness furthermore finds an excellent symbolization in his particular sexual symptomatology. Far from being restricted to sexual behavior, his anger, hostility, and destructiveness were evident in all spheres of living; it was only in the sexual realm that through his impotence the rejecting hostile orientation became so obvious. The understanding of his symbolizing processes can be carried further, for in his particular symptom he also expressed simultaneously a good deal of insight, which stated: I am barren and impotent as rejective behavior and blind fury are barren and impotent; my hostility makes me impotent, deprives me of any meaningful satisfaction, makes me literally sterile. This inner sense of sterility and unproductiveness was expressed in the symbol of impotence, hostility and sterility being synonymous. Small wonder that the patient also engaged in rather extensive masturbation, expressing symbolically concern with the question whether he was at all capable of detecting some inner life, whether his hostility had destroyed him completely, whether he was still alive, be it to whatever small degree. □

This is an example of universal symbolism. The inner experience of destructiveness, vicious anger, and hatred—something writers and artists may depict in wasteland, in scorched earth, in barren land incapable of producing growth—is reflected in a personal and yet at the same time universal symbol: impotence. The patient's first dream while in therapy is also quite illustrative of the expressive nature of symbolizations:

□ The therapist had made some tentative comments in the direction outlined above. One night the patient dreamed that he was visiting Bing Crosby, whose first wife Dixie was lying ill in another room, and that he was talking to the singer about his wife's illness. Suddenly there was a commotion in the next room and upon rushing in, the patient saw Dixie vomit profusely. She seemed cured after having thrown up and the patient felt that she was going to be well from then on.[2]

Understanding the dream was not too difficult once it was learned that the patient had always been much impressed by

---

[2] At the time of the dream, newspapers carried accounts of Mrs. Crosby's incurable illness.

Crosby. He now meets a *singer* and the meaning of the pun is clear, a *singer* by whom he is impressed, something generally rare for the patient, and reveals to him his childish hope for the cure of cancer—throwing up his problem, his hope that once he has revealed his problem he will be miraculously well, will have gotten rid of what internally destroys him.

The symbolic connection between his hostility and his passivity reveals itself: even in the process of becoming well he wants to live out his hostility by being and remaining inactive, by simply vomiting up his disease. He symbolizes his interest in therapy but also his interest in remaining inert, sends a message that he intends to remain passive and hostile. It was a tipoff that one should be prepared for long years of work. ☐

Vomiting is actually a rather common symbolization of hostility expressed through passive resistance.

☐ A patient dreamed that she was throwing up, but as she looked she discovered that it really was not vomitus but instead beautiful precious stones that she had brought forth. The dream occurred after the second interview and as therapy progressed it became apparent that she was extremely passive and hostile; despite overt self-derogation she was quite haughty beneath all her humility. The idea that she thought of herself as one who cast pearls before a swine was quite obvious. ☐

Similarily, the male patient discussed earlier was, despite all his self-berating verbalizations, extremely conceited, knew everything better than anybody else, belittled everybody. Parenthetically, vomiting is such a common symbol for passive hostility because it represents perhaps the only and most adequate way children have at their disposal for expressing resistance to having something crammed down their throats, first literally and eventually figuratively. Vomiting becomes the child's passive resistance *par excellence* and indeed, both patients had been raised in homes where parents tried eagerly to indoctrinate their offspring.

The concrete representation of inner states via symptom

formations can be seen even more readily in disturbances of childhood and adolescence. Symptoms of these stages are more transparent because repressive cultural forces have not yet had a chance to work so intensely and long as in the case of adults and consequently communications are not yet as subtle, halting, and defensive, but are more open and direct. Some school phobias, for instance, have been ascribed to the child's concern and worry about his status in the home (Waldfogel, Coolidge, & Hahn, 1959; Johnson, Falstein, Szurek, & Svendsen, 1941). It is as if the child wanted to say: "It is not so much that I am afraid to go to school as I am of being away from home, for I do not trust that I will find it the way I left it." The specifics of the distrust are, of course, not manifest from the phobia *per se* but require more specific knowledge of details.

☐ A seven-year-old boy was plagued by the fact that in school he would hear about geological events, such as the ice age, and the idea arose in him that a new ice age would come while he learned about such past events. This, he thought, would make it impossible for him to return to his home; tremendous mountains of ice would trap him in school. He conveyed rather pointedly the sense of icy coldness he felt between him and his parents, his sense that his status in the home was tenuous and how likely abandonment was were he to stop being on guard against such desertion. Furthermore, his symptom revealed his belief that he would be rejected were he to grow up and mature, that being accepted was contingent upon immaturity. ☐

While detailed understanding and awareness of these feelings were out of consciousness, the feeling tone which they evoked was obviously portrayed in his phobia. Other problems youngsters manifest, such as learning problems, have similar message value and have been described in those terms in the literature (Blanchard, 1946; Plank & Plank, 1954; Roswell & Natchez, 1964).

A few words concerning the clinical illustrations. They

frequently deal with sexual disturbances and sexual symbolizations despite the apparent rejection of libido theory and the
refusal to place sexuality at the center of all considerations.
This apparent contradiction is reduced if it is clear that the
rejection of libido theory does not entail a disregard for or
even a diminution of the importance of sexual impulse and
behavior. What is presented here is a point of view which
conceives of sexual disturbances and problems as pointed reflections of wider and more general difficulties in living, reflections of the person's outlook and orientation vis-à-vis himself
as a physically independent unit and his concomitant outlook
upon others. A person's sexual behavior is then seen as a manifestation of his orientation rather than its cause. This view is
then quite similar to that advanced by Fromm-Reichmann
(1950) and to Sullivan's (1953) insistence that the position
human beings take in relation to their biologically given lustful
impulses and in relation to the lustful needs of others characterizes most pointedly their relatedness to their own life and
the life of others. Sullivan (1947) also pointed out that the
character of this relatedness is essentially culturally determined
and must be understood in terms of particular cultural experiences:

> The lurid twilight which invests sex in our culture is pri-
> marily a function of two factors. We still try to discour-
> age premarital sexual performances; hold that abstinence
> is the moral course before marriage. And we discourage
> early marriage; in fact progressively widen the gap be-
> tween the adolescent awakening of lust and the proper
> circumstances for marriage. These two factors work
> through many cultural conventions to make us the most
> sex-ridden people of whom I have any knowledge [1947,
> [pp. 28–29].

Sexual symptomatology is prominently associated with psychopathology because sexuality lends itself more readily than
any other behavior to symbolic expression of attitudes toward
oneself, others, and life itself. Through one's genitalia and
erotic relationships the inner situation is, paradoxical as this
may sound, most concretely symbolized. The difference be-

tween the Freudian position and the thought presented here can be illustrated readily by drawing upon some of Freud's discussion. In elaborating on the dream work, Freud (1900) referred to Federn's belief that many dreams about flying have sexual implications. Citing from mythology such symbolic images as the "winged phallus," Freud suggested that the connection between flying and male sexuality lies in the fact that both flying and penile erections defy the laws of gravity. Therefore, he argued, flying lends itself well to the symbolic representation of male sexuality. It seems more pointed, however, to suggest that the affective tone associated with flying may be one of defiance of restrictive ties (Icarus myth); of exhilaration in conquering space; or of frenzy when one is confronted with demands which no human being can really fulfill—to name only a few. The dream symbol of flying may represent any of these inner constellations, and these emotional reactions may be associated with sexual and/or nonsexual issues that occupy the dreamer.

☐ A man in his late twenties dreams that he is flying like a bird from the center of town to its outskirts and the seashore, near which he lived as a child, and then hops along the beach like a sandpiper. This was a person who constantly felt called upon to perform superhuman feats, whether professional, personal, educational, or sexual in nature. He was utterly convinced that unless he performed miraculous feats nobody would ever pay any attention to him.

How deeply ingrained this attitude was revealed itself in another dream that occurred during the same night. He dreamed that he was walking naked on a busy avenue, specifically the street on which the therapist's office was located, and nobody but nobody would even turn around and look at him. He was apparently quite upset by the fact that the therapist to whom he had related some of his feats the day before refused to be terribly impressed by certain "accomplishments." ☐

A final illustration will further indicate the symbolic message value of the symptom.

☐ A young woman comes to therapy obsessed by the thought that a good many of her acquaintances will meet a terrible fate: their eyes will suddenly, while she looks at them, transform into transparent stone balls devoid of pupils. Detailing the genesis of the symptom is unnecessary here; however, it is quite clear that the patient was preoccupied with the fantasy of others becoming blind. She said in effect: "It is within my power to blind others." To what end she wished to exercise this power is also irrelevant here, but clearly in the fantasy she reduced others to a rather unfortunate status. This is, of course, at least in part what she did not want them to know or to *see:* how eager she was for them to be blind to her particular brand of dominance needs, how eager she was for them to be helpless and eventually dependent upon her. ☐

Obviously even the most seemingly bizarre and unintelligible symptoms have definite communicative value. All symbolizations, including symptoms, contain, as Fromm (1951) has put it, several elements. They contain conventional, accidental, and universal symbol facets. Sometimes one, at another moment other facets are more prominently noticeable in the symbolization, but in most instances all three aspects are observable.

A point already touched upon requires further elaboration: the symbolizations in dreams in general and the initial dream in therapy in particular. Among others, Gutheil (1951) advanced the thought that the first dream in therapy is of special relevance, and Bonime (1962) held that it excellently depicts the dynamic situation of the patient. The small amount of systematic research dealing with this idea has been quite inconclusive (Bondel, 1958). Clinical evidence points in this direction, although more research is needed to shed further light upon this hypothesis. The following examples of initial dreams illustrate what Tauber and Green (1959) have referred to as the "diagrammatic significance" of initial dreams.[3] A woman patient reports in her twenty-third interview the following dream, the first dream she can remember since she started therapy:

[3] Erikson (1954) expresses similar thoughts about the significance of dreams.

☐ A girl friend of mine and I and a man I cannot identify are at the beach. The man seems kind and wants me to go into the ocean and swim, even though he does not say so directly. I finally go in but do so fully dressed. I stay in the shallow water, do not swim, I just wade. I feel greatly refreshed and wake up. ☐

She seems puzzled by the dream. Associations reveal that she had been to the beach the preceding day and that she is an excellent swimmer who has won several amateur swimming contests. The patient had thought about certain decisions she had to make and contemplated taking significant actions the following day, among them the decision to look for work. Although she was excellently trained for profitable and creative work she had never been gainfully employed. The idea of finding work had arisen because she thought she wanted to pay for therapy herself rather than simply depend on her parents' financial resources. She ruminated about the possibility of the man in the dream being the therapist, a decided likelihood.

Aside from the obvious symbolizations referring to the patient's sense that therapy might prove invigorating, the dream also revealed her character structure succinctly. Although she was an excellent swimmer, she entered the water quite reluctantly, wanted to be coaxed, made believe that she did not know how to swim, and once in the water remained in shallow areas. The idea emerges that she was a person given to a good deal of dissembling, eager to give the impression of helplessness. Above all, the need to create such impressions was so strong that it led to self-defeating behavior: she remained fully dressed while entering the water even though it proved refreshing. Most strikingly, she expressed her knowledge that she could defeat the analyst who was eager to see her enter the water; a certain amount of pleasure in frustrating his efforts also seemed expressed in the dream. Involvement in analytic work appeared antithetical to her need to control.

In her dream she employed conventional symbols, common words and common images, but she used them in accidental and personal fashion. The accidental facts that she was a superior swimmer and that she was at the beach while thinking about important decisions to be made enter significantly. A person who is a poor swimmer or cannot swim at all could not symbolize make-believe helplessness and ineffectualness by dreaming that she is wading in shallow water. This would be quite realistic for such an individual, but it reflects the importance of creating misleading impressions when the dreamer is quite capable of deriving a good deal of satisfaction from swimming. The universal symbolisms of ocean, immersion, and getting wet should also be noted. The significance with which most cultures invest bathing is well known. The bathing rituals of the ancients and the ritualistic water rites of Christianity are but a few examples of the symbolic value men attach to bathing: an inner, not just an outer cleansing, rebirth via such a cleansing, a starting anew. The phrase "getting one's feet wet," denoting a change from detachment to involvement, points in the same direction. In her dream the patient depicts her inner situation quite well. She portrayed the temptation to become involved with her life, being reborn through involvement, and simultaneously her marked hesitation to do so, how pleasing the pretense of helplessness was, her reluctance to reveal herself and really to "get her feet wet."

This is, then, the dream of a highly self-depriving (one is tempted to say masochistic) woman. She had been raised in a home which placed a high premium on childishness, a home in which one could get anything provided one acted helpless and most immature. Such behavior always brought rewards and acceptance—maturity and growth, however little, inevitably brought scorn and rejection. The dream ends on an ominous note: despite the ineffectualness of the bathing behavior, or perhaps because of it, the patient feels refreshed. The make-believe was pleasing and refreshing rather than depressing, and her leaving therapy should have been expected. Anguish, anxiety, and dissatisfaction are absent, even though she remained uninvolved. The patient in fact terminated therapy shortly after reporting the dream.

The following initial dream comes from a man in his late twenties. Marked depression, vacillating indecision, and a resultant sense of paralysis brought him to therapy.

☐ I am in high school, but I seem much younger, as if I really belong in grammar school. I am on a big field and my classmates and I are playing football. I am very small and we are wearing a peculiar uniform, not our school colors but blue shirts and white shorts. The going gets rough, it's a difficult match, we are playing a tough team and I am scared and run off the field and hide behind a big barnlike building and wait until the game is over. Suddenly my teammates have disappeared and I notice a woman who reminds me of my father's second wife and I ask her where my teammates went. She points to some other field where a party seems in progress and she says that I cannot join them. She seems to sneer. I am very depressed and wake up. ☐

For present purposes it is unnecessary to grasp the meaning of all details of this dream; its partial understanding, however, requires the information that it occurred within a few days of the end of the abortive war between Israel and Egypt and that the patient came from a Jewish home, characterized by the urge for total assimilation and renunciation of Jewishness. The uniform in which he played is readily associated with the Israeli colors; on this association hinges a good deal of the understanding of the dream. The patient senses deeply that he is a coward, that in the course of his life he has run out on many of his convictions because he too was constantly concerned with fitting in, despite his protestations about the value of individuality and honesty of position. He felt that he had often deserted what he deemed a just cause, felt that he lacked the courage of conviction, felt therefore isolated and depressed. The dream also revealed why he had so often felt that he must run out on himself, why he deemed it imperative to sell himself down the river, although discussion of this aspect of the dream is not germane here.

Some final comments on the nature of symbolizations: First, a word of caution concerning universal symbols. Many of the so-called universal symbols have the peculiar quality of symbolizing seemingly diametrically opposed tendencies and qualities. Freud (1900) dealt with this phenomenon when he suggested that anything may be represented by its opposite and Fromm (1951) has discussed this issue in some detail from still another viewpoint. But some additional remarks are nevertheless appropriate. Consider the symbol "fire." To be sure, one may associate it with death and destruction, hostility and rage. But fire is also associated with the eternal flame, the fire of life and the perpetuity of life. Fire symbolized the solstice, the return of warmth for the pagans and self-assertive victory for the Maccabeans.

Similarly the snake, aside from its phallic implications, has often been thought of as a symbolic representation of deadly treachery, of viciousness and of poison. Yet many a poison, used judiciously, has helpful effects and therefore medical practice employs induced illness to protect man's health. And so the snake has also become the symbol of cure and is part of the emblem of the medical profession. Furthermore, the snake has long stood as a symbol of wisdom, as reflected in the story of Adam and Eve, when the snake whispered that man could acquire reason and in so doing approximate his creator. But, as Fromm (1947) has pointed out, in the course of gaining reason and only through its application does man learn the inevitable limits of his reason. The recognition that the sharp awareness of one state is intimately and inevitably associated with the awareness of its opposite suggests an additional basis for the peculiar quality of most symbolizations, their ability to represent thesis and antithesis. Whatever the foundations of this dualism, the importance of viewing so-called universal symbols in broad terms must be remembered.

It must also be remembered that a variety of accidental circumstances can make for accidental symbolizations. Personal events in the life of the individual as well as accidents of language contribute to the development of such symbols. The former variety has already been illustrated by case material. The latter group, accidental symbols brought about by language peculiarities, requires some amplification. Puns are the prototype of this group. One encounters rather revealing "accidental" puns in the dreams of patients:

□ A woman dreamed that she was on a trip to Lapland. The scenery was beautiful, the sky full of miraculous and colorful northern lights. Everything was exciting but it was also terribly cold and the patient woke up shivering and freezing. □

She had finally realized how icily cold despite its deceptive beauty her life in the lap of her family had been. That she actually came from a northern country contributed to the accidental symbol formation. Another dream, by a man in his twenties, further illustrates the point:

□ I was in your [the therapist's] office but it seemed located in the basement of a building and the walls were terribly thick. The color of the walls was different also and on one of the walls there was a strange and fascinating mosaic which attracted my attention very much. My wife and my mother were also in the room and I wanted to leave but felt that they wanted me to stay. I woke up very angry and depressed. □

In order to understand the pun in the dream as it reflects an accidental symbol, it is necessary to know that the patient comes from an orthodox Jewish home, which he had always experienced as rather oppressive and he had consciously thought of his mother as enveloping, demanding, and emphasizing family ties. He had had similar feelings about his wife. In this particular dream he depicts a tomblike or perhaps womblike structure with a mosaic; he dreams about what seems to him a mosaic (synonymous with Jewish) womb which "fascinates" him. Transference elements—the patient's feeling that the Jewish therapist keeps him tied—are also obvious.

The dream like any expression is a symbolic and yet concrete representation of an inner situation, whether a wish, a hope, a fear, or an insight. Its significance for psychotherapeutic work lies in the fact that this representation is less schematized than the statements often made in waking life. Freud (1900) commented that he thought of dreams as guardians of the sleep and that man censors in his dreams in order to remain unperturbed so that he may continue his rest. But he also observed that such censoring controls are loosened in the dream and therefore saw the dream as the royal road to the unconscious. His observations were indeed profound. Yet it is likely that much less censoring in man's dream life than one is often led to believe actually occurs, that a good deal of what Freud and some of his students thought was censorship reflects in reality the individual's addressing himself, in his sleep, to more profound and central aspects of his existence than he is capable of in waking life. When a woman dreams in terror of a snake she may be much more insightful than the psychoanalyst who insists that she is afraid of the male genitals and of sexuality because of some incestuous conflict, even though the analyst may be correct in a limited sense. The woman may be saying in much more dynamic terms that she is afraid of all knowledge—in the Biblical sense or in any other sense—and that she is eager to avoid such knowledge because it would be antithetical to her remaining incestuously rooted in the familiar. Under such circumstances the symbolization appears not only in the service of repression and repressive censorship but also represents a more elemental statement of experience and perception. And via this central and elemental expressive mode the dream and its symbols truly become this "royal road to the unconscious."

► *Summary* ◄

1. All behavior is communicative—expressive of inner states even when it seems designed to obscure an inner situation. Such attempts to becloud reflect an emotional constellation in its own right.

2. Since feelings are not directly communicable, they are expressed in symbols, which are then inevitably devices in the service of expression—even when they express the desire to repress.

3. A person's symbolizations are understood by another indi-

vidual through nondefensive projection—through empathy. The therapist's ability to understand the patient's symbolizations rests upon the fact that "we are all simply more human than otherwise." Specifically, symbolizations can be understood by the therapist

    a. If in the course of his own life he has become familiar with the particular emotion the patient symbolizes and is not removed or alienated from that type of personal experience; and

    b. If he can conceive of himself as symbolizing such an experience in terms similar to those employed by his patient.

4. Symptoms are *de facto* communicative symbols depicting simple or complex feeling states and therefore symptoms, if properly understood, reveal the clash of motivational systems within the individual. Although aspects of the motivational systems are out of awareness, the symptoms symbolize the nature of the system.

5. Similarly, dreams and the symbols employed in dreams reflect inner states in pointed fashion. They reveal to the observer, whether the patient himself or the therapist, the essence of underlying feelings. Dream symbols help both the patient and therapist grasp the dreamer's inner life sharply.

6. In symbol and/or symptom formation one finds conventional, personal-accidental, and universal-expressive terms.

CHAPTER FIVE

Patient and Therapist:
Needs and Expectations

THE PATIENT'S INNER ATTITUDE TOWARD THERAPY IS INEVITABLY ambivalent and his view of therapy necessarily colored by conflictual tendencies. He must experience some longing for life and freedom to exert himself, to be and become active; at the same time he has promptings to remain chained and passive. Were the former lacking altogether, the patient would never present himself at the therapist's office; he could not imagine the possibility of another way of life. He would see no need for therapy at all—how can anyone search for something of which he cannot even conceive? Were the latter aspects missing, the person would not be a patient, would not be in need of therapeutic intervention. What therapy was to bring about would already be present.

In most instances, therefore (the exceptions will be discussed later), the patient brings to therapy some rational, positive, life-furthering tendencies, expressed in his rational expectations. The patient hopes to receive from therapy something new so that he may become somebody new; there must be some nucleus of rationality in those hopes, otherwise therapeutic work is impossible. Freud (1922a) had spoken about something similar (though he eventually went off in a different direction) when he concluded that the so-called transference neuroses were treatable while the psychoses (narcissistic neuroses) were not amenable to analytic therapy. He suggested that the "necessary and sufficient conditions for therapy" include prominently the patient's capacity to form rational relationships with others. The rationality of the patient's relationship to the therapist then includes, to whatever small degree, the hope that he will be helped toward genuine change no matter how much the very idea of change may frighten him. Of course, by genuine change is meant a move in the direction of genuine activity as defined in Chapter 3 rather than a mere maintenance of old ways in "prettied-up" form.

Unfortunately, the hope for such simple "prettying-up" is all too prevalent among human beings. There are several reasons for the widespread belief and this common hope that psychotherapy can or will bring about such "improvements." First among them is the presentation to the general public of psychological information and a model of man as developed by some academic psychologists; second, one notes a wide acceptance of this model among people in search of help. A basically stimulus-response-oriented psychology has sold the belief that man is essentially a machine and that like any machine, he is capable of being simply "fixed up"—tuned up like a car, or, as the prevalent term has it, helped to "adjust." The development of conditioned-response therapy (Salter, 1952) and similar systems (Wolpe, 1958) widely written about and advocated has been a logical outgrowth of this particular psychological heritage. Chein (1962) has shown that without detracting from some contributions made by stimulus-response psychology, its models are incomplete and insufficient for the understanding or modification of behavior. There is little doubt that in an era which has witnessed spectacular advances in technology, men (therapists or patients) look with hope to a machine model of man. If machines are perfectible, why should not people be equally malleable? So the patient, by definition terrified of being human, finds some false comfort in an image of non-humanness and the unrealistic, irrational hope of being made a more effective machine. In this hope he of course reveals the depth of his pathology, for in effect he states that he looks toward the perpetuation of passivity, expects that he may remain basically passive, a machine activated by an outside source of energy, hopes that he may remain creature without becoming creator—and do so without discomfort. The most hopeful aspect about any patient is the discomfort he suffers, because this agony about his self-dehumanization indicates that he has not given up the ghost altogether, is not satisfied to be and remain the type of aberration described so eloquently by Čapek and Orwell. Finally, the pathological belief and hope that psychotherapy can and will aid one in finding happiness by bringing about "adjustment" is so prevalent precisely because it pacifies man's most penetrating anxieties, anxieties which center around the problems of freedom and responsibility, growth and change, the latter being inevitable predicates of freedom and responsibility.

Fortunately, some of the investigators best equipped to appreciate the usefulness of machines in the performance of tasks which were at one time thought to be exclusively the province of human ingenuity have stated unequivocally that machines cannot do what is essentially human, that likening human beings to machines is grossly misleading. Neisser (1963), for instance, points out that although the sheer quantity of data processed by a modern computer is creative and this quantity leads to creative insights impossible without the aid of such devices, he is also fully cognizant of the limitations of machines in the imitation of man:

> The deep difference between the thinking of men and machines has been intuitively recognized by those who fear that machines may somehow come to regulate our society. But computer intelligence is indeed "inhuman": it does not grow, has no emotional basis, and is shallowly motivated. These defects do not matter in technical applications, where the criteria for successful problem solving are relatively simple. They become extremely important if the computer is used to make social decisions, for there our criteria of adequacy are as subtle and as multiply motivated as human thinking itself [p. 197].

Yet it is precisely in the realm of social decision-making that patients hope to become "effective," a euphemism for machine-like.

To abandon freedom, without serious consequences to his well-being, is so tempting because in the final analysis it absolves man of responsibility. The profound interrelationship between human freedom and responsibility was eloquently expressed by Buber (1926). Between World War I and World War II, at a moment in history when the specter of coming events was obvious to men of penetrating thought, Buber addressed the Third International Educational Conference at the University of Heidelberg. His topic was "The Development of the Creative Powers of the Child" and on that occasion he made remarks of considerable relevance for the present discussion:

Freedom—I love its flashing face: it flashes forth from the darkness and dies away, but it has made the heart invulnerable. I am devoted to it, I am always ready to join in the fight for it, for the appearance of the flash, which lasts no longer than the eye is able to endure it, for the vibrating of the needle that was held down too long and stiff. I give my left hand to the rebel and my right to the heretic: forward! But I do not trust them. They know how to die, but that is not enough. I love freedom, but I do not believe in it. How could one believe in it after looking in its face? It is the flash of significance comprising all meanings, of a possibility comprising all potentiality. For it we fight, again and again, from of old, victorious and in vain.

It is easy to understand that in a time when the deterioration of all traditional bonds has made their legitimacy questionable, the tendency to freedom is exalted, the springboard is treated as the goal and a functional good as a substantial good. Moreover it is idle sentimentality to lament at great length that freedom is made the subject of experiments. Perhaps it is fitting for this time which has no compass that people should throw out their lives like a plummet to discover our bearings and the course we should set. But truly *their* lives! Such an experiment, when it is carried out, is a neck-breaking venture which cannot be disputed. But when it is talked about and talked around, in intellectual discussions and confessions and in the mutual pros and cons of their life's "problems" it is an abomination of disintegration. Those who stake themselves as individuals or as a community, may leap and crash out into the swaying void where senses and sense fail, or through it and beyond into some kind of existence. But they must not make freedom into a theorem or a program. To become free of a bond is destiny; one carries that like a cross, not a cockade. Let us realize the true meaning of being free of a bond: it means that a quite personal responsibility takes the place of one shared with many generations. Life lived in freedom is personal responsibility or it is a pathetic farce [pp. 91–92].

Buber insists that freedom and genuine activity are synonymous, for freedom requires the activity implicit in the taking of responsibility for oneself and by implication for one's brother.

Fromm (1941) has elaborated on the same theme extensively and has often commented how difficult it is for man to endure freedom because of the responsibility implied in it. Although his thinking is in many instances at variance with Buber's, Fromm too maintains that the sense of being isolated frequently accompanies freedom, making it an experience difficult to bear. To be sure, Fromm also sketches a road to freedom that does not lead to feelings of isolation, nor does he suggest that isolation is an inevitable consequence of being free, but he is equally insistent that the sense of responsibility for the welfare of one's fellow man and one's own behavior in relation to others make the desire to escape the burden of freedom understandable. This burden, he suggests, becomes especially heavy within the framework of modern capitalism and leads him to conclude at one point that

. . . freedom has a twofold meaning for modern man: that he has been freed from traditional authorities and has become an "individual," but at the same time he has become isolated, powerless, and an instrument of purposes outside of himself and others; furthermore, that this state undermines his self, weakens and frightens him, and makes him ready for submission to new kinds of bondage. . . .

Freedom has reached a critical point where, driven by the logics of its own dynamism, it threatens to change into its opposite [1941, p. 270]. . . .

He [man] is alone inasmuch as he is a unique entity, not identical with anyone else, and aware of his self as a separate entity. He must be alone when he has to judge or to make decisions solely by the power of his reason. And yet he cannot bear to be alone, to be unrelated to his fellow men [1947, p. 43].

Fromm believes that freedom is not a bed of roses, that it entails almost unbearable burdens. It is for this reason that certain aspects of Herberg's critique of Fromm are startling:

Fromm, on the other hand, in contrast to Freud is a most manifest Rousseauean, for to him natural man is born free and good, only to be enslaved and corrupted by an evil society. Freud finds the evil drive in man's biological nature ("The tendency to aggression is an innate independent and instinctual disposition in man"), whereas Fromm sees man's aggressive antisocial tendencies to be the result of social pressures, particularly social frustrations and insecurities. As a natural consequence, Freud refuses to reassure us by holding out the possibility of a cure for the "discontents" of civilization; Fromm has his program all ready [1957, p. 153].

Herberg's interpretation seems untenable in view of Fromm's repeated insistence that the "existential dichotomies" (1947) inevitably make for problems in living and that constructive answers are neither simple nor easy to find.

Emphasis upon active freedom, reflected in autonomous genuine activity, is sorely lacking in a good deal of the popular image of emotional well-being and in the conscious desires of many a patient. In many instances the reduction or absence of such strivings for autonomy is strongly stressed (especially when the patient is "sent" to get "straightened out"). Yet without some such longing the therapeutic contact is doomed to failure from the beginning. The realistic hopes of the patient as he contemplates entering therapy include the hope that he will encounter a human being who can help him achieve this autonomous freedom and become active despite his promptings to remain machinelike, nonautonomous, inactive. Therefore it is realistic for the patient to hope that he will meet a person who respects his dilemma, that this respect will enable the therapist to hear the symbolic presentation of the dilemma's facets and help the patient grasp their nature fully. Such respect for the dignity of the patient is of course not identical with "sympathy" in the usual sense of the word or with an "agreeable" attitude, behavior which reflects disinterest at best, hostility and false flattery at worst. Weigert has put it very well when she says:

> True sympathy enables the therapist to look through the patient's false front. It is easy to recognize the deceptions of a bad actor who tries to express emotions that are not really his own. It is more difficult to understand unconscious emotional distortions beyond the volition and grasp of the patient who has become the slave of defensive habits. His false front is a powerful protection against a panic that might transiently overthrow his rationalizations and his self-control [1961, p. 193].

Thus the rational anticipations of the patient also include the hope that the therapist will be interested and courageous enough to see through false fronts and to deal with them, even though their reduction may entail some panic. This type of sympathy is the reflection of commitment on the part of the therapist. It is a commitment to the patient's growth into well-being and active participation in his own life and a reflection of the therapist's willingness to serve such ends. This type of commitment is, of course, the antithesis of false and empty promises of an easy and "adjusted" life.

Respect for the dignity of the patient expresses itself also in the therapist's realistic appreciation of what he may expect from the patient in terms of financial and similar sacrifices. While Freud (1913) had pointed out the need for demanding sacrifices from the patient—sacrifices of an essentially economic nature—in order to overcome what he deemed the patient's natural tendency to resist therapy, he was also brutally frank with himself in admitting that certain of his demands were motivated by his own desire for creature comforts. This honesty is in line with Freud's total life style. But it does seem ludicrous to demand sacrifices from a patient which entail his leading a most undignified existence under the guise that this will somehow motivate him to exert greater efforts toward self-investigation. Such talk sounds all too often like a grand rationalization for not admitting what the therapist's personal demands happen to be. His demands must also be honored—it would do the patient little good if the therapist acted like some benevolent angel—and therefore realistic solutions are called for, solutions which violate neither the patient's dignity nor the therapist's demands. It is not the province of this book to outline practical and practicable solutions in this area, but it should be remembered that only when it is carried out under realistic and honest circumstances can the therapeutic process bear fruit.

If the patient's rational expectations concerning therapy are defined by hope for the development of freedom of action, his irrational anticipations are defined by the expectation that nothing really significant will happen, that his essential inactivity and bondage, no matter how troublesome, will be permitted to perpetuate themselves. What is suggested is that resistance (see Chapter 10) is willy-nilly present from the very beginning of therapy—indeed, is present before the patient even makes the initial step toward establishing contact with the therapist. It will be shown that the reasons for such resistance must be found in the patient's more or less deeply ingrained belief that there is no real alternative to his present way of life and in the profound fear that the therapist will deprive him of his single road to survival, ineffectual and limited as it may be. If being inactive has had significant survival value, it is only understandable that the patient will hope that the therapist will help him remain inactive, will help him learn bigger and better methods of self-deception and more approved methods of deceiving others in this area. If being an authoritarian controller of the fate of others has had survival value, one should not be surprised if the patient hopes that the therapist will help him to control others more effectively and socially acceptably, help him dominate his spouse, his family, his colleagues more adequately. In other words, the nucleus of the patient's irrational approach to therapy is the expectation that his life style will not be disturbed through the therapeutic contacts, that his character structure will remain unchanged but that at the same time his anxieties about his behavior and way of relating to others will be alleviated. The following illustration exemplifies a patient's conflict between the rational and irrational hopes in relation to therapy as she contemplated entering analysis.

☐ A professional woman beset by many difficulties in her relationships with her husband, her children, and her co-workers sought therapeutic help. She decided to consult an analyst who had written extensively. She had read several of his publications and was therefore quite familiar with his thinking. After having called to arrange for an appointment, she sat down and decided in her own mind how often she was willing to see him, at what times, and what fee she was going to offer. Although quite knowledgeable about analytic procedure, she decided on this course of action and during the first interview presented the therapist with the "conditions" she had thought out. (She literally referred to them as "my conditions for entering treatment with you.")

Characteristically, her difficulties with her family and colleagues centered around deep convictions that nobody could do right by her, that everybody was unreliable and that it was of paramount importance to be in control always and "on top of things." This was how she had established security in her life; small wonder that she also attempted to live out her neurotic strivings, both in anticipation and from the very beginning of therapy. Yet simultaneously, on the basis of her information about the analyst, she knew very well, as she later admitted, that he would not let her "get away with it," would deem unilateral laying down of conditions as unacceptable to him and would inquire into the roots of such behavior. And, as it turned out, she had also deeply hoped that he would pursue this position, would force into the open an investigation of this life style. Even though this style was for defensive reasons near and dear to her, it was enough at variance with her image of life to make her hope for the development of a different orientation. ☐

This illustration recalls the thought advanced in Chapter 1 that the patient's rational hopes in relation to therapy are determined by the degree to which he can envision a life differing significantly from his present one. The patient's rational hopes are brought about by his deep though unconscious knowledge that fundamentally he has failed in fulfilling his constructive human potentials and by his conflicts attendant on this failure. For this reason prognosis is always better in those instances in which such a conflict is present. This is simply a reformulation of what has often been said—that some conscious anxiety and discomfort are positive prognostic indicators (Arieti, 1955; Fenichel, 1945; Freud, 1936; Fromm-Reichmann, 1955; Weigert, 1949). The basis for this old assertion has often been the belief that the discomfort engendered by anxiety will spur the patient to more strenuous self-investigative efforts than might be hoped for were anxiety absent. The present formulation, similar to that advanced by neo-Freudians, suggests that anxiety indicates the presence of dissatisfaction in the face of some knowledge of what one could be. Furthermore, this understanding of anxiety also suggests that the patients who experience such discomfort are closer to well-being than those who do not feel anxious: the former are closer to the awareness of having betrayed their human potential than those who are nowhere near the knowledge of self-betrayal.

It will be well to consider here the nature of the conflict between rational and irrational needs in those patients who do not voluntarily seek the aid of a psychotherapist. This group is made up of individuals markedly varying in motivation and therefore it is best to deal with subgroupings. First, there are children and adolescents who are introduced to therapy by parents and other authorities. Their being brought to a therapist may be occasioned by what such authorities consider problems in school, formal learning, or social learning. Here one encounters, of course, youngsters who either do or do not think they have difficulties in living, who may or may not experience any conscious sense of conflict or anxiety. To the extent to which they do experience discomfort their inner situation, their conflict, and their motivations are of course similar to those of the adult self-referring individual; they differ only insofar as their age and economic and social circumstances preclude self-referral; in most instances the young patient has not even been aware of the fact that therapeutic services are available.

More complicated is the situation in the case of those individuals, young or adult, who do not consider their lives fraught with conflict and anxiety, who have managed to eliminate awareness of discomfort. They come to therapy only because others believe that their actions indicate the presence of conflict. In effect the patient has no hopes in relation to therapy because he sees no need for personal and emotional change. Such instances of course present a rather difficult picture, for here the pathology is already so intense and the pathological defenses against anxiety so well organized that dissatisfaction with self has been eliminated and (to use the term employed above) the person has no knowledge of his betrayal of self or others. His behavior appears to him rational, logical, and from his viewpoint realistic and devoid of conflict. Indeed, it is likely that a good deal of the behavior which makes others bring him to a therapist is precisely designed to eliminate discomfort altogether. It is outside the scope of this book to discuss specific therapeutic procedures necessary in such instances, but it is apparent that the conceptual framework presented here requires helping the patient develop a sense of dissatisfaction with himself, a sense of conflict, and ensuing anxiety. In this process the patient may seem to "regress," but this worsening is illusory because to become anxious and conflict-ridden is more in line with well-being than to short-circuit one's conflicts automatically in irrational though anxiety-free fashion.

This conflict of inner needs, conscious or unconscious, the conflict between the urge to remain who one is and the desire to change in spite of it, this conflict and the hopes and fears associated with it are the initial attitude the individual brings to therapy.

The therapist may also bring rational and irrational needs and desires to his meeting with the patient. Hopefully the latter will be minimal, the former maximal. Hopefully, he will bring to this encounter the characteristics of well-being as they were defined in Chapter 3, a desire to fulfill himself in productive effort, and the inner freedom to be fully active. Such expectations raise an often-asked question: Is it necessary that the therapist be free from conflict and emotional problems in order to help his patient? Freud (1937) answered the question in an unmistakably clear manner. As mentioned earlier, he believed that "a considerable degree of mental normality and correctness" (p. 248) were essential requirements for doing analytic work. But it will be recalled that "mental normality" was to Freud's mind not synonymous with a Pollyanna type of happiness or freedom from problems in living. Indeed, Freud (1951) thought discontent was inevitable and therefore also an inevitable part of the analyst's life. By mental normality he meant an adequate management of one's impulse life and reality forces through sublimation without taking refuge in repressive devices. Analysis was to lead to health by awareness and the presence of heightened awareness in the analyst was Freud's demand. Fromm-Reichmann (1949b, 1952) also suggested that the therapist's emotional well-being is a prerequisite for effective work; she too believed that health was characterized by a willingness to know oneself rather than by an artificial absence of the inevitable problems life presents or by a sterile conventionality. That Sullivan (1949) also maintained that psychotherapists must be emotionally healthy (while at the same time rejecting the common notions of "adjustment") is clearly implied in one of his discussions on training in psychiatry:

> There is such an accumulation of handicap in the case of some people that it is relatively impractical to undertake their training. These are in general people who are quite content with themselves, their present and their foreseen probable future. These genuinely complacent people can scarcely be said to have promise for psychiatry [p. 196].

The belief that psychological well-being is synonymous with awareness and constant search for self-knowledge and that health defined in these terms is an essential prerequisite for effective work as a psychotherapist is at least implicit in discussions by authors of such diverse orientations as Boss (1963), Tarachow (1963), and Rogers (1951). (Also see Chapter 1.)

If the definition of emotional health is search for self-knowledge (a position maintained throughout these discussions), it would seem reasonable that therapists can be quite useful to their patients even when they themselves are beset by conflicts, problems, and difficulties in living of their own—provided they do not abandon hope and a continuing search for insight into themselves. So long as the therapist remains his own patient or if need be seeks the help of a colleague, he does not reject active living, maintains hope for freedom, and is therefore potentially capable of doing effective work. The question then is never how many or how much of life's problems the therapist has solved already but much more how much he continuously strives toward increased understanding and subtle solutions of issues in his life, how much he cherishes his own struggle for freedom and active involvement; or conversely, how much he has given up this effort, how defeated and resigned he is, how much he despairs about his own life and rejects the value of growth. It is suggested that only the psychotherapist who believes in the possibility of his own freedom to know and to choose is capable of helping the patient to know and to choose. That the therapist will encounter conflicts in the course of fully attaining this freedom of action is obvious; that he dare not give in to the temptation of abandoning his quest for it is equally clear. (Also see Chapter 3.)

Assertion of his own freedom has important consequences for the therapist's behavior toward his patient and his hopes in the therapeutic situation. It is rational for the therapist to derive satisfactions from his work with an individual and to hope for various satisfactions. They range from the desire to derive income to support himself and his family in comfort, thus satisfying his desire for creature comforts, to the satisfaction derived from the knowledge that one has contributed to another person's growth. The therapist becomes to some extent dependent upon his patient, not only for income but also for the satisfactions work and the utilization of one's energies bring about. A mutually interdependent situation in which both partners derive rational benefit from one another is inevitable. More will be said on this topic later; what is relevant here is the recognition that the therapist's rational hopes include his desire to engage in a collaboration that will prove profitable in all meanings of the term.

The therapist will not derive general satisfaction from his work unless he feels free to work with a given patient or to reject seeing another. In effect, he must experience in his own professional life little if any irrational compulsion. One of the most dangerous compulsions, the urge to appear angelic, is often tempting, but like any other compulsion it must be eliminated by the therapist. He may, for instance, become disturbed by his reluctance to work with a particular type of patient; he should feel free to investigate the meaning of this reluctance. In the course of such self-examination the therapist may learn something new and very important about his own psychological make-up, but he must wait until he has learned more about himself before he starts working with people he would rather not see lest he deal irrationally with such patients.

Furthermore, the therapist must feel free to acknowledge such common desires as the wish for income and satisfactory working conditions, including specified hours during which he does engage in work; he must feel ready to admit his desire for leisure and vacation time, and so on. These are rational needs and rational hopes, and to deny them reflects the therapist's refusal to know himself. Their denial indicates his irrational and exploitative tendencies. The reasons for this implication will be discussed later on in this and in the following chapter. The discussion so far can be summarized by saying that the therapist's rational hopes in his work with his patient are expressions of his striving for unhampered creative activity, creature satisfactions, and self-fulfillment.[1]

---

[1] An interesting attempt to develop a catalogue of neurotic and emotionally healthy needs in psychotherapists comes from Bugental (1964), and Wheelis (1958) has dealt with this question in a provocative manner.

His irrational needs, however, are circumscribed by pathological features as they operate in the therapist's personality
and they express themselves in destructive hopes, conscious or
unconscious, and in behavior detrimental to the patient. Psychotherapy, like any other educative process, lends itself
exquisitely to the acting out of destructive needs. Most prominent among them is the desire to dominate and control the
lives of others, even though such dominance needs may be
rationalized by the therapist through attempts to convince
himself that he is merely exercising "rational authority"
(Fromm, 1947) and meeting his responsibilities. Basically
such needs and the desire to satisfy them are reflections of the
therapist's urge to bolster a shaky sense of self-esteem: through
dominating his patient the therapist hopes to reduce his own
anxieties.

The wish to reduce his own anxieties may induce the therapist to engage in many operations more or less subtly
destructive to the patient. The setting of fees, insistence upon
specific hours, demands that the patient see him a specified
number of times per week, and the selection or rejection of
particular patients may have more to do with the amassing of
prestige in the eyes of colleagues, supervisors, or students, and
the achievement of worthwhileness in his own eyes than with
his rational demands and the realistic needs of the patient. The
common notion, especially among neurotics, that an expensive
service must be better and more desirable than a lower-priced
effort may lead the therapist to set unrealistic fees and to urge
a patient who cannot afford such expenses to make unbearable
sacrifices. Furthermore, prestige needs may operate within the
therapist in such a fashion that the accumulation of money *per
se* without regard to his realistic needs and desires unduly
determines his patient choice. He may die leaving a large
estate but hardly a large circle of individuals who have benefited from their association with him.

The insistence upon a given frequency of contacts may well
be related to irrational prestige desires. The therapist may well
labor under the unfortunate notions that being an "analyst" is
more prestigious than being a "psychotherapist" and that the

distinction between the two groupings is determined by frequency of interviews rather than their content and aims. It is probably true that more profound self-understanding by the patient can be achieved more readily through frequent contact, that closely spaced interviews enable him to search in greater depth than seeing the therapist relatively infrequently. The reasons for this likelihood will be discussed later, but there are also undoubtedly circumstances which make relatively infrequent contacts more desirable than frequent sessions. The irrational need to think of himself as an "analyst" ("analysts see their patients at least X times per week") may make the therapist overlook the desirability of infrequent meetings or referral to a colleague capable of working effectively in widely spaced sessions.

As already noted, it is also possible for therapists to try to impress themselves and others through irrational and therefore destructive benevolence. This may take the form of largesse or insistence upon working exclusively with extremely difficult patients who have not been helped by other therapists. It is of course not suggested that one should refuse to work with a given patient just because some other professional person had failed with him or had thought that he could not be of service to him. This would be absurd in the face of the well-established fact that different therapists happen to be effective with different patients. But eagerness to work with a patient just because somebody else has failed or recognized his own limitations vis-à-vis that individual is highly irrational and destructive. In such instances the patient is simply exploited in whatever power or prestige struggles the therapist happens to be engaged. Such problems loom especially strong when therapy proceeds within the framework of an agency. The private practitioner working in relative anonymity and without direct observation of his competence is less likely to find himself in a situation that lends itself readily to competitive struggles with colleagues than the clinical worker in an institution or agency. It should be noted that the private practitioner, even though direct competition is somewhat reduced by the nature of his work situation, is not immune to such irrational strivings, for obviously he can, if this is a dominant need within him, fantasize about his superiority in comparison with his colleagues. The problem discussed here becomes even more complicated in those instances in which the clinician is a student working under supervision, because then several additional dangers arise. First and simplest, the student therapist may out of his desire to impress his supervisor discuss with him only that part of his work in which he believes he is doing well—an obvious waste of time for both and of course derogatory to the supervisor who in this process is deprived of his *raison d'être,* that of being a teacher. Even more destructive to patient, therapist, and supervisor is the possibility of outright falsification in the reporting of material in order to create favorable impressions and to compete "successfully." In a different context Ullman (1958) discussed the dangers of competitiveness in the psychotherapist. Its destructive potential in the supervisory relationship seems equally clear.[2]

Irrational needs of the therapist, then, are expressions of his feeling driven, his lack of real freedom, and his avoidance of personal responsibility. Yet the attainment of genuine freedom of action is precisely what he is to help the patient achieve. The therapist will succeed in discharging this responsibility only to the extent to which he cherishes and hopes to increase his own sense of involvement in free and self-determined action. Since psychotherapists are human and not supernatural beings, it is unreasonable to expect from them an immunity to broad cultural pathological features such as competitiveness, exploitiveness, and anxiety in the face of freedom and responsibility. But it is not unreasonable to expect that the therapist be relatively free of such pathological features or that he be

[2] It should also be noted that various "pathological" features of the therapist may appear in the therapist-supervisor interaction not so much because they are really prominent aspects of the therapist's personality, but much more because he has unconsciously gleaned them as facets in his patient, without recognizing them. In his interactions with the supervisor and in his reporting the therapist may communicate these dimly noticed features of the patient's make-up. Tauber (1954) and Searles (1955) have discussed this possibility in provocative papers and a more detailed examination of the issue will be offered in the presentation of counter-transference (Chapter 11).

aware under what circumstances they do arise. Furthermore, it is imperative for the therapist to feel free to refuse work if and when a particular patient or a particular problem presented causes him to react destructively. In other words, he may not be free of all pathology, but he must be free from one particular emotional difficulty: the pathology of feeling compelled to engage in "activity" which he knows he cannot pursue; he must be free to know when to say "no," must not feel compelled to say a forced "yes." In addition, he must feel free to search himself whenever he encounters a work situation that he cannot adequately handle, must be free to acknowledge to himself that he may need help from a colleague in clarifying aspects of therapeutic problems to be faced. In this process the therapist is also likely to achieve greater self-understanding. This type of freedom, which may lead to termination or referral of the patient to another therapist, is essential. Indeed, this has been recognized so fully that the thoughts presented above are incorporated in the code of Ethical Standards of the American Psychological Association (1953). It is therefore the hallmark of a good agency to allow its clinical workers the opportunity to select patients so that they feel comfortable in their work and not to insist that any therapist must be able to deal adequately with any patient. If, within such a setting, a therapist discovers that he cannot work with *any* of his prospective patients, then he is of course confronted with the pressing necessity to examine himself, to see why this happens, and possibly leave the field at least temporarily. Similarly, a patient cannot be expected to work adequately with any therapist, no matter how generally competent the clinician may be, and the patient must be encouraged to desist from making hasty choices in selecting a therapist. Unfortunately, patients rarely if ever feel free enough to be that rational and the usual arrangements in agency structures do not permit them this latitude. Deplorable as this may be, it is a fact and needs to be recognized and dealt with in the therapeutic exchange from the very beginning, for undoubtedly many patients experience some coercion of "having to see the assigned therapist." Their situation is similar to that already touched upon, in which individuals come to therapy unwillingly and demand immediate exploration. The discussion will return to this issue in the following chapter.

Rational and irrational needs and hopes of patient and therapist as they bring them to the therapeutic encounter will be expressed more or less subtly by the participants from the very outset. This communication will take place through various symbolizations, verbal and nonverbal, and it is therefore utter folly for the therapist to believe that he can possibly remain an unknown entity, because even in his eagerness to remain unknown or a "blank screen" he communicates something very important about himself. Above all, the therapist must come to the therapeutic meeting knowing that he cannot fool the patient about his nature and that any desire to trick the patient will be detrimental to growth; a tacit admission that the therapist does not believe in real freedom of action. The need to obscure and to fool are reflections of the therapist's sense of being compelled and obsessed, reflections of his sense of inactivity and lack of freedom (see Chapter 3).

► Summary ◄

1. Both therapist and patient bring to the therapeutic contact rational as well as irrational needs and attitudes.

2. While this admixture defines the nature of being a patient, it may exist in therapists (though hopefully to a lesser degree) at least to the extent to which all human beings wrestle with problems in living and are not immune to culturally promoted irrationalities and existentially given anxieties.

3. It is essential, however, that the therapist experience freedom of action, that he cherish his ability to make choices, including the ability to determine his working conditions. Above all, the therapist must feel free to acknowledge at least to himself the multifaceted nature of his motivations, no matter what it might be.

4. The motivational systems of patient and therapist will reveal themselves in symbolic fashion to both participants even though they may not be aware of their self-revealing activities.

The Initial Interview

THE INITIAL MEETING OF THERAPIST AND PATIENT POSES SEVERAL important problems. The most immediate question is, of course, the definition of their relationship to each other.

Obviously their meeting is an occasion where one person, the patient, consults another, the therapist, to derive benefits from his training, background, and efforts. By definition it is not a meeting between equals but rather between an expert and his client or potential client. The most succinct statement defining the relationship in these terms may be found in Sullivan:

> As I see it, such an interview is a situation of . . . communication . . . on a progressively unfolding *expert-client* basis for the purpose of elucidating characteristic *patterns of living* of the subject person, the patient or client, which patterns he experiences as particularly troublesome or especially valuable, and in the revealing of which he expects to derive *benefit* [1954, p. 4].

Sullivan employs the term *expert*, but a common synonym for expert is the term *authority*. The ease with which these words are interchangeable has led to a good deal of debate because the question has been raised whether it is really beneficial for the patient to meet an authority.

There are several aspects to this debate. One facet, which

can be disposed of relatively easily, revolves around the fact that two similar-sounding but conceptually totally different adjectives are commonly associated with the term "authority": *authoritarian* and *authoritative*. It is self-evident that an authority may be authoritative without being authoritarian even though many authoritative individuals may simultaneously act in authoritarian fashion. And unfortunately many self-styled authorities act authoritarian without being authoritative. It is not too difficult to understand how and why this semantic confusion has arisen. Quite a few neurotics resent authoritative individuals either because this characteristic is also associated in their minds with authoritarians they have known in the past or because, more often, they envy persons who can be involved with material so diligently and thoroughly that they become authorities in their fields. At any rate, the distinction between the terms and concepts is real enough.

Fromm recognized this distinction and devoted a good deal of discussion to it. Although he does not use the particular semantic differentiation made here, he does distinguish conceptually between authoritative and authoritarian when he discusses what he calls "rational authority" and "irrational authority." He defines the former as authority exercised by an individual with superior knowledge in a given area, for the express purpose of reducing inequality between him and another person who initially lacks such knowledge, ability, or skill. It is essentially the ideal parent–child and the ideal teacher–student relationship. Somewhat analogous though not identical is the physician–patient relationship; here too the expert, the physician, exercises his authority for the avowed purpose of reducing the "inadequacy" of his patient, not in terms of knowledge but in terms of physical well-being.

Irrational authority Fromm defines as authority exercised for the explicit or at least implicit purpose of perpetuating a state of inequality between the authority and a subordinate person. Its fundamental model is the master–slave relationship. The crucial differentiation, Fromm suggests, lies in the intent with which authority is exercised. He insists that such differences in intent are brought about by differences in self-evaluation. Specifically, he believes that rational authority originates in a personal sense of strength, irrational authority in a personal sense of weakness:

> *Rational authority* has its source in competence. The person whose authority is respected functions competently in the task with which he is entrusted by those who conferred it upon him. He need not intimidate them nor arouse their admiration by magic qualities; as long as and to the extent to which he is competently helping, instead of exploiting his authority is based on rational grounds and does not call for irrational awe. Rational authority not only permits but requires constant scrutiny and criticism of those subjected to it; it is always temporary, its acceptance depending upon its performance. The source of *irrational authority*, on the other hand, is always power over people. This power can be physical or mental, it can be realistic or only relative in terms of the anxiety and helplessness of the person submitting to this authority. Power on the one side, fear on the other, are always the buttresses on which irrational authority is built. Criticism of the authority is not only not required but forbidden. Rational authority is based upon the equality of both authority and subject, which differ only with respect to the degree of knowledge and skill in a particular field. Irrational authority is by its very nature based upon inequality, implying differences in value [1947, pp. 9–10].

It is clear that the ideal expert–client relationship envisioned by Sullivan is permeated by the therapist's rational authority. His insistence upon what he calls "consensual validation" (p. 93), a procedure which demands the constant questioning of particular understandings developed by the therapist, is ample evidence of Sullivan's emphasis upon an authoritative yet non-authoritarian approach to the patient. That the expert role of the therapist may lead him to authoritarian pronouncements while he deludes himself that he is merely authoritative need barely be mentioned. Assuming authority and responsibility is always fraught with dangers and it is only too easy to rationalize one's needs to dominate and domineer as indices of genuine interest in the welfare of one's charges and of one's fellow men. The history of mankind is replete with illustrations of mass murder being committed in the name of love, brotherhood, and the common good. Similarly, the old saw "This hurts me more than it hurts you" is more often than not a rationalization of sadistic tendencies than the indicator of loving concern, whether uttered by a parent engaged in manhandling his child, a teacher engaged in humiliating a student, or an agent of society violating the life and dignity of some person over whom he happens to have power. This general point will need re-emphasizing in the following chapter when the discussion will turn to the setting of limits in psychotherapy; what should be stressed here is simply that constant vigilance must be exercised by the therapist through self-investigation to make his behavior authoritative rather than authoritarian.

Doubting voices have asked profound questions concerning the value of the therapist's authoritative position. Rogers (1942) has been one of the most searching critics of the therapist as an authority. His criticism of so much pomposity that often passed as counseling or psychotherapy had an extremely salutary effect upon psychological practices in the United States. But his skepticism went further than a mere attack upon stuffy silliness. He wondered whether authoritative knowledge on the part of the therapist could possibly be beneficial, no matter how nonauthoritarian the therapist. He was obviously convinced that human beings gain insight through exploration of their feelings and the recognition and acceptance of their feelings by the therapist without what he deemed the dubious benefit of authoritative comments offered. He insisted that no matter how well meant the therapist's interpretive comments, they will be at best useless to the patient, at worst destructive to his growth. Rogers makes the important point that many people—especially those suffering from emotional problems in living—are terribly dependent and passive persons, always looking to others as potential masters of their fate. The point of view presented by practitioners who identify themselves as nondirective therapists maintains that it cannot be helpful to the patient if the therapist in his meetings with the patient does anything but accept and in "reflecting" clarify the client's expressed feelings. Rogers summarized his position:

> The counselor accepts, recognizes, and clarifies these negative feelings. Here is a subtle point which seems to be very difficult for students to grasp. If the counselor is to grasp these feelings, he must be prepared to respond, not to the intellectual content of what the person is saying, but to the feeling which underlies it. Sometimes the feelings are deep ambivalences, sometimes they are feelings of hostility, sometimes they are feelings of inadequacy. Whatever they are, the counselor endeavors, by what he says and what he does, to create an atmosphere in which the client can come to recognize that he has these negative feelings and can accept them as part of himself, instead of projecting them onto others or hiding them behind defense mechanisms. Frequently the counselor verbally clarifies these feelings, not trying to interpret their cause or argue in regard to their utility—simply recognizing that they exist, and that he accepts them. Thus such phrases as "You feel pretty bitter about this," "You want to correct this fault, but still you don't want to," "What you are saying sounds as though you feel pretty guilty," seem to crop out rather frequently in this type of therapy, and nearly always, if they are accurate portrayals of feeling, allow the individual to go forward in a freer fashion [1942, pp. 37–38].

The therapist's expertness, as Rogers understands it, lies in accurate reflection of his client's feelings after the client has assumed responsibility for expressing them. These expressions are therefore not in response to the usual questioning traditionally associated with interviewing, but spontaneous, more or less clearly defined statements of the patient's inner situation. The assuming of this responsibility for expression and the therapist's encouragement of such an attitude, Rogers suggests, make for growth and the development of maturity. The importance of not assuming the position of an authority when examined from the nondirective viewpoint lies in the therapist's insistence that the patient must assume responsibility for his own communication, for the choice of what he communicates, and for his following up some clarifying reflection by the counselor. This emphasis upon helping the patient by encouraging him to assume responsibility for the conduct of therapy is a persistent motif through Rogers' writings and reports. In this he is of course not unique; others operating within markedly different theoretical frameworks have made similar proposals. Kaiser (1955), for instance, though clearly not a Rogerian, expressed thoughts along similar lines when he said that to cure the patient is to help him assume responsibility and to help him assume responsibility is synonymous with curing. But Rogers is unique in his insistence that the therapist must never be an authority. He even confused, at least at one time, the meaning of authoritative and authoritarian:

> Therapy and authority cannot be coexistent in the same relationship. If this statement is amplified in terms of the description of the counseling situation which has been given in this chapter, the reasons for the incompatibility are plain. There cannot be an atmosphere of complete permissiveness when the relationship is authoritative [1942, p. 109].

Fairness to Rogers demands the recognition that in the context of this quotation he meant to say *authoritarian,* but it is of interest to note that he did not consider rational authority as potentially permissive, encouraging, and supportive.

Systematic study of Rogers' publications leads to the conclusion that his position has evolved to a point where he pays less attention to the specifics of the therapist's words and actions, so that he is relatively undisturbed by the possibility of the therapist's being a rational authority. He seems to have come to a point of view which focuses upon the intent of the counselor's behavior (1951). The therapist's desire to understand and sharply grasp the client's feelings is now Rogers' main concern and he suggests that failures in this endeavor are not so crucial as he had thought previously, provided the intent to understand is genuine:

> . . . as the client is genuinely exploring the unknown, the counselor becomes wholly engaged in trying to keep step

with this puzzled and puzzling search. His attention is completely focused upon the attempt to perceive from the client's frame of reference, and thus it is no longer a technique in operation, but the implementation of an absorbing personal purpose. In this attempt to struggle along with the client, to glimpse with him the half-understood causes of behavior, to wrestle with feelings which emerge into awareness and slip away again, it is entirely possible that the simple concept of "an accurate reflection of feeling" no longer fits the therapist's behavior. Rather than serving as a mirror, the therapist becomes a companion to the client as the latter searches through a tangled forest through the dead of night. The therapist's responses are more in the nature of calls through the darkness: "Am I with you?" "Is this where you are?" "Are we together?" "Is this the direction you are heading?" As might be expected, the answer to these questions is sometimes "No," sometimes "Yes." The counselor is sometimes with the client, at times may be on ahead, at times he lags behind in understanding. Such minor deviations from the course are relatively unimportant since it is so clear that the therapist is in general saying, "I am trying to keep right with you as you make this perilous and frightening search" [1951, pp. 112–13].

The definition of the relationship as it emerges in client-centered therapy is quite different from the one developed in what Gill and his associates (1954) have called the "traditional diagnostic interview." It was precisely against such traditional diagnostic interviewing that Rogers and his followers inveighed, because it leads to "the doctor . . . treating the patient like an inanimate object to be thumped at will according to some predetermined routine of his profession" (Gill *et al.*, 1954, pp. 76–77); in doing so he violates the patient's dignity. This type of interviewing, which demands that the patient respond to a series of prearranged questions by reporting events in his life, readily suggests to the patient that he has relatively little to do with his own growth and development, that in effect he can remain passive and yet be "cured," an obvious contradiction in terms.

This impression is conveyed by therapists who—their protestations to the contrary notwithstanding—labor under the misconception that it is *they* who somehow cure the patients. Their orientation is of course strongly influenced by the traditional physician–patient relationship in which an expert, the physician, employs prescriptive and manipulative procedures on behalf of his patient. He exercises his authority in areas and ways unfamiliar to the patient. The psychotherapeutic relationship, even though still an expert–client relationship, is completely different insofar as its aim is not to ameliorate a condition for the patient but to aid him in becoming the ameliorative agent—to help him become his own healer. While such a goal is patently inappropriate in matters of physical medicine, this growth to personal maturity is precisely the psychotherapeutic aim. Because the expert–client relationship in psychotherapy differs so much from its counterpart in medicine, Freud (1927b) suggested that medical training often seriously hinders the development of psychotherapeutic skills. The therapist's authority derives from his ability to grasp, understand, or—in terms usually employed—diagnose those inner constellations (and their historical bases) which interfere with the patient's attempts to develop a meaningful and satisfying life. Therapeutic authority is also based on the ability to engage the patient in collaborative behavior designed to remove these roadblocks to self-fulfillment and active living.

These comments lead to a consideration of the concept and the role of diagnosis in psychotherapy. Again the difference between medicine and psychotherapy becomes apparent. While good medical practice rests heavily upon the detailed and adequate grasp of the existing condition by the physician so that curative procedures based on a correct diagnostic understanding by the physician can be instituted, the situation in psychotherapy is quite different. First of all, psychological diagnosis is an extremely protracted process and the therapeutic process becomes paradoxically a diagnostic investigation, in which the inner situation of the patient unfolds in ever-sharpened form; and second, equally paradoxically, the diagnostic process is in itself the therapeutic process. It is clear that the term *diagnosis* as used here does not denote affixing a categorical label to the patient's condition; by diagnosis is not meant classification of the patient along Kraepelian or any other phenotypical lines, but much more the development of a genotypical understanding and dynamic grasp of the patient. If the aim of psychotherapy is the patient's gaining insight and knowledge concerning the nature of his existence, his profound grasp of his "diagnosis" is synonymous with a good deal of cure. To restate the issue in simple terms: While in medicine diagnosis and therapy are separate though related processes, in the psychotherapeutic endeavor they are almost synonymous; diagnosis becomes therapy and therapy becomes diagnosis. Both patient and therapist are engaged in a collaborative search concerning the patient's genuine inner situation, the therapist being skilled in the methods of searching and methods of helping patients learn the ways of self-inquiry. Such a position has certain important consequences for procedures customarily associated with psychological diagnosis—diagnostic psychological testing. Thoughtful observers have voiced doubts concerning the usefulness of testing procedures if the all-important issue is not simply the therapist gaining knowledge of the patient but much more the patient's gaining insight (Rogers, 1951).

To appreciate fully the problem involved, several pertinent factors must be remembered. First, the fallibility of the therapist must be kept in mind. Physicians dealing with physical problems, where criteria are much more clear-cut, are fallible; therefore doctors employ a variety of laboratory procedures to check on their clinical hunches and impressions and, mindful of their own shortcomings, they employ consultants to validate their understanding of physical circumstances or to help them along in their investigations of the patient's condition. The situation may be thought of in similar terms in psychotherapy. Psychotherapists, too, may have blind spots which interfere with their grasp of the patient's fundamental belief systems and motivations, interfere with the understanding of what Kelly (1955) called the patient's personal constructs, and therefore they too may require consultants to aid them in sharpening their vision, making the collaborative effort of patient and therapist more efficient and effective.

Second, such blind spots are more likely to occur in dealing with matters psychological than in the investigation of physical problems because some problems in living dissociated by the patient may also operate in repressed fashion in the therapist. It is conceivable that the therapist for his own defensive reasons may avoid or even actively interfere with the patient's search, lest it uncover simultaneously within the therapist something he is eager to keep repressed. This potential difficulty will be dealt with in greater detail under the rubric of *counter-transference;* what must be noted here is that psychological test findings when interpreted and reported sensibly and with sensitivity can alert the therapist to some patient characteristic potentially avoided by the therapist for reasons of his own.

Finally, it must be remembered that the therapist's inability to see the patient's security operations sharply is frequently a failure in gleaning resistance maneuvers. It will be shown in Chapter 10 that resistance will develop inevitably in the psychotherapeutic process because human beings are loath to part with the security operations which have had survival value for them. Whatever helps the therapist to heightened awareness of his patient's particular modes in holding on to ways that have been at least partially successful in the pursuit of some security —including information gathered from psychological tests— will enhance the therapeutic process. Unwitting and neurotic collaboration between the therapist's counter-transference and the patient's resistance is all too common and has been described well by Lindner (1955). Psychological test data are valuable when the diagnostic consultant is able to offer a preview of the interpersonal resistive operations that may be expected from the patient, so that the therapist will be less likely to overlook them and be better prepared to examine and avoid his potential counter-transference reactions, reactions which play into the patient's neurotic and resistive hand.

The pertinence of this awareness lies in the ability of the neurotic and the psychotic to be attuned to the security needs and operations of people in general and the therapist in particular. While patients often distort the meaning and the broader significance of the therapist's personality facets by tearing them out of context, and while they frequently employ their insights about the therapist for their own defensive ends, their sensitivity to personality variables of the therapist is omnipresent. When Gill and his associates (1954) reported how a patient told his interviewing psychiatrist that he hoped the interviewer would pass his test (the interview had been part of an examination procedure), they reported on the patient's sensitivity and his correct perception of the interviewer's primary concern with the examination and lack of interest in learning worthwhile and useful data. Thus, grasp of the therapist's motivations can be sharply focused in the patient's awareness or, dimly sensed, it may proceed subliminally or on the basis of minimal clues (see Chapter 2). But the very capacity of people to perceive another person's motivations suggests that the patient's reactions to the personality of the therapist start from the moment the two establish any contact with each other and that from the earliest moments on, patient and therapist can develop a potentially ever-broadening knowledge of each other.

Whether the therapist knows it or not, through his behavior he constantly defines and redefines himself to the patient, whether by acts of commission or of omission. What the therapist pays attention to and what he seems less interested in; what questions he asks and what questions he does not ask; whether he asks any questions at all are only some of the indicators which are communicated and make for the therapist's definition in the eyes of the patient. Conversely, in his reactions to the self-revealing behavior of the therapist the patient reveals himself, defines and describes in action his personality and the premises by which he lives. From the very beginning the patient's statements and his reactions to the therapist's responses to them have diagnostic and therefore, as pointed out previously, therapeutic value. Inevitably and for better or worse, therapy starts from the earliest moments of the patient–therapist encounter.

Concrete material is necessary. Most frequently the patient will discuss in his remarks the reasons for consulting a therapist. He will state just what he sees wrong with himself and his life, what has moved him to ask for help. Through these statements the patient reveals aspects of his value system, aspects of what he believes is essentially human and what he considers contrary to human essence (Chapter 1). Just as the patient's presenting complaint defines at least in part his value system, so does the therapist's response define a great deal about his orientation. This does not mean the therapist's simple agreement or disagreement with the client, but rather that any comment or even the absence of any remark says something about the values of the therapist. Through this inevitably self-revealing behavior the therapist sets the stage for further self-revealing communication by the patient, triggering a chain reaction of exchange and interaction. Here is an illustration.

□ A man in his mid-twenties consulted a therapist and after a good deal of initial hesitancy and with some embarrassment he started to talk about his reasons for seeking a consultation: even though he was married, father of three children, and a respected man in his community, he frequently felt the urge to masturbate. He considered this abnormal, experienced guilt feelings about such urges and even more profound guilt and shame when he gave in to them. Recently there had been a decided increase in his masturbatory impulses and activities and he believed that this was decidedly pathological and hence was seeking the aid of a therapist to counteract what he thought were manifestations of mental illness.

The therapist, after listening to the patient's statement for a while, inquired about the man's reasons for thinking that his behavior was so pathological. The client looked up with amazement, as if he thought the therapist were insane. It had never occurred to him that any person in his right mind would question what seemed to him self-evident truth: that masturbation at his time and station in life was a reflection of pathology. □

The therapist had of course neither denied nor confirmed the patient's belief, but he had defined himself as an individual who took little if anything as self-evident, as a person who deemed inquiry important and was eager to hear the foundations of the man's belief. At the same time the therapist's question was also experienced by the patient as a challenge confronting him with his apparent reluctance to question his beliefs searchingly and his tendency to take much for granted despite—as it developed later—his pride in independence of thought and action. To repeat: Any relevant comment or question expressed by the therapist defines him to the patient; abstaining from comments and questions has a similar effect. There exists a mass of experimental evidence indicating that the most innocuous noises produced by the therapist are picked up by patients as signs and signals concerning the therapist's attitudes and that they will be responded to consciously or unconsciously (Salzinger, 1959). For instance, an investigator's consistent responding with a simple "Mhm" immediately following the subject's use of a noun resulted in a significant increase of nouns in the verbal behavior of experimental subjects demonstrating their perception of what the experimenter seemed to respond to and what he seemed to ignore, as if his selective grunting of "Mhm" somehow defined him to the subject.

The following example further illustrates how the therapist's comments define him to the patient.

☐ A young woman, in describing the reasons for her seeking help, thought that what she considered her selfless kindness and consideration caused her much harm and pain. In contact with most people—tradespeople, colleagues, friends and acquaintances, or her fiancé—she acted too retiringly. She allowed tradespeople to cheat her in blatant fashion (like selling her shoes that were clearly too small, letting her garage man charge for washing her car though it was obviously not cleaned); her colleagues knew that the slightest hint saw her always ready to shoulder work that was rightfully theirs and she was therefore known at her place of work as "the sweetest thing on earth"; her fiancé had succeeded in making her change her food preferences, her hobbies, and her interests.

While she had a ready "Oh, that's all right" for any demand or imposition, she inwardly raged and fumed until eventually she would break into wild temper tantrums. Then she would stop shopping where she had been taken advantage of, she would terminate friendships abruptly, and engage in violent quarrels with her affianced.

The therapist listened to her report for a while and then asked her if she could describe in some detail the facets of her angry reactions when she felt taken advantage of. This seemed very difficult for her and therefore she returned to making general statements about her conviction that people were grossly inconsiderate, that the overwhelming majority of mankind was eager to exploit, that it was dreadful that one could not trust others, that people were just plain mean, at least most people she had ever met. While she expressed these thoughts she seemed much calmer than at the beginning of her account and occasionally smiled as if lost in some private unrevealed reverie.

The therapist finally commented that it seemed as if she did not include herself in this overwhelming majority of "meanies" and that he wondered why she allowed the people she knew to reveal themselves as such "beasts." The patient seemed startled, expressed some annoyance with the therapist's question but immediately proceeded to report that she had consulted a psychotherapist for several years but that recently she had stopped seeing him because he "was not good enough," had been incapable of helping her to be firmer with all those selfish people. Indeed, she felt it was generally very hard to help her. In college she had gotten A's in most courses despite the fact that she had cut classes and had rarely done assignments and readings. All that was needed was some "fantastic story and excuse," most instructors would buy it and she would wind up with a good grade. She had not attended classes because the lecturers had been "inferior," had not read because the assignments had been "infantile."

With a smile the therapist responded to the effect that most everybody she knew seemed either mean or stupid or both. And with a pointed look directed toward her he remarked "But undoubtedly there are exceptions, too—occasionally one meets a superior product of creation." At this point the patient became very anxious but also eager to discuss her sudden fright and confusion. □

Whether one agrees with the therapist's response or deems his interpretive comments premature, he had grasped a significant facet of the patient's inner life: the importance she attached to thinking of herself as morally and intellectually superior to others and that a haughty and contemptuous superiority was concealed behind a mask of injured and self-righteous indignation. This was of course a diagnostic insight but to the extent to which the interview brought this personality feature into focus and awareness, to that extent was the diagnostic insight used for therapeutic ends. In the exchange just described the therapist defined a good deal about himself. He conveyed to the patient his attention to her feelings, that he thought that she harbored attitudes which were outside the realm of her awareness yet revealed themselves in her behavior, and that he did not hesitate to express how the patient happened to strike him. In effect the therapist tried from the very onset to engage her in searching self-examination.

It can be argued that the therapist's behavior represents what has been called "wild analysis" (Freud, 1910) because no historical material was available to him; that his confrontational manner was uncalled for because a historical framework for the patient's feelings is necessary; that even were the therapist right in his grasp of the patient's experience, and even if she were able to be aware of such feelings, this could result in nothing but damaged self-esteem because the patient would be left with a sense of being "bad" and a sense of having been beaten over the head. It might be argued that some masochistic characters would enjoy reactions which resemble verbal shock treatment because they may help guilt-ridden individuals fleetingly in atoning but that they are ineffectual in bringing about any real personality change.

These would be perfectly reasonable arguments if a therapist were satisfied to confront the patient with insights and leave it at that. Such behavior would come dangerously close to sadism. Therapist and patient must gather in their early meetings data concerning the make-up of the patient and recognize his genuine emotional reactivity because these data and recognitions define for both participants the areas of future search: the ever-expanding grasp of the emotional forces which motivate the patient, the underlying belief systems from which these forces spring, and last but not least the historical factors which gave rise to such belief systems and their consequent emotional manifestations (also see Chapter 9). To use the illustration offered earlier: were one simply to take the patient's lamentation at face value, little could be accomplished by patient and therapist. They could either bemoan the stupidity and hostility of mankind, consoling each other and themselves with the knowledge that there are fortunate though rare exceptions to all this destructiveness and banality; or the therapist could try to help the patient learn some ways of not being bothered by this sad state of affairs; or perhaps try to teach the patient some new ways of being "more assertive." If one were to accept the patient's story, nothing else could be done; no amount of talk could change the sad picture of the universe presented by the patient. The therapeutic exchange is not designed to modify the world or people in the life of the patient—the only person who can change is the patient, the only variable in the equation subject to change is the patient.

It is therefore incumbent upon the therapist to define the therapeutic relationship as early as possible in terms which allow both participants to address themselves to an examination of those forces within the patient which cause him grief and harm. There is no denying the importance of outside forces that contributed to the development of a patient's nonproductive orientation, but the investigation of the history of a phenomenon requires first and foremost the full grasp of its nature. Understanding the historical determinants of a personality constellation demands first of all a precise knowledge of the present personality make-up. On this basis psychotherapy follows truly the road of all scientific inquiry in which sharp naturalistic observation and pointed description of all relevant facets inevitably precede historical and causal understanding. Unfortunately the importance of establishing the *what* of the patient's existence is frequently disregarded because too often young and inexperienced therapists think that this *what* refers merely to overt behavioral manifestations, overlooking the fact that it also includes present dynamic though not psychogenetic constellations which make for observable events.

Additional reporting of the initial contacts between the young woman and her therapist further illustrates this point.

□ In her second interview she informed the therapist how disturbed she had been by his comments, how she had resolved not to come back but how she also felt at the same time that she had to return. She mentioned that she feared and in some ways hated him for what he had said but—oddly enough, she thought—had also felt strangely relieved. Furthermore, his comments had brought up many memories. She had remembered that in high school she had often been thought snobbish by her classmates, that she had indeed affected a stand-offish air and had not wanted to mix with them. She had frequently thought them inferior to her, even though she had gone to an "elite" private school where admission requirements were quite high and where selection procedure had been very rigorous. She remembered how she had always been a "loner" and had prided herself on this even though it had caused her some pain. In any case, the therapist's comments had released a flood of associations and memories long forgotten, most of them centering around an awareness of some snobbish contemptuousness.

At one point during these reminiscences the therapist mused aloud: he wondered where and how she had developed this haughtiness, how and where she had adopted this attitude.

After an immediate attack of anxiety, a severe headache, and a lengthy silence, the patient started to discuss her family. She came from an economically well-to-do upper-middle-class family; however, the cultural and educational level of her background lagged sorely behind her family's financial affluence. She described the all-pervasive belief of her family that most anybody could be bought, had to be bought, and should be bought.

Her father had always liked to impress on her and her siblings how easy it was to do business if one only had enough power. He had actually managed to amass enough money and power to have his family and associates in business dance to his tune, was able to manipulate most anybody and seemed pleased by his ability to do so. He was always involved in big deals which kept him out of the home from dawn to late at night and the children had learned early to look up to him as a tycoon who made the world go round, an exaggerated picture the mother had deliberately painted for the children.

As the patient discussed this it struck her also that evidently the parents had had relatively little to do with each other, that all the members of the household lived past each other, "passed each other like ships in the night." It occurred to her that there had been a remarkable lack of companionship between her parents, that the father had acted as if he did not need his wife at all, that all the mother seemed to want from her husband was physical support.

The patient, who had recently divorced her husband because she just "did not love him, never had loved him, knew that I did not love him as we were being married," now began to recount her feelings of not needing her husband for anything except as an escort to nice places and reminisced about feeling pleased when she entered a crowded restaurant with her unusually handsome husband "because he made such a striking appearance." At the same time, she remarked, she had resented the very pleasure she derived from this type of "dependence." She finally commented that she thought she could see a connection between the spirit with which she felt she was imbued from earliest times and her relationship to her ex-husband.

The therapist nodded and remarked that her haughty attitude toward her teachers seemed similarly in line with this "I don't want to need anybody" attitude. But he also suggested that it seemed to him that in any indoctrination process two parties were necessary, "an indoctrinator and one who is willing to be indoctrinated." He commented that "It takes two to tango."

Again the patient became visibly flustered, anxious, and annoyed and once again after a short while went on to describe how today, as a grown woman with a relatively well-paying professional position, she constantly got into economic difficulties. She described how her family would have to bail her out of financial troubles, inevitably raising a fuss about it but then always refusing the patient's admittedly feeble attempts to pay back loans that had been extended to her. □

This material is reported to illustrate how the development of historical perspectives, the learning of the patient's history, need not be a sterile or mechanical enterprise and to show that the reporting of historical material by the patient springs from an examination of the "what" of today. The therapist's somewhat challenging and confrontational comments on the patient's characterological make-up gave rise to meaningful and emotionally significant recall of early environmental features. In her third visit and under the impact of the therapist's comment "It takes two to tango," the patient began to describe her relation to her father, including certain peculiarities in his attitude toward her and how they had pleased her. These details need not be pursued because they do not contribute to the general point being examined here: historical material is important and meaningful but assumes therapeutic value only if developed within the immediate context of emotional experience and not when simply offered or collected for the therapist's illumination.

The development of historical perspectives is useful only when it becomes an integral part of the therapeutic process itself and a procedure that neither smacks of detective work nor conveys to the patient the idea that once the therapist knows all about him he will "straighten" him out. When the collection of historical material is an integral part of the therapeutic effort it reflects the therapist's intense desire to understand the patient as a human being, his strengths and his foibles. Then it indicates the therapist's urge to learn the essential meaning that the patient gives to his life, the premises on which this meaning is based and the events in his past that convinced him that the premises and methods he chose were the most adequate ones in developing a personal meaning.

The process of defining the patient's problems Sullivan (1954) called the "reconnaissance," a procedure he distinguished from what he called the "detailed inquiry." But examining what goes on in the "reconnaissance" and comparing it with the "detailed inquiry" one finds that conceptually and procedurally the two periods differ little from one another. Of course, later stages of inquiry are based upon material already produced and data accumulated later are understood in terms of previously gained insights, but as Sullivan described it all parts of the therapeutic process can be thought of as a progressive unfolding of the person's characterological picture and its historical antecedents. All of therapy can be conceived as an extensive historical investigation and simultaneously as a grasp of the present, the interrelation of the present with the past, the present picture, and past influences. All of therapy, the initial interviews and later stages, may be thought of as a continuing effort in self-exploration that includes the exploration of factors which contributed to the development of the present self. As previously mentioned (and discussed in much greater detail in Chapter 13), the very process of searching is curative, not merely the finding of connections; the patient's self-diagnostic efforts, which require his examination of his past and present, constitute therapy. The distinction between initial interview periods and later stages is therefore somewhat arbitrary, moving Gill and his associates to comment:

> No one has supplied us with a more brilliant discussion of the therapist-patient relationship in a broad cultural context. It seems to us surprising, therefore, that Sullivan still adheres to a relatively formal "reconnaissance" and "detailed inquiry." Even he cannot entirely free himself from the shackles of the established sequence of psychiatric history taking, at least as he reveals himself in these two papers [1954, p. 62].

Yet there is a meaningful distinction between initial contacts and later stages of therapeutic work: the initial interviews set the tone for what is to follow, create the atmosphere and the climate for later developments, and therefore represent a period more crucial for the therapeutic enterprise than any other stage in the patient-therapist relationship. If human beings need psychotherapy because they have abandoned the essential features of their activity and consciousness, and because they believe that events have taught them not to take themselves and their lives seriously; and if achieving emotional well-being is synonymous with a regaining of consciousness, activity, and seriousness, the therapist must emphasize the importance of these qualities in his own behavior toward the patient from earliest moments. The therapist must indicate to the patient from the beginning that he takes his own life seriously and that on the basis of this self-respect he values the patient's life. The communication of this serious interest cannot wait. The intense urgency of the therapist to learn to know the patient must not be diluted by inquiry into trivia, concern with history for history's sake, and an orientation which implies that tomorrow is another day. The patient has undoubtedly experienced only all too painfully expressions of disrespect for his time and his life by significant persons in his past. To perpetuate such pain by delay in the therapeutic sessions must disastrously reinforce a depreciation of self.

Some observers might say that such urgency on the part of the therapist can easily arouse the patient's anxiety and subsequent defensive behavior to ward off unbearable terror. This undoubtedly represents a real enough possibility. However, this arousal of anxiety and even the appearance of defensive maneuvers are not necessarily undesirable because, if properly examined and understood by both participants, they afford opportunities for the development of profound insights into the characterological structure and organization of the patient. The following example illustrates this.

☐ A young man seeks help for a variety of distressing symptoms, such as insomnia, inability to concentrate, difficulties with his employer, and similar problems. Somewhat sophisticated psychologically, he makes reference to his "anxiety," his tendency to "repress," and his "high level of aspirations." Somewhere toward the end of their first meeting the therapist asked him to describe exactly what he meant by "having a high level of aspirations."

The patient acted as if taken aback, as if he did not understand the question. The therapist simply repeated the request, and when no response was forthcoming and it became apparent that the man was becoming increasingly anxious and fidgety, the therapist explained that he liked to hear a somewhat detailed description of the feelings which the patient identified in this particular fashion, a description of some of the nuances of experience referred to by the patient when he talked about "high levels of aspiration."

At this moment the patient became obviously angry, insisted that the therapist was teasing him, that he must know what was meant, that he was not in the mood to waste his time, and that they ought to get on with their business.

When the therapist simply raised his eyebrows and gave him a quizzical look the patient became intensely anxious, started to sweat profusely, and shortness of breath set in. There was no glib talk of anxiety—a full-fledged anxiety attack was in progress. While the patient was of course incapable of discussing the nuances of his experience, it was perhaps the first time he had paid some attention to what he had been fond of discussing with his friends—his anxiety. □

Thus a very important facet of the patient's personality revealed itself. The patient had somehow learned to avoid awareness of anxiety by talking about it, such talk serving him as an escape from experience, from observation of self, and from the potential discomfort self-observations entail. Instead he had developed a remarkable array of debilitating symptoms.

The initial interview also serves as a period during which the patient can be educated to face the tasks involved in the therapeutic process, can learn about his responsibility in the coming meetings with the therapist. As early as 1913 Freud saw the importance of this early educative process when he recommended that the "fundamental rule" had to be offered and insisted upon from the very beginning:

> This [fundamental rule] must be imparted to him [the patient] at the very beginning. 'One more thing before you start. What you tell me must differ in one respect from an ordinary conversation. Ordinarily you rightly try to keep a connecting thread running through your remarks and you exclude any intrusive ideas that may occur to you and any side-issues so as not to wander too far from the point. But in this case you must proceed differently. You will notice that as you relate things various thoughts will occur to you which you would like to put aside on the ground of certain criticisms and objections. You will be tempted to say to yourself that this or that is irrelevant here, or is quite unimportant, or nonsensical, or that there is no need to say it. You must never give in to these criticisms, but must say it in spite of them—indeed, you must say it precisely *because* you feel an aversion to doing so. Later on you will find out and learn to understand the reason for this injunction, which is really the only one you have to follow. So say whatever goes through your mind. Act as though, for instance, you were a traveller sitting next to the window of a railway carriage and describing to someone inside the changing views which you see outside. Finally, never forget that you have promised to be absolutely honest, and never leave anything out because for some reason or other, it is unpleasant to tell' [pp. 134–35].

Freud (1913) also fully recognized how difficult it was to follow this rule. His "injunction" and hope that a patient could really obey it bear potent testimony to Freud's abiding confidence in the power of rational thought, a quality in Freud discussed extensively by Fromm (1959). It is as if Freud somehow believed that rational thought could overpower irrational emotions and oddly enough hoped that the patient would be capable of mustering enough determination to follow the "basic rule." But if an individual were really capable of being so open to his thoughts and experiences and so trusting of another person that he felt free to communicate to him all that came to his mind, what earthly business would he have in a psychotherapist's office? The intimate self-knowledge and the capacity to pay attention to and concentrate on one's sensations and emotions, qualities which are prerequisites for following the "basic rule," are reflections of psychic well-being, end stages and outcomes of therapy rather than requirements for therapy. Because emotionally disturbed people are out of touch with their feelings other writers have suggested that the therapist inquire most carefully concerning exactly what the patient means by any given expression or verbalization rather than assume that he knows the nature or intent of the communication. Sullivan, for instance, remarked:

> The psychiatrist, the interviewer, plays a very active role in introducing interrogations, not to show that he is smart or that he is skeptical, but literally to make sure that he knows what he is being told. Few things do the patient more good in the way of getting toward his more or less clearly formulated desire to benefit from the investigation than this very care on the part of the interviewer to discover exactly what is meant. Almost every time one asks, "Well, what do you mean by so and so?" the patient is a little clearer on what he does mean. And what a relief it is for him to discover that his true meaning is anything but what he at first says, and that he is at long last uncovering some conventional self-deception that he has been pulling on himself for years [1954, p. 21].

Sullivan thought that the educative process toward self-discovery must start from the very beginning, notably at a time when the patient still needs help in achieving a "more or less clearly formulated desire to benefit" and that the development of this desire is therapeutic in itself. Sullivan explained the basis of his thinking:

> Thus whenever the psychiatrist's attempt to discover what the patient is talking about leads the patient to be somewhat more clear on what he is thinking about or attempting to communicate or conceal, his grasp on life is to some extent enhanced. And no one has grave difficulties in living if he has a very good grasp on what is happening to him [1954, pp. 23–24].

The initial interview also affords the therapist an opportunity to assess the patient's suitability for psychotherapy. Freud (1904) had originally proposed that this is defined by his educatability. Freud's (1937) later statement that success of therapy depends on the degree to which the patient's instinctual demands can be "tamed" represents a refinement rather than a change in position; it was the result of experience gained during more than a quarter of a century of work. Other theorists concerned with the importance of the initial interview have also seen this stage as a period for prognostic evaluations and they too equated prognosis with "educatability," though they differed in their criteria for it because they disagreed on ultimate aims in therapy. Youth, for instance, was an important criterion for Freud (1904); he believed that instinctual demands could be "tamed" more easily when this taming process started early in life. Because "taming the instincts" as a therapeutic aim was alien to Jung's (1933) thinking, youthfulness was not an important prognostic criterion for him. He thought that the aims and goals of therapy before forty and after forty were different and therefore he considered factors which had little to do with the likelihood that instincts could be tamed when he assessed treatability during his early contacts with the patient. Sullivan (1956) went so far as to think that youthfulness in some instances was a drawback for therapeutic progress and was much more concerned with the ability of patient and therapist to agree on an outline of difficulties in living for the patient, and the patient's genuine conviction that it was important to investigate these difficulties and their meaning. And Gill and his associates (1954), without using the term, proposed that the patient's educatability be determined early and that this assessment revolved around the patient's motivation and realistic resources for change.

Finally, the initial interview also serves most psychotherapists as a period for defining to the patient the conditions of employment they are willing to accept. Regardless of one's willingness to admit it freely, it is obvious that the patient employs the therapist for specified services requiring at least implicitly an employment contract. Most authorities suggest that the conditions of this contract be made explicit. Specific demands made will differ from therapist to therapist. They will be determined by several factors:

First of all, personal needs, hopefully rational in nature, will enter (see Chapter 5).

Second, the therapist's orientation will be a determining factor. If he is convinced that even under the best of circumstances human beings are extremely reluctant to change, that the ability to engage in free association and to combat one's resistance depends upon the frequency of sessions, he will insist upon daily interviews. On the other hand, those therapists whose experience and theoretical thinking lead them to believe that human beings can engage in much productive self-investigation outside the therapist's office will not insist on daily visits. The setting of fees is also somewhat influenced by theoretical issues. Those who conclude with Freud (1913) that the educative process is furthered by a modicum of frustration will insist that fees must be high enough to cause the patient some economic distress; otherwise, so the argument runs, patients who are reluctant to move into maturity anyhow would be deprived of an important spur in their self-examination. Those who have other opinions about man's willingness to grow into maturity consider economic hardship at most a minor motivating force and therefore such considerations do not enter into their setting of fees.

Third, and also closely related to the theoretical orientation of the therapist, the specifics of the psychological condition of a given patient may influence the working conditions insisted upon by the therapist. While he may believe that certain patients will benefit from individual therapeutic sessions, he may believe that the particular psychological make-up of other individuals warrants their becoming members of a therapy group. In any case, the initial interview is an appropriate time for determining and clarifying to the patient the circumstances under which the therapist will work with him. In other words, the formal arrangements governing the therapeutic contacts are spelled out.

Obviously all this—the development and definition of the patient-therapist relationship; the gathering of some historical data relevant for a broad diagnostic impression; the initiation of therapeutic exchanges and orienting the patient to the therapeutic process; the assessment of prognosis or the patient's suitability for therapy; and the working out of practical and practicable arrangements for the proposed contacts—cannot be accomplished in one meeting.

It is therefore commonplace to think of the initial interview not as one session but as a series of interviews—as many as are needed to determine salient factors. Consequently the initial interview is thought of as an essentially experimental period. Freud (1913) was most explicit in stating that this was his position. Other authors have discussed this period in similar terms, at least by implication (Freud, 1946a; Gill, Newman & Redlich, 1954; Sullivan, 1954). They think of this period as an experimental stage because it provides for patient and therapist an opportunity to learn whether a genuine need for therapy exists and, if it does, whether they can work with each other productively. It may turn out that their interaction seems doomed to failure. If on the basis of his experience and self-understanding the therapist considers such failure probable, he has no ethical choice other than to terminate and to refer the patient to someone else. This can be quite a blow to the patient, but whenever necessary it must not be avoided. It would be much more cruel were the therapist to disregard his impressions, delude himself, or grudgingly continue despite his knowledge that nothing fruitful is likely to come from his contacts with the patient.

The initial interview is not only the starting point; it is also part and parcel of the therapeutic process. The specific facets of the process, the concepts and constructs that describe and make psychotherapy comprehensible, will be sketched in the following chapters.

► *Summary* ◄

1. The therapist's expertness casts him inevitably in the role of an authority, though hopefully a rational authority rather than an irrational authoritarian.

2. In his gathering of relevant data the therapist defines

himself as a person genuinely interested in meeting the patient as a human being, even though his own anxieties may tempt the therapist to gather information for collecting's sake.

3. Learning the *what* of the patient's life, who he is and what he feels, must precede the knowledge of the *why* of his ways. To state it differently: the development of a dynamic picture forms the basis for psychogenic investigation.

4. Careful and sensitive diagnostic inquiry into the present life of the patient and the premises by which he lives is itself therapeutic. Conversely, therapy is ultimately a diagnostic inquiry into the *what* and *why* of the patient's character and life style. In this sense the initial sessions do not differ markedly from subsequent interviews.

5. However, the initial interviews do differ from later contacts because during the early meetings the therapist is in an excellent position to set the tone for the psychotherapeutic process and is in a position to convey a sense of urgency and immediacy, directness, and seriousness. Through this behavior he expresses respect for the patient and makes the psychotherapeutic search a truly unique experience for his client.

6. During the initial interviews the patient's education for the psychotherapeutic collaboration takes place. Careful inquiry by the therapist shows the patient the road to painstaking self-investigation. Consequently these early contacts afford the participants the opportunity to investigate the patient's motivations for seeking therapy. Understanding these motives has important implications.

7. The initial interviews are also the time for arranging the formal aspects of patient–therapist collaboration.

8. The initial interview must also be thought of as an experimental period during which patient and therapist have an opportunity to learn something about each other so that they may come to a rational decision concerning the feasibility of working with each other.

CHAPTER SEVEN

The Concept of Limits in Psychotherapy

IN THE TWO IMMEDIATELY PRECEDING CHAPTERS IT WAS SUG-gested that therapists have definite, hopefully rational, needs. It was furthermore indicated that the nature and expression of these need systems define the personality of the therapist and that these self-definitions communicate themselves to the patients from the earliest moments of the therapeutic exchange. In this inevitable self-defining process the therapist willy-nilly sets "limits," establishes his personal outline and limits beyond which the patient must not go.

The concept of setting limits and its importance has been discussed prominently since its inception in the literature on child therapy (Allen, 1942; Arline, 1947; Freud, A., 1928; Klein, M., 1960; Redl & Wineman, 1951; Rogers, 1951). The type of limits set and the methods employed in establishing them differ in adult therapy from their counterparts in child therapy. Yet conceptually and in its rationales and broad consequences the process of setting limits is similar for both settings, even though the techniques and the areas in which it is employed vary. There are, of course, instances in psychotherapeutic work with adults when the limits imposed and the techniques establishing them are identical with those found in working with children. The therapist will not permit children to assault him physically in play therapy; it would also be utter folly to allow adults to harm the therapist. There are two obvious reasons for preventing physical attack: first, the therapist sets such limits because he genuinely values his well-being and nobody who values his welfare can allow others to interfere with it; second, in not allowing the patient to harm him the therapist prevents activities which must ultimately produce a profound sense of guilt in the patient. The spark of desire for freedom, reason, and personal responsibility somewhere alive in the patient—and its nurture and development are the fundamental goals of therapy—will ultimately cause him to suffer intense guilt engendered by his hostile acts and assaults. Patients come to therapists because they feel guilt about what they have done to themselves and to others and because they have built defensive operations obscuring their knowledge in this area (see Chapter 1). It would be quite detrimental to the patient were the therapist to structure their relationship in such a way as to make for the development of more destructiveness, more guilt, more defenses against guilt—more pathology.

When a therapist assumes an unduly permissive stance toward a patient's destructive actions, indicates that "it's all right," that he really does not mind or that he has no negative reactions, he enmeshes the patient in a tormenting bind, imposing an even greater burden of guilt because the patient is really crushed and feels doubly guilty for having assaulted such a "wonderful" and "angelic" person. There is nothing "wonderful" or truly understanding or accepting about such behavior by a therapist. The only understanding, acceptance, and therapeutic approach to an act of violence on the part of the patient is to acknowledge one's reaction to it, acknowledge that one does not like it and that the patient and the therapist need to explore the patient's experience, the real meaning of the incident and what triggered it. This may lead to true understanding, while making light of such an incident seals avenues of exploration and insight.

Honest limit-setting responses by the therapist are much

more reassuring to the patient than playing a benevolent role; they convey that he is genuinely accepted *despite* his pathology, despite his destructiveness, not simply *because* the therapist blinds himself to it consciously or unconsciously. The latter type of avoidance is likely to make the patient live in constant terror of the day when the therapist stops deluding himself and sees the nature of the patient's impulses fully. Of course, the opportunity to act "wonderfully" is tempting, especially if the therapist permits himself to engage in a competitive struggle with some significant person in the patient's life and tries to show the patient how "good" he is. Such artificial comparisons may prove self-flattering to the therapist, but they will do nothing but harm the patient, adult or child. He will have been manipulated once again to serve the irrational and self-aggrandizing needs of another person; once again he will have been somebody's tool (undoubtedly the patient has been exploited innumerable times before by others, circumstances basically responsible for his adoption of pathological ways). Neither will a therapist's simple moralistic and moralizing condemnation of the patient's destructive behavior or the assuming of an injured air further growth and well-being. These gambits pointedly interfere with the patient's and therapist's learning meaningful material (see also Chapters 5 and 6).

"Assaults" upon another person are not necessarily physical; they include infringements upon the rights and dignity of others. Assaults may take the form of interfering with the rational needs of the therapist by making unreasonable demands upon his time. Some patients tend to call the therapist at all times of the day and night, interrupting his work, his play, and his sleep with inquiries about trivia and by posing all kinds of inconsequential problems. It must be kept in mind that there are a good many people who are thoroughly convinced that to irritate is their only chance for maintaining contact with another human being; their nuisance calls must be understood as expressions of this conviction. The meaning of their behavior lends itself to fruitful exploration only when its annoying character has been fully acknowledged without condemnation and an attempt is made to stop it.

Some patients attempt to infringe unreasonably upon the time of other patients by trying to stay for longer than the appointed time, or in child therapy youngsters may try to interfere with the rights of other children by destroying toys. The setting of limits in these instances is important for the reasons mentioned earlier (destructiveness eventually leads to guilt and complicating defenses against it) as well as an additional significant consideration: such limits will convince the patient more than words that the therapist genuinely respects the rights of others, and this genuinely protective attitude furthers the patient's development of trust in the therapist's rational concern with him personally. Assaults may, of course, also take the form of economic infringement, the patient's attempts to manipulate and inconvenience the therapist through delayed payments and broken appointments. Again it is necessary for patient and therapist to learn the inner meaning of these activities, but here too limits must be set lest the investigation of the patient's destructive behavior is made impossible. The patient can learn to develop some self-respect, can learn to see self-respect as a possibility in his own life, only in contact with a therapist who respects himself.

A few additional observations concerning the beneficial aspects of setting limits are in order here. The patient, child or adult, will derive from limits imposed the relieving sense that he is not omnipotent. Contrary to the often-voiced and popular belief—prevalent even among the psychologically sophisticated—the feeling of omnipotence is one of the most disturbing and troublesome human experiences imaginable, because it entails feelings of unreality and paradoxically a sense of nothingness and nonexistence. It is indeed terrifying to feel that everything somehow turns out magically the way one wants it to happen, magically because events take place without any apparent rhyme or reason; that actually, if there were reason in one's universe, things would turn out quite differently and that therefore things happen in unpredictable and ununderstandable fashion: things are simply not real. The terrifying consequence of such circumstances is the feeling that nothing has reality because nothing has boundaries and definition, and "if nothing has definition, I have no definition either; if nothing around me is real I cannot be real either." It is enlightening to watch how often youngsters will persist in provocative behavior until finally the adult calls a halt to their impositions and annoyances and to observe the obvious sense of relief when the child discovers that the other person will not permit further infringements. One can even hear youngsters exclaim with great satisfaction when physically punished that now they know "Mommy is for real." In a similar vein, patients repeatedly express great satisfaction, some verbal protestations to the contrary notwithstanding, when the therapist disallows unreasonable requests and indicates firmness. The patient takes comfort in knowing that he is meeting a real person who will not permit some outlandish action because the therapist, in defining his reality through the establishment of his limits, simultaneously establishes the reality of his patient.

The comfort derived from such development of reality boundaries was pointedly described by a nine-year-old boy while sitting on a beach and watching the waves intently. An adult friend of his family sat next to him and after observing the boy's intense concentration inquired about its object. The boy replied that he had been watching the patterns of the waves coming in and going out. After a while, he added, something strange had occurred to him. He had concentrated upon willing the waves to come in and go out in reverse rhythm. But no matter how hard he concentrated, he could not change the pattern of the tides and he said that this was fine by him; in a way it made him feel good. Eventually he indicated that it was reassuring to him that the waves moved independent of his wishes, for then he could be sure that things were real. He evidently meant that then he could be sure that he was real too. Whatever the causes of his doubts concerning his own reality, he had found some reassuring sense of reality in the "integrity" of the surf. One can hope that a human being learns to sense his reality in a more personal and intimate setting, but at least he had this rather impersonal evidence.

Lack of adult integrity, reflected in the parents' failure to set limits, is often terror-provoking in children because this failure in setting limits reduces the child's sense of his own reality. His terror in the absence of realistic limits was explained by a patient in his early thirties who had sought therapy in the hope of finding relief from extremely severe mood swings.

☐ During his intense depressions the patient would lose all interest in work, family, friends, and acquaintances; he would live in utter despair, totally incapable of utilizing his genuine enough talents. At those moments nothing seemed real to him, the world was distant and meaningless. One day while talking about these depressive moods and the sense of unreality associated with them, he recalled the following episode from his youth.

He had been reared by his maternal grandparents and he felt that he had loved his grandmother deeply because she had been "so understanding"; yet whenever he thought of her he became sad. His home had been in a medium-size town in mountainous country. The winters had been long and cold with large accumulations of snow and he had enjoyed immensely playing in the fresh snow. One day (he was probably in third or fourth grade) a lot of snow had fallen, and upon leaving school the children had engaged in a snowball fight. The patient remembered how he had made a snowball, let it melt a bit in his hands, and then let it refreeze to make it good and hard; how he had aimed at a little girl across the street and then fired with all his might. To his terror he hit her on the head and she ran screaming back into the school to be comforted by a teacher. Panic-stricken, the little boy ran home.

As soon as he got there he decided that he had to stay out of school for a few days and wait until the episode blew over or was forgotten and so he began to scheme. Next morning he told his grandmother that he had a sore throat, that he didn't feel well, and that he should stay home. The grandmother nodded, but asked him to open his mouth and let her look at his tonsils. Frightened of being found out, he opened his mouth and was amazed when his grandmother nodded agreement, said he must have a lot of pain for it was "such a bad red and sore throat." He became even more amazed when she took his temperature and announced that he had some fever, even though he knew full well this was not so—nothing bothered him—and when he secretly took his temperature a short while later it was perfectly normal.

In recalling this episode the fantastic unreality of the scene struck him, how he had thought he was crazy, how he had thought he could magically control the world, how nothing made sense. This and similar episodes had been terrifying in their implication that neither of the participants was real. □

The illustration will illuminate the positive and reality-enhancing aspects of the setting of limits and the potential destructiveness of their not being imposed. Although the patient might have been in a bit of trouble, had the grandmother insisted that he go to school or tell her just why he was so eager to stay home, such insistence would have spared him the nightmarish quality of seeing reality vanish. To be sure, the setting of limits brings in its wake what Sullivan (1953) called the "shrinking to life size," but the avoidance of setting limits inevitably results in lack of definition, in diminution of the sense of reality and subsequent terror. Alexander (1946c) referred to psychotherapy as a process of exposing human beings to "emotionally corrective experiences." The limits imposed in the course of psychotherapeutic work represent "emotionally corrective experiences" for individuals who experience themselves and others as foggy and unreal. They reflect the therapist's integrity and help the patient achieve what Erikson (1950, 1953, 1962) so aptly referred to as "identity" (also see Chapters 13 and 14).

The illustrations offered make it clear that the setting of limits occurs primarily although not exclusively around the formal aspects of the patient–therapist interaction. It is also apparent that setting of limits poses a dilemma. It may easily prevent the patient from activities which would reveal impulses deeply buried yet invaluable in the development of insight and understanding of the patient. One might argue, as has been done often (Benedek, 1946; Fenichel, 1945; Fromm-Reichmann, 1950; Tarachow, 1963), that the setting of limits is an injunction against "acting-out" behavior but not an injunction against the experiencing of impulses toward certain actions and that therapy is concerned with the investigation of impulses rather than their behavioral manifestations. This position makes a good deal of sense on first sight; but it must also be borne in mind that most human beings are not thoroughly attuned to their desires, that they engage in many actions unconscious of what they have done and unaware of the impulses triggering their behavior. They have a good deal of trouble in really "catching" their motivations. Most pointedly—and by definition—is this true of emotionally disturbed people. They probably would not be patients if they possessed the capacity for gleaning their motivational forces as they arise. As a matter of fact, they may not even view some of their so-called acting-out as being in need of investigation because their actions seem to them most rational.

A good deal of character pathology reveals itself precisely through "acting-out." A patient may see nothing wrong in inconveniencing another person by keeping him waiting, his basic assumption being that life is a continuous power struggle anyhow; he who inconveniences others is, so far as the patient can see, the more powerful—"and what is wrong with wanting to have the upper hand?" Were the therapist to make it clear from the very beginning that he will not tolerate lateness, were promptness for appointments a limit imposed and were the patient to accept this demand, his secret longings for power through inconveniencing others might not reveal itself so readily as it might were such an injunction not imposed. In setting limits the therapist steers a course between the Scylla of loss of self-respect, of well-being, and of dignity and the harmful, nontherapeutic implications of this loss for both him and his patient and the Charybdis of interfering with behavior throwing significant light upon important areas in the patient's motivational structure.

Therefore limits must be set sparingly and must be rational. This is true of those limits which govern the patient's and therapist's behavior in relation to each other and limits the therapist might impose upon the patient's behavior outside the therapeutic setting. A good deal has been written about what Freud (1915a, 1919) originally called the "rule of abstinence." This "rule" requires that the therapist deny the patient's cravings for satisfaction:

> The treatment must be carried out in abstinence. By this I do not mean physical abstinence alone, nor yet the deprivation of everything that the patient desires, for perhaps no sick person could tolerate this. Instead, I shall state it as a fundamental principle that the patient's need and longing should be allowed to persist in her, in order that they may serve as forces impelling her to do work and to make changes, and that we must beware of appeasing those forces by means of surrogates [1915a, p. 165].

Once again Freud advanced the theme that runs so prominently through his thinking: cure and emotional well-being are the outcome of judiciously applied deprivations and frustrations. In addition to this familiar theme and his belief that the patient's cravings for the love of the therapist are manifestations of transference and resistance, Freud advanced another, more potent argument, at least by implication (see also Chapters 10, 11, and 12). He pointed out that were the therapist to give in to demands in order "to eventually get the patient around" he would violate the most fundamental premise of analytic treatment—he would engage in sham and dishonesty.

In addition, the "rule of abstinence" includes the therapist's insistence that the patient refrain from any major changes in the arrangements of his life during the course of therapy. Such a rule immediately runs into a definitional problem: what is "major"? Obviously what appears major to one can be trivial to another. The more the patient's life activities are restricted, the less the opportunities for patient and therapist to observe his reactions and feelings when confronted with life's issues. A stringent injunction against the patient's changing jobs while in therapy would prevent both participants from learning and examining fully his reaction in a new setting; it would interfere with both understanding the forces that threaten him, and under what conditions of employment he feels comfortable. Most therapeutic interviews would be devoted at best to interesting speculations, but the investigation would lack the convincing evidence that naturalistic data provide.

The value placed upon obtaining direct and immediate experiential data does not reduce the importance of verbal exploration of impulses and actions the patient plans to take: there is a world of difference between his announcing to the therapist that he had married yesterday a woman he had been seeing for three years but had never even mentioned in his sessions and the behavior of the patient who relates that he had been at a party the night before, that he had become infatuated with someone there and had spent the rest of the night in her bedroom. Were he to resist his impulse until he had thoroughly discussed his possible motivations for it in abstract and academic terms, therapy would become the pathetic farce cartoonists and satirists often imply it is. In the former instance the therapist might question why he is consulted at all if the patient does not care to discuss and explore present or anticipated events in his life; in the latter instance the patient is confronted with his spontaneous experience, affording him an opportunity to observe subtleties of his feelings and reactions contributing important knowledge.

A rational formulation of the "rule of abstinence" suggests that *all* the patient's behavior, current or anticipated, is subject to scrutiny and is legitimate and potentially fruitful material for investigation, but this does not imply an injunction against spontaneous acts except for those bringing irrevocable consequences and harm to self and/or others. "Major" activities or decisions, then, are those which are irrevocable or irreversible. Since there are relatively few actions and decisions which have such consequences, the rule of abstinence is less restrictive than one might think at first sight and therefore the setting of limits is also less arbitrary than it might appear to some. Rational limits are simply limits devoid of arbitrariness established solely for the rational benefit of the patient and people around him, including the therapist. So defined, the concept of rational limits parallels closely Fromm's (1947) concept of rational authority. Of course, the temptation to play God can easily be rationalized by insisting that the limits set are "for the good" of the patient—but this is unfortunately how all despots (benevolent or malevolent, political, familial, or therapeutic) can rationalize their tyranny (see Chapter 6). It must also be remembered that the psychotherapeutic situation lends itself particularly to the disguised acting-out of irrational dominance needs and therefore the therapist inevitably has two patients to deal with, two people whose motivations he must scrutinize and understand—the patient and himself.

Another imposition of limits that has been written about extensively concerns the patient-therapist relation outside the therapeutic setting. Since the day Freud (1913) recommended that the patient lie on a couch while the analyst sits "behind him out of his sight" (p. 133) so that the patient's communications remain uninfluenced by the therapist's behavior, it has been proposed that they have no contact with each other except their regularly scheduled meetings. Therapists have been urged to avoid any situation which might bring about meeting the patient in a social setting or similar circumstances. The main reason offered in support of this limitation is the belief that the less the patient knows about the therapist the more likely it is that his reactions toward the therapist will be transferences, fantasies, and attitudes which are really feelings basically harbored for some significant person in the patient's past, now displaced upon the therapist. The argument concludes that the less a patient knows about the therapist the *purer* will be his transference reactions. Therapists are consequently counseled to reveal as little as possible about themselves to their patients. While this limitation has a certain degree of validity—to be dealt with extensively in Chapter 11—it also has its drawbacks. Prominent among them is the loss of opportunity for examining the patient's reactions to the therapist in other than office settings. Seeing the therapist in another setting often sets off a flood of associations, thoughts, and transference reactions leading to useful awareness and insights lost or delayed in the absence of such outside contacts. This episode will serve as an illustration:

☐ A female patient participated in a celebration which was also attended by the therapist. In the course of the event drinks were served and the therapist had several cocktails. The patient observed this, became acutely uncomfortable when she noticed it, and reported her discomfort and annoyance about the therapist's "unreasonable consumption of alcohol" in her next therapy hour. While consciously she had been rather critical of her grossly puritanical and oppressively self-righteous mother, who had on innumerable occasions spoken to the daughter derogatorily about the father's drinking habits; and while she had always felt that she had sided emotionally and intellectually with the father, in the course of investigating her discomfort it became apparent to her and the therapist that secretly she was quite identified with the mother and harbored basically equally haughty and contemptuous attitudes toward men in general and the father in particular. These attitudes had emerged pointedly in her discomfort when she observed the therapist in this social situation. ☐

It is likely that her genuine feelings would have come to the fore sooner or later under different circumstances, but the observations made by the patient were useful insofar as they facilitated awareness of dissociated attitudes.

Observing the patient in an extratherapeutic setting can also help the therapist achieve deepened understanding of the patient's character structure:

☐ A therapist working with a young professional woman had experienced what seemed to him irrational annoyance with her on several occasions when she had expressed feelings of depression and a sense of extreme loneliness in all her social activities. He had puzzled about this and discussed the matter with her but no meaningful understanding had developed. One day he happened to see her at a professional meeting and observed her seemingly genuine animation while she conversed with other participants of the conference. When the patient eventually noticed the therapist a few yards away her expression changed immediately; she became gloomy, stopped her conversation abruptly, and assumed an air quite in line with what she had often described in her sessions. The therapist suddenly noticed his sense of annoyance once again while observing the rapid change in the patient's mood. ☐

It became transparently clear that a good deal of her "depression" and gloominess were reflections of certain transference tendencies, and the understanding of her desire to present herself to the therapist as lonely and depressed was materially furthered by this chance meeting.

▶ *Summary* ◀

1. Limits are designed to facilitate the patient–therapist relationship and to protect the patient's welfare by preventing behavior which entails irreparable and irrevocable harm.

2. In order to be growth-furthering, limits must be rational —free of arbitrariness and imposed only to make their imposition in the future unnecessary. Some limits, however, interfere with the unfolding of relevant and meaningful material. Rigidly limiting contacts between therapist and patient to the therapeutic sessions will enhance the development of some relevant transference material, but it can simultaneously prevent the airing of other revealing transference attitudes.

3. The setting of limits has important emotional consequences for the patient. It prevents the development of unnecessary feelings of guilt; it reduces the patient's uneasiness that the therapist might be taxed beyond endurance; and it enhances the patient's sense of reality, helps him toward self-definition and awareness by bringing him face to face with the reality and definition of another person. Rational limits, insofar as they reflect integrity, suggest to others that the development of self-respect is a real possibility in human existence.

Memory, Recall, and
Free Association

THOSE PSYCHOLOGICAL THEORY-BUILDERS AND THEIR CLINICAL
followers who believe that awareness is the hallmark of well-
being insist that the therapeutic enterprise be concerned with
the reduction of inner forces which interfere with the emergence and maintenance of this vital attribute. This, they say,
requires foremost the dissolution of motivations which make
lack of awareness tempting. They hope that this dissolution
will help the patient acquire those new qualities they consider
in harmony with and prerequisites of self-fulfillment (see
Chapter 3). Therefore theorists whose systems are rooted in
"dynamic psychology" maintain that the basic procedure of the
therapeutic transaction is the undoing of repressive processes,
dissociative tendencies, and self-alienating forces.

Classical psychoanalytic theory pointedly developed this line
of thinking. Fenichel, for instance, exemplified this approach:

> In psychoneuroses some impulses have been blocked; the
> consequence is a state of tension and eventually some
> "emergency discharges." These consist partly in unspe-
> cific restlessness and its elaborations and partly in much
> more specific phenomena which represent the distorted
> involuntary discharges of those very instinctual drives for

which a normal discharge has been interdicted. Thus we
have in psychoneuroses, first a defense of the ego against
an instinct, then a conflict between the instinct striving
for discharge and the defensive forces of the ego, then a
state of damming up—a compromise between the opposing forces. The symptom is the only step in this development that becomes manifest; the conflict, its history, and
the significance of the symptoms are unconscious [1945,
p. 20].

If this "damming up" process is the crux of a person's problems
leading eventually to difficulties in deriving pleasure from
work and love, the curative road is clearly mapped: what is
called for is the resolution of the "damming up," the lifting of
the repressive defenses of the ego and the substitution of more
adequate mechanisms for dealing with instinctual impulse.
Fenichel's thinking is quite consistent when he later maintains:

But now at least we know what necessitates this long
duration [of psychoanalytic therapy]: the education of
the ego to tolerate less and less distorted derivatives, until
the pathogenic defense is undone [p. 572].

Since in Fenichel's system all defenses except sublimation are
"pathogenic," the ultimate therapeutic aim is the substitution
of sublimatory defense for any of the others. But such a substitution process can take place only when the originally repressed impulse is no longer repugnant to the patient. The
impulse itself need not necessarily become acceptable as a
basis for action but must become acceptable as part of oneself.
Therefore the recovery of memories of past impulses which
were repressed assumed crucial therapeutic importance. Even
though he refined his system and thinking considerably, this
remained Freud's (1937) position to the very end and Munroe
was quite correct when she commented:

In so far as the pathological symptoms are conceived as
the direct consequence of the exclusion from consciousness of infantile wishes and fears *which remain active as
such*, their emergence during the analysis becomes the
sine qua non of deep analytic therapy [1955, p. 315].

Implicit in this position is the belief that the recovery of child-hood memories, the lifting of the infantile amnesia has curative effects. This recovery of memories seems, however, the outcome rather than merely the path of cure. This paradoxical situation has been touched upon already (Chapter 6) and will be dealt with in detail in Chapter 13, but it should be noted here that Freud (1914a) recognized this somewhat dimly in a brief paragraph and Alexander (1946a) has meaningfully elaborated upon it. In any case, the patient's recall and reporting of childhood events assumed a central position in psychoanalytic treatment precisely because the psychoanalytic theory of pathology maintains that neurosis is the result of repressed experience and lost memories.

The paradigm Jung outlined is both similar to and also quite different from Freud's conceptions. Jung too proposed that neurosis is a reflection of repression, the result of the individual's attempts to deny something operating within him. The essential similarity with Freudian thinking lies in Jung's insistence that the neurotic evades awareness, that he reduces consciousness by self-fragmentation, and that this process does gross injustice to his potentialities. The following quotation is typical of Jung's approach:

> Only a unified personality can experience life, not that personality which is split up into partial aspects, that bundle of odds and ends which also calls itself "man" [1953, p. 105].

To Jung (1956b) neurosis was a miscarriage of the individual's attempts to survive as a person. In this respect his theory did not differ grossly from Freudian thinking or, for that matter, Adler's ideas. For Freud, neurosis was the individual's vision of what will bring salvation: repression. For Jung, neurosis also reflected the neurotic's ideas as to what would bring salvation; Jung too thought that the neurotic saw salvation in repression. But Jung was convinced that the neurotic did *not* repress infantile incestuous cravings but totally different aspects of himself, aspects Jung considered basic to any individual—just as Freud thought incestuous strivings were integral parts of every human being. Therefore Jung also envisioned as crucial the recall of that which interfered with the integration of all aspects of the organism. Such recall, he hoped, would make for the development of a unique individuality in which all aspects could live harmoniously, completeness could be established, no function of mental life or type of relatedness remaining in oblivion. Jung was quite unequivocal:

> But it would be quite incorrect simply to emphasize the pathological aspects of the unconscious. Usually the unconscious is pathological or dangerous only because we live in disharmony with it and in doing so live contrary to our instincts.
>
> If we succeed in bringing about a functioning which I refer to as transcendental, then this lack of unity is resolved and then we may enjoy the helpful aspects of the unconscious. For then the unconscious gives us the support and help which a benevolent nature has provided for man in most ample supply. For the unconscious has potentialities of which the conscious is totally devoid; it has at its disposal all subliminal psychic contents, has at its disposal all that has been forgotten and has been overlooked and in addition the wisdom and the experience of uncounted millenniums, a wisdom and experience laid down in the pathways and pathway potentials of the human brain [1929, p. 162; translation E.S.].

Jung's aim was the liberation of the unconscious and the removal of forces which interfered with this liberation—the removal of repression. Events in the life of the patient were understood as agents, interfering with the benefits which the wisdom of the unconscious has to offer. Jung (1933) thought that these events could be personal mishaps, but more pointedly he believed that such unfortunate experiences were culturally determined, for Western civilization as he saw it was vehemently opposed to man's availing himself of his potential inner wisdom.

Rogers (1942, 1951) also thought something is to be uncovered in psychotherapy. His emphasis upon the patient's free expression and the eventual clarification of his feelings are potent reminders of Rogers' view that neurosis is the reflection of feelings, motivations, and attitudes existing outside the client's awareness. He thought, as most other theorists do, that insight develops when aspects outside one's awareness come into focus of consciousness. Rogers did not insist that this required the client's recall of events and situations in his early life, but he did maintain that the repression of affective states is pathogenic. Thus Rogers (1951) suggested that repression is the foundation of emotional disturbances and that patients' difficulties are caused by their repressing affects which for some reason or other are not in harmony with their self-concepts. Rogers obviously did not refer to repression in the usual specific psychoanalytic sense of the term, but he did believe that in neurosis aspects of self are dissociated and that the aim of therapy is their acceptance by the patient and their reintegration into his personality.

While in Rogers' system the reporting of events and experiences does not serve to help the patient gain an understanding of his past and its influence upon his present state—an important feature of the Freudian framework—this reporting does serve the function of helping the patient gain awareness of who and what he is, even if the whys remain unexplored.

Sullivan (1947, 1962) saw pathological disturbances—or, to be more precise, disturbances in living—reflected in a variety of security operations; he considered dissociation and selective inattention as the most common among them. He thought that these devices were learned methods in the service of avoidance or at least the diminution of anxiety. But he also thought that they were specious and potentially disruptive solutions and therefore his therapeutic inquiry was designed to study carefully their historical origins and present-day settings through the participant observation of doctor and patient. He believed that these security operations had serious consequences, reducing effective living even when they were "successful" because they prevented the individual from learning anything of value about himself and others. Thus, Sullivan thought that, ultimately, processes which foster exclusion of awareness are not only at some point conducive to a schizophrenic way of life but also that in their less ominous forms they preclude expansion of self. It was therefore Sullivan's (1947) fundamental therapeutic aim to help the patient dispense with his dissociations and to help him reintegrate dissociated dynamisms so that the patient would become known to himself. To accomplish this, Sullivan thought, the recall of past events by the patient was crucial:

> Each recurrent recognition of a particular parataxic distortion of the physician brings with it more data as to the historic, personal source. The time comes when the patient recalls vividly a series of highly significant events that occurred in interpersonal relations with this person. This recall gradually expands into a more or less comprehensive insight; first, into the 'effects' of this earlier relationship on the subsequent course of the patient's dealings with others, on the formulation of ideals of conduct and relatively fixed valuational judgements of behavior [pp. 116–17].

These admittedly fragmentary sketches should demonstrate more precisely what was said in Chapter 1: that despite divergent theoretical views concerning the nature of repressed material, most schools agree that obliviousness to self is a striking index of pathology. Therefore they also agree on the need to help the patient lift his repressions, and uncover and recover his repressed experiences so that curative insight can develop. These schools of thought insist that the process of talking about himself, his experiences, and the events in his life will further the patient's efforts in this direction.

The intricate system Freud (1915b) developed to explain why memories are buried need not be reviewed here, save his insistence that memories are repressed because of their noxious affective qualities, his belief that these "forgotten" events were "traumatic." But by "traumatic" Freud did not mean what is so often erroneously ascribed to him. In popular usage a traumatic event is an incident in which the person experienced himself as assaulted or severely threatened by some outside agent—a parent, an authority, a dangerous stranger. This is *not* what Freud meant. He thought that the infantile trauma is the result of a clash between some wish, thought, or fantasy arising in the individual, between the clamoring of some primitive impulse to make itself heard and the individual's fear of the consequences were he to act on his impulse (Freud, 1938). It was postulated that the child's anxiety about his own impulses is brought about by his fear of severe punishment at the hands of others who would not tolerate his impulse life. Eventually, at least in Freud's thinking, the dangerous impulse which had to be repressed became identified as the Oedipal impulse; the child was said to fear castration as the punishment for his incestuous wishes.

Other authors have rejected this particular formulation, rejected Freud's theory of anxiety, and advanced their own conceptions concerning events in the child's life which are anxiety-producing and hence repressed by him (May, 1950). But they are all in agreement that the noxious quality of certain events causes the individual to repress and that in this repressive process he loses part of himself. Consequently, they say, the therapeutic process requires the recovery and reintegration of these lost fragments.

From the beginnings of systematic psychotherapy one finds marked emphasis upon the recall and recovery of repressed or dissociated elements in the patient's life. Freud originally thought that the hypnotic method offered an excellent vehicle for the unearthing of buried material. With his early collaborator Breuer he developed this technique and was able to demonstrate that the hypnotic recall of "forgotten" material was often followed by a startling and dramatic decrease of troublesome symptoms. But Freud (1922a) soon became dissatisfied with hypnotic procedures. The discharge of pent-up affect was important, but he also saw clearly the limitations of hypnotic procedures. Aside from his recognition that he was not a very good hypnotist, other considerations entered, which Freud summarized:

> It soon appeared that the therapeutic hopes which had been placed upon cathartic treatment in hypnosis were to some extent unfulfilled. It was true that the disappearance of the symptoms went hand-in-hand with the catharsis, but total success turned out to be entirely de-

pendent upon the patient's relation to the physician and thus resembled the effect of "suggestion." If that relation was disturbed, all the symptoms reappeared, just as though they had never been cleared up. In addition to this, the small number of people who could be put into a deep state of hypnosis involved a very considerable limitation, from the medical standpoint, of the applicability of the cathartic procedure. For these reasons the present writer decided to give up the use of hypnosis [1922a, p. 237].

Now the emphasis shifted to the basic procedure of psychoanalysis: the demand on the patient that he recall and report recent and past events.

This recalling and reporting can take various forms. Aside from the unfortunate possibility that a person can report trivia and in chatty fashion can busy himself with material that is inconsequential, the report then becoming smalltalk, consequential and substantial data can be recalled in at least two ways. They may be reported as a trained journalist describes the facts of an event he covers for his paper: when it occurred, where it took place, who was involved, how it ended. The patient may even report how he felt at the time of the event, relate that he was very frightened, that he was overcome with joy, that he was very excited, and so on. In this type of reporting the person remembers and discusses just what took place. The affect associated with events is often mentioned, intellectually recalled, but not re-experienced. This type of reporting has a stale quality and, although it can be helpful to learn exactly what took place in an individual's life, events recalled in this manner are experienced by the listener as if they had come through a filtering screen—they lack the enlivening and crucial dimension of re-experienced affect. It is as if the speaker were detached from what he remembers and from the feelings he experienced when the event took place. Under such circumstances recall is at best partial.

Free association, the procedure Freud instituted in place of hypnosis, often has this unfortunate quality of detached recall. Freud's instructions to the patient how to go about associating and the difficulties in following them have already been mentioned (Chapter 7). What complicates matters even more is the possibility that the patient may truly recall and verbalize what comes to his mind without affectively re-experiencing the emotional impact of what he recalls, even though he may be able to tell correctly what he had felt at that time.

The causes of this type of sterile recounting and reporting are not difficult to find. Western civilization has placed a premium upon the intellectualized, not necessarily the intellectual, management of human affairs, has placed a premium upon objectivity often synonymous with detachment. Great achievements, it has been claimed, result from the individual's capacity to assume a detached stance and are the reflection of lack of passionate involvement. Somehow youngsters learn from earliest days of formal or informal training that passions and emotions presumably interfere with their capacity for achievement, that detachment will bring success and that this detachment is to take place vis-à-vis others, life's events, and themselves. Somehow the young are taught the value of standing outside and looking in, whether outside the other person, outside an event, or outside oneself. The emphasis of rationalism has always been upon analytic moving around an object, even if this object is the self, rather than upon the intuitive and empathic entering of the object. This culturally approved rationalistic orientation interferes drastically with a capacity for genuine free association and, even though some voices have been raised against the exclusivistic claims of rationalism in man's attempt to understand himself (Ben-Avi, 1959; Boss, 1963; Fromm, Suzuki, & de Martino, 1960; Fromm-Reichmann, 1950; Jung, 1933; May, 1953; May, Angel & Ellenberger, 1958; Tauber & Green, 1959), it remains a most powerful influence in the psychological development of human beings. And Bergson opened his *Introduction to Metaphysics:*

> There are two profoundly different ways of knowing a thing. The first one implies that we move around the object; the second that we enter into it [1912, p. 1].

The second road suggested by Bergson was the road of intuition and introspection, a road leading to a profound knowledge of self, of capturing the uniqueness of one's own or another's experience. Thirty years later Jung, critical of Western rationalism, exclaimed scathingly:

> Whether from the intellectual, the moral or the aesthetic viewpoint, the undercurrents of the psychic life of the West present an uninviting picture. We have built a monumental world round about us, and have slaved for it with unequalled energy. But it is so imposing only because we have spent upon the outside all that is imposing in our natures—and what we find when we look within must necessarily be as it is, shabby and insufficient [1933, p. 247].

This emphasis upon objectivity, upon the spectacular achievements of an objective scientific method, and upon analytic understanding is a fundamental cultural barrier that interferes with free association because this type of objectivity denies the value of nonschematized inner experience, belittles man's paying attention to its nature and committing it to memory. There are other and more personal forces which reduce emotional experience, the activity implicit in experience, and its recall in free association; they will be dealt with later. What needs stating here is that genuine free association inevitably requires that the patient overcome these inner and outer restrictions and interfering forces lest free association deteriorate into expensive talk.

Why all this emphasis upon affective recall, upon the re-experiencing of events—what value does it have, what purpose does it serve? Broadly speaking, there are two fundamental reasons why the re-experiencing of affective states associated with past events is deemed of utmost importance. First, it can be demonstrated both clinically and through ingenious experimentation that the persistence of certain affective states sets off physiological processes leading to deleterious bodily changes. Ever since Dunbar (1954) summarized data then available on this issue, more and more refined investigations have supported the general hypothesis that specific emotions can and do produce bodily changes—directly, indirectly, and in simple and complex ways. The basic formulation suggests that banishing affects from awareness does not do away with them. This banishment of affect, reflected in intellectualized recall, merely prolongs the effective presence of certain emotional states and their harmful consequences. Further, it has been suggested that affective recall results in what has been termed "abreaction" (Breuer & Freud, 1957, pp. 8–11) and that recall culminating in "abreaction" causes a discharge of emotional energy with subsequent removal of those tension states which, although operating only outside the awareness of the individual, cause structural change. The idea has also been advanced that the persistence of unconscious and disavowed emotional reactions results in generalized tension, a state in which the individual is constantly on guard against the awareness of his repressed affective tendencies. This generalized state of tension and the alert defensiveness it implies has deleterious physical consequences.

Second, the inability to recall and thereby to become fully aware of previous emotional reactions entails serious psychological consequences: the extent of this inability defines the degree of feelings of incompleteness and lack of rootedness a person experiences. This loss of roots in the emotional past, not synonymous with nostalgia, carries with it a tragic byproduct. Individuals who find it difficult or impossible to recapture experience of times gone by have the same difficulty with being aware of experiences in the present (Edwards, 1962) and, instead of finding a center and a sense of self in their own feelings, they concentrate on outside events. Such people act as if they were eager to find guidelines externally imposed and willingly adopted in the hope that these will obviate the necessity to pay attention to their genuine attitudes. It appears that he who cannot recall his past emotional life is not only alienated from his background but equally estranged from the present and his contemporary sense of self. In addition, the estrangement from past and present personal experience does not result in the sharper awareness of outside events. When estrangement from autocentric experience occurs, the attention to external circumstances is shallow and remote, defensive rather than inquiringly interested, sterile rather than conducive to the development of new and profound allocentric experience. This phenomenon is not difficult to explain. To the degree to which an individual must constantly guard against the development of potentially threatening inner states, to that extent is he forced to exclude perception of outer stimuli in order to prevent them from triggering recognition of his inner tendencies. A host of studies by investigators (Eagle, 1962) concerned with the problem of "subliminal perception" lend themselves to this interpretation.

These are the consequences of a person's inability to recall emotional reactions; psychotherapeutic procedures designed to help him recall past experiences are vehicles which aid him in recapturing and resurrecting from oblivion important aspects of himself. Such resurrection results in his regaining a sense of identity, aids him in the development of self-awareness and self-definition. No matter how painful the affects brought back, their recall enhances the person's feelings of completeness—an experiencing autonomous entity with outlines and individuality. The suggestion, admittedly teleological in nature, is close at hand that the inability to recall emotional states is the reflection of the individual's desire to avoid such identity, the urge to evade experiencing himself as an autonomous unit, a determined attempt to reduce self-awareness and self-definition. This avoidance is in the service of salvaging life itself, as if the patient had learned that the development of identity and definition would be grossly disapproved and hence so anxiety-producing as to make life unbearable. The following clinical material illustrates this point:

☐ A man in his middle twenties, well educated and highly successful in his chosen profession but seriously troubled by both somatic disturbances and interpersonal difficulties making for extreme loneliness and frustration, found it almost impossible to recall any feeling reactions and emotional experiences of his youth. Sophisticated and well-read person that he was, he found this inability quite disturbing and at least intellectually realized that this barrier to memory of times gone by represented a serious roadblock to his progress and to finding ways for satisfactions in living. All he could do was infer that his inner sense in childhood had been so terrifying that he had divorced himself from all knowledge, shut himself off from awareness of his emotions in his youth.

He had been talking about this for quite a while and the therapist's attempts to help him come closer to grasping what he had felt as a youngster were relatively fruitless. Further attempts to interpret his resistance and transference reactions proved equally unsuccessful.

During this therapeutic impasse his brother, several years his junior, developed a psychotic episode, the third within a two-year span. The young man, who clearly showed symptoms of an insidious paranoid schizophrenic process, had been hospitalized on both previous occasions and was now to undergo his third series of electro-shock therapy. His older brother had experienced a good deal of guilt because he had not intervened before, had never asked his parents to call in a consultant, and had never suggested intensive psychotherapy for his brother. This time he decided at least to visit the treating psychiatrist with his parents and inquire about this possibility.

During the consultation the physician informed the three that he was of the opinion that psychosis could not be dealt with psychotherapeutically, that one could not expect the young man to recover, that the family would have to resign itself to the fact that he was incurably sick and that shock treatment would at least produce more or less lengthy periods of lucidity and effectiveness.

Parents and brother were horrified by this news and upon the latter's insistence they consulted a psychiatrist who had become prominent for his psychoanalytic work with schizophrenic individuals. After a consultation with the young man he expressed his belief that the patient was analytically reachable and recommended initiation of analytic therapy. He indicated that he thought it would be a long and slow process but that within a year or so the patient might be at the point of starting work, living on his own, and generally getting on his own feet, even though he most likely would have to remain in analysis for a considerable time beyond this.

At this point the patient noticed a sudden change in the mother's reactions. Serious upset over the son's condition gave way rapidly to direct and immediate hostility toward the psychiatrist, and later all she could remember were the analyst's comments about her son's trying life on his own within a year. The mother now started to agree with the position of the other psychiatrist that they were really dealing with an incurable process and commented that as sad as it was they would have to make the best of their cross in life.

The brother was horror-stricken. In a flash he experienced for the first time what he had somehow known intellectually all along: that his mother was a grossly possessive individual, a person who at least unconsciously deeply resented any attempt at independence by her children, a woman who enjoyed playing the matriarch who controlled a rather weak and ineffectual husband, one pathetically dependent son, and another moody, depressed, lonely, and unhappy older son. (Characteristically, the boy's overt psychosis had occurred first toward the end of his junior year in college, the third episode in the second term of his senior year while he was planning a trip to Europe with some of his friends following graduation. Needless to say that graduation and travel had to be postponed indefinitely.)

For the first time the patient experienced a childlike rage of impotence and for the first time his insights were not just intellectual but were based on a flood of affectively charged memories. He finally knew how furious he was, did not just infer this or think it, and suddenly he also realized how terrified he had been of knowing in depth his mother's dominating fury. Events he had reported at one time with sarcastic and humorous resignation, events which were to illustrate the "nuttiness" of the family, were now recalled with tears and with rage. Painful as it was, an aspect of inner life was liberated from oblivion. Following this episode the patient's productions started to resemble free association instead of intellectualized talk. □

What gave him the courage finally to break through the self-imposed security barrier of "forgetting" his feelings? The indications are that there were two relatively simple and at the same time profound reasons for this change. First there was the therapist's patience. He had sat with him for years without being discouraged, and when he was dismayed by the patient's preoccupation with trivia and his emotional detachment he had never made a secret of it. The patient had also learned, though in painfully slow fashion, that his acceptability did not depend exclusively on just how much he pleased the therapist's vanity or supported his self-esteem by dealing in healthier ways with his past, present, and future.

Second, what seemed to have convinced him more than anything else that it was possible to live with knowledge was the therapist's obvious interest in the fate of the brother and his recommending the consultant who had held out some hope for the brother—all this despite his and the patient's knowledge that the patient harbored marked ambivalence toward his brother.

These observations lead to a simple conclusion. If contemporary security operations are methods a person has learned in order to reduce his anxiety and to prevent anxiety-arousing emotional recall, only enormous trust can move him to abandon those methods which have previously proved themselves life-sustaining. A patient will expose himself through free association and the accompanying recall of emotions, and will discard his basic self-protective security operations only if and when he is deeply convinced that revealing himself will not result in scorn, disapproval, and subsequent additional anxiety. Free association, recall, and self-revelation are then contingent upon complete trust, specifically the sense that self-esteem will not be shattered by disapproval and rejection. It is as if the courage to face himself depends on the patient's conviction that the therapist can bear the patient's revelations without anxiety and defenses of his own.

Such a formulation has important consequences for the theory of the therapeutic process. Its logical consequence is the recognition that free association, recall, and self-revealing are not merely the vehicles by which therapy progresses but, much more, their occurrence indicates that important changes have already taken place. Patients who by definition are eager to avoid anxiety and therefore develop operations designed to keep themselves distant, detached, and removed from others and themselves are individuals who cannot trust themselves or other human beings, cannot trust that they themselves or anybody else will deal with them without violating their dignity; they are therefore both consciously and unconsciously reticent about revealing their inner reactions and remain detached from experience. Their fundamental distrustfulness makes it necessary for them to remain constantly on guard, and repression of affect and remoteness from experience is basically a manifestation of such guardedness.

Genuine free association, affective recall, and the ability to reveal oneself indicate that the basic premise of "be on guard" in relation to others and in relation to oneself has been loosened, has less potency as a maxim in living. This represents a momentous advance in the individual's life. The capacity to remember, to recall what really was and to be familiar with one's emotional past and present requires the capacity to discard particular premises in living and the specific security-bringing schemata for experience produced by them. The patient who has learned to examine all events in the light of his fundamental distrust can recall only if and when he has learned to abandon the very premise upon which his life is built. The topic of insight will be treated in its own right in Chapter 13, but it may be pointed out here that in any act of learning, of insight, of change—change being implied in insight and learning—there is to be found a process of unlearning, abandoning, forgetting. This recognition is expressed by Shaw (1962) when in *Major Barbara* Barbara's father remarks to her: "You have learnt something. That always feels at first as if you had lost something" (p. 128).

A clinical example will further illustrate this general point:

□ A woman in her late thirties, troubled by work problems and marital frictions, brought about by her constant denigrating and derogating behavior toward her husband, had come to recognize that her contemptuous reactions to him were not "reality based," although this recognition was more intellectualized than genuinely experienced. She had ruminated about the origin of this orientation and had speculated about the possibility that she identified unconsciously with her highly efficient and competent yet equally cold mother. She was a woman who had hardly made a secret of her own disdain for womanhood and the "ineffectualness" of men. The patient toyed with this idea, saw it as an interesting intellectual construct but seemed unable really to capture her feelings of contempt for men in general or her husband in particular. They always seemed to her realistically deserving of derision because she felt she could always demonstrate their incompetence all too easily.

Aimlessly ruminating one day about the pleasure she derived from gardening, she suddenly recalled the following episode. She remembered how, one day when she was about five, she had been running exuberantly down a hill on a farm and how her father, who had been standing at the foot of the hill, had playfully tried to catch her in his arms as she came careening down the hill. She recalled that she had noticed him standing there trying to catch her, had swiftly sidestepped him, and had triumphantly come to a halt a few feet away from him with a sense of "I don't need your help, I can do it myself." But she had also noticed a peculiar expression on his face, an expression she had never forgotton or understood. Recalling the incident, the patient burst into tears. She experienced her feelings of contempt for her father and sensed how she had hurt him in her haughty self-assertion. ☐

Once again it must be emphasized that the full recall of such feelings is extremely difficult and that it would be folly to expect it from patients during the early phases of their self-investigation. This type of recall occurs at moments that seem sudden and dramatic, but they are really climactic instances in the slow development of trust and the painful unlearning of defensive self-detachment.

Schachtel, perhaps more searchingly than anybody else, has addressed himself to the investigation of memory and the difficulties human beings experience when they try to recall in depth *les temps perdus*. He too suggests that the abandoning of memory has certain adaptive functions, that modern adult life cannot proceed without some loss of man's capacity for profound emotional experience:

> . . . the biologically, culturally, and socially influenced process of memory organization results in the formation of memory categories [schemata] which are not suitable vehicles to receive and reproduce experiences of the quality and intensity of early childhood [1959, p. 284].

Why are adult memory categories so unsuitable "to receive and reproduce" intense experience? Schachtel indicates some of the reasons for the development of adult memory schemata:

> The world of modern Western civilization has no use for this type of experience; in fact it cannot permit itself to have any use for it; it cannot permit the memory of it, because such memory, if universal, would explode the restrictive social order of this civilization [pp. 284–85].

As Schachtel sees it, the recall of man's capacity for experience and the sharp recall of deep experience would entail feelings of being lost in a world and a civilization which do not allow for such a rich sense of being. Education for the reduction of consciousness starts very early in life and is furthered by a variety of social institutions and conventions. A man who regains the capacity for deep experience loses his moorings in a world which frowns upon all intense affects and denies the individual the right to some experiences altogether. Freud (1905b) himself was a victim of this hypocritical denial when he was viciously attacked for showing how the erotic impulses and experiences exist in human beings from the very beginning and for demonstrating that the repression of sexual impulses is dangerous to man's well-being. Little has changed since Freud raised the mirror to a hypocritical world if one is to believe Sullivan's (1947, 1953) characterization of present-day American civilization as the "most sex-ridden" of which he had any knowledge. Sullivan too was convinced that contemporary mores deny human beings the right to be aware of lustful impulses.

No matter in what theoretical frame an author writes, he

inevitably refers to the difficulties human beings encounter in their attempts to remember in depth, to re-experience fully what was, and the subsequent difficulties when they try to become aware of what they experience in the present. Different theorists hold different sets of factors responsible for this type of amnesia. But no matter who they are and how much they may feud with each other or how much they may change the theoretical wrinkles they themselves introduce in the course of their careers, they all refer to *strife* and *conflict* as the responsible forces. They insist that instinctual conflicts or social conflicts or existential conflicts or any combination of them are responsible for difficulties in living and for difficulties in getting well, for the loss of penetrating and affective memory, and for difficulties in free association which is to bring about a reawakening of memory, recall, and conscious experience. They may quarrel with each other about the models they propose to account for the development of strife-induced amnesia and particular schematizations in place of memory and experience. Some of them may propose that certain types of schematizations are valuable, as Freud (1914b, 1933) did when he insisted that schematization through sublimation leads to man's highest cultural achievements; others, like Sullivan (1933), may insist that all substitutive schemata designed to reduce anxiety have some restrictive consequences for the ultimate growth of the individual.

Different authors categorize the schemata human beings develop along different lines of classification and each suggests that his system of classification is more valid and useful than another's outline. Obviously, processes usually referred to as defenses, or methods in dissociation, or types of alienation, and so on, are *de facto* modes of schematizing perceptions and experiences to keep affective states of the past and present hidden and to perpetuate emotional amnesia and lack of consciousness. What are usually referred to as syndromes are but overt manifestations and outcomes of particular schematization processes (see Chapters 1 and 3). Hysteria is one way of keeping buried what the person is eager to keep forgotten through the use of certain schematizations; obsessions and compulsions are other ways of repressing past and present experiences; schizophrenia is still another way of schematizing to prevent remembrances of things past from coming to the surface.

Theorists often differ in delineating reasons for the patient's avoidance of past emotions, but they do maintain a common insistence that the recapturing of the capacity for emotional experience is central to the psychotherapeutic endeavor; many suggest that the recall of past emotional reactions is essential for psychotherapeutic reeducation to emotional life. They are also in essential agreement that strife and conflict are responsible for the amnesiac loss of affective experience and the maintenance of emotional alienation through different types of schemata. They differ about the types of conflicts responsible for this amnesia and continued repression, but they agree that strife and conflict (no matter how defined) are responsible for these developments. The psychotherapeutic community is indebted to Schachtel for a concise and beautiful summary of this issue:

> Hesiod tells us that Lethe (Forgetting) is the daughter of Eris (Strife). Amnesia, normal and pathological, is indeed the daughter of conflict between nature and society and the conflict in society, the conflict between society and man and the conflict within man. Lethe is the stream of the underworld, of forgetting, the stream which constantly flows and never retains. In the realm of Lethe dwell the Danaides, who are condemned eternally to pour water into a leaking vessel. Plato interprets this as the punishment of those unwise souls who leak, who cannot remember and are therefore always empty. But Mnemosyne is an older and more powerful goddess than Lethe. According to Hesiod she was one of the six Titanesses from whom all gods stem. And it was one of the world-founding deeds of Zeus that he begot the muses on her. Memory cannot be entirely extinguished in man, his capacity for experience cannot be entirely suppressed by schematization. It is in those experiences which transcend the cultural schemata, in those memories of experience which transcend the conventional memory schemata, that every new insight and every true work of art have their

origin, and that the hope of progress, of a widening of the scope of human endeavor and human life, is founded [1959, pp. 321–22].

Active recall of emotional experience is not simply a vehicle for psychotherapy, but like any other activity a goal of therapy itself. In encouraging their patients to recall events of the past fully and to revive the past with a sense of immediacy while reconstructing it (Wyatt, 1963), therapists encourage their patients to practice a type of living which does not truncate experience through the use of schematic devices. Through this emphasis they encourage their patients toward an awareness of the past and the present, they encourage the development of courageous self-consciousness, and they discourage the security of self-oblivion.

▶ *Summary* ◀

1. Despite theoretical differences concerning the causes of repression, of dissociation, and of alienation, most authors agree that the central aim of psychotherapy is the reduction of these processes so that the patient can achieve consciousness and self-awareness.

2. Emphasis has shifted from efforts to help patients simply recall events through hypnosis or free association to aiding them in reviving repressed or dissociated affective states and reactions. Therefore the aim of recall in psychotherapy has become the reliving of buried or disregarded experience rather than the mere reporting of events.

3. Psychotherapists stress the importance of affective re-experiencing for several reasons. Dissociated and repressed affective components bring in their wake tensions which can produce deteriorative bodily changes. Second, efforts to prevent awareness of emotional reactions result in a generalized defensive guardedness, producing ever-increasing gradients of dissociation and repression. Finally, through recall and growing awareness of past affective states, the individual recaptures

an essential part of himself. This recapturing leads to the development of a growing sense of identity and definition.

4. Difficulties in reviving past experience in genuine recall and free association are linked with:

   a. Cultural demands which minimize the value of subjective experience, emotional reactivity, and awareness thereof, and which maximize the importance of objective detachment, reserved indifference, and uninvolved chronicling;

   b. The individual's successful reduction of anxiety through dissociation and repression of affective experiences in his past.

5. To engage in free association is so difficult because this process requires enormous trust and at least a partial willingness to abandon the familiar and security-producing schematizations in memory organization and ultimately in living. Therefore a patient's ability to engage in genuine free association not only furthers his therapy but is also an indication that a good deal of personal change has taken place within him.

The Concept of Interpretation

IF THE RECALL OF AFFECTIVELY CHARGED MATERIAL AND THE development of awareness are such difficult but essential tasks in the process of achieving emotional well-being, what are the inner and outer agencies that help the patient overcome obstacles in recalling and gaining awareness, and by what means do these agents accomplish their difficult mission?

The inner agency opposing self-oblivion and lack of consciousness is part of the patient himself. In Chapter 2 were offered data which suggested that the organism inherently strives toward self-fulfilling behavior and is in constant search for relatedness and interaction with the world around him, even though life events can stunt this basic tendency. Neurosis and psychosis were therefore defined as roundabout, self-defeating, inappropriate, ineffectual expressions of a self-actualizing impulse—an impulse toward survival which, no matter how miscarried, is always at least minimally present and observable. When Freud (1922a) suggested that the successful application of psychoanalytic treatment required intelligence of and "a certain amount of psychical plasticity from its patients" (p. 250), he seemed to be emphasizing the crucial dependence of psychoanalytic success upon life-furthering tendencies in the patient. And when Freud (1904b, 1919) speculated about applying psychoanalytic principles to the treatment of ever-widening circles of patients, he seems to have envisioned Eros (in the widest sense of the term) as at least minimally effective in the lives of all human beings. When Jung (1933) described neurosis as a failure of man's search for meaning and when Sullivan (1953) referred to so much that is called neurotic symptomatology as "remarkable manifestations of human dexterity in living" (p. 11), both men suggested at least implicitly the existence of man's tendency to seek survival and to reject psychological death, even if efforts in this direction are all too often unsuccessful.

The basic premise of the present discussion is that this drive toward self-actualization represents the internal force which makes the patient dissatisfied with his neuroticism, moves him to seek help, or at least makes him to some degree available to the help offered by others. The more this inner tendency has been stunted by events in the patient's life, the more circumstances in his background have convinced him that the only way he can survive at all is through total oblivion, dissociation, and withdrawal, the more difficult it will be to aid him toward the pursuit of self-investigation, recall, free association, and ultimate revival of awareness. The inner agent which helps the patient in overcoming roadblocks in the path to consciousness is the patient's own urge toward life and health and the means of this urge is his dissatisfaction with the *status quo* of his existence (also see Chapters 5 and 10).

Where this urge is strong, the tendencies toward self-exploration and growing awareness will be prominent and no therapist will be needed; the person is and will remain his own therapist. But where historical curcumstances have been of such a nature as to reduce the effectiveness of this inner urge to grow, intervention by an external force allied with the remnants of the urge is required. The therapist is this external force prompting the patient toward growing self-knowledge and awareness, and the therapist's behavior vis-à-vis the patient is the instrumentality designed to further the process of personal fulfillment. The therapist's comments and communications, verbal or nonverbal, are designed to bring about this ultimate goal of experience and knowledge, to facilitate within the patient processes which will bring about his self-recognition. The process of *interpretation* is the method Freud (1922a, 1923, 1925a) proposed to help patients toward these ends by offering his insights about them and by simultaneously encouraging them to use these insights in a diligent search for additional self-knowledge.

The concept of "understanding" presents yet another thorny definitional problem. "Understanding" refers to at least two markedly different processes. A man may understand the functioning of an apparatus, under what circumstances it will break down, what makes for the breakdown of such a piece of equipment, and what steps are necessary to put it in working order again. Such reasoning processes may be either adequate or incorrect and reflect the person's fund of information and intellectual acumen. In any case such understanding is usually not complicated by emotional reactions. Whenever one deals with so-called objective events, this type of intellectual understanding can be quite useful and may advance the analysis of an event and the decision on steps to be taken.

The original model of psychoanalytic therapy follows similar lines, the lines of thought customarily employed in scientific undertakings, including medical practice. The therapist's and patient's clear understanding of the sequence of events in the latter's life was to lead to his psychological well-being. Once the patient learned what dangerous and therefore noxious thoughts and wishes he had entertained; how and why they were unacceptable to him; how and why they were repressed; and how they now live on hidden and disguised in his symptoms, repressive and therefore symptom-producing forces would no longer be necessary and the patient could, on the basis of his newly achieved consciousness, go on to live productively and symptom-free. This state of self-understanding was to be advanced through the interpretations—the analyst's explanations concerning the meaning of the patient's thoughts, fantasies, associations, and dreams; what they revealed about his real intentions, past and present, and his true attitudes toward important people in his life.

This remarkably sturdy faith in the powers of reason (more

precisely, the powers of intellectual understanding) is intricately associated with the historical roots of psychology in general and psychotherapy in particular. It has been shown how these roots extend into the Era of Enlightenment; Freud's (1922a) constant emphasis upon his "scientific" work bears testimony to his rootedness in a *Zeitgeist* which saw man's salvation through intellectual achievement (see Chapter 1). This led to the almost paradoxical situation that the study of man's irrationality was to be pursued by highly rational investigation and that this irrationality could be banished by presenting man with rationality in a didactic manner. When Freud presented his famous essay on religion he again showed his belief in rationality:

> The more the fruits of knowledge become accessible to man, the more widespread is the decline of religious belief, at first only of the obsolete and objectionable expressions of the same, then of its fundamental assumptions also [1953, p. 68].

Freud was not alone in this faith. Fromm, despite his criticism of Freud's overevaluation of rationality as an agent of change (Fromm, 1959), at one time also maintained a remarkable degree of confidence in reason as capable of reducing man's need to adhere to irrational ideas:

> Man turned to the gods to satisfy those practical needs which he himself could not properly provide for; those needs for which he did not pray were already within his power to satisfy. The more man understands and masters nature the less he needs to use religion as a scientific explanation and as a magical device for controlling nature [1950, p. 104].

This sounds rather hopeful and on first reading similar to Freud, somehow implying that understanding and reason will conquer all. But mankind has witnessed remarkable manifestations of primitive idolatry by highly educated men who had scientific tools for rational observation at their disposal. There is no doubt that Freud and Fromm recognized this phenomenon, and yet it was apparently difficult for Freud to acknowledge the obvious limits of intellectual grasp as an agent bringing about personal change in behavioral manifestations. Fromm came much closer to acknowledging the limits of rationalistic approaches when he criticized Freud on precisely this point. He could object to Freud's emphasis upon "reason" and yet maintain his own confidence in its powers because he defined reason in terms quite different from those employed by Freud. He remarked that Freud accepted as rational only thought and not emotion, that Freud viewed all feelings as irrational by definition, and Fromm commented that this position led Freud to his gross overvaluation of rationalistic approaches:

> In speaking of Freud's passion for truth and reason, one point must be mentioned here. . . : for him reason was confined to *thought*. Feelings and emotions were per se irrational, and hence inferior to thought. The enlightenment philosophers in general shared in this contempt for feeling and affect. Thought was for them the only vehicle of progress and reason to be found only in thought. They did not see, as Spinoza had seen, that affects, like thought, can be both rational and irrational and that the full development of man requires the rational evolution of *both* thought and affect. They did not see that, if man's thinking is split from his feeling, both his thinking *and* feelings become distorted, and that the picture of man based on the assumption of this split is also distorted.
>
> These rationalistic thinkers believed that if man understood intellectually the causes for his misery, this intellectual knowledge would give him the power to change the circumstances which caused his suffering. Freud was much influenced by this attitude, and it took him years to overcome the expectation that the mere intellectual knowledge of causes for neurotic systems would bring about their cure [1959, p. 7].

Discussing what seems to him the central theme in Freud's system of thought ("Psychoanalysis is the instrument destined for the progressive conquest of the Id") Fromm exclaimed: "Freud expresses here a religious-ethical aim, the conquest of passion by reason" (p. 93). Fromm would consider useless interpretation whose central aim is the reduction of feeling and the substitution of thought for affect.

His emphasis upon intellectual reason and the importance of the therapist as a force allied with it to help the patient overcome irrational emotions is a constant theme throughout Freud's writings, even though he *seems* to have had misgivings about the power of reason:

> It is a long superseded idea, and one derived from super-
> ficial appearances, that the patient suffers from a sort of
> ignorance, and that if one removes this ignorance by giv-
> ing him information (about the causal connection of his
> illness with his life, about his experiences in childhood
> and so on) he is bound to recover. The pathological fac-
> tor is not his ignorance in itself, but the root of this
> ignorance in his *inner resistances;* it was they that first
> called this ignorance into being, and they still maintain it
> now [1910, p. 225].

While seemingly opposing *simple* instruction of the patient concerning what he does not know, Freud actually only shifted the focus of instruction from telling the patient about "connec-tions" to telling him about his reasons for being so ignorant, for staying so ignorant, for wanting to remain so unknowing. Freud apparently recognized this as a mere shift concerning the content of interpretations and did not abandon procedures of intellectual enlightenment. In the paper quoted above Freud said:

> Since, however, *psycho-analysis cannot dispense with
> giving this information,* it lays down that this shall not be
> done before two conditions have been fulfilled. First, the
> patient must, through preparation, himself have reached
> the neighbourhood of what he has repressed, and sec-
> ondly, he must have formed a sufficient attachment
> (transference) to the physician for his emotional rela-
> tionship to make a fresh flight impossible.
> Only when these conditions have been fulfilled is it pos-
> sible to recognize and to master the resistances which
> have led to the repression and the ignorance [pp. 225–
> 26, emphasis supplied—E.S.].

The central theme of this approach to interpretation was the adequate preparation of the patient so that the explanations to be offered would be more readily acceptable to him. Ultimately Freud thought of interpretations as explanations with curative power when they were properly presented by the analyst.

Yet many years later, shortly before his death, Freud seemed to recognize painfully how often these interpretations he had offered his patients failed to bring about the desired results:

> At no point in one's analytic work does one suffer more from an oppressive feeling that all one's repeated efforts have been in vain, and from a suspicion that one has been 'preaching to the winds', than when one is trying to persuade a woman to abandon her wish for a penis on the ground of its being unrealizable or when one is seeking to convince a man that a passive attitude to men does not always signify castration and that it is indispensable in many relationships in life. . . . We often have the impression that with the wish for a penis and the masculine protest we have penetrated through all the psychological strata and have reached bedrock, and that thus our activities are at an end. This is probably true. . . . It would be hard to say whether and when we have succeeded in mastering this factor in an analytic treatment. We can only console ourselves with the certainty that we have given the person analysed every possible encouragement to re-examine and alter his attitude to it [1937, pp. 252–53].

That explanations and the powers of the intellect often failed to bring about personal change Freud acknowledged in his gloomy epilogue.

This growing realization caused many to question the value of interpretation, at least as an attempt to reconstruct the events in the patient's life designed to help him see the connections between his behavior, his ignorance, and his resistance to insight. The interpretative efforts shifted gradually from enlightening the patient about his life to helping him capture the nature of his emotional life in intimate detail—to help him focus more sharply upon *what* he experienced than upon *why* he experienced what he claimed to feel. The emphasis moved from the understanding and explaining of connections to concern with the present and interest in immediate awareness of emotions. This focus on present experience can be found in many authors writing on matters psychotherapeutic; for this discussion the thinking of only a few will be discussed.

Rogers (1939, 1942, 1951) is quite unequivocal. Since 1939 he has developed the theme that the main function of the therapist is helping the patient clarify his feelings by making comments which will sharpen for the patient the nature of his experience (1942, p. 38; see pp. 129–31 in this book). His is a concept of "interpretation" totally different from Freud's—if the term is admissible in this context. It is the essence of the experience which is clarified and interpreted, in the sense of being made more sharply conscious for the patient than it had been until then. Rogers has elaborated on this idea over the years; in 1961 he commented:

. . . I should like to cite very briefly, some of my own experience. I started from a thoroughly objective point of view. Psychotherapeutic treatment involved the diagnosis and analysis of the client's difficulties, the cautious interpretation and explanation to the client of the causes of his difficulties, and a re-educative process focused by the clinician upon the specific causal elements. Gradually I observed that I was more effective if I could create a psychological climate in which the client could undertake these functions himself—exploring, analyzing, understanding, and trying new solutions to his problems. During more recent years, I have been forced to recognize that the most important ingredient in creating this climate is that I should be *real*. . . . The essence of therapy . . . is a meeting of two *persons* in which the therapist is openly and freely himself and evidences this perhaps more fully when he can freely and acceptantly enter into the world of the other. . . . The client finds himself confirmed . . . not only in what he is, but also in his potentialities. He can affirm himself, fearfully to be sure, as a separate, unique person. . . . What this means is that because he is more open to his experience, he can permit himself to live symbolically in terms of all the possibilities [pp. 87–88].

The therapist's clarifying comments are part of his being "real," are to bring about the patient's growing openness to experience and the development of a meaningful existence. Rogers' "real" responding of course demands that the therapist fully grasp his patient's feelings even though the client is unaware of the emotional content of his communication. It furthermore requires the therapist's sensitivity to nuances of expression and to their meaning, to their thought content, but much more to their emotional tone. Reconstruction of the past becomes unimportant and is not a primary therapeutic concern; indeed, it is often wasteful, so far as Rogers is concerned. Reflective clarification of feelings is to Rogers the only meaningful and legitimate interpretive effort.

Sullivan's thoughts on the concept and the place of interpretation in psychotherapy were rather unique. His was a position which at times approximated Freud's, at others seemed similar to Rogers', and yet was distinctively different from either:

These results [certain therapeutic changes] come partly from the interpretation of clearly documented facts, the building of inferential bridges that carry one from particular concrete instances to a generalized formulation, and partly from considering alternative hypotheses for misleading formulations [1947, p. 92].

The advocacy of building an interlocking system of inferences about the patient's past experiences and present behavior sounds very much in the spirit of Freud. But Sullivan was quick to remind his audience that "The supply of interpretations, like that of advice, greatly exceeds the need for them" (p. 92). He seemed rather scornful of the analyst's private reveries and constructs which were to account for the patient's development; he was inclined to believe that all too often analysts place the data presented by their patients on a Procrustean bed to make them fit cherished theoretical preconceptions. Aside from these differences with other psychoanalysts, the interpretations he offered in his work with disturbed individuals seemed anything but overly concerned with issues of intricate psychogenetic development, quite devoid of explanation, and much more pointed in the direction of helping the patient become aware of what it was that he actually felt. When one hears some of Sullivan's comments to patients one is struck with their dearth of construction:

> Living is simple. Are you not aware that you have a tendency to complicate it?

> It takes a great deal of competence to entertain as complex a mental disorder as you do.

> You have copied your mother's paranoid psychosis with some improvements on it.

> Was it not actually rather grandiose for one to assume that he could be entirely responsible for being such an evil person? The grandiosity might well be looked at [White, M. J., 1952, pp. 132–33].

In response to a patient's expressing affection and appreciation for the therapist after the patient had been able to correct a "major fiction that he had been peddling all his life" Sullivan commented:

> Yes, when one corrects a major fiction in the presence of another person, one is apt to have a warm feeling for that person [White, M. J., 1952, p. 135].

Here one sees the clinician at work, entering the world of the patient and trying to make conscious for the patient what he actually did experience. This does not imply neglect or a depreciation of historical events which influenced the patient to move in particular directions and to develop specific security operations. The exact opposite is true. Sullivan was very much interested in the patient's history (Chapter 6), but he used such data not to explain how the present behavior came about but concisely to glean the experiential meaning of present behavior. Complicated and confusing communications were seen by Sullivan as roundabout expressions of inner states and his knowledge of significant developmental facts helped him to grasp more precisely the meaning of the patient's behavior. In this connection White reported:

> Another colleague controlled his work with a schizophrenic boy with Dr. Sullivan. After about six months of work, in which there had been no talk of sex matters at all, Dr. Sullivan suddenly said, "You know, I think this man is one of those very unfortunate youngsters who wants to be a woman but cannot be a satisfactory woman because he has a penis, and is very concerned about his homosexuality and his penis's size, and so on." This also proved later true [1952, p. 148].

She explains how Sullivan developed this insight. It was based on his awareness of historical details in the patient's development and his understanding of their emotional consequences in the particular familial constellation. This understanding led him to the grasp of the patient's present feelings, behavior, and verbalizations. Conversely, Sullivan was apparently also disposed to infer historical data from his intuitive hunches which were based on the patient's present behavior:

> One colleague was working on a patient's recurrent delusion that he was the Assistant Secretary of State. Dr. Sullivan in a supervisory hour said, "You know, I think this fellow has the feeling that he has made a fool of himself somewhere." This was worked on and validated by the patient; the delusion did not recur [White, M. J., 1952, p. 148].

The interpretation, offered not to the patient but to his therapist, addressed itself once again to the inner situation of the person, and this understanding of the patient's inner sense resulted in the uncovering of corroborative historical material.

The striking difference between these interpretations and what might be offered from a Freudian frame of reference is the absence of explanations and the emphasis upon the reality of the patient's experience. In this respect Sullivan's thinking approximates that of Rogers, with the important variation that while the inquiry into historical and developmental details is something Rogers frowns upon, while to his mind the accumulation of such data does not aid the therapist in his efforts to understand the emotional life of the patient, Sullivan deems such material quite important in arriving at correct interpretive comments, even though the nature of meaningful interpretations is seen by Sullivan and Rogers in essentially similar terms.

Sullivan's student, friend, and colleague Fromm-Reichmann has addressed herself extensively to issues associated with therapeutic interpretation. Her thinking telegraphed itself clearly in her definition of an interpretation:

> Interpretation means translating into the language of awareness, and thereby bringing into the open, what the patient communicates, without being conscious of its contents, its dynamics, its revealing connections with other experiences, or the various implications pertaining to its factual or emotional background [1949a, pp. 94–95].

The affinity to Sullivan's thinking is striking. The focus is not upon the divining of "bedrock" universal and ultimately biological problems and processes and their psychological consequences but upon the clarification of present experience and its particular and individualized antecedents. Fromm-Reichmann made this very clear when she discussed the purposes of the interpretive procedures:

> The purpose of interpretation and of interpretive questions is to bring dissociated and repressed experiences and motivations to awareness and to show patients how, unknown to themselves, repressed and dissociated material finds its expression in and colors verbalized communications and behavior patterns such as their actions, attitudes, and gestures [1950, p. 70].

Fromm-Reichmann maintained that these "dissociated and repressed experiences" are not simply events of the past but are present though unconscious inner situations. Consequently Fromm-Reichmann believed that they must not be dealt with simply as manifestations of a distant past but rather as reflections of contemporary, significant character facets. Repeatedly she showed how the patient's reactions to the therapist and other persons can be understood as expressions of his present defensive modes against anxiety. That such defensive modes have their historical roots is obvious, but apparently Fromm-Reichmann focused first on grasping the defensive character of the behavior or communications and only secondarily on the understanding of its historical development.

The following vignette illustrates Fromm-Reichmann's general position on the question of interpretation:[1]

A patient broke through prolonged periods of compulsive silence by asking the psychiatrist questions about his personal life. The therapist did not fall into the trap of interpreting this as an expression of the patient's curiosity engendered by her attachment to him. He understood that the same anxiety which had kept the patient silent so far was now operating in her verbalizations. Therefore, his response to the patient's questions about him was to the effect that, should she remain interested, he would have no objections to answering these questions at some later date. For the time being, however, he was more interested in and therefore wished to investigate the patient's interest in the reasons prompting her to replace therapeutic curiosity about herself with concern about the doctor's personal affairs. After that the psychiatrist could demonstrate to her that the anxiety she felt in dealing with him, which she tried to ward off at all costs was the reason for her remaining silent or talking about him instead of discussing her problems. Subsequently, this became a starting point for the therapeutic investigation of the same pattern used in the patient's interpersonal dealings with people at large. The patient had been reared to lead the life of a self-sacrificing, kind, generous, and charitable person. As a result, she had developed intense feelings of resentment and hostility, primarily

[1] Fromm-Reichmann was here discussing the work of one of her colleagues.

against those who had forced upon her the yoke of this self-sacrificing attitude. After that her "kindness" became a reaction formation to the resentment and the destructive fantasies against those close to her and quite frequently against the recipients of her charitable generosity. This was her "secret," of which she was only dimly aware, however. Fear of her own disapproval as well as of the disdain of others prompted her to hide the "secret" as best she could. Therefore, the patient had assumed the obsessional pattern of evading an answer to any personal question asked her, whether it was by a friend or a mere casual acquaintance. Her automatic response to any personal question was to ask in return a personal question which expressed her concern with the affairs of the friend or acquaintance [1950, pp. 108–9].

Thus her approach to interpretation was quite pointed: neurotic behavior and inappropriate reactions in therapeutic and in other settings must be understood and interpreted as security measures. This recognition leads to the eventual grasp of their historical roots. The therapist's interpretation—his recognition that the patient was anxious and tried to defend herself against anxiety—had little to do with historical interpretation and explanation but had the freshness of the here and now, brought the patient face to face with her experience, and thereby helped enlarge her horizons of consciousness. The therapist's behavior afforded the patient what she needed most —an opportunity to experience something—and avoided what she needed least—an explanation.

In some ways this position is seemingly not too divergent from thoughts expressed by theorists operating within the orthodox psychoanalytic tradition. A good deal of Fenichel's (1945) discussion of interpretation is somewhat compatible with Fromm-Reichmann's. There is little to be found in Fenichel which would make one think that he cherished intellectual explanation. He too emphasized the importance of experience and helping the patient feel his repressed impulses. The main difference between his thinking and that of others presented here centers about the insistence of the orthodox psychoanalytic system that correct interpretations will inevitably lead to a particular and, to the analyst, already known source of conflict: to the Oedipus complex, to the incestuous and regressive instinctual strivings of the organism.

Interpretations in Freudian thinking deal predominantly with resistance behavior and these resistances—whether obvious transference reactions or their more disguised derivatives—inevitably oppose the recognition of Oedipal problems. This explanatory principle is the hub of the system, and unless the patient is capable of consciously re-experiencing his Oedipal strivings no change can take place. The strivings about which Freud thought "disclosures" had to be made to the patient are inevitably urges of the past even though they operate now on a transference level in the present. What is missing from this intricate and often powerful construction is the recognition that particular resistances and transference reactions are not simply repetitions of the past, not simply mechanical S–R sets as suggested by the psychologists eager to integrate psychoanalytic theory and classical behavioristic learning theory. Far more are resistances and transference reactions security operations in the present designed to prevent the catastrophe of losing what the patient considers his only hope for alleviating anxiety and ultimately for survival. This will be discussed in detail in Chapters 10 and 11; suffice it to indicate here that the emphasis upon past connections evades the patient's present desperate search for anxiety avoidance, for a bolstering of self-esteem, and for security. For instance, it may be true that a good deal of "love" often expressed by patients for therapists is simply transference love (Freud, 1915a) and is therefore in need of analytic investigation. Yet harboring neurotic feelings toward the therapist does not mean that the patient simply relives his infantile strivings toward the parent without acknowledging them; his neurotic "love" for the therapist may reflect a basic mode in achieving security, by ingratiation, attempts to reassure the other person, or insisting that he is deeply indebted. Attempts to understand this phenomenon in terms of previous attitudes toward others diminishes the experience of the moment and evades, at least in part, the anxiety which lurks behind transference phenomena. The interpretation of transference reactions in terms of past relatedness robs the therapeutic situation of the vitality of the here and now. To the extent to which all neurotic reactions, including transference feelings, are viewed as security operations designed to avoid anxiety *today*, to that extent their interpretation demands that the therapist deal with them in the present either of the doctor–patient relationship or of the patient's other relationships (Fromm-Reichmann, 1950).

This brief survey of ideas advanced by some authors indicates that a gradual shift in emphasis has taken place since Freud first started writing on the topic of interpretation; interpretive comments and questions have become less genesis-oriented and less concerned with unearthing specific historical connections between present behavior and antecedents. This is particularly evident in the recent modifications of psychoanalytic thought presented by the so-called culturally oriented schools and groups. Although members of this group accept the basic idea that interpretations will bring back to the patient's consciousness repressed affects, they focus on helping him become conscious of present security operations vis-à-vis anxiety engendered by contemporary situations. Through this shift interpretations have become confrontations of the patient with his experiences, his anxiety, the nature of the anxiety-arousing situation, and his character defenses against such discomfort.

A clinical illustration from the author's work highlights this:

☐ A young woman had discussed at length some of her reactions to her husband. Somehow, no matter what gifts he brought her, she always felt dissatisfied with them, she always found them wanting—even when they were things for which she had expressed great desire. In addition, she felt that their sexual life was quite unsatisfactory. During intercourse, she constantly caught herself thinking about all kinds of things, the following day's schedule of activities, arrangements to be made at home and at work, social events, etc. All this made her dissatisfied with herself, distressed her markedly, but her pattern of behavior and her dissatisfaction persisted over the years despite prolonged analytic investigations with two previous therapists.

She commented frequently that she was quite aware that she was very "castrating," that this undoubtedly had something to do with her repressed "penis envy" but also that she could not get to these "underlying feelings."

The therapist pointedly disregarded her formulation and simply inquired why it was so important for her not to allow another person to be of any use to her. He expressed the idea that it sounded to him as if she were eager to deny vigorously another person's usefulness. He thought that this inference was further supported by the patient's frequent derogatory comments about his thinking, the location of his office, his appearance, etc. Furthermore, she had similar feelings about her previous therapists, yet had continued to see them for several years and had obviously derived benefit in some areas of her life from them.

This interpretive question opened a vista of experience for the patient. It caused her the anxious recognition of a dreadful fear of dependence, of terrifying anxiety about ever really needing somebody, and of her need to belittle anybody useful lest she become dependent upon him. This recognition led eventually to her awareness of a deep sense of betrayal, of having been betrayed and wanting to betray others. It led her to recall how she had resolved to arrange life's circumstances so as to prevent herself from ever again being betrayed or betraying others. □

What the therapist had done was acquaint the patient with the way she happened to strike him and with his reactions to what she had told him. But at the same time, while he confronted her with what seemed to him the meaning of her reactions to others, he also tried to move the investigation a step further: he led the patient toward an examination of feelings and motives responsible for her behavior. Furthermore, the interpretation moved the discussion from the exclusive investigation of her reactions outside the office to a simultaneous inquiry into similar attitudes toward the therapist, which increased the sense of immediacy in their discussions.

Another example may further clarify the essential difference between interpretation and confrontation:

☐ An apparently intellectually highly gifted research worker sought help with marital problems, claiming that his wife was totally "unresponsive" to him. He explained that he felt that she did not treat him as a person with whom she wanted to share emotions, thoughts, and reflections, nor was she interested in hearing about her husband's difficulties with the chairman of his department, who was also said to be "disinterested" in the patient's particular research concerns.

While he reported these supposedly very distressing situations, he acted as if he had nothing to contribute to the deeper understanding of his difficulties; he would sit for long periods as if devoid of any idea or feeling, and nothing he said seemed to interest him. It was as if he were waiting for the therapist to offer some explanations for his depressing circumstances, circumstances which had led to a legal separation from his wife and the imminent danger of losing his job.

Whenever the therapist made the unfortunate mistake of advancing an explanatory formulation, the patient would agree with it and sometimes nodded vigorous support. But agreement was so quick that the therapist became suspicious. It seemed likely that the patient had entertained similar ideas long before the therapist had made his remarks, albeit ideas and feelings he had not expressed.

One day when the therapist remarked that he had the distinct impression that the patient was somehow secretly ridiculing his chairman and his colleagues, that he somehow gave them to understand that they really did not know anything and were fools, the patient disagreed vehemently. On the contrary, he said, he had always tried to make sure not to offend their sensitivities. At conferences and informal professional discussions around the lunch table he would remain very silent even when the discussion dealt with his particular esoteric specialty.

Suddenly the therapist caught on and he exclaimed, "By

God, this is how you rub my nose in dirt, too." The patient was quite startled by the therapist's admission that he had often felt foolish when he had offered a comment—that he had frequently had the distinct impression that his remarks had been old hat to the patient; that they expressed thoughts the patient seemed to have harbored all along; and that he (the therapist) had felt silly as if he had belabored the obvious.

The therapist added that although the patient's inability to explore his thoughts and feelings seemed designed to convey overtly polite deference, it felt like the covertly derogatory statement, "I will let you play the smart one," or an even more derogatory invitation, "All right, let's see what you have to say and I will give you enough rope to hang yourself."

The patient sat for a long time in silence, then slowly nodded his head and merely inquired several times, "Do I really make you feel this way?" During the night following this interview the patient dreamed about having protected his wife from an assault by her mother but in helping her kept her in a basically infantile setting and position. He fully grasped the message of the dream without any comment by the therapist. And this led to an airing of the patient's pervasive distrustfulness, triggered by his own resentments, of his subtly contemptuous defenses in the face of anxiety, and the eventual unfolding of the psychogenesis of the man's profound depression. □

Confrontations differ from traditional interpretations in their avoidance of explanations and historical reconstructions and in their emphasis on the patient's behavior and experience. Thus, confrontations aid the patient in becoming acquainted with who he is and what he feels, and how he affects other people, including the therapist (also see Chapter 6). In dealing with the here and now of behavior, confrontations aid the patient in grasping directly and with a sense of immediacy his present experience. They do not lend themselves to intellectualized talking about and talking around causality, therefore the usual questions about the correctness or incorrectness of interpretations become irrelevant because no inferences are drawn concerning the "deeper meanings" and historical roots of the patient's behavior. All that is stated and exposed is his impact upon others. Questions concerning the ultimate reason for the patient's behavior or whether it is reasonable do not enter into the therapeutic transaction when confrontational comments are offered. The patient's explorations in these directions are, however, stimulated by confrontations.

Yet there is a striking similarity between confrontational remarks and more traditional interpretations. Psychotherapists were repeatedly admonished by Freud (1914a, 1922a) to focus their interpretations on the patient's transference behavior and resistance reactions. By confronting the patient with his effect on the therapist, his transference and by implication the manifestations of his resistance are dealt with directly (see Chapters 10 and 11). Thus confrontations do not prevent investigation of transference reactions; on the contrary, they bring the patient's transference behavior out into the open, making it amenable to detailed inquiry. This procedure is not designed to the end that the patient eventually be "persuaded to give up" his infantile wishes, or simply to "show" him the irrationality of his strivings, but solely to help him become familiar with the nature of his experience. The essential conceptual shortcomings of explanatory, "rational" interpretations have been summarized by Hobbs:

> In the Freudian prescription for the handling of transference one finds the great psychoanalytic paradox: The cure for unreason is reason. Freud gave us a twentieth-century discovery that unreasonable (i.e., neurotic) behavior is determined by specific life experiences, thousands of them probably, and that neurotic behavior is unconscious and pre-eminently nonrational in origin. He could have said that neurosis is a summary term describing an extensive matrix of conditioned responses built upon a lifetime of hurtful relationships with important life persons, hardened around an armature of assumed guilt. He might further have observed that no man by taking thought becomes neurotic. But for this twentieth-century diagnosis, Freud had a nineteenth-century prescription: Be rational. Transference represents the neu-

rosis in microcosm; when transference appears it should be interpreted. As Fenichel so clearly instructs us, the client should be shown that he is behaving in an irrational manner [1962, p. 744].

It may be argued with some justification that confrontational comments may fill the patient with horror and fright because they jolt him into facing how his behavior affects others without the palliative of immediate attempts to "explain" it. Of course, the patient is likely to see something about himself that is not very noble, and what he sees may indeed arouse intense anxiety within him—it does quite often. At the same time, the therapist's recognition and open admission of the patient's motives and feelings without turning from him in horror can be nothing but enormously reassuring (also see Chapter 7).

Insights brought home to the patient through confrontations are of course about feelings potentially available to the patient, operating often on a preconscious level. Frequently the patient had some glimmering awareness of those tendencies before he was confronted with them, although a variety of reasons made him studiously avoid full and conscious knowledge of their presence. The causes for the repressive evasion of self-knowledge need not be re-examined here; they have been touched upon in earlier chapters. Through confrontational interpretations the patient is effectively told that his attempts at evading awareness and hiding from others have failed, that a denouement has taken place. Patients always fear this denouement—but there is little doubt that at the same time they also hope for it.

It is most difficult to live with the gnawing suspicion that one is hiding unpleasant truths and to live in constant fear that someday somebody will notice them. On this dreaded day, the patient is convinced, all hell will break loose and punishment will be visited upon him. In the therapeutic situation and the transference relationship he is often convinced that he will incur the analyst's disapproval, his wrath, rejection, and punishment. Being "found out" by the therapist without the expected catastrophes taking place is likely to bring profound relief, and yet, for reasons to be discussed in Chapters 10 and

11, an almost inevitable increase of anxiety for the patient. At that moment he experiences a sense of fundamental and genuine acceptability as a human being. He realizes that the therapist does not labor on his behalf because he views the patient as some wonderful being but despite his now exposed and apparent shortcomings and defects. Through the confrontational comments the therapist expresses directly and in action his acceptance of the patient as a fellow member of the human community. Conversely, it is almost disastrous for the patient to feel that the therapist avoids seeing what he could see or what the patient at least thinks the analyst should see because he infers that "the man is just too scared to see how terribly defective I am," and he dreads the day when the therapist will finally realize the extent of what the patient considers his pathology. Then he imagines that the therapist will turn away in anger, with disapproval and with disgust. Unfortunate and all too common attempts to reassure the patient that his behavior can really be understood as "meaning this or that" and that "this is really not so bad at all" merely reinforce the patient's sense that the therapist is eager to reassure *himself* to avoid a hideous vision, but that eventually the inevitable knowledge will dawn on him and dreaded consequences will ensue. Confrontations, on the other hand, are genuinely reassuring because they clearly tell the patient: "You are known and yet not cast out." (See Chapter 8.)

Some clinical illustrations will further show this point:

□ A young woman, somewhat physically handicapped by congenital defects of a vital organ, had been working with a therapist for quite some time. She had entered therapy in the hope that she would be helped to make a more reasonable adjustment to her real enough ailment and to rid herself of a multiplicity of symptoms, including her inability to find or keep any meaningful job despite her adequate academic preparation. She also felt socially isolated, had no friends, for no sooner had she struck up a friendship than it seemed that people just "dropped" her. She blamed a good deal of her difficulties on her physical condition, which did not allow her to socialize as much as she thought she would like. Despite two years of analytic effort, basically little had changed. To be sure, she managed her life better, finally had found and held on to a relatively rewarding job, had developed enough courage to undergo difficult surgery to remove the defect, and had some minimal social life—but fundamentally she remained lonely, detached, and isolated.

In the course of her life the patient had developed an extremely witty manner, could be quite entertaining, and took pride in her repartee and her clever and sophisticated remarks. She saw these facets as definite assets despite the fact that others seemed to tire of them quickly. One day the therapist came to the waiting room to ask her into the office about five minutes past her appointment time. Upon entering, the patient quipped flippantly about being kept waiting, made some seemingly half-facetious and half-serious cracks and finally added: "I am quite angry about your being late." The analyst had the distinct impression that the patient was not the least bit angry and remarked with some annoyance: "I wish you really were angry instead of simply trying to make me feel guilty."

Making others feel guilty had been a prominent defensive device in the patient's life and she usually employed her wit to make her accusations more palatable. This behavior had been a common theme in the therapeutic explorations but the patient always managed to avoid facing its impact on others by quickly insisting that these maneuvers were necessary to compensate for her physical inferiority and to maintain some self-respect at home and in contacts with others. But she had always avoided such maneuvers with the therapist and so interpretive attempts which had to deal with interactions reported by her were always somewhat stale. But now she could not avoid the therapist's irritation and she had to take note of what his reaction had been.

The patient was silent for a long time and then started to sob bitterly. She finally commented that she had been able to feel her desire to make the analyst feel uncomfortable and the awareness of this inner experience moved her to some fruitful inquiry into her pervasive anxiety and her urge to make others feel guilty in order to evade it. □

There was little doubt that this confrontation, despite its pain-producing aspects, was greatly relieving to the patient.

But it must also be remembered that some patients do not become anxious when they anticipate or are subjected to reactions which most people would consider critical, derogatory, disapproving, or outright hostile. Instead they react with anxiety to approving and affirming behavior by others. In fact, some individuals seem to thrive on hostility directed toward them. This is often the result of a peculiar attitude in which the person equates hostility with contact and agreement with isolation. Historically, such individuals experienced meaningful contact with significant persons primarily around arguments, disapprobation, and conflict. Any agreement between them and others had resulted in withdrawal by the adult, disinterest, and neglect, as if he had said: "If there is nothing to disapprove then there is no basis for our having anything to do with each other." Characteristically such patients react with anxiety to comments and interpretations which tend to affirm or support them, and once again direct confrontation rather than interpretive explanations seems the only device which helps them experience the essence of their inner situation. The following example illustrates such an instance:

☐ A highly argumentative and contentious but gifted man had sought therapy. Among some of his difficulties were constant disagreements with colleagues. One day he reported again how "unreasonable and stupid" his colleagues were. He had discussed some of his ideas at a staff meeting and had run into a good deal of opposition. He claimed to have felt slighted, depressed, and angry, but his tone in reporting these events seemed instead highly animated.

At one point the therapist commented that the ideas he had discussed seemed to her quite ingenious and intriguing, and she wondered why the patient's colleagues had reacted so negatively. The patient reacted most vehemently to this comment: "Here you go again, knocking me down like they did." The therapist, who had taped the session, asked the patient if he cared to hear the tape. The patient was most eager but it took several replays before he realized that she had said "ingenious and intriguing" and not "infantile and intimidating" as he insisted he had heard it.

When he finally heard correctly he broke out in a cold sweat, became highly anxious and agitated. The therapist's comment: "You do seem to love arguing with me, even if it requires mishearing—is this really all you think you are good for, to be knocked down and argued with?" brought forth even more anxiety but also a marked decrease of agitation and the patient's sudden awareness that indeed he cherished arguments lest he feel totally abandoned. A flood of memories about his loneliness when he was little and a good boy ensued. It soon became apparent to patient and therapist that the very manner in which he had discussed his ideas with his colleagues was designed to precipitate what he craved—opposition. □

This vignette and the issue it illustrates lead to a point already alluded to: the observation that confrontations do not simply relieve the patient and reassure him, but that they also simultaneously heighten his anxiety. The reason for this seeming paradox is twofold. First, the confrontation is anxiety-producing because it goes straight to the heart of the character pathology and threatens to rob the patient of his illusions, his defenses, his self-oblivion no matter how defined, while simultaneously holding out the very reassuring hope that life without such props is possible. This hope is also the second and more important source of heightened anxiety because this possibility and this hope threaten the patient's world order, his premises, and his "secure knowledge" that he has figured out the universe and has learned to deal with it. If one accepts the position that anxiety is engendered by the individual's sense that he will be punished by retaliations ranging from castration to isolation for experiencing inner promptings (be they Oedipally regressive or personally expansive); and if the patient learns in the confrontation and acceptance that punishments are not inevitable and universal reactions of others, it is likely that this recognition, relieving as it may be, will also bring forth first confusion and then rage against those who through their actions have contributed to the development of the patient's world picture. This confusion and rage brought about by his realization that he has been duped and, what is worse, that he has gone along with a lie is extremely anxiety-arousing for the patient. The broader aspects and consequences of this dilemma will be dealt with in Chapters 10 and 11, especially in the discussion of "negative transference."

Another type of interpretive approach deserves note. Since the late forties Rosen (1947) has written extensively about what he calls "direct analysis," a psychoanalytic technique in which confrontational interpretations are offered quickly and in rapid succession.[2] Since this volume is not concerned with psychotherapeutic techniques but with concepts developed by various authors and practicing therapists, a discussion of the technical aspects of Rosen's work is irrelevant. In some ways his theoretical conception of the interpretation parallels the concept of confrontation outlined earlier. In stressing the importance of the analyst's entering the patient's world, Rosen suggests that confronting patients with one's grasp of their experiences is of paramount importance and that this very grasp and its communication help the patient to rid himself of anxiety caused by his inner experience. But Rosen's understanding of emotional states tends to follow predetermined lines; his understanding is inevitably anchored in a libidinally and psychosexually determined developmental framework. Therefore his interpretations often have an explanatory flavor even though they are offered with a good deal of apparent emotional involvement, conviction, and sincerity.

Rosen's work and that of others lead to the question of the timing of interpretations, an issue that has concerned writers on psychotherapeutic concepts since earliest days. As noted earlier Freud (1913) suggested two guiding principles for choosing opportune moments. He believed that they ought to be given after the patient has developed a positive attitude toward the analyst and also has come close to gaining understanding of his motives and attitudes on his own. This, Freud

---

[2] Interestingly enough, Rosen's work with grossly disturbed adults somewhat parallels Klein's (1960) procedures in her therapeutic efforts with children.

insisted, will occur after resistances to insight have lessened; their diminution was seen by him partially as a function of the positive transference and partially as a function of the successful interpretation of resistance itself. But the interpretation of resistance itself could be undertaken only if and when a positive transference had developed. Freud believed that any attempt to interpret, whether resistances or later on instinctual conflict material, was contingent upon and could not take place before the patient had developed a strong emotional attachment to and dependence upon the therapist. Many years after Freud had developed these ideas Fenichel assumed a similar stand:

> Actually resistances are attacked not only by interpretation; other means of influencing people to do something unpleasant are used as well. The analyst tries to convince the patient that the unpleasant task is necessary; his friendly feelings toward the analyst are utilized [1945, pp. 25–26].

Fenichel obviously believed that these "friendly feelings" are the bases which make interpretive processes possible.

A similar yet different outlook was presented by Alexander. He said of one of the illustrative cases he reported:

> Only because of the patient's great confidence in the physician, which he confessed at the very beginning of the second interview, could he allow himself to face his intolerable insecurity [1946b, p. 154].

This ability to face truth was brought about by a very pointed interpretation the therapist had offered during the session.

> The analyst continued in a dramatic fashion, "And they come and beg you. But you remain adamant. You say, 'No. I am going to retire; I have had enough of fight and struggle. You do it yourself!' You are taking a malicious satisfaction in their impotence to solve the mathematical equations. In your own eyes you are fully rehabilitated. You can say, 'I may no longer be a great hero in the field of sexuality, but I am still better than the younger generation. I am better in what really counts.' All this you

cannot permit yourself to feel frankly. You must have some alibi, and this you receive from your illness. You are depressed, you cannot sleep, you cannot stop weeping, you do not want any recognition. Why should you feel guilty? In this way you can have satisfaction and still not feel bad about it because at the same time that you hurt others you also hurt yourself. But would you be so generous if you were not sure they could not accomplish your work without you? sure that even if they could, they would certainly give you the credit? Your martyrdom is only a cover for a vindictive triumph over your colleagues—whose only crime is that they are younger than you" [p. 151].

This is certainly quite an interpretation for any patient at any time in his therapy—and here it was offered in the *second* meeting. In its wording, in its avoidance of "explaining" and directly relating present behavior to historical material, the comment comes closer to being a confrontation than anything else. No matter how deep the patient's confidence in the analyst, his acceptance seems less born of "confidence" than of the fact that the doctor spoke to him with candor about things that mattered. The therapist was not "clever" but to the point, was not dazzling but unmasking. What undoubtedly impressed the patient was the therapist's courage to see, his honesty in telling, and his willingness to accept the patient despite what he saw. And so the point is not how much positive transference *has* been established, but how much genuine rather than irrational respect *is* established—and forthright confrontations establish rational respect. Alexander showed that this *can* be established in the second interview.

It was probably with such thoughts in mind that Fromm-Reichmann remarked:

As soon as a workable doctor–patient relationship has been established and as soon as the psychiatrist approximately knows with whom he is dealing, he should be ready, in principle, to approach his patients with active therapeutic moves. The fact that they may not be able to accept them immediately is not necessarily a sign that the approach is counterindicated. The suggestions offered may have to be repeated, and their results may have to be worked through innumerable times, but that should only rarely be a reason for refraining altogether from therapeutic intervention [1950, p. 151].

Fromm-Reichmann obviously believed that interpretations should be offered early, even though they may be rejected by the patient or may require later modification. By "workable doctor–patient relationship" she did not mean a positive transference in the traditional sense of the term but rather a relationship which is characterized by the doctor's respect for the patient and serious attempts to understand him, and the patient's recognition that these are his therapist's basic attitudes. Her thinking was in marked contrast with Fenichel's:

> . . . in general one can say that an interpretation to which the patient objects is wrong. That does not necessarily mean that it is wrong in content, that, for instance, the impulse which the analyst surmised and imparted to the patient had never been operative. The interpretation may be correct in content but incorrect dynamically or economically, that is, given at a moment when the patient could not grasp its validity or get any farther with it [Fenichel, 1945, pp. 31–32].

Fenichel's position also differs markedly with another thought expressed by Fromm-Reichmann:

> This suggestion is not intended to exclude the possibility of establishing a therapeutically valid relationship with a patient by offering interpretive reactions to his manifestations. In the hands of a skilled and experienced person who is not afraid of the hostile outbursts with which some patients may respond, favorable time-saving results may be obtained with the use of this technique [1950, p. 151].

Later, however, Fromm-Reichmann added:

> As a rule, it will be wise to offer interpretations and to try to elicit interpretive responses from a patient after he has reached a stage bordering upon an awareness of the subject of interpretation. It is then that the psychiatrist may

be most successful in conveying to patients the experience of discovering their final interpretations by themselves. . . . This suggestion should not be followed, however, at the expense of directness and spontaneity in the doctor's attitude [pp. 151–52].

This last comment has become the guiding principle in the timing of interpretations and confrontations. The analyst's honesty, directness, and spontaneity in interpreting appear the instrumentalities most theoreticians view as ultimately curative in the psychotherapeutic enterprise. The warnings against "ill-timed" interpretations have given way to a more profound caution against destructive interpretations, which are not designed to help the patient understand crucial issues in his life but sound as if they were offered in a spirit of "smartness," bravado, and haughty superiority. Under such circumstances the patient is used and experiences himself as used, exploited, and violated. Such "interpretations" are indeed disastrous to a human being who has suffered long enough from the effects of having been exploited in the past. Withholding interpretive and confrontational comments for the sake of maintaining an august theoretical position, disregarding the possibility that the patient could benefit from learning about another person's rational efforts in understanding him is also disrespectful and therefore harmful to the patient. Implied in such withholding is the statement: "The theory is more important than you, the patient." And so in withholding confrontational comments the therapist deprives the patient of the reassurance which follows active therapeutic efforts and exchanges.

No discussion of the concept of interpretation and confrontation can avoid at least brief mention of the concept of "working through." Freud recognized that many interpretations seemed in need of repetition, that resistances required often repeated interpretations; that, in effect, the patient needed time to assimilate the knowledge he had gained and that this assimilation demanded what contemporary psychologists call "re-enforcement."

One must allow the patient time to become more conversant with the resistance with which he has now become acquainted, to *work through* it, to overcome it, by continuing, in defiance of it, the analytic work according to the fundamental rule of analysis [1914a, p. 155].

Note once again the similarity between Freudian psychoanalytic thinking and S–R learning theory. Repetition and the re-enforced building up of connections was to effect the patient's gaining insight. Freud wrote sparingly about "aha experience," the illuminating sudden grasp and insightful understanding. He believed that:

> This working-through of the resistances may in practice turn out to be an arduous task for the subject of the analysis and a trial of the patience for the analyst. Nevertheless, it is a part of the work which effects the greatest changes in the patient and which distinguishes analytic treatment from any kind of treatment by suggestion [1914a, pp. 155–56].[3]

The same emphasis upon repetition as the dynamic force in learning can be found in the writing of Freud's faithful student Fenichel:

> Systematic and consistent interpretive work, both within and without the framework of transference, can be described as educating the patient to produce continually less distorted derivatives until his fundamental instinctual conflicts are recognizable. Of course, this is not a single operation resulting in a single act of abreaction; it is, rather, a chronic process of working through, which shows the patient again and again the same conflicts and his usual way of reacting to them, but from new angles and in new connections [1945, p. 31].

The slow and patient building up of connections is the basic model of S–R psychology and psychoanalytic theory.

Fromm-Reichmann does not differ significantly from Freud or Fenichel here. She also thought that:

---

[3] The last comment in this quotation seems a *non sequitur* because one is left to wonder why repeated "working through" of a particular defensive structure or conflict is less "suggestive" than a single interpretive exposure.

. . . any understanding, any new piece of awareness which has been gained by interpretive clarification, has to be reconquered and tested time and again in new connections and contacts with other interlocking experiences, which may or may not have to be subsequently approached interpretively in their own right. That is the process to which psychoanalysts refer when speaking of the necessity of repeatedly "working through" . . . [1950, p. 141].

Fromm-Reichmann apparently held that this repeated "working through" is an essential aspect of psychotherapeutic practice; while she was not as explicit as others in suggesting that learning and insight proceed through repetition, she left the impression that this was her belief.

This position is of course quite different from Alexander's (1946b) previously cited confidence in single key-interpretations. Most of the cases reported by Alexander and French (1946) lack any prolonged "working through" period. One is led to believe that profound insights and profound changes can occur on the basis of little repetition and working through. This leads one to a curious speculation. Is it possible that the importance of repetition for psychotherapy is analogous to the value Lewin (1942) ascribed to practice for the learning process? Contrary to popular belief prevalent even among some psychologists, Lewin never denied the value of practice and repetition. He firmly believed that repetition was valuable because it offered many opportunities for the occurrence of the *single* insight-producing moment. The "working through" process can be thought of in similar terms. By and large, interpretations and confrontations are always at best close approximations of the patient's true inner life. At the beginning of their contact the therapist's grasp of the patient's feelings is likely to be fragmentary and consequently his comments are apt to be first approximations. As the therapist's and patient's insights become refined, chances will improve that genuine and more penetrating understanding will force itself upon them. But this does not preclude the possibility that sudden illuminating awareness can occur early and forcefully, making the "working through" period more or less obsolete or at least not so long as is often thought inevitable. The "working through" period, then, may well be thought of as a period during which the therapist gains insight and corrects his misapprehensions about the patient.

But even the most profound and penetrating interpretations offered in a spirit of genuine dedication will often fail to move the patient. He often seems neither "convinced" nor even interested in what the therapist has to say because his prime concern is the question "How sincere is the therapist?" The "working through" period may also represent a time span during which the patient tests the sincerity and honesty of the therapist.[4] The behavior of these patients is governed by the abiding sense that they dare not trust others or themselves; therefore they cannot trust their own reactions and certainly dare not trust expressing them to others. The intensity of this distrust is directly proportional to the patient's conviction that awareness of his inner life, making for a sense of separate and individual existence, will result in his being cast out and abandoned. Thus the patient's distrust is heightened by the degree to which the price of experiencing as an independent and unique entity was unbearable loneliness (Fromm–Reichmann, 1959). During the "working through" period the patient hopefully learns that independent life and personal experience are not synonymous with or inevitably followed by loneliness and rejection. Hopefully, he will learn to accept himself as a human being and face all facets of his experience so that he may end ready to exclaim: *"Homo sum; nihil humani a me alienum puto."*

The basic condition which makes this realization possible is the therapist's genuine acceptance of the patient as a fellow human being. This does not mean benevolent or condescending approval by the therapist—the mere concept of approval implies a haughty, patronizing orientation. Much more, genuine acceptance implies an understanding beyond approval or disapproval. Confrontational interpretations are direct acts expressing this type of acceptance because they convey to the

---

[4] Subsequent chapters will be addressed to much of what is here merely sketched.

patient more than explanations ever can that the therapist at least tries to hear him and that he will not be cast out for revealing the nature of his inner life. Thus interpretive efforts become acts of compassionate acceptance, acts of love which must be repeated over and over until the person learns to trust again. In this connection one is reminded of a passage in Goethe's *Faust*. After his Easter promenade Faust returns to his study to devote himself to his favorite task, the translation of the New Testament into German:

> It says: "In the beginning was the *Word*."
> Already I am stopped. It seems absurd.
> The *Word* does not deserve the highest prize,
> I must translate it otherwise
> If I am well inspired and not blind.
> It says: In the beginning was the *Mind*.
> Ponder that first line, wait and see,
> Lest you should write too hastily.
> Is mind the all-creating source?
> It ought to say: In the beginning there was *Force*.
> Yet something warns me as I grasp the pen,
> That my translation must be changed again.
> The spirit helps me. Now it is exact.
> I write: In the beginning was the *Act*.
> [Kaufmann, 1962, p. 153].

Indeed, psychotherapeutic intervention leading to the rekindling of life and growth also cannot start with a mere giving of the word, or with rationalistic constructs no matter how forcefully offered—but with a deed, an act of acceptance, of the impassioned struggle to understand him who is in need of being understood. This life-furthering act is the pointed confrontational interpretation.

▶ *Summary* ◀

1. The concept of psychotherapeutic "interpretation" has undergone significant reformulations since it first appeared in the literature. Freud shifted the emphasis from interpreting

the nature of the patient's core conflict to interpreting the patient's resistance and the reasons for his resistance to becoming aware of instinctual conflicts. Despite this shift, however, Freud continued to believe that interpretations were essentially rationalistic explanations offered to the patient, a point of view still prevalent in many quarters.

2. But interpretations may also be thought of as attempts by the therapist to confront the patient with the impact he makes upon others. Confrontations are attempts to acquaint the patient with aspects of his hidden characterological *what* rather than with the *why* of his behavior. Only after the basic *what* of his behavior has come sharply into the focus of his awareness can the patient adequately understand the *why* of his behavior.

3. Continuing to help a patient overcome his difficulties in living despite the fact that a denouement has taken place represents a genuine and unmistakable act of acceptance and spares the patient agonizing fears about future consequences if and when he will be "found out." Therefore interpretations are not comments to be offered only after the patient has developed positive affective bonds toward the therapist; confrontational comments are precisely the instruments making for the establishment of such ties.

4. The "working through" period has often been considered the period of time during which the patient gradually becomes convinced of the existence of certain instinctual conflicts, learns to avoid repressing them, and learns to sublimate instead. An alternate interpretation of the "working through" is that it is the time during which the patient gradually refines the interpretations and insights gathered and during which he tests his therapist's sincerity.

CHAPTER TEN

The Concept of Resistance

PSYCHOTHERAPISTS FROM THE FIRST HAVE OBSERVED AND WRITTEN about the tendency of many patients frequently and vigorously to reject offered interpretations (Fenichel, 1945; Ferenczi, 1909; Freud, 1922, 1936, 1937; Menninger, 1946). In addition to outright rejection of the therapist's words and efforts, subtly rejecting behavior was noted and reported. Individuals ostensibly seeking psychotherapeutic help were reported, despite their obvious distress, to carry out various maneuvers which undermined and sabotaged the therapist's efforts on their behalf, despite their having consulted the therapist voluntarily, and despite the considerable amounts of money and time they expended in this search for emotional well-being.

There are, of course, untold opportunities for sabotaging the therapeutic process, and patients can use a variety of conscious and unconscious methods to carry it out. The pointed avoidance of relevant material with a concomitant expenditure of effort in the elaboration of trivia; the reduction of time available for collaboration with the therapist by being late or by completely forgetting appointments; and the inability to remember, selective omissions, or conscious censoring in reporting fantasy material, dreams, or even recent events are striking methods of circumventing therapeutic investigation. The sudden development of quickly disappearing symptoms which are followed by new ones often gives the impression that the patient is eager to spend his time in cursory discussion of transitory problems in order to reduce the time available to him for the exploration of characterological traits, attitudes, and significant events which would throw some light upon his personality make-up. However, although some of these "new" symptoms superficially resemble avoidance behavior, upon careful investigation reveal some significant aspect or problem of the patient and therefore cannot be considered manifestations of *resistance,* the generic term which encompasses all behavior that seemingly interferes with therapeutic uncovering and understanding. The following clinical excerpt is an example of revealing rather than resistive new symptom formation.

☐ A young woman shortly before termination of therapy (a termination precipitated by both marked personality changes and moving to another city where she and her husband had secured very desirable employment) suddenly developed the obsessive idea that she was rapidly losing her hair. There were hardly any indications that this was fact rather than fiction and the numerous dermatologists and internists consulted by her concurred that if there was any loss at all it was minimal, what might reasonably be expected, and that there were no realistic reasons for anticipating dreaded baldness.

The therapist's immediate impression was that this was simply another expression of the patient's resistance to investigating severe anxiety attacks that seemed associated with the drastic changes that were to occur in her life: new living arrangements, economic advancement, increased status, and generally heightened satisfactions. Careful inquiry as to just when the thought that she might become bald struck her brought merely the response that it had first occurred to her on a short vacation, the first in many years, during which she had enjoyed herself immensely.

One day the patient appeared for her appointment very disturbed—her panic over losing her hair had intensified the night before and frantic ruminations had developed. Suddenly and for no apparent reason the therapist tried to remember what he had done the evening before: he had watched a television rerun of *For Whom the Bell Tolls*. Spontaneously, he inquired if perchance the patient had watched television the night before. She confirmed this and to the amazement of both the patient reported that she had watched the rerun.

Associations led the patient to recall that she had seen *Hiroshima Mon Amour* on her vacation when the obsession arose. Both films, of course, have as central characters girls whose heads were shaven because of traitorous behavior. And therein lay the key to the understanding of the obsession. The patient was deeply imbued with the sense that she was betraying her mother by developing a life of her own—and a successful life at that—and that the punishment that would fit this crime was the public branding symbol of the traitor. Because mother and daughter also had lived in intense competition with each other over which of the two was the more attractive, loss of hair seemed an especially appropriate punishment since it would bring about a loss of feminine charm. A Snow White conflict was expressed and solved by the patient through her new symptom formation. □

Far from being a manifestation of resistance, the obsession was the reflection of the patient's intense effort to capture her inner sense and to communicate it as concretely as possible even though at first the new symptom development could have been misconstrued as resistance (also see Chapter 4).

It must also be remembered that practitioners of psychotherapy are not necessarily oracles of wisdom and therefore the patient's outright rejection of some interpretation or confrontational comment often represents anything but resistance in the traditional sense of the term: it is frequently a sign of remarkable well-being. Indeed it would indicate gross pathology were a patient to accept as gospel truth the therapist's misconceptions or inconsequential and irrelevant interpretations. (Or he would have to be very hostile to the therapist, because in accepting his silly pronouncements and pontifications the patient would allow the therapist to live unchallenged in a fool's paradise.) Yet, despite these considerations and reservations, patients do engage in behavior which interferes drastically with the therapeutic enterprise. Their resistance may be subtle (such as blind and mechanical agreement with interpretations) or open rejection of therapy, leading to forthright termination. And in between one notices roundabout expressions of desire to terminate: for instance, a patient may suddenly develop a subway phobia which prevents further consultations with the therapist.

In any case the phenomenon of resistance was observed, and all behavior which interfered with the uncovering process of therapy and with the avowed aim of therapy—making conscious what was unconscious and helping the patient to substitute sublimation in place of other defenses—was subsumed under this rubric. The phenomenon of resistance had to be taken seriously, and theories of resistance were soon formulated. Because each theorist tried to understand resistance from his particular orientation, every theory of resistance reflected its originator's ideas about the nature of man and man's motivations. Consequently early formulations described resistance as something akin to repression—or more precisely as the handmaiden of repression, a reflection of the general repressive tendencies of patients. These formulations suggested that it was quite understandable and to be anticipated that patients would resist becoming aware of what they were eager to keep repressed.

Freud (1933) admitted that this idea had occurred to him during attempts to fit resistance into the wider framework of his thinking and concluded that "the resistance can only be the manifestation of the ego" (p. 97), because he believed that it was the ego's function to support the individual in the real world against his id impulses which were unacceptable to the world and would get him into difficulties. Therefore the ego had to busy itself and keep impulses repressed. This repressive albeit inadequately performed function of the ego (performed adequately there would be total repression, no symptoms, and no need for therapy) was said to express itself as resistance in the therapeutic exchange.

As Freud (1933) elaborated on his thoughts he ascribed the origin of the resistance less to ego forces and more to those aspects of the ego he called the "super-ego." It is of historical interest to note that this reconceptualization of the meaning and the origins of resistance was responsible for the development of ego-psychology and ego-analysis. They assumed their position in psychoanalytic theory and practice because Freud now felt justified in saying that certain aspects and facets of the "ego and super-ego themselves are unconscious" (p. 98) and hence they too (not only the id, as he had assumed earlier) were to be explored analytically. The idea that both ego and super-ego may have unconscious and pathological features and therefore need therapeutic investigation was by no means Freud's alone. It was expressed in somewhat sketchy fashion by Reich (1928) in the late twenties and developed in his thinking in more detail later:

> Rarely are our patients immediately accessible to analysis, capable of following the fundamental rule and really opening up to the analyst. They cannot immediately have full confidence in a strange person; more importantly years of illness, constant influencing by a neurotic milieu, bad experiences with physicians, in brief the whole secondary warping of the personality have created a situation unfavorable to analysis. *The elimination of this difficulty would not be so hard were it not supported by the character of the patient which is part and parcel of the neurosis* [1949, p. 40; emphasis supplied—E.S.].

This new emphasis on unconscious and potentially pathological aspects of the ego and the super-ego had significant implications for the total theory of resistance and led Freud (1933) to conclude that masochism (the need for punishment) brought about by the patient's severe super-ego is prominently responsible for the development of resistance. The patient is eager to remain neurotic, to suffer and atone for what he considers his guilt; he does not really wish to feel better because he does not believe that he has yet fully atoned. The dissolution of the neurosis would deprive him of opportunities for suffering and atonement. Therefore the patient holds on to his neurotic symptoms, continues his self-punishment, resists the resolution of the neurosis and rejects insights which would bring about a resolution and subsequent alleviation of his condition. This construction led inevitably to a heightened interest in masochism as a dynamic force in human beings and the masochistic character, presumably the resisting character *par excellence*, became a focal object of inquiry.

When Freud (1933) developed this intricate and clever formulation he also insisted that his constructs were really not startling because, after all, they were highly consistent with his general theory and concept of man. Long before he had penned his detailed thoughts on resistance he had advanced the notion that the super-ego incorporated paternal aggression, an outgrowth of the boy's adopting the father's hostility against his son's incestuous tendencies. The very fact that a boy developed a super-ego was evidence, Freud (1924b, 1925c) thought, for his identification with the aggressor, with the jealous, wrathful, and castration-threatening father. In developing the super-ego through this identification process the boy was thought to express the attitude "I am now on father's side" and to continue by saying "Father's anger with me is justified and from now on I shall act as if I were he, as his agent against myself." In becoming this self-punishing agency the super-ego will resist a lessening of punishment and the diminution of neurotic suffering. This identification process Freud (1951) proclaimed as absolutely essential for the development and perpetuation of civilization, but of course discontent was its inevitable consequence. Thus resistance was finally considered as operating in the service of atonement for incestuous impulses, an atonement the patient felt was necessary to prevent castration.

What about women and their resistances? Clearly they cannot be threatened with castration and therefore Freud (1936) thought that they could not develop super-egos similar to those of men. Since they cannot be punished by castration and cannot develop punishing super-egos they also cannot want to atone for their instinctual strivings unless they have never given up the desire for and secret fantasy of being a man and therefore act in their neuroses like men. Penis envy, the fear of loss of a fantasized phallus, and similar constructs had to be developed in order to account for the obvious fact that women do become neurotic and show as much resistance as male patients. Consequently the analysis of penis envy, of its masochistic consequences, and of the inability of some women to "resign" themselves to the lot of womanhood—facts thought central to the etiology of neuroses in women—became singularly important aspects in the analytic treatment of neurotic women (Deutsch, 1925, 1930, 1932; Freud, 1937).[1]

There is an additional fundamental trend in Freud's thinking about resistance, a strain once again very much in harmony with his concept of man. Even though this facet was abandoned by many of his later followers, it is still maintained by some and represents really a *sine qua non* for the system he built. Thanatos, the death instinct, and its expression in the conservative (more aptly, regressive) character of nature and man appear prominently in Freud's theory of resistance. Although Freud (1924a) somewhat haltingly rejected Low's elevation of the death instinct to the Nirvana principle, he did maintain to the end that masochism was older than sadism, that the tendency toward self-elimination preceded outward-directed hostility (1933). And so resistance in Freud's thought was not only intricately associated with repression but was more fundamentally a manifestation of that force which gives rise to repression, was at least in part a derivative of regression. If man's inherent tendencies and strivings are regressive in nature it would, Freud (1933) implied, be reasonable to expect his resistance to the development of new insights because their growth *per se* is antithetical to these basic regressive strivings. Freud in effect suggested that human beings resisted insights not only to avoid *what* they revealed but even more basically because they revealed *anything* at all. If their revealing quality broadened man's horizons and increased his awareness of himself as a differentiated organism, regressive man had to resist them. If man is essentially against himself he must resist all that brings about awareness of himself.

[1] This formulation of the origins of pathology and by implication of the resistance in women has been modified considerably by Thompson (1929a, 1949b, 1949c, 1950b).

Munroe's (1955) appraisal of Freud's theory of resistance as "complex" is obviously correct. Fundamentally, resistance was to Freud a natural phenomenon because it is in line with what he proposed was the inherent nature of man. The neurotic, essentially libidinally fixated character is bound to resist what might dislodge him from his natural tendency toward fixations. These resistances to the awareness of id impulses were said to protect the patient from the consequence acting on them would bring—castration, presumably dreaded by the boy primarily because it would forever preclude the fulfillment of man's ultimate hope: regression through union with the mother or her substitute. In order to maintain some minimal though sublimated thread of hope for this ultimate reunion man must guard against the awareness of his impulses, against acting out these promptings, against the punishment such actions would bring by developing a super-ego which will not only prevent him from such behavior but will also punish him for ever having had forbidden impulses. It would be less than prudent, Freud thought, to expect patients to become readily aware of all this and thereby to jeopardize their elaborate defensive structure.

Different ideas about man's basic strivings gave rise to different theories of resistance. Adler's theory of resistance can be inferred from his general theory of man. Because Adler's man was primarily concerned with and dominated by a quest for superiority and mastery, he implied that resistance will rear its head whenever the patient senses that his feelings of superiority are threatened and that feelings of inferiority are likely to follow. Despite Adler's failure to present anything even approximating in detail Freud's exhaustive theory of resistance it is clear that the two men saw eye to eye on one aspect of the topic: both agreed that resistance is directed against noxious insights. They differed in delineating the ideas and feelings which they thought human beings were eager to keep out of awareness, and because Adler completely rejected Freud's ideas about and emphasis on the death instinct he did not conceive of resistance as a reflection of instinctive regressive processes.

As one examines other authors on "dynamic psychiatry," to use Fromm-Reichmann's (1956) term (perhaps "dynamic psychology" would have been more appropriate), a similarity in thinking becomes apparent: that resistance is a mechanism in the service of avoidance, in the service of keeping buried what the patient hopes will remain buried because he wishes to avoid the anxiety that would ensue were this material not repressed. Thus all schools of thought view resistance as opposition to the unearthing of anxiety- and terror-provoking material. Jung's (1956a) particular theoretical outlook somewhat complicated his theory of resistance, yet he wound up eventually where most other authors had: resistance is a manifestation of dread and dread-inspired repression. He insisted that the unconscious contains not only personal experiences that are repressed because of their anxiety-producing potential but also past collective experiences of mankind. Even though these collective experiences are outside the individual's consciousness, this lack of awareness is not a result of repression. Anxiety, Jung believed, sets in when the person feels that some of the "irrational forces and images" which constitute either his personal or his collective unconscious are about to break into awareness. This invasion is experienced as dangerous because "this possible upsurging of irrational material constitutes a threat to the orderly, stable existence of the individual"—to quote May's (1950, p. 136) apt formulation—is a threat to the niche the person for better or worse has established for himself in this world. Jung believed that resistance opposes awareness of these potentially disruptive feelings:

If we follow the history of a neurosis with attention, we regularly find a critical moment when some problem emerged that was evaded. This evasion is just as natural and just as common a reaction as the laziness, slackness, cowardice, anxiety, ignorance and unconsciousness which are at the back of it. Whenever things are unpleasant, difficult, and dangerous, we mostly hesitate and if possible give them a wide berth. I regard these reasons as entirely sufficient....

The symptomatology of incest, which is undoubtedly

there and which Freud saw, is to my mind a secondary phenomenon, already pathological [1956a, p. 33].

Jung's (1939) suggestion that total avoidance of this upsurge is unfortunate because the wisdom of the collective unconscious used properly is more to be treasured than feared is challenging but irrelevant for the present discussion. Jung (1933) sadly admitted that Western civilization frowns upon and rejects this wisdom of the past, and therefore its upsurge does represent a realistic threat to the individual's existence.

The essential similarities and differences between Freud's thinking and that of more recent theoreticians are even more obvious when one examines Sullivan's position. As Freud understood resistance in terms of his particular theory of nature and man, so Sullivan conceived of resistance from the vantage point of his own theory of human behavior:

> Disregarding for our present purpose the derivation of the term and its earlier definitions, I would say that in general it has come to mean *something that opposes what was presumed to be helpful*. I have no great quarrel with the idea that anxiety may be regarded as resistance. Anxiety is always a handicap to adjustment, or a block to communication in the therapeutic situation or anywhere else. Any concept which carries along with its other qualities some hint that it will reflect unfavorably on the therapist's esteem of the patient will rouse anxiety in the patient and provoke "resistance" [1954, p. 219].

Strikingly akin to Freud's thinking is Sullivan's belief that resistance is engendered by a sense of danger and the idea that danger is sensed when personally unacceptable material is touched upon. The two men, however, are miles apart in their respective definitions as to what constitutes "danger."

A generalization can be developed on the basis of these persistent similarities and differences: the meanings attached to resistance vary from school to school insofar as their respective theories of anxiety differ. To the extent to which all schools of thought believe that the organism is eager to avoid anxiety, to that extent they agree that resistance represents an attempt to stave off anxiety brought about by the therapist's interpretations, confrontational comments, attempts at exploration, or any other procedures experienced as potentially increasing awareness. In orthodox psychoanalytic thinking resistance operates in the service of the neurotic compromise between the essentially regressive forces of the pleasure principle and the propelling demands of the reality principle, operates in the service of maintaining neurosis presumably dear to the patient because it permits an at least partially unsublimated perpetuation of his infantile strivings.

Those who do not accept the Freudian model of neurosis (but insist that neurosis is the reflection of the patient's attempts to survive and to salvage some aspect of his indivuality and sense of dignity under circumstances which demand from him the renunciation of essential aspects of himself) see in the resistance and its particular manifestations the patient's heroic efforts to survive and the particular methods he considers essential to fight successfully. Examined in this framework, the theoretical difference between the two viewpoints is obvious; in the former resistance is viewed as serving regression, in the latter as serving survival. As this latter group sees it, what is neurotic about resistance is the patient's implied inability to appreciate the fact that the valid premises for survival of yesteryear are not necessarily valid today. Sullivan expressed this position:

> For years and years psychiatrists have been struggling to cure this-and-that distortion of living as it came up in patients. Some of these distortions have proven extraordinarily resistant. I am inclined to say, when I don't feel that too many people are hanging on my words, that some of the cures have probably just been the result of mutual exhaustion. And why has this been so? Well, the present indication is very strongly in the direction of the wrong thing having been tackled. There was nothing particularly wrong with that which was allegedly to be cured. *It was a pretty remarkable manifestation of human dexterity in living* [1953, p. 11; emphasis supplied —E.S.].

Sullivan maintained that a good deal of what is considered neurotic is a reflection of "dexterity in living" under trying circumstances. Fromm-Reichmann (1946) has expressed similar thoughts and Thompson, one of Sullivan's most devoted friends and colleagues, often insisted that the main thing she could see wrong with patients was their difficulty in learning that time marches on and that the premises of yesteryear are not the premises of today.[2]

Psychoanalytic theorists who have moved away from the idea that man is dominated by regressive tendencies in general and the death instinct in particular, who have advanced the idea of an originally autonomous ego (Erikson, 1950, 1953; Hartmann, 1939, 1964; Kris, 1952; Rapaport, 1951, 1958), have also come to view resistance in the service of survival—at least by implication. Rapaport (1958) suggested in one of his last theoretical papers that the ego when threatened by id demands calls upon reality forces to combat these attacks, and vice versa; when the ego feels the danger of being swamped by reality demands it calls upon the id forces to help combat oppressive reality features. The only trouble, as he saw it, was the sticky quality of these forces: once called upon, they often behaved like the man who came to dinner—they refused to leave; they tried, indeed, to take over. Pathology, Rapaport believed, was the outcome of this taking-over process by erstwhile allies originally called in by the ego to combat a threatening force. Rapaport held that it would seem reasonable for the ego to resist interpretation concerning the presence of id forces if these id forces had been experienced as so overpowering that reality forces had to be called upon to assist the ego's struggle against them, even though the excessive pressures of these reality forces now themselves became bothersome.

Rapaport's formulation, although somewhat suggestive of reification, comes close to positing that pathology reflects a desire for survival—not simply the desire to sink into oblivion —and therefore resistance can be understood within his framework as opposition to demands to give up what one realistically considers essential for survival. This is precisely the position Fromm-Reichmann (1946) took when she postulated a dialectic process in psychopathology. She saw each pathological manifestation as simultaneously showing a life-enhancing

[2] Personal communication to the author.

feature; she therefore believed that one ought not be surprised by the patient's reluctance to abandon mechanisms which at least at one time helped him in his struggle for survival and in his quest to maintain a sense of continuity (1952).

In the evolution of psychotherapeutic thinking resistance has come to be regarded *less* a reflection of an inherent and inevitable regressive pull when the educative process has failed to counteract it early and instead created libidinal fixation points through too much and/or too little frustrations in the rearing process; resistance is now viewed by many *more* as an expression of the patient's conviction that he has found some way, no matter how painful otherwise, to minimize anxiety and maintain some semblance of self-esteem, dignity, and life. If the latter position is accepted some further implications are clear: resistance reflects both the patient's disbelief in an alternative way of life, reflects his desperate holding on to familiar self-esteem-furthering operations and at the same time his intense fear that any other approach to living would be self-esteem-shattering. Some clinical illustrations of this formulation follow:

☐ A fairly well-to-do young man always made it a point to be quite far behind in his payments to the therapist. Neither economic difficulties nor strong desires to inconvenience the therapist were apparent; as a matter of fact, at one point when the patient thought that his lateness actually inconvenienced the therapist he settled his bill immediately, only to fall back in his payments once again. Inquiry revealed that he systematically delayed paying bills owed to people of whom he seemed fond. His telephone bills, electricity bills, and similar obligations were settled rapidly. But he always delayed paying his rent; characteristically, the owner of the house in which he lived was a close friend of long standing. Similarly, he delayed paying the lawyer who handled the legal aspects of his business—a classmate from college and a dear friend also.

He fiercely resisted the therapeutic investigation of these delays, grew extremely sulky and angry when the therapist tried to examine all this, threatened to terminate, felt that "nobody really needs to worry—I am good for the money, I'll never walk out on any obligation; I don't know what all the fuss is about." Eventually after many a stormy session and accompanied by intense anxiety the picture unfolded. He lived with the deep conviction that people would remain concerned about him and continue seeing him only if he could somehow keep them "interested" in him and the only way he felt he could do this was to owe them money—then they would continue dealing with him; otherwise they would just not care and drop him as a friend, as a patient, or as a client. ☐

Discussion of the origins of this unconsciously harbored conviction, in a way reminiscent of what Sullivan (1953) called "malevolent transformation," is unnecessary. The transference elements in such behavior will be dealt with in Chapter 11 when the relationship between resistance and transference is discussed. This illustration presents evidence for the observation that resistance, reflected in his delaying tactics and reluctance to examine its meaning, served the patient in two ways: it was designed to maintain behavior which seemed to the patient life-furthering, and at the same time to avoid the self-esteem-damaging awareness of its dynamics and origins.

Another illustration will clarify the problem in a different context:

☐ A young married woman had sought psychotherapeutic help for a variety of reasons, among them the hope that she would become capable of freeing herself from an extramarital love affair which she claimed had caused her a great deal of emotional anguish. She had ruminated in her therapeutic sessions for weeks about her inability to break with her lover. Yet her resistance to discussing the affair only grew in intensity when the therapist asked her to describe some of the mechanical details in their arrangements for rendezvous, because it seemed to him that they carried on right under the noses of their respective mates and he had some (as it turned out, erroneous) notion that the two were looking for trouble— hoping to be found out, seeking scandal and perhaps divorce.

The patient insisted that this was not so, that the arrangements were "foolproof" but vehemently refused to divulge the specific nature of this "foolproof" set-up. She said that she was afraid that the therapist would reveal the arrangements and then she would really be in trouble. (The transference element need not be elaborated upon here.) Finally, and with utmost reluctance and terror, she disclosed their methods for meeting. They were certainly ingenious, but the degree of anxiety associated with these mechanics seemed quite disproportionate to the anxiety aroused in revealing them, especially in view of the fact that discussion of the affair itself was not anywhere near as panic-producing as the discussion of the mechanics.

The details cannot be revealed here but it can be stated that they included behavior on the part of her lover which must have been extremely humiliating to him, made him seem ridiculous to the therapist and, it could be established eventually, to the patient also. It was also established that the patient enjoyed seeing her "lover" in this absurd and ridicule-provoking situation more than she enjoyed the affair itself. This was indeed what she had resisted: the discovery of her hostility to this man and how she relished the belittling of people she claimed to love deeply. □

Once again one notes resistance in the service of behavior which the patient deems essential for survival, in this instance the perpetuation of expressions of hostility through subtle humiliation. Humiliation and self-humiliation had been persistent integrative modes in her family. To humiliate was an all-important pursuit for the patient because she felt that she would be "swallowed up" were she not to maintain "integrity" somehow; this was to be accomplished by humiliating others. The very thought of abandoning such "integrity"-enhancing acts filled her with despair because she felt that then she would have no way to salvage some self-esteem.[3]

[3] In a similar vein patients often resist the exploration of what they claim is a very bothersome personality feature: their shyness. Frequently they claim that they "fear rejection" and therefore are "naturally" shy. Of course, under the respectable mantle of shyness they engage in a good deal of rejecting behavior of their own, reject others who extend their

The basic idea is that the patient experiences his particular neurotic behavior as the only possible way of maintaining himself, despairs about the absence of an alternative, sees no alternative in survival, and will therefore resist any efforts which may interfere with his "single" way of sustaining life. Since investigation of the presumably anguish-producing symptoms or problems might bring in its wake interference with if not outright dissolution of specific anxiety-avoiding integrative methods, resistance to this inquiry is essential lest in the absence of such integrations—so far as the patient can see, the only self-respecting methods of relating open to him—despair takes over. (The term *despair* is used here in the sense of complete doubt that an alternative is available and not in the sense in which some existentialist writers, notably Tillich, have employed it. The theoretical relationship between the existential and the present use of the term will be clarified later in this chapter.)

Just as resistance reflects the patient's despairing conviction that an alternative in living is impossible, so the therapist's persistent efforts in investigating resistance indicate his lack of despair, his conviction that there is an alternative in living, experiencing, and dealing with others. The therapist's attack upon resisting behavior, no matter how anxiety-producing to the patient, is his vote of confidence in the patient's ability to find an alternative and therefore ultimately a very reassuring process. By investigating the resistance and uncovering the patient's secret convictions, the mainsprings of his neurotic life, the therapist expresses his deep belief that these underlying premises cause the patient's anguish, that they are faulty, and that the patient can grow to develop new foundations for living. Thus the investigation of resistance is really the exploration of the deepest layers of the patient's psychic life because it is an inquiry into and an attempt to help him redevelop the unconscious premises of his existence.

For these reasons Rogers' (1951) position on the topic of

---

hand to them and in doing so express their own hostility. The investigation of such "shyness" can prove extraordinarily provocative of resistance, for the patient has found a socially acceptable method of venting his anger and is loath to become aware of it and to give it up.

resistance is untenable. Rogers saw clearly the intricate relationship between anxiety and resistance, saw that any procedure that challenged the patient's security would produce anxiety and consequently would be opposed by the patient. He therefore proposed a therapeutic approach which did not challenge the patient's established methods of finding security; he concentrated upon "reflecting" the patient's expressed feelings and suggested that in his own time the patient will become aware of his feelings. In this process of gaining clarity about his feelings the patient was said to develop constructive ways of relating to others. There is a good deal of merit in this theory but it is very much to be doubted that a human being can reorganize the very foundations of his existence, can give up the premises by which he lives, abandon one *Weltanschauung* and develop a new one in emotional and not just intellectual terms, experience a loss of old moorings and familiar roots, and do all this without being anxious. Rogers has full confidence that man can develop new foundations, that he can go through revolutionary changes because Rogers has complete faith in man's inherent and fundamental strength. Rogers is in good company; his thinking is similar to that expressed by Goethe in *Faust* when (in the Prologue in Heaven) he has his God say to Mephistopheles:

> A good man in his darkling aspiration
> Remembers the right road throughout his quest.
> [Kaufmann, 1962, p. 89.]

The fundamental optimism posited earlier as the indispensable ingredient of the psychotherapeutic enterprise is fully reflected in Goethe's thought and Rogers' theory. Nor is the possibility of growth questioned here. What is questioned is whether man can grow, can give up his neurotic foundation in living for another basis of life without the active presentation of such an alternative; whether man can exchange dissociation, self-restriction, and self-oblivion as a way of life for self-awareness, openness to experience, and emergence without the active presentation of this type of fulfillment as an alternative; and above all, whether man can do all this without experiencing anxiety in the process.

The presentation of this alternative implicit in the therapist's behavior, in his readiness to hear, in his attitude (which willy-nilly challenges the premises of the patient) will inevitably cause the patient conflict and hence anxiety and resistance. If neurotic solutions are "remarkable manifestations of dexterity in living" even though their premises are not valid any more, it is rather unlikely that human beings who have found such useful devices for survival will be willing to abandon them without trepidation. The therapist cannot help but become anxiety-provoking because his behavior is a thorn in the side of the patient's orientation. By being a therapist he states implicitly that there is an alternative, and this statement challenges the patient's world system. Of course, it may be argued with justification that were the patient totally enamored of his neurosis and its survival value he would not come to therapy, that he must have already experienced some dissatisfaction with his life, otherwise he would not look for therapy (see Chapter 5). This conclusion is correct but does not negate the possibility that both orientations live side by side, that the patient is ambivalent toward his own neurosis, is not only troubled by his neurosis but also feels somewhat pulled to neurotic behavior and integrations because they were life-saving and are still expected to support life.

While resistance represents his desire to hold on to time-tested aids in survival and reveals his doubt that there are other methods for maintaining himself, the patient's continuation with therapy despite his doubts indicates his hope and faith that he can find an alternative. The therapist, in allying himself with the patient's hope, inevitably becomes party to the inner struggle between this hope and despair; he thereby activates anxiety and resistance. This alliance of course requires the therapist's conviction that life does offer various choices; were he to believe differently it would be ludicrous to hope that his patient would give up that faithful servant, the neurotic road to survival. The analysis of resistance can proceed fruitfully only when the therapist, although capable of empathizing with the patient's restrictive view of his existence and the choices available to him, harbors a totally different vision, for only then will he have the courage and fortitude necessary to withstand the patient's resistance and continue the therapeutic investigation despite the patient's constant obstruction of the inquiry. The analysis of resistance is therefore the therapist's expression of faith in an alternative in living, the patient's giving up resistance is his admission that he sees such a possibility. The therapist's own despair is the force which most potently reinforces the patient's resistance. To the extent to which the therapist unconsciously despairs about his own life and/or the patient's life will resistance appear heightened because his despair will subtly prevent the therapist from analyzing the patient's despair as it expresses itself in resistance, and the patient will not feel free to emerge from his neurotic dexterities in living. The following clinical example will illustrate the important role of the therapist's despair in the therapeutic transaction:

□ A young and relatively inexperienced therapist had worked with a markedly depressed woman who masked her depression with much psychopathic and overtly cruel behavior. Her steadfast resistance to any real self-investigation made him seek the help of a colleague. He reported some typical behavior of the patient to him. She would make sure to inform her husband of an affair she was having, berating and generally humiliating him. For his own reasons, he was very "indulgent" and went so far as to make sure to leave a hall light on when she was out with her lover so that when she returned from a rendezvous she would not stumble. She also treated the lover shabbily. She ridiculed him mercilessly, exploited him financially, demanded his total attention. One day she informed him that she was pregnant and was quite sure that he was the father, a statement he accepted despite his knowledge that they had had intercourse only once, that he had used a contraceptive, and that the time at which coitus had taken place (about six months earlier) was at a point in her cycle which made fertilization quite improbable. Yet he was frantic. After the patient had observed him squirm and in hysterics, she laughingly told him that it was all a hoax, that he was "too stupid" for words and berated him in similar fashion.

The supervising therapist asked how the "lovers" did spend

their time together, coitus and other sexual contacts being of minimal interest to them. The therapist apparently had wondered also, had inquired, and had learned that what the patient relished in the relationship was spending the night huddled up against her "friend," clutching him and literally warming her body on his. The patient's enormous dependence and her strong need for support and cuddling became obvious despite her flamboyant and grandiose attempts to act like a big shot and a most "independent cuss." This impression was supported by the supervising therapist's sudden visual association of an advertisement for a Tennessee Williams movie playing on Broadway at the time. The advertisement for *Baby Doll* depicted a young but rather grown girl huddled up in a crib. The supervisor commented to the therapist that this was how the patient was likely to feel—infantile, helpless, and cold, feelings she tried to obscure with all kinds of bravado.

The therapist sat for a moment in silence and then shook his head in amazement, commenting that the patient had reported a dream in their last session, that he had meant to discuss the dream but it had somehow slipped his mind. The patient's dream was that she had come for an appointed hour to the therapist but had brought some tiny little girl along, an infant she could not identify. While she was sitting in the waiting room, the therapist had come out of his office, had looked at her without recognizing her, had wandered around in the waiting room for a short while, and then had returned to his office, closed the door behind him and had never asked her in. The patient felt very hurt, left, and woke up.

The story in its broad outlines was quite clear: the patient had wanted to expose some aspect of herself, specifically her infantile nature, but she had also felt that the therapist did not want to see it. Discussion with him validated this impression. Yes, he was quite reluctant to see the dependence of this woman and admitted to himself his doubts concerning her capacity really to change. He admitted he had despaired about her capacity for growth. The patient's resistance was a reflection of her despair which was shared by the therapist. □

A general discussion of why therapists often despair appears in Chapter 12.

Two more points must be dealt with. First, it can be noted that the methods a patient employs in resisting may often give a clear clue to the particular modes he has developed in his attempts to maintain some integrity. In broadest terms, one can distinguish between passive and active resistance, between a subtle and disguised avoidance of the threat and a more direct and vehement offense as the best defense. Thus one encounters people who habitually "have nothing to say," who seemingly listen to what is said by another—in this case the therapist—but find it impossible to respond or to "carry the ball" themselves. They seem to disappear into thin air. Others express agreement and then add material seemingly supportive of some interpretation; but on closer inspection such "corroboration" often turns out to be a denial of the therapist's understanding. Still others have their inevitable "but" always handy and in employing "buts," "howevers," and the like deftly deny the utility of the therapist. There is a host of more direct evasions of the therapist, thereby avoiding the threat which self-understanding brings in its wake: the possibility of losing what has proved useful in maintaining existence. Whatever the method of resistance, it reflects the preferred operation in survival in the face of what is experienced as threat:

☐ A young woman, whose romance with one of her colleagues had just been terminated by his marriage to somebody to whom he had been engaged for a long time, lamented her sadness and upset about this turn of events, although she had known of the engagement long before she became romantically interested in the young man. It had not been the first time she had experienced such "disappointments" and the therapeutic investigations had focused on her need either to actually feel miserable or at least try to give the world the impression that everything went wrong in her life.

A compulsive eater, she was extremely obese and she did her utmost to dress unattractively. Work offered her minimal satisfaction but she insisted that she was trapped in her job. She had terminated her education under some pretense shortly before earning the advanced degree necessary to secure a—to her—presumably desirable position and at the same time found all kinds of "reality" reasons which made the return to school and completion of training impossible.

She had resisted vehemently the idea that she had a stake in her "unhappiness" even though there was good evidence that the sadder she appeared in her home the more she was "appreciated," and that any sign of competence had been met with sarcasm, ridicule, and manifestations of outright annoyance. At the end of the hour following her boy friend's marriage she said that all these discussions made little sense and that she felt very "discouraged and hopeless."

As she left the therapist commented that these feelings might well be the ultimate triumph of hostility but that indeed this would be a rather Pyrrhic victory. He referred to a frequent theme in their discussions, one she vehemently resisted: the idea that her resistance was an attempt to make the therapist useless and ineffectual while at the same time she tried to ingratiate herself and gain approval by remaining pitiable and pathetic. Within half an hour the patient called the therapist to tell him that on the way out she had broken into tears, had known how right he had been in his appraisal, and that she really hadn't felt hopeless at all. On the contrary, she had felt more hopeful than ever because she had felt that now she could really start anew. She added that she could not bear telling this to the therapist directly, that she had been tempted to run back into the office to say all this to him, but that she could not bring herself to do so. She admitted that she did not want to talk about it the next time and her calling, while on the one hand an effort to break the resistance by facing something squarely, was at the same time an attempt to avoid direct investigation.

Needless to say, the therapist did not permit the issue to lie dormant and in the course of subsequent sessions the patient was able to contact a part of her determination not to agree, as if any agreement openly expressed meant the loss of any shred of integrity. Any agreement with the therapist was experienced as identical with agreeing openly to the negative appraisals and expectations she had experienced in childhood. ☐

This illustration demonstrates the intricate and intimate relationship between resistance and transference, a theoretical issue to be discussed in the following chapter. The patient's method of resisting by direct denial paralleled a long-established and preferred way of surviving in the parental home. She had always openly denied and rejected most vociferously the negative appraisals that had been offered, maintaining that all was well with her, that she was adequate and happy, even though—perhaps because—in her day-to-day living she fulfilled the negative expectations placed upon her.

Finally, resistance, it was maintained, is the reflection of despair and despair was defined as disbelief in an alternative. The concept and the sense of despair have appeared prominently in the writings of existentialist philosophers and their thinking on despair has bearing on the view presented here. Sartre, commenting on despair, offered this succinct definition:

> As for despair, the term has a very simple meaning. It means that we shall confine ourselves only upon what depends upon our will. . . . When Descartes said, "Conquer yourself rather than the world," he meant essentially the same thing [1957, p. 29].

Fundamentally, says Sartre, there is no alternative, "no exit" from the realization that man defines his own meaning by his actions and the way he leads his life; in this respect he cannot hope for an alternative which will relieve him of ultimate responsibility. Despair in this sense is the recognition of the essential meaninglessness of life and the existential responsibility for giving meaning to one's being. As a Protestant theologian, Tillich had to arrive ultimately at conclusions somewhat different from those advanced by the atheist Sartre, but he approached the problem of despair in similar fashion:

> If life is as meaningless as death, if guilt is as questionable as perfection, if being is no more meaningful than nonbeing, on what can one base the courage to be?

The answer must accept its [the courage to be's] precondition, the state of meaninglessness. It is not an answer if it demands the removal of this state; for that is just what cannot be done. He who is in the grip of doubt and meaninglessness cannot liberate himself from this grip; but he asks for an answer within not outside the situation of his despair. He asks for the ultimate of what we have called the "courage of despair." There is only one possible answer, if one does not try to escape the question: namely, that the acceptance of despair is in itself faith and on the boundary line of the courage to be. In this situation the meaning of life is reduced to despair about the meaning of life [1952, pp. 174–75].

Existential despair, says Tillich, is the result of a man's recognition that only he can give meaning to his life and that there is no alternative to this responsibility for self-definition; the full acceptance of this immutable fact of life, Tillich maintains, is an act of faith in itself because it implies a man's faith in his capacity to define and assert himself. This recognition and faith lead to his ultimate awareness that in his pursuit of self-definition, self-affirmation, and self-assertion he can choose among the infinite varieties of human activity. In effect both Sartre and Tillich exclaim: "I have no alternative to affirming myself—but this opens to me many choices in self-affirmation!"

The patient's resistance (which denies his ability to affirm himself by rejecting the fact that he has made personal choices based on personal though unconscious motivations) is a struggle against the awareness that his life has no predetermined meaning and therefore demands his personal self-definition. Resistance as one encounters it in the psychotherapeutic process obliterates the fundamental despair about which Sartre and Tillich write. In rejecting insights and in avoiding self-understanding—in resisting—the patient expresses his preference for the despair implicit in the statement "I have no choice" over the despair inherent in the recognition "I have all choices." It is here that the comments on the meaning of resistance offered in the preceding pages of this chapter meet Tillich's thoughts. To the extent to which the patient resists does he try to avoid the knowledge that he *has chosen* and in having chosen *has self-affirmed* himself, even if his choices no longer rest on valid premises. His resistance denotes his unwillingness to acknowledge that *he and nobody else has chosen* for him, that *he has affirmed himself* even if this particular self-affirmation has led to at least partial self-denial, has led to his giving up part of himself in order to survive at least in crippled form.

Resistance in psychotherapy is then the patient's refusal to admit freedom despite the obvious fact that he has always chosen (also see Kaiser, 1955). The intensity of his strenuous disavowal of past and present freedom will vary directly with the patient's conviction that he must not admit that he has affirmed himself or affirms himself now, be it ever so minimal, inadequate, and ineffectual. In resisting the patient not only agrees with Sartre (1956) when he cried out that man was "condemned" to be free and with Buber's (1926) observation that freedom is a "cross" one must bear, but he goes further in maintaining "And to know that one is free is worse than not knowing it." (Also see Chapters 1 and 3.)

The analysis of resistance is the therapist's attempt to help his patient abandon the despair of *no* choice and instead to accept the despair of *all* choices so that he may ultimately acknowledge that he has made choices and in so doing has tried to affirm himself. The therapist, in pursuing the analysis of resistance, affirms his conviction that human beings can live productively with the knowledge that ultimate responsibility for self-definition inevitably rests within the person and not outside him, and that life with this desperate knowledge is bearable.

The therapist must be fully aware that even though this knowledge is "bearable" it is tremendously difficult to bear. One can hardly expect a person not to resist the knowledge that he is condemned to be free and that he must bear his cross of freedom and responsibility. The particular insights avoided by the patient in his resistance are insights about the particular self-denials he has chosen to impose upon himself in the hope of accomplishing simultaneously two ends: somehow to affirm himself, and at the same time to obscure from himself and others the knowledge that he has engaged in such at least partial self-definition. The premises for his particular modes of self-affirmation and his desire to obscure such self-assertion may have been quite appropriate at one time; in the neurotic they are inappropriate today.

▶ *Summary* ◀

1. Resistance expresses the patient's attempts to remain unaware of anxiety-provoking aspects within him.

2. Since each theory maintains that resistance occurs when the therapeutic investigation touches upon crucial anxiety-provoking conflicts, there are as many theories of resistance as there are theories about the origins of anxiety.

3. Because Freud thought that neurosis was an attempt to maintain regressive tendencies without incurring punishment, he believed that resistance worked in the service of salvaging regressive instinctual and incestuous id impulses. Others who have a different view of neurosis maintain that resistance is an effort to hold on to those security operations and integrative methods which have proved themselves at one time at least partially life-furthering.

4. Whatever the patient's motivations, the analysis of the resistance is geared toward his gaining awarenesss of them and the development of his knowledge that all his behavior is motivated personally, that all his actions reflect his attempts to define himself and that he ultimately is responsible for all he does and all he experiences.

5. In attempting to break through the wall of resistance with which the patient fends off these insights, the therapist expresses his conviction that human beings can and must live with this knowledge, even if it is painful, because the type of despair caused by it is infinitely preferable to the despair of neurosis.

The Concept of Transference

ANY DISCUSSION OF THE TRANSFERENCE PHENOMENON MUST start with Freud's definition:

> What are transferences? They are the new editions or facsimiles of the tendencies and phantasies which are aroused and made conscious during the progress of the analysis; but they have this peculiarity, which is characteristic of their species, that they replace some earlier person by the person of the physician. To put it another way: a whole series of psychological experiences is revived, not as belonging to the past, but as applying to the person of the physician at the present moment [1905a, p. 116].

Freud proposed that his patients were capable of effecting a substitution and of reacting to the analyst as if he were really another person or a conglomeration of people they had met earlier in their lives. He cited illustrations of this substitution process; so have innumerable observers of human behavior since. The examples in the literature and surveys of this topic such as Wolstein's (1954, 1960) present irrefutable evidence for the existence of such a substituting tendency.

Relatively soon various theoreticians—including Freud—found it unnecessary to question the validity of their observations and became increasingly concerned with understanding the origins and foundations of this substitution process. Eventually their theory of transference, this curious reactivation of attitudes once harbored toward others and now brought into a relationship with a totally different person, was delicately integrated into Freud's system of thought and the phenomenon explained on the basis of formulations he had advanced earlier. In turn the explanation was used to advance new concepts and to bolster already existing theoretical propositions. Some of the concepts utilized in the explanation of transference have already been touched upon in Chapters 1 and 2, but it is necessary to mention them briefly once again because they are intricately associated with the classic psychoanalytic thinking on transference.

A consistent theme in Freud's theorizing was the idea that matter has a basic tendency to return to previous states of organization and that man exhibits this tendency to return to past states in both physical and behavioral terms, that man tends to repeat previous acts over and over again. Zoological observations and data collected by comparative embryologists had been called upon and marshaled as evidence of an inherent regressive striving in physical life. The assertion that "ontogeny recapitulates phylogeny" had been accepted uncritically and was considered proof for the universality of such regressive strivings in nature. Animal behavior, notably migratory patterns of birds and fish (including the peculiar spawning behavior of the salmon), seemed to Freud (1933) supportive of the hypothesis that in behavior as in physical existence a regressive tendency inevitably operated, and he decided to refer to this tendency as the *repetition compulsion* (1942).

This repetition compulsion became *prima facie* evidence for the assertion that nature is fundamentally conservative. If all nature were conservative, Freud could conclude that the nature of the libido would also be controlled by such conservative tendencies; it would be perfectly reasonable to conclude that libidinal organization and attachments tend to exhibit this conservatism, that they too tend to regress and in regressing repeat previous states. The whole theory of psychosexual development was based on this idea. Fixations were thought to reflect this natural tendency of the libido to linger rather than to advance. So the amount of libido available for mature genital life varied with the parents' ability to prod the child on, to prevail on him to give up, albeit reluctantly, early stages of his libido utilization. Only prodding could move the organism; without it he would remain fixed and fixated, would regress rather than advance. The educative process was viewed as a system of incentives (rewards or punishments) designed to move the reluctant child toward maturity.

A careful course had to be steered in this educative prodding: regrettable as it seemed, some libidinal gratification had to be allowed at each stage in development because, unless some such gratification was offered, the libido would balk altogether and refuse to make progress. Equally, if not even more important, libidinal frustration was also necessary lest all motivation for progressing and moving on be lacking. Only frustration, carefully controlled and administered in appropriate dosages, would stir man out of his lethargy. The function of the educative process was to help the individual overcome his inherent regressive tendencies, to sublimate them so that he might move on toward genital primacy or what Erikson (1950) has called generativity (see also Chapters 1 and 7).

It was assumed that in the case of the neurotic something went awry in this frustration-satisfaction sequence, that his regressive tendencies were therefore never adequately sublimated and consequently would appear in his neurosis. But these tendencies would appear not only in the distorted and disguised forms of symptoms but also in the patient's attitudes toward the analyst. Transference phenomena became dramatic manifestations of the generally regressive and repetition tendencies of neurotic man. Classic psychoanalytic theory proposed that this struggle between the unsublimated pull toward regression and opposing reality demands and ego as well as super-ego forces rages in all neuroses. In the analytic process, it was suggested, one witnessed this conflict between man's desire to maintain id tendencies and his fears of disastrous consequences if they were maintained. The patient was said to relive this ancient conflict with the analyst directly and more openly than would be possible in his daily life and was therefore likely to reveal his instinctual id impulses in purer form. The expression of id impulses toward the analyst in therapy was considered reflective of attitudes originally maintained toward significant persons in the patient's past.

Several questions suggest themselves immediately. First, why should the patient engage in such a re-enactment? A variety of reasons were offered. The regressive tendency of human beings, markedly heightened in the neurotic, was immediately suggested, and since it was said that the neurotic had by definition failed to develop critical ego functions, it would be relatively easy for him to substitute uncritically one or several individuals of his past for the person of the present, the therapist. The generally permissive and encouraging attitude of the therapist would allow the patient to let his deeply hidden impulses and feelings come to the fore. Furthermore, the patient's knowledge that it was the function of the analyst to help him abandon his infantile strivings (such a renunciation in itself was considered counter to nature) would resurrect deeply hidden negative feelings toward parental figures who also were at one time agents opposed to his infantile desires. Finally, the deliberately induced mystery which was to surround the analyst (the patient was not to know anything about him, was not even to look at him during his session) was thought to facilitate a rearousal of the feelings of awe which the patient had presumably experienced in his childhood relations with his parents. These factors were said to combine in bringing about a relatively unhampered resurgence of instinctual tendencies and attitudes—the childhood neurosis. Early orthodox psychoanalytic theory proposed that making the infantile conflicts accessible to consciousness and the resultant reduction of repressive efforts would lead to an abatement of symptoms (see also Chapters 13 and 14).

Another question remains: What is the precise nature of the instinctual impulses as they come to the fore in less disguised form in the therapeutic process? The answers Freud (1905a) and his students provided were equally obvious and in keeping with the general theory Freud had developed. Generally the instincts that would reveal themselves were thought to be regressive in nature, primitive in striving, and clearly infantile. More specifically, they would center around the core problem of human existence as Freud saw it—the Oedipus conflict. The primitive, instinctual, and libidinal attachment of the individual to the mother would come into the open and be transferred to the analyst. Old incestuous cravings, hostile impulses toward those who had interfered with them, and fear of punishment by castration were said to come to the fore. Because the Oedipus complex was the core of all neuroses, indeed was the central problem each individual had to face and solve, and because man's regressive tendencies forced him to return to this central problem until he had solved it, Freud (1914c) thought that this nucleus of man's dilemma would appear inevitably and in pure culture during the course of analysis. This formulation was considered valid for men and women, but in the case of the female the matter would be a bit more complicated since the Oedipus conflict in the girl was understood in more complex terms (see also Chapter 10). And so in the transference the patient was said to relive with the therapist his infantile Oedipal neuroses, the original inner traumas (impulses), and the dangerous outer realities (castration threat) which demanded the repression of instinctual impulses. For these reasons, the transference reactions were looked upon as vehicles which afforded patient and analyst a view into the patient's past and a glimpse of the forces responsible for the development of his neurosis (Freud, 1905a).

The patient's feelings toward important people around him during the critical Oedipal period and the reactive modes he had learned during that period were said to come to the fore in his transference behavior. Expression of incestuous promptings, hostility against the frustrator of these strivings, and defensive counter-reactions to avoid tabooed impulses and the anticipated castration threat were expected. Thus, in orthodox psychoanalytic theory transference was defined specifically as the patient's reliving of the Oedipal situation during analytic therapy (Thompson, 1950).

This conceptualization explains why Freud (1904b, 1911,

1914b) for most of his life and many of his followers thought that the psychotic was not amenable to analytic therapy. (Only rarely did Freud [1904b] concede the possibility that psychotics might be amenable to modified psychoanalytic treatment.) If the etiology of neurosis hinges on something going awry in the sublimation of the Oedipal impulses and if the development of Oedipal attachments and hostilities is contingent upon the child's emergence from pre-Oedipal stages—periods presumably characterized by an absence of object attachments and the dominance of primary narcissism—only those patients who in their libidinal development had progressed to the Oedipal level could develop attitudes toward the analyst and had something to relive in the analytic exploration.

Because the Oedipal conflict is the inevitable struggle the individual faces as he emerges fully into an era of object-relatedness and starts on the road to socialization and because neuroses are developmental failures during this period (due to prior fixations), the central problem of psychoanalytic treatment is the removal of these Oedipal problems during the analysis of the transference. But in instances of pre-Oedipal fixations so extremely severe that the individual has never reached the Oedipal stage or if so only minimally (psychoses), analytic treatment was considered impossible or at best very difficult because transference reactions are then either absent altogether or extremely tenuous. Therefore Freud (1922a) referred to disorders called in contemporary psychological language neuroses as the *transference neuroses* and spoke of the *narcissistic* disorders when he discussed what are classified today as psychoses.

The Freudian approach to the concept of transference rests squarely on the basic assumption of an inborn and fundamental regressive tendency in man and the assumption that this tendency expresses itself prominently in the repetition compulsion. No matter how one may try to get around it, the death instinct enters significantly here. The experimental evidence on Thanatos and the tension-reduction hypothesis was summarized in Chapter 2 and it was concluded that little evidence could be found supporting the insistence that such an inherent regressive pull operates in living organisms. Nobody can deny that human beings engage in repetitive behavior, but what is needed is an explanation of this repetition phenomenon without taking refuge in Thanatos.

White's (1959) concept of "competence" lends itself well for such an alternate explanatory formulation and his point that Hendrick's (1942) thinking had followed similar lines is well taken. In proposing an "instinct to master" Hendrick had advanced a construct which also lent itself well to the understanding of the repetition compulsion and the understanding of transference without resorting to concepts such as a "regressive pull" or the death instinct. The thinking of some of the proponents of so-called ego-psychology, notably Rapaport's (1958) ideas, also raised the possibility of understanding repetitive behavior and transference phenomena as a person's efforts to maintain his independent ego-apparatuses and not simply as expressions of some regressive pull. But it should be fully recognized that the usual point of departure for ego-psychologists is a statement by Freud which is indicative neither of his willingness to abandon his ideas about inherent regression nor suggestive of a new emphasis by Freud on "independent" forces active in ego development. If anything, this famous passage in one of Freud's last papers expresses an adherence to the concept of the repetition compulsion and denies the ego any "independent" strength:

> But we shall not overlook the fact that id and ego are originally one; nor does it imply any mystical overvaluation of heredity if we think it credible that, even before the ego has come into existence, the lines of development, trends and reactions which it will later exhibit are already laid down for it. The psychological peculiarities of families, races and nations, even in their attitude to analysis, allow for no other explanation. Indeed, more than this: analytic experience has forced on us the conviction that even particular psychical contents, such as symbolism, have no other sources than hereditary transmission, and researches in various fields of social anthro-

pology, make it plausible to suppose that other, equally specialized precipitates left by early human development are also present in the archaic heritage [1937, pp. 240–41].

Aside from the interesting similarity of these ideas with those Jung (1956b) advanced, Freud also expanded the repetition compulsion to include the ego's compulsive return to hereditarily determined reactions. His thought is therefore a reaffirmation and an extension of the repetition compulsion's power.

But if so little that is substantive can be found in support of the repetition compulsion as an expression of inherent regressive tendencies; and if, as Schachtel (1959) suggests, repetitive behavior can be explained more parsimoniously and more in line with empirically verifiable facts as a manifestation of a progressive trend in human nature, what is to become of the foundations of the transference phenomenon? If lack of evidence forces one to abandon these foundations, what new constructs can be substituted, what constructs are more in accord with accumulated data? Of course, one could do as Rogers did, and insist that transference is some kind of artifact, a behavioral manifestation observed only when the therapist threatens the patient and provokes his anxiety. Advancing his tentative ideas about the origins of transference behavior cautiously, Rogers suggested:

> When the client is evaluated and comes to realize clearly in his own experience that this evaluation is more accurate than any he has made himself, then self-confidence crumbles, and a dependent relationship is built up. When the therapist is experienced as "knowing more about me than I know myself," then there appears to the client to be nothing to do but to hand over the reins of his life into the more competent hands. This is likely to be accompanied by comfortable feelings of relief and liking, but also at times by hatred for the person who has thus become so all-important [1951, pp. 215–16].

It is this threat, real or fancied, that the therapist will take over which Rogers held responsible for the development of clinically observable transference reaction. He postulated nothing concerning inherent regressive tendencies and suggested that patients can overcome their transference attitudes with relative ease when they learn that they are not judged or evaluated but are genuinely accepted. Then the client "must" see that the attitudes he imagines the therapist harbors are really his and consequently he will give up his own tendency to project and to distort the reactions of others. Here is how Rogers put it:

> Why is this accomplished so quickly and so readily? It would appear that one reason is that the therapist has so completely put aside the self of ordinary interaction that there is no shred of evidence upon which to base the projection. For four interviews this woman has experienced understanding and acceptance—and nothing else. There has been no evidence that the therapist is trying to "size her up," diagnose her, evaluate her scientifically, judge her morally. There is no evidence that he approves or disapproves of anything she does—of her behavior, present or past, of the topics she chooses to discuss, of the way she presents them, of her inability to express herself, of her silences, of the interpretations she gives to her own behavior. Consequently when she feels that the therapist is passing a moral judgement upon her, and when this feeling too is accepted, there is nothing upon which this projection can hang. It *must* be recognized as coming from herself, since every evidence of her senses makes it plain that it does not come from the therapist, and the complete lack of immediate threat in the situation makes it unnecessary to insist upon the feeling in defiance of the evidence of her senses [1951, p. 203].

One admires Rogers' unfailing confidence in the capacity of human beings to listen to their own reason and to the evidence of their senses if they are only given half a chance to do so. But other authors have reported far less gratifying results, patients far less willing to listen to their senses; even Rogers reports disappointing cases.

Thus Rogers dealt with transference reactions and explained the phenomenon without resorting to such concepts as the repetition compulsion, inherent regressive tendencies, and similar constructs. But while he accounted for the circumstances under which it manifests itself, he did not account for the bases of the transference potential and failed to offer a metapsychology of transference. His central theme is "threat" but Rogers did not explain why under circumstances of threat the organism resorts to repetitive behavior and to transference reactions except somewhat indirectly in his general theory of personality. There he maintained that *"The organism has one basic tendency and striving—to actualize, and enhance the experiencing organism"* (1951, p. 487). If this be the basic tendency of the organism, he must also have understood transference as an expression of this striving. It can easily be inferred from Rogers' thinking that he deemed transference behavior as life-furthering because, as he saw it, transference reactions erupted when the patient justifiedly tried to ward off the therapist's threats embodied in his disrespectful treatment of the patient. This threatening disrespect was said to manifest itself in the therapist's probing interpretations, direction-giving, and so on. Other theorists would disagree and insist that such activities do not necessarily imply disrespect. Yet they may fully agree, though for different reasons, with Rogers' implied conclusion that transference behavior reflects some effort in self-actualization. However, these authors also suggest that the patient's self-protective and heroic struggle as it is observed in his transference behavior is based on pathological premises.

Sullivan's (1953) thought that anxiety engendered by disapproval is the most unbearable of human experiences, and his suggestion that human beings develop methods of avoiding anxiety-provoking situations and interactions from the earliest days of life, led to the reasonable expectation that in later life in situations which reactivate old anxieties the individual will employ—or, more correctly, will tend to re-employ—patterns of anxiety avoidance which have proved useful at some previous time.

To avoid anxiety the individual will resort to any previously developed security operation, including the distortion of potentially anxiety-arousing events. According to Sullivan (1953) anxiety-reducing processes assume a variety of forms, but basically they are learned procedures in the sense that they were at least at one time demonstrably valuable. Sullivan further postulated that this learning starts at a relatively early age, at a time when the child experienced and understood connections between his emotional life and events around him in terms of simple contiguity, as if he believed *post hoc ergo propter hoc.* Sullivan (1953) referred to this form of experiencing as the parataxic mode. In an often-cited passage Mullahy described what Sullivan meant:

> As the infant develops and maturation proceeds, the original, undifferentiated wholeness of experience is broken. However, the "parts," the diverse aspects, the various kinds of experience are not related or connected in a logical fashion. They "just happen" together, or they do not, depending on circumstances. In other words, various experiences are felt as concomitant, not recognized as connected in an orderly way. The child cannot yet relate them to one another or make logical distinctions among them. What is experienced is assumed to be the "natural" way of such occurrences, without reflection or comparison. Since no connections or relations are established, there is no logical movement of "thought" from one idea to the next. The parataxic mode is not a step by step process. Experience is undergone as momentary, unconnected states of being [1948, pp. 287–88].

Yet Sullivan was careful to point out that even though the child may assume that events "just happen" together, he also tries to identify patterns as they recur and to generalize on the basis of his observation. Consequently, it is as if the child tried to bring some rhyme and reason into what he experiences by employing an essentially phenotypical process of systematizing. Sullivan said:

> The identifying of differences can make very useful contributions to behavior in the satisfaction of needs; and the generalizing of experience so that the significant common factors mixed in with the differences are identified or connected with one recurrent pattern of experience . . .

elevates the complexity or elaboration of experience from the prototaxic to the parataxic mode of experience [1953, p. 84].

The parataxic mode is characterized by attempts to generalize; inappropriate generalizations are likely to be developed. To complicate matters, it is entirely conceivable that some generalization, if developed in a mechanical (phenotypical rather than genotypical) fashion, will prove singularly successful in certain settings but will be totally inadequate under other superficially and mechanically similar though dynamically totally dissimilar circumstances. In any event, these generalizations lead to what Sullivan (1953) called "dynamisms of difficulty" (p. 304), processes employed by the individual to avoid anxiety and to maintain or establish his euphoria. He referred to the aggregate of these "dynamisms of difficulty" as the "self-system" (p. 164). This "self-system," this collection of security operations, had but one aim: the avoidance of anxiety.

> The self-system thus is an organization of educative experiences called into being by the necessity to avoid or minimize incidents of anxiety [p. 165].

Generalizations developed through parataxic experience give rise to "parataxic processes," a term synonymous with "dynamisms of difficulty." Here is how Sullivan put it:

> In further commenting on the critical opposition of anxiety and the self-system to favorable growth in late adolescence, I would like to call attention to the parataxic processes in avoiding or minimizing anxiety. These processes extend from selective inattention—which to a certain extent covers the world like a tent—through all the other classical dynamisms of difficulty, to the gravest dissociation of one or more of the vitally essential human dynamisms.[1] And incidentally, while I once liked the

[1] Here is one of the difficulties so prominently associated with the study of Sullivan. Unfortunately, he employed the term "dynamism" in referring to two distinct concepts: (a) self-protective, anxiety-reducing processes such as dissociation; and (b) vital, biologically given needs and forces within the organisms, such as lust. Consequently there are some confusing passages in Sullivan's writings which state that a particular

rubric, dynamism of difficulty, it has lost its charm over my years of attempting to teach psychiatry, because the conviction grew among some of the people who encountered this usage that these dynamisms represented peculiarities shown by the morbid. On the contrary, I believe that there are no peculiarities shown by the morbid; there are only differences in degree—that is, in intensity and timing—of that which is shown by everyone. Thus whenever I speak of dynamisms I am discussing universal human equipment, sometimes represented almost entirely in dreadful distortions of living, but still universal. And the distortions arise from misfortunes in development, restrictions of opportunity, and the like. Thus the interventions of the self-system which are striking in this late adolescent phase—that is, in chronological maturity —cover the whole field of what we like to talk about as being psychiatric entities—mental disorders, if you please [1953, pp. 304-5].

When human beings in later life react to others (including the psychotherapist) on the basis of early-developed parataxic patterns of generalizing, they carry out what Sullivan has called "parataxic distortions." In their quest for security and freedom from anxiety they distort others to make previously learned patterns of anxiety avoidance appropriate. Thus Sullivan's concept of parataxic distortion runs parallel but is certainly not synonymous with Freud's concept of transference.

For the sake of clarity it may be useful briefly to sketch and recapitulate here the essential similarities and differences between the concept of transference and the concept of parataxic distortion. In both concepts reactions and attitudes harbored toward significant individuals of one's past are seen as reactivated in the person's dealings with others. But Freud by and large reserved the term transference for such a reactivation in the analytic relationship; Sullivan was convinced that these distortions, such a recasting of one's contemporaries in the image of people in one's past, appear in all interpersonal contexts. Furthermore, transference specifically denotes a re-expe-

---

dynamism *learned* in the search for security may interfere with other *inherent* dynamisms essential for the achievement of satisfaction.

riencing of the therapist within the framework of the Oedipal conflict; but the process of parataxic distortion implies no such restrictions, essentially because Sullivan did not consider the Oedipal conflict central to neurosis. Perhaps most important, both theorists believed that the processes they described were reactions to anxiety and to those threats which caused anxiety.

Freud and Sullivan both saw the origins of anxiety and consequently understood reactions to anxiety in totally different terms. Transference behavior revealed to Freud Oedipal tendencies, reactions to them and anxiety associated with them; to Sullivan parataxic distortions revealed the patient's sense that loss of self-esteem was around the corner and methods of preventing this threat from materializing. Freud saw in the transference reactions how the individual went about trying to maintain his regressive and hostile Oedipal impulses without bearing dreaded consequences; Sullivan saw in the parataxic distortions learned behavior which the individual assumes will help him survive. Freud saw the potential for engaging in transference behavior in what he thought was the essentially regressive characteristic of nature, basically expressed in the repetition compulsion; Sullivan saw the potential for parataxic distortions in the organism's constant tendency to maintain himself necessitating a reduction of anxiety.

Fromm-Reichmann's position on the concept of transference was—as could have been anticipated—closer to that of Sullivan than to that of Freud. Although she used the term *transference* quite frequently and often avoided the somewhat cumbersome *parataxic distortion,* it was obvious that she meant parataxic distortion instead of transference when she wrote:

Transference in its special application to the therapeutic process naturally means transferring to the therapist, as a present-day partner, early experiences in interpersonal relatedness. Such significant carry-overs from people's early relationships with the parents of their childhood, of course, will also affect their later relationships with their family doctor, dentist, minister, etc. Even the mere anticipation of consulting any kind of qualified helper, including the future psychiatrist, may pave the way for the development of transference reactions [1950, p. 97].

By "transference reactions" Fromm-Reichmann did not mean Oedipal tendencies or their derivatives in classical psycho-analytic terms; her accent was placed upon the individual's reaction to a *helper* rather than his attitudes toward a libidinal partner and/or rival. Her point of view revealed itself even more clearly in another of her comments:

> Frequently the reports of patients about their early at-tachments to their parents may lend themselves to sexual misinterpretation. However, in evaluating these data, the psychiatrist should keep in mind the possibility of pa-tients' difficulty of expressing feelings of friendliness to-wards the doctor and his own problem of accepting them. People in Western culture do not seem to find it too difficult to talk about sexual attachments, falling in love, etc., but . . . many of us are reluctant, if not afraid, to speak about the friendly, tender, asexual loving aspects of our interpersonal relationships. This holds true not only for adult relationships but also for feelings of attach-ment to the parents of one's childhood as viewed and reported by adult patients. Moreover, the psychiatrist's own fear of a friendly give-and-take, if not recognized, may encourage these misconceptions [p. 99].

Since Fromm-Reichmann did not address herself frequently to metapsychological issues and was more concerned with the practice of psychoanalytic therapy, it is not too surprising that she did not deal extensively with questions about the transfer-ence potential. Her conceptions on this issue can nevertheless be pieced together from various sources. In one of her papers (1946) she suggested that all emotional disorders ought to be understood as the patient's attempts to preserve some aspect of life no matter how minimal or distorted; later (1950) she re-ferred to transference reactions as parataxic *misjudgments,* leaving the distinct impression that she thought transferences were reflections of the patient's desire to find his way in a world which confused him.

Fromm-Reichmann thought that in order to cope with his

baffling universe the patient would fall back upon judgments, albeit *mis*judgments developed at one time in the service of survival. This led her to reject thoroughly Freud's (1935, 1949) suggestion that transferences are not noticeable in the analytic behavior of the psychotic. On the contrary, she insisted (1950), what she observed in the psychotic was little else but transference reactions. As she saw it, the trouble with the psychotic was that he fell back mechanically and persistently on judgments he had developed in relation to significant people earlier in his life and applied them later in almost rote manner, utilizing unchecked and uninvestigated associative bonds. In other words, she suggested that it was not quite correct to say that the psychotic was withdrawn from human relationships but that it was more correct to conclude that he conducted them on the basis of rigidly maintained, early-developed, and potentially inappropriate judgments—that his behavior was based primarily on parataxic distortions.

The thoughts of Rogers, Sullivan, Fromm-Reichmann, and others who maintain similar views lend themselves to an integrative formulation of the bases, origins, and functions of transference. If human beings abandon expansion, growth, and development for self-protective purposes, if neurotic and psychotic self-restrictions represent "remarkable manifestations of dexterity in living," it is reasonable to expect that the patient's general self-protective efforts will also reveal themselves in his specific reactions to the therapist. If neuroses and psychoses are ways of life designed to protect life itself, though on a reduced, caricatured, distorted, and often pathetic level, one can expect this way of life also to express itself in the patient's behavior and attitudes toward the analyst. The more profound the patient's pathology, the more far-reaching his abandoning growth, vision, and awareness, the more pervasive his deeply ingrained belief system about the nature of his fellow men, what they will tolerate and what they will condemn, under what circumstances they will let him live and what will occasion their wrath and anxiety-provoking behavior. To the extent to which this belief system includes the conviction that personal growth and self-actualization will be frowned on, imagination, intellect, inquiry, and ability to understand will be given up and in their stead mechanical and robotlike transference reactions will be noticeable. The rigidity of adherence to this belief system determines the extensiveness of transference behavior.

This rigidity is a function of the number of situations the patient has encountered in his life which forced him to develop his particular system of beliefs. The more the person has learned to generalize, the more one will notice transference reactions based on the conviction that everybody, including the therapist, denies the patient's right to growth and creative insight. The more massively and early in his life the patient has encountered insistence on self-restriction, the more readily will he have developed such once-and-for-all parataxic generalizations.[2]

As in resistance, the development and maintenance of parataxic distortions and transference reactions is occasioned by the patient's despair about an alternative, by his conviction that nobody will tolerate whatever alternate way of living he may choose. The patient's view of the therapist is simply a specific instance of his general perception of man. What the patient has learned (or thinks he has learned) about human nature in contacts with significant figures during his formative years reveals itself in his attitudes and his conscious and unconscious reactions to the therapist. The despair about finding an alternative in living, which was held responsible for the inception and maintenance of resistance (Chapter 10) is ultimately based on the patient's abiding doubt that people are capable of behavior which is at variance with the generalizations he has developed about man's nature. His desperate conclusion that he must continue to live the way he does and see events and people around him the way he has learned to view them—that he has no choice—runs parallel to his conviction that people in general and the therapist in particular are also not free, that nobody can choose, and that the behavior of all people is dominated by some immutable laws of nature over

[2] For a discussion of the importance of belief systems for behavior see Rokeach (1960).

which they have no control. In the face of this conclusion the patient re-employs procedures which have brought him earlier at least minimal salvation. This leveling belief in the universality of some determinism toward malevolence makes it easy for the patient to engage in the substitution procedures of transference. Viewed in this light the intimate and intricate connection between resistance and transference becomes obvious.

A particular world image is maintained through transference and attempts to dissolve it are resisted because it provided reference points for the patient and aided him in anticipating and avoiding anxiety.[3] The therapeutic attack on this minimally sustaining world image is resisted even if outright distortion of persons and situations is necessary. In many instances this maintenance demands behavior of the patient which may eventually prove so trying and so unbearable to the therapist that he may start treating the patient in an actually destructive fashion and may in his reaction develop the characteristics ascribed to him by the patient. Even though this process ultimately proves harmful to the patient and is dreaded secretly, it is at the same time experienced by him as relieving because then he can say somewhat triumphantly—though it is a Pyrrhic victory—"My perception was right, I have seen the world and its people correctly; I can now fall back once again on my well-learned lesson." Additional psychological foundations for the patient's desire to demonstrate the uselessness, inadequacy, and outright destructiveness of the therapist will be examined later in this chapter. Chapter 12 will discuss the danger that the patient's transference will trigger the therapist's counter-transference hostility (see also Chapter 10).

Before proceeding to an examination of the customary differentiation of transference into "positive" and "negative" transference, let us note the limits of transference. A good deal of the patient's behavior toward the therapist is undoubtedly dominated by a more or less rigid and robotlike application of his world image; the patient will engage in transference reac-

---

[3] Freud (1912a) also considered the possibility of transference reactions in nontherapeutic interactions, but he preferred to keep the term reserved for the phenomenon he observed in the analytic relationship.

tions for, Rogers notwithstanding, this robotlike application of early perceptions defines the person's state of emotional disturbance and reveals that he has given up the essential qualities of emotional well-being as defined in Chapter 3. The more deeply disturbed the patient is, the more decidedly he has abandoned his ability to experience and grasp his own nature and the nature of others correctly, and the more trying his transference reactions will be. But if he has any shred of sanity left, if he has not abandoned his constructive human potentials totally, he will also perceive some situations and relationships adequately, experience some interactions in undistorted fashion, and see some events realistically. And he may perceive and experience some of the therapist's behavior and reactions correctly even though the therapist himself may not be aware of his own behavior and motivations. There are many instances in which patients are capable of sensing and seeing the doctor's reactions clearly and of detecting aspects within the therapist which are far from flattering—even damaging to the analyst's self-image. It behooves the therapist to remember that in any patient's make-up there are islands of sanity, to respect them, and to aid him in expanding them rather than to assume a defensive stance.

If a patient is informed that once again he has seen things incorrectly, has distorted even though a careful examination would have shown how correct his perception was, he cannot help but feel hurt and discouraged, for some of his worst fears as well as some of his fondest (albeit pathological) hopes have come to pass once again. He must conclude that human beings as represented by the therapist are inevitably concerned with showing that they are noble, right, and smart, and that he is wicked and wrong. He must conclude that his world image is correct, that this type of hostility is part and parcel of men and that they cannot change their nature. The patient will be led to believe that he had better stick with what he knows and stop the pursuit of presumably more adequate perceptions because it must seem to him that he has positive proof that what he "knows" is more correct than what he is to learn. A frank admission on the part of the therapist that the patient has seen something correctly can prove of extreme therapeutic benefit. The following incident illustrates:

☐ A grossly distorting and highly obdurate woman had been in therapy for about a year. She had often expressed the desire to leave a therapeutic session abruptly because she had felt at those moments that the therapist was not interested in her, was bored, and had other supposedly more important things (to him) on his mind than to listen to her difficulties in living. These transference attitudes had been examined by them for many hours. One day the therapist received a phone call during one of their sessions. He was notified that one of his dearest friends and colleagues had just suffered a heart attack. Although the therapist's replies on the phone were minimal and confined to "I'll call you back very soon" (it had been his intention to finish his session with the patient), the woman recognized the analyst's change in mood instantaneously and said: "I want to leave again, I think I'll leave." The therapist hesitated for a moment, looked at her and replied: "Thank you, I think that is wise," and the patient left. She reported the next time how greatly relieved she was, that the incident during the hour had been crucial because it confirmed that she could see at least some things correctly. ☐

It would have been disastrous, grossly dishonest, and inhuman had the therapist tried to investigate the patient's desire to leave at this particular moment as a transference reaction. In a similar vein a psychiatrist reported:

☐ She had been at the beginning of her first year of residency and had been assigned to a small ward of extremely disturbed patients. Their bizarre behavior had frightened her considerably, but she had eventually grown less fearful and had developed the sense that she was capable of working with them. While this conviction grew within her, she was notified one day that her father—who lived in another town—was ailing. He had been ill before but had made good recoveries from his sickness. She thought that she was not worried about his condition until one morning when she came on the ward every one of the patients asked to see her and one after the other informed her that he was well and ready for discharge from the hospital. The young psychiatrist was stunned by this uniformity and wondered about this strange occurrence when she suddenly realized that this time she was much more worried about her father's condition than she had been on previous occasions. It seemed clear to her that her patients had sensed her concern and in effect had suggested to her that she was not needed desperately now and could take a leave. She decided to apply for a leave, went home, and indeed the father's condition was much more critical than it had ever been. He died a few days after her arrival. □

A final example will illustrate the general point that even odd behavior that may seem as if it were resistance and transference must often be understood in totally different terms.

□ The staff of a psychological clinic had been thrown into turmoil and confusion by the announcement of new personnel practices which threatened the positions of some and forced others whose jobs were not in danger to do some soul-searching as to whether they wanted to continue working for an agency which promulgated what seemed to them arbitrary and capricious procedures. It was noted during this period that the number of broken appointments jumped dramatically, that many patients suddenly expressed their desire to terminate therapy, that a surprising amount of what seemed "regressive" transference reactions occurred.

These facts came into the open at a staff conference and it was decided to discuss with the patients whether they had possibly sensed their therapists' distraction and to investigate how much this had influenced them. While it must be kept in mind that certain data gathered in this instance may have been contaminated by the desire of some therapists to use them in their dealings with the clinic administration, it became obvious that the frank airing of the therapists' concern with extratherapeutic problems did result in a return of the number of broken appointments to the usual precrisis level. □

The therapist must always keep in mind the patients' sensitivity to nuances in his emotional life when he tries to assess the intensity and function of their transference reactions. Interestingly enough, the more profound the patient's emotional disturbance, the greater his sensitivity to even the most subtle shifts in the therapist's mood. Nondefensive investigation of the patient's bases for reacting to the therapist without immediately assuming that one is dealing with neurotic transference behavior is therefore of utmost importance. Such investigations may lead to a good deal of clarification and benefit for both patient and analyst. It must also be remembered, however, that psychologically sophisticated individuals sometimes insist that the doctor is bringing his problems into therapy, is burdening the patients with his difficulties in living, and employ this tack in their resistance. They try to concentrate on what they defensively label the therapist's "counter-transference" difficulties. While the therapist's constant investigation of his potential counter-transference feelings is of crucial importance for the success of psychotherapy (see Chapter 12), a patient's insistence that the therapist is in the throes of counter-transference reactions often represents a subtle transference maneuver in itself. But his comment to that effect is worth consideration. Regardless of its accuracy, it is likely to lead to important revelations.

Transference reactions take diverse forms. Traditionally transference has been considered under two rubrics: positive transference and negative transference. As the terms suggest, the former refers to what seem the patient's positive feelings toward the therapist; the latter refers to the patient's negative attitudes toward his helper. But both positive and negative transferences are said to be "new editions" of attitudes the patient harbored toward significant figures in his past and do not constitute realistic feelings. Freud (1912a) recognized that both types of transference will reveal themselves in analytic therapy. He insisted that the positive transference was a *sine qua non* for the psychoanalytic transaction because such positive transference made the patient amenable to accepting interpretations about his resistance. Its origins were explained by Freud in one of his most important contributions on this topic:

> Positive transference is then further divisible into trans-
> ference of friendly or affectionate feelings which are
> admissible to consciousness and transference of prolonga-
> tions of those feelings into the unconscious. As regards
> the latter, analysis shows that they invariably go back to
> erotic sources. And we are thus led to the discovery that
> all the emotional relations of sympathy, friendship, trust,
> and the like, are generally linked with sexuality and have
> developed from purely sexual desires through a softening
> of their sexual aim, however pure and unsexual they may
> appear to our conscious self-perception. Originally we
> know only sexual objects; and psycho-analysis shows us
> that people who in our real life are merely admired or
> respected may still be sexual objects for our unconscious
> [1912a, p. 105].

When Freud discussed Breuer's work with Fräulein O., he remarked:

> In his treatment of her case, Breuer could make use of a
> very intense suggestive *rapport* with the patient, which
> may serve us as a complete prototype of what we call
> "transference" today. Now I have strong reasons for sus-
> pecting that after all her symptoms had been relieved
> Breuer must have discovered from further indications the
> sexual motivation of this transference, but that the uni-
> versal nature of this unexpected phenomenon escaped
> him, with the result that, as though confronted by an
> "untoward event," he broke off all further investigation
> [1914c, p. 12].

Freud's position is abundantly clear: positive transference is the reflection of unrepressed but adequately sublimated, social-ized, and therefore emotionally mature (though originally in-fantile) sexuality. Positive transference is seen by Freud as a manifestation of the nonpathological aspects of the person-ality; he advocated that the therapist ally himself with this healthy aspect of the individual and in turn the positive trans-ference would become the analyst's strongest ally in his strug-gle with the patient's pathological facets.

In fairness to Freud it must be noted that very shortly after he had advanced the thoughts cited, he modified his position somewhat. Commenting on the frequently observed phenomenon that some patients habitually fall in love with their therapists and that this makes them change analysts several times, Freud (1915a) came to the conclusion that this type of "positive" transference must be understood as anything but positive in the sense he had outlined earlier. Rather than advancing therapy it retards progress and is therefore a manifestation of resistance. Freud also saw that this type of resistance through transference-love (as he called it) is bound to lead to the analyst failing in his *raison d'être* unless he is skillful enough to analyze the situation successfully, investigate the transference-love courageously, and help the patient rid herself (or himself) of such unrealistic attachments. But Freud also thought that there are patients who cannot give up their transference-love:

> With such people one has the choice between returning their love or else bringing down upon oneself the full enmity of a woman scorned. In neither case can one safeguard the interests of the treatment. One has to withdraw, unsatisfied; and all one can do is turn the problem over in one's mind of how it is that a capacity for neurosis is joined with such an intractable need for love [p. 167].

These are indeed profound and penetrating observations. Yet why should not the analyst face the "full force of the mortified woman's fury"? Of course, to face it is a most difficult undertaking, but Freud never suggested that analysis was child's play. This negative transference masquerading as positive attachment must be dealt with as one would deal with any other manifestation of resistance: by analyzing it, not by withdrawing. But more importantly, from a theoretical point of view, it would be quite interesting to examine what one would arrive at if one contemplated the patient's behavior "at leisure," how the "capacity for neurosis" comes to employ such devious ways of maintaining itself.

The answer may not be too far afield, for *de facto* such

patients succeed in defeating those who are mandated to help them, seem singularly bent upon demonstrating their capacity to shatter the sense of self-esteem in the analyst, seem particularly adept in what psychoanalytic jargon calls "castrating" the analyst (although this castration takes place in forms more fundamentally devastating than mere physical mutilation). Patients who exhibit this particular potential to devastate the therapist are perhaps not just "children of nature who refuse to accept the spiritual instead of the material" as Freud suggested; their particular "love" is like the kiss of death and a pointed manifestation of a world image which they try to maintain at all costs, an image dominated by the theme "Nobody, but nobody, shall be capable of being helpful and useful in my life; everybody must turn out to be inadequate and useless. Only when I see everybody pathetically impotent can I have a modicum of peace, only then can I understand the world and find my way in it." And it is precisely this premise in living which cries out to be dealt with therapeutically.

The problem of negative transference in its more obvious forms was also discussed by Freud. He saw negative transference as a vehicle prominently employed in the service of resistance:

> Thus the solution of the puzzle is that transference to the doctor is suitable for resistance to the treatment only in so far as it is a negative transference or a positive transference of repressed erotic impulses [1912a, p. 105].

Freud suggested that negative transference is an attempt to keep Oedipal attachments repressed by developing reaction formations in the face of these tendencies. The patient, in his effort to avoid facing his instinctual strivings, will engage in many operations—including distortions to keep buried what is at least partially hidden. The theoretical foundations Freud advanced for this urge to resist have been dealt with in Chapter 10; it is only necessary here to recall that orthodox psychoanalytic theory conceived of neurosis as an attempt to maintain primitive instinctual strivings while simultaneously avoiding the dreaded consequences of this persistence. Resistance in the Freudian framework is opposition to giving up a "having-one's-cake-and-eating-it" solution; negative transference reactions were explained by assuming that the patient wants to maintain this neurotic solution and by suggesting that he relives in the negative transference feelings presumably associated with his original infantile Oedipal neurosis.[4] The transference reaction was consequently for Freud the laboratory situation in which these infantile attitudes were revealed directly, in which they were understood explicitly, leading to eventual and effective sublimation. For that reason he concluded:

> It cannot be disputed that controlling the phenomena of transference presents the psycho-analyst with the greatest difficulties. But it should not be forgotten that it is precisely they that do us the inestimable service of making the patient's hidden and forgotten impulses immediate and manifest. For when all is said and done, it is impossible to destroy anyone *in absentia* or *in effigie* [1912a, p. 108].

What are the viewpoints of theorists who deviate from classical thinking when they examine positive and negative transference? While there is reference to the topic in the contributions of Fromm-Reichmann (1950), Reich (1949), Jung (1946),[5] and others, the distinction has disappeared in many circles. Reich's (1949) formulation, for example, stated that all of the patient's defensive character traits—whether revealed in positive or negative transference reactions—function in the service of resistance. Transference was therefore to him no longer a repetitive reliving of Oedipal feelings. Although Thompson (1950) has discussed Reich's point explicitly, a brief résumé of his thoughts seems in order because they represent to some extent a turning point in the history of the

---

[4] This construct is stated succinctly by Loewenstein:
During analysis, when the transference is "negative"—i.e., dominated by hostile feelings once experienced towards the father—the . . . doctor is regarded as . . . dangerous and sinister . . . [1952, p. 31].

[5] Jung considered positive transference a "synthesis of opposites" (p. 165n) and therefore really not a neurotic problem at all.

theory on transference. Reich came to understand all positive transference reactions as disguised manifestations of negative attitudes:

> These three types of seemingly positive transference— undoubtedly, further study will reveal others—drown out such rudiments of genuine object love as have not yet been consumed by the neurosis. They are in themselves results of the neurotic process, in that the frustration of love has given rise to hatred, narcissism and guilt feelings. They are sufficient to keep the patient in analysis until such time as they can be dissolved; but if they are not unmasked in time, they will provide the patient with strong motives for breaking off the analysis [1949, p. 121].

Reich saw that much of the so-called positive transferences obscured negative and defensive attitudes and believed that it was crucial to bring these negative tendencies into the open so that they could be analyzed and dissolved. Although he remained firmly rooted in libido theory and if anything tried to expand the concept beyond its original formulation, he did contribute significantly to the understanding of transference by insisting that positive and negative reactions are essentially irrational attitudes which reveal the patient's anger and hatred. He understood positive transference in terms similar to those used by Freud when he discussed "transference-love." In contrast to Freud, who was reluctant to consider transference-love an expression of the patient's character pathology, Reich maintained that all positive transference was pathological and therefore a subject for therapeutic investigation from the very beginning of analysis.

Operating within a totally different theoretical framework, Fromm-Reichmann's thoughts on positive and negative transferences were closely similar to those of Reich. She too thought the patient's early expressions of affection for the analyst were likely to reveal themselves eventually as his characteristic method of resistance, which had to be investigated. She did not deny that patients may have feelings of genuine affection for their doctor, but like Sullivan (White, M. J., 1952) she was inclined to think that genuine affection for the therapist can set in only when the doctor has really helped the patient and that early expressions of admiration are unrealistic and therefore are likely to disguise negative feelings:

> In the psychoneurotic, such talk [about the psychiatrist instead of submitting their problems] should immediately be discouraged as irrelevant, and its significance as resistance should be brought to the patient's awareness. ... The same holds true of the attempts of psychoneurotic patients to delay interpretive psychotherapy by discussing at great length their relationship with the doctor, especially its positive aspects [1950, p. 112].

Thus Fromm-Reichmann saw in such "positive" transference and the patients' talk about it negative resistance, an evasion of therapy and the therapist's basic function. She was extremely interested in the analysis of these negative attitudes because she believed that they were intricately related to the total picture of the patients' emotional disturbances. It is therefore not surprising to hear her say:

> Active interpretation of patients' hostility will be necessary, though, if and when it is part of their attempted security operations with the doctor. Freud's recommendation that priority be given to the interpretation of resistance over that of the rest of a patient's manifestations should be repeated in this connection. Sullivan's recommendation of giving interpretive priority to patients' security operations should be mentioned here in the same vein [p. 102].

These security operations and resistances may take seemingly positive avenues while disguising negative feelings.

The general trend in the literature and the thinking on transference thus indicates a gradual rejection of the distinction between positive and negative transference in some quarters and the emergence of the position that all transference is by definition negative. But in addition to what has been outlined so far, there is another, perhaps even more basic, reason for considering all transference reactions reflections of negative feelings. To transfer, it has been said, is to generalize in relatively unquestioning terms. To do this requires a more or less prominent disregard of the therapist as he actually is, demands pressing him into a mold no matter how much it violates his reality. To distort another person by ascribing angelic qualities to him is by no means less disrespectful than to invest him with diabolic tendencies. In either case his personality is disregarded and attacked. To be sure, the foundations of such behavior, in which individuals are substituted as if they were identical pawns on a chessboard, are all too easily understandable and are undoubtedly themselves the results of unfortunate experiences. But this does not detract from the essential disrespectfulness embodied in substitution processes. It reflects the patient's contempt by saying pointedly: "I have figured you out without bothering to learn who you are and I shall deal with you on the assumption that you have no individuality. I shall apply my stereotyped patterns of understanding to you just as I apply them to others." All this is certainly done in the worthwhile pursuit of freedom from anxiety, no matter how it is defined or how its origins are understood. In applying these schemata to the therapist the patient reveals not only his hostility but also simultaneously exposes the outlines and the details of his world picture. He exposes his assumptions about the nature of human beings and reveals his beliefs about universals of human nature. One cannot disagree with those authors who suggest that the nature of the patient's disturbance emerges in the transference, not because the Oedipal problem in its restricted orthodox meaning comes to the fore, but because in the transference or the parataxic distortions the particular attitudes and convictions the patient harbors are revealed as is his technique for avoiding anticipated anxiety. His "personal constructs," to use Kelly's (1955) term, lead the patient to anticipate that others will treat him shabbily and cause him anxiety. All transference is negative because it reflects derogatory beliefs about the other person. At the same time all transference reactions are self-debasing because they express an abandoning of one's capacity to see, learn, and understand and a derogatory self-evaluation which insists that all the person is capable of is robotlike mechanical substitutions.

Before offering an explanation of the often amazing stubbornness with which transference attitudes are maintained, some clinical illustrations must be examined. The analysis and understanding of the case material will lead to a reformulation concerning the function and persistence of transference reactions.

In Chapter 9 the behavior of a patient who ridiculed and mocked others, including the therapist, by subservient agreement and overtly retiring deference was discussed (pp. 205–06). The meaning of his transference reactions will now be examined further:

□ After the therapist had confronted the patient with his derogating attitude, his flow of associations led the patient to recollect how he had mocked other people by agreeing with them. He recalled that many years ago he had befriended a man of considerable prominence in scholarly pursuits. He had been a most pompous and overbearing individual who demanded constant agreement and flattery. The patient had recognized his abilities but also found him pathetically inadequate in his relationships with others, singularly insensitive, and so bent on receiving adulation that he did not even notice when he was being mocked and agreed with in ridiculing fashion. The demands of this man became so unbearable that the friendship was eventually ended.

The patient now had the distinct sense that he reacted to the therapist as he had toward this "friend" of years ago. The inquiry led to his discussing his mother's overbearing and terribly demanding behavior. She had always been the dominant person in his childhood and the father had played a nebulous background role. Eventually the patient had developed a convenient way of dealing with her demands, nodding agreement but secretly disregarding her demands. Vain and self-absorbed woman that she was, she was less interested in actually being obeyed than in having people ceremoniously pay their respects to her superior knowledge and ability. Once that was acknowledged she lost interest. In his transference reaction the patient now pictured the analyst in similar terms, as a vain, overbearing, pompous, and smugly detached person who wished to be flattered, humored, and entertained, instead of being taken seriously. ☐

Here is an instance of what seemed overtly positive agreement with the therapist, positive transference, and being agreeable while secretly though unconsciously the analyst was being mocked. What at first appeared positive transference was actually negative reactivity, and a good deal of further evidence corroborated the hunch that the patient expressed his hostility toward the therapist and others in feigned modesty, in setting traps which gave his colleagues a chance to make fools of themselves, and by provoking people into patronizing behavior toward him when he made himself appear a most inadequate person. People were continuously cast in ridiculous or pompous roles and the patient enjoyed seeing them as stupid fools. Everyone, including the therapist, was placed in such a role and the unsuspecting would step right into his traps. Characteristically enough the patient was involved with a woman who, troubled herself, was very much in need of flattery and deference. The patient could secretly laugh at her while openly lamenting her lack of consideration, demandingness, and tyranny. With such people he felt at home and he knew how to deal with them. Those who seemed genuinely interested in him and concerned with his welfare he feared; he shunned them and found them "uninteresting."

Another illustration reveals a transference reaction in which a patient seemed eager to demonstrate the therapist's inadequacy in order to deny his potential usefulness.

☐ A therapist had moved his office from one suburban location to another. He had mimeographed detailed instructions for reaching the new location and had given them to all patients before moving. A woman patient who seemed dominated by an unconscious and unadmitted conviction that she must never depend on anyone came to her first appointment at the new office over half an hour late. She arrived fuming with anger. She insisted that her "worst fears" about the therapist's inadequacy had been justified because he did not even know how one could reach his office and had given wrong directions.

"You should really know the difference between left and right! You must make a right turn at X Street to get here and you printed here *Make a left turn!*" she exclaimed, pushing the printed instruction sheet at the therapist.

He looked at it and returned it, asking her to reread it. After considerable effort the patient realized that she had misread the directions; they actually did call for a right and not a left turn. This little incident proved a turning point in her analysis, for it finally became apparent to her that she was terribly eager to distort in order to prove the inadequacy of any man—the therapist, her husband, a friend, or a colleague. □

The patient had been raised by a mother who had often belittled her husband to the little girl. Actually quite successful in her own work, the mother had enormously exaggerated her accomplishments at the expense of others, who were either subtly ridiculed or openly held in contempt for their "inadequacies." The patient herself had often enough been the victim of both types of derogation. Yet she had managed to identify with her mother—despite her protestations to the contrary—and had dedicated her life to finding the "terrible shortcomings" in "inadequate and dependent" men.

In the final vignette to be presented here, transference reactions overtly quite different from those just described are encountered.

□ A young woman in her early twenties became increasingly abusive toward her analyst, occasionally destroyed fixtures in his office, and appeared totally unmanageable. He was the fifth therapist she had consulted within a span of eighteen months. Her behavior with other therapists had been similar, leading either to the therapist's refusal to continue working with her or, failing this, she invariably started to think that he was just a "stupid ass" and terminated analysis.

The dynamics of her behavior were relatively simple. She

was a woman who, in her youth, had experienced an inordinate amount of teasing from her family and who seemed love-starved. Her background was characterized by a markedly seductive father whose busy concern with her clothing and whose interest in her diets so that she would look slim and smart were clearly erotically tinged; at the same time he rejected with obvious panic the daughter's responding to his advances. The mother, on the other hand, constantly found something wrong with her, always insisting that corrections suggested were for her child's benefit, but the girl had at some time apparently noticed that the more there could be found to be wrong, the better the mother seemed to like it.

Early in life the patient had discovered hypocrisy and pretentious deceit and she now insisted that she saw them all around her. Somewhere along the line she had resolved not to be teased any longer and later, whenever she felt affection for anybody—classmates, boy friends, or her therapists—she did everything in her power to destroy the relationship. (Characteristically, she sought therapeutic help for failure in precisely those college courses which she claimed had interested her and were taught by instructors she had admired.)

She worked diligently to protect herself from the anxiety brought on by her affectionate impulses by denying them, and tried strenuously to alienate her therapists by attempts to tease and threaten them. It was not surprising to find a character structure full of suspicion that everybody was "a rejecting hypocritical son of a bitch—and that goes for you too—especially." Obsessive ruminations, so often the outcome of experience with hypocritical unreality, were striking and included constant doubt that she was actually her parents' child and endless speculations about a mix-up in the hospital. Since nothing could be trusted, the very origin of her existence was in question.

After she had worked with a particular therapist for about a year, he became ill, had to be hospitalized, underwent major surgery, and was forced to interrupt his work for several months. About three days after he had undergone a serious operation and while he was acutely ill the patient appeared at his bedside at midnight. She had managed to get into the hospital and then past the nurses in a highly ingenious manner. This included the rental of a nurse's uniform, sneaking around corridors and waiting until the therapist's nurse had gone out for a short break. The patient woke the therapist and insisted upon visiting with him, claiming that this was the only time she had to see him. When the therapist seemed anything but delighted by the call she became furious, berated him for being unsympathetic and rejecting and stormed out, saying that she hoped he died and in any case she would never want to see him again.

After his convalescence, the therapist contacted her, ready to resume his work with her. She refused adamantly. But several weeks later she called and insisted that now she was ready to resume therapy. He explained to her that he had no free time (it is quite possible that he was just as glad that he did not have time) but that he would be glad to refer her to somebody else. After a vehement outburst about the therapist's "selfishness," the patient consented and was referred to another analyst.

Her behavior now deteriorated rapidly, she became increasingly destructive and self-destructive and hospitalization seemed imminent. Shortly before a transient psychotic episode (from which she eventually recovered) the patient managed to write a letter to the previous therapist. Most abusive in language and often quite incoherent, the note nevertheless included the statement: "I thought you had helped me, I really thought so. . . . I loved you dearly for it and it also made me furious with you, you bastard, you. . . . I hate you." ☐

The patient's transference reactions epitomized her general defensive mode and the foundations on which her defenses rested. It was all-important for her to avoid any sense of closeness and to forestall any development of positive attitudes by deliberately provoking rejection lest she become attached or develop friendly feelings. These operations were carried out not only with therapists but also with employers, teachers, classmates, and assorted "friends" and were based on her deep conviction that "everybody is a son of a bitch" out to destroy her—and she was not going to give them a chance to do so. So long as this outlook could be maintained she was quite content and relatively anxiety-free. Only if the anticipated rejection did not occur, when a therapist challenged the patient's system by accepting her, did panic ensue, spurring her on to greater efforts and eventually provoking rejection. Rejection was often quite relieving to her because the likelihood of developing positive attitudes was diminished and the danger of being teased once again was reduced.

At the same time being rejected brought about another outcome equally important to her: the image of the world as she saw it was kept intact and she could remain oriented in a world she understood. Finally, it was striking how she apparently enjoyed a constant state of warfare with other people. While she was derisive toward her "friends," caused them discomfort and anxiety, she was always very reluctant to give up her conflict-laden relationships as if she genuinely enjoyed them. Since she was starved for contact, it was quite understandable that she did cherish being with others—provided of course that her relationships with them were scratchy, nagging, biting, and warlike. This helped her maintain a world system dominated solely by conflict and totally devoid of cooperative interchange. Her transference behavior must therefore be understood not simply in terms of a reliving of some infantile conflict but also as an effort in determined perpetuation of her view of the world.

This illustration raises an important theoretical point. Rogers had insisted that transference reactions are brought about by the threatening behavior of the therapist, and he equated threatening behavior with some form of nonacceptance. But it must be remembered that from the patient's viewpoint—or to maintain Rogers' favorite framework, in his phenomenological field—acceptance can be experienced as a threat. Therefore it is a mistake to believe that acceptance will necessarily be experienced without anxiety. Actually, for patients in whose life a "malevolent transformation" (Sullivan, 1953) has taken place, the exact opposite is true. It is therefore well-nigh impossible to conceive of any therapeutic endeavor without recognizing that it will inevitably create anxiety and consequently defensive and resistive transference reactions (see also Chapter 10). This suggests of course that patients harbor, in addition to obvious and apparent self-actualizing tendencies, forces which seem to insist upon a maintenance of the *status quo* and seem bent upon a continuation of customary ways. But if one rejects the death instinct, and if one believes that all behavior is governed by a tendency to self-actualization, this attempted and clinically observable perpetuation of the *status quo* requires an explanation in those terms. The following pages are devoted to such an explanation.

What was strikingly similar in the behavior of the patients discussed was their inordinate capacity somehow to structure their view of the world and the people around them in highly familiar terms and their insistence that everyone they met was possessed of similar qualities, usually negative and destructive in nature.[6] It was as if they insisted that they had learned their lesson well and were loath to admit shortcomings in their understanding of human behavior. And the more prominent this reluctance, the more likely is the patient to engage in transference distortions as if desperately eager to prove his point. What self-actualizing purposes can this remarkably stubborn adherence to rigid perceptual stereotypes which interfere with growth, satisfactions, experience, and expanding vision possibly serve?

A continuation of the *status quo* and of a fixed world image has important consequences for the patient: it markedly reduces chances for the development of self-awareness. If everything is static, rigidly fixed, there are no contrasting stimuli to call forth varied reactions, and in the absence of varied reactions self-awareness cannot take place. This idea can be clarified by drawing on an illustration frequently used in introductions to the theory of relativity. It is well known that a coin tossed into the air by a person traveling on a rapidly moving

---

[6] In some instances to be discussed in the following chapter, patients managed to irritate the therapist to a point where he actually assumed in his counter-transference the negative characteristics ascribed to him by the patients.

train will come to rest once again in his palm. It will not land somewhere behind him, even though he and the train have moved some distance while the coin was rising and then falling. In effect, his coin-tossing does not help the traveler learn that he is in a moving vehicle because the awareness of movement requires the perception and recognition of changed relationships between contrasting fields. The traveler could develop awareness of his movement only by observing contrasting changes in the landscape outside his window or by noticing changing and contrasting sensations occasioned by the rocking of the vehicle, or by sensing other internal and external changes which make comparisons possible.

Transference attitudes also interfere with awareness of one's behavior, inner state, and actions because they prevent the possibility of making comparisons—there is nothing to compare when everything is always the same: A man who is and always has been angry without variation in intensity of anger is totally incapable of knowing that he is angry. Only if he can compare his inner state and reactions from one moment to the next (and such a comparison would require variations of intensity) can he grasp the fact that he is angry. A persistent and unvaried inner state minimizes contrasts demanding attention and reduces experience because any feeling reaches consciousness and assumes meaning only to the extent to which it is sometimes present and other times absent. Transference reactions interfere markedly with the development of self-awareness by reducing the most vital element necessary for it: changing and contrasting reactions.

In the final analysis, the patient who engages in massive transference behavior employs the basic operation which makes for a marked diminution of his sense of self. By not experiencing varied reactions he does not experience at all; in not experiencing he remains unaware of himself. In this way he may well protect himself, but he pays a horrible price: not being. Transference is the vehicle for self-elimination.

But this formulation does not answer several questions. Why are some human beings so eager to reduce their experience and to eliminate their sense of self? Why do they avoid experience *per se* and the sense of self associated with experience? Why do patients determinedly avoid the sense of personal reality by distorting outer reality? What is it they avoid by avoiding experience and a sense of self? This avoidance is especially difficult to understand when one notices how often they furiously mistake acts of kindness for acts of malevolence and seem much more satisfied when they have managed to reconstruct the kind behavior of others into hostility.

The answer is simple. They avoid outer contrasts and any possibility of differentiated inner reactions. The woman who insisted that everybody was a vicious "son of a bitch" sought security in this conviction. If everyone was what she called mean, then nobody was really vicious toward her personally. If everybody was equally destructive, she could not be angry with anybody or feel hurt by anything. Another patient eager to avoid the full impact of his feelings once put the matter concisely. Asked if he were angry with the underhanded behavior of one of his associates, he replied: "Why should I be? What he did is simply human nature; everybody is that way. It would be foolish to be angry. Are you angry with the sun for rising in the east and setting in the west? Are you angry because you have only two eyes and not four? I have nothing to be angry about. I don't even know what you people mean when you say 'angry'; it seems like a lot of nonsense to me."

If the patient who mockingly nodded feigned agreement could succeed in structuring the universe so that everybody was pompous, overbearing, and constantly demanded cere-monial deference, then the pain he had experienced when he had actually encountered such disrespect would be lessened. His mother's behavior could pain him only if he thought she had been free to choose and could have behaved differently. But in his transference reactions he expressed the conviction that this was impossible, that her behavior was the essence of human nature. This conviction reduced his pain significantly— and, what was even more crucial, it helped him allay his anx-iety and anger with her. This is the important link between resistance and transference. Through his transference distor-tions, the patient can avoid real anger, full awareness of himself as an angry person, responsibility for feeling angry with those whom he had once experienced as tormentors, and retaliatory punishment for being angry and expressing hostility. Thus the patient's transference reactions are, from his point of view, decidedly life-furthering functions because they interfere with the awareness of feelings, feelings for which he fears he will be punished severely. It is then as if inner life were abandoned for the sake of sheer survival. Only when the patient learns that he can survive despite self-awareness and despite his awareness of disapproved feelings can he abandon his transference distortions.

These considerations make readily understandable certain difficulties which often bewilder beginning and seriously dedicated therapists. They frequently report discouragement when they observe their patients' frantic attempts to misconstrue the therapists' behavior, observe the patients distorting any genuine act of kindness into some hostility, and notice the patients' eventual fury. Their fury is their reaction to the threat of losing a systematic and undifferentiated image of the world. This image had helped them avoid emotional experience and self-awareness. A somnambulant but also survival-guaranteeing state is threatened by the therapist's behavior, making for the patient's more strenuous efforts to perpetuate a relatively painless equilibrium in which all people are seen as essentially similar. Through this leveling process he reduces his anger with his genuine tormentors and eliminates the threatening consequences of his fury.

Even more striking are reports from many genuinely sincere and originally enthusiastic teachers who work in so-called "problem schools." They are often startled by the frequency with which acts of interest and concern are met with rising hostility and resentment, as if the youngsters were eager to provoke their teachers into hostile actions. One can only sympathize with these well-meaning and unfortunately all too often disillusioned educators who were guided by their belief that "love cures all." Indeed, many youngsters in "problem schools"—like so many of their adult counterparts—are terribly eager to provoke hostile behavior so as to find or re-establish a similarity and uniformity in the attitudes of others. This uniformity helps them avoid experiences analogous to those called forth by the therapist's challenge of his patient's convictions. In subsequent pages this issue will be discussed again, when the presentation turns to the consideration of the concept of counter-transference, because some transference behavior provokes, accidentally or by design, reactions which then prevent the resolution of the patient's pathological generalizations.

In simplest terms, transference behavior can be understood as a "whitewash." By ascribing destructiveness in general and even in its more specific manifestations to all human beings (including the therapist), by making such behavior an inevitable, universal, and pervasive aspect of human nature, the patient removes the onus of destructiveness from his real tormentors, past or present. This whitewash eliminates or at least reduces differentiated experience, subjectively felt anxiety, sadness, and loneliness. It reduces ensuing hostility against real tormentors, and the internal and external consequences (self-awareness and retaliation, respectively) of anger and indignation.

► *Summary* ◄

1. The orthodox psychoanalytic point of view maintains that transference reactions represent a reliving of the Oedipal conflict in the therapeutic relationship in which the therapist is substituted and reacted to as if he were any or all participants in the patient's early instinctual struggles. This point of view rests on the belief that transference behavior is an instance of the repetition compulsion and the conservative character of nature.

2. Some authors reject this understanding of clinically demonstrable transference reactions. They do parallel Freud's thinking by viewing transference reactions as attempts to reduce or eliminate anxiety, but to the extent to which they conceive of the origins of anxiety in other than the terms of

libido theory they consider the origins and functions of transference differently. Specifically, one encounters the position that transference reactions represent learned and persisting reactive modes of avoiding loss of self-esteem rather than of avoiding the threat of castration.

3. Similarly, one finds general agreement among theorists that transference can be understood as operating in the service of resistance. But again they differ in their assumptions about the types of problems that human beings are eager to avoid. Therefore transference is seen by some as serving the maintenance of regressive tendencies and is understood by others as aiding the individual in his quest for survival.

4. All transference is essentially negative because it requires and perpetuates a distortion of the therapist. A differentiation between positive and negative transference seems logically indefensible.

5. Transference reactions reduce self-awareness by helping patients maintain a world image in which all people are seen in essentially identical terms, thus eliminating differentiated experience. This leveling process minimizes the patient's awareness of the hostility directed against him by others, reduces his potential anger with them for the way they behaved, and therefore he attempts to whitewash them. This whitewashing operation reduces past and present anxiety.

The Concept of
Counter-Transference

Any honest analyst will admit that, even though he is very thoroughly analyzed, he does better work with certain types of patients than with others. However, this difficulty should never reach a degree at which work with certain personalities becomes entirely impossible. An analyst has to have the width of empathy to work with any type. If the reality in this respect differs too much from the ideal state of affairs, the mistake may be the analyst's; it may be rooted either directly in a negative counter-transference or in a disappointment because a certain type of patient does not fulfill some expectation that the analyst unduly and unconsciously connects with his work; in such cases the analyst should be analyzed more thoroughly [Fenichel, 1945, p. 580].

THIS DEFINITION OF COUNTER-TRANSFERENCE[1] AS AN UNCONsciously determined attitudinal set held by the therapist which interferes with his work is widely though not universally accepted.

Counter-transference is understood as a development highly analogous to transference. It is assumed that its appearance is

---

[1] For a detailed survey see Wolstein (1959).

governed by essentially the same processes, drives, and tendencies which authors posit in their respective explanations of the transference phenomenon. An author who insists that transferences are the patient's overt manifestations of unsublimated regressive instinctual tendencies experienced by him toward the analyst will also propose that counter-transference manifestations are expressions of the analyst's unsublimated regressive instinctual strivings brought to the fore by his contacts with the patient. Those therapists who support the position that parataxic distortions are essentially methods of dealing with anxiety by generalizing and then applying deeply ingrained schemata also maintain that counter-transference is similarly a device employed by the therapist to avoid his anxiety. They conclude that just as the patient's transference reactions must be understood as parataxic distortions designed to avoid loss of euphoria, blows to his self-esteem, and loss of approval, so must the therapist's distortions and unrealistic reactions to his patient be understood as manifestations of the analyst's search for euphoria, self-esteem, and approval. And they propose that the appearance of counter-transference indicates that the therapist feels these highly cherished states threatened and therefore engages in parataxic distortions.

Examination of the relevant theoretical and clinical literature will reveal that theoreticians consider the dynamics of counter-transference in precisely the terms in which they understand the dynamics of transference. For instance, Tarachow, writing within a relatively orthodox analytic frame of reference, observed:

> Just as transference is the source of danger, so is counter-transference. Psychiatrists have been seduced by female patients, and by male patients too, I suppose. On the patient's side there are many dangers. A patient may act out her transference love for a therapist by having an affair on the outside. I know of a therapist who became angry and perhaps jealous of his female patient for doing just that, and threw her out of treatment instead of interpreting the transference acting out. The therapist acted like a rejected lover [1963, p. 99].

Most therapists and theoreticians would agree that the psychiatrist discussed by Tarachow was made quite anxious by his patient's affair. They may disagree with Tarachow's explanation that the therapist's anxiety was related to his unconscious sexual promptings toward the patient.

If one turns to Fromm-Reichmann for an examination of the phenomenon from a different point of view it becomes apparent that her view of counter-transference was similar to her understanding of transference. She made this abundantly clear when she presented examples of counter-transference. A patient she discussed had engaged in chatter for a long time and the therapist had become so bored that he failed to hear that the patient had suddenly started to discuss meaningful data. Fromm-Reichmann commented:

> It may also be true that the psychiatrist's special sensitivity to the patient's meaningless chatter, hence his failure in being alert to the changed contents of the patient's communication, could be due to a pertinent experience in his own childhood. Suppose the doctor as a child had had to listen to the endless inconsequential talk of an elderly grandmother, to the point of becoming unable in his early years to pay attention to any significant communications of hers or of any other person's, which may have been interpolated into grandmother's chatter [1950, p. 5].

Evidently Fromm-Reichmann was able to understand the counter-transference phenomenon without resorting to such constructs as regressive instinctual tendencies. She focused on understanding how the therapist had learned defensive operations in his struggle for survival and how he then applied them inappropriately and in generalized fashion to later therapeutic interpersonal contexts.

Ruesch was perhaps more explicit than most authors when he stated frankly that as far as he was concerned, theoretical considerations of counter-transference were identical with those on transference:

> Countertransference is transference in reverse. The therapist's unresolved conflicts force him to invest the patient with certain properties which bear upon his own past

experiences rather than to constitute reactions to the patient's actual behavior. All that was said about transference, therefore, also applies to countertransference, with the addition that it is the transference of the patient which triggers into existence the countertransference of the therapist [1961, p. 175].

Consistent with the observation that counter-transference is viewed by theorists in the same way in which they consider transference is Rogers' (1942, 1951) position. It will be recalled that he considered transference an artifact and therefore he felt justified in ignoring the topic altogether. Nonetheless he dealt with behavior on the part of the therapist which others would term reflections of counter-transference. He did this under the rubric of the "therapist's attitude" toward his client. Thus Rogers commented in his discussion of trends in training of client-centered therapists:

> It has become apparent that the most important goal to be achieved is that the student should clarify and understand his own basic relationship to people, and the attitudinal and philosophical concomitants of this relationship. Therefore the first step in training client-centered therapists has been to drop all concern as to the orientation with which the student will emerge. The basic attitude must be genuine [1951, p. 432].

Elsewhere, discussing "failures" in therapy, Rogers remarked: "Clinically it is probably true that our most frequent explanation of failure is that the counselor somehow failed to build a therapeutic relationship" (p. 189). Unfortunately, Rogers did not comment on the dynamics and processes presumably operating within the therapist and responsible for preventing him from building a therapeutic relationship—or, in Rogers' own terms, from assuming a genuinely accepting attitude. As in the case of transference one can only infer from Rogers' general theory of personality the dynamics he held responsible for this failure. In his theory he maintained:

> *When the individual perceives and accepts into one consistent and integrated system all his sensory and visceral experiences, then he is necessarily more understanding of*

others and is more accepting of others as separate individuals [p. 520].

It would follow that the therapist who cannot establish a therapeutic relationship is characterized by some self-rejection; while Rogers did not say so specifically, he implied his belief that certain patients (at least aspects of some patients) may trigger self-rejecting tendencies in therapists. Rogers thought that the bases of such self-rejection by the therapist were similar to the patient's bases for self-rejection: his efforts to maintain a consistent sense of self, aiding him at least partially in preserving some feelings of identity and well-being. Since Rogers understood all behavior as goal-directed (its goal being "maintenance and enhancement of the organism"), he had to see self-rejection as also directed toward these ends. Rogers therefore spoke at least by implication about counter-transference, whether he liked to employ the term or not, though of course in terms quite different from those employed in orthodox psychoanalytic thinking. He had tried to avoid discussion of transference but wound up writing about it in most cogent terms; the situation was much the same when he came to counter-transference.

As each system's theoretical propositions concerning the origins and functions of counter-transference parallel its general theoretical formulations of transference, so the operational indices for counter-transference reactions (or rejecting attitudes) advanced by an author parallel his indicators for resistive transference. The therapist's forgetting of appointments, his inability to pay attention to the patient's productions, his dearth of associative responses to what is presented, his irrational attitudes toward the patient (positive or negative), and all the other signs usually cited as manifestations of counter-transference parallel closely those manifestations usually thought of as indicative of transference.

The point that irrational attitudes, *positive* or *negative*, reveal counter-transference requires an expansion of Fenichel's (1945) definition quoted earlier. Fenichel seemed to speak of negative counter-transference exclusively. This is not too surprising because Freud (1912a), whose model Fenichel followed carefully, concerned himself primarily with negative transference. Of course Freud (1915b) also warned the therapist extensively against certain aspects of positive transference, but he saw the patient's positive transference as a primary aid in the therapist's endeavor. But just as positive transference must be understood as a reflection of essentially negative attitudes (see Chapter 11), so positive counter-transference reveals the therapist's essentially defensive and negative orientation toward his patient.

When a therapist becomes irrationally enamored of some of the patient's genuine assets to such a point that he cannot see his pathology, when the therapist allows the patient to blind him and permits himself to be blinded, the therapist has *de facto* abandoned the patient even though he and the patient may get along fabulously well. To all intents and purposes, he has stopped helping the patient in his struggle toward emotional growth. This abandoning of the patient by the therapist may be occasioned by a variety of processes in the analyst. They are triggered by a multitude of facets operating in the patient; some concrete examples of this complex interaction will be presented shortly. The general point made here is simply that a distortion, whether perpetrated by patient or by therapist and regardless of its overt form—irrational admiration or irrational dislike—is inevitably negative and pathological in the sense that it bespeaks a reduction of personal awareness and simultaneously does violence to the other person.

Preceding the presentation of a point of view which stresses the potential usefulness of counter-transference reactions provided they are carefully examined, it is necessary to call attention to the obvious fact that not all reactions to his patient on the part of the therapist must be undersood as reflections of irrational attitudes. On this point Thompson commented:

> Freud always knew that it was sometimes not possible for the analyst to remain entirely out of the picture, that sometimes, in spite of everything, he would react personally to the patient and what he said or did. This he saw as counter-transference, by which he meant that analysts sometimes transfer elements of their past (or

present) problems to the analytic situation. Thus one might be susceptible to the flattery of a patient's erotic interest or one might be hurt by a hostile attack on a vulnerable spot. Because of the stress on the unfortunate aspects of the analyst's involvement, the feeling grew that even a genuine objective feeling of friendliness on his part was to be suspected. As a result many of Freud's pupils became afraid to be simply human and show the ordinary friendliness and interest a therapist customarily feels for a patient. In many cases, out of a fear of showing counter-transference, the attitude of the analyst became stilted and unnatural [1950a, p. 107].

In another of her publications Thompson (1952) dealt with the problem of negative counter-transference and showed how important it was to distinguish between realistic negative attitudes such as annoyance with a patient's excessive and unreasonable demands and impositions on the one hand, and genuinely irrational negative reactions to a patient, reflections of the therapist's personal problems, on the other. Her general point was that the therapist had to distinguish carefully between his genuine rejoicing over a patient's real accomplishment and false encouragement and praise for the sake of pleasing an intimidating person; that the therapist had to separate with equal concern his displeasure occasioned, for instance, by a patient's insistence upon calling him at all hours of the night from anger with some of the patient's mannerisms. Yet even such irrational anger, as will be shown, can prove therapeutically valuable if the therapist carefully investigates its foundations.

What emerges from an examination of the theoretical literature is a widely held position which suggests that counter-transference appears when the therapist is made anxious by the patient, when he fears feelings and ideas which therapeutic investigation may arouse in him, and when his desire to avoid anxiety and its dynamic roots force him into assuming defensive attitudes. They in turn are said to interfere with his genuine therapeutic understanding of the patient. Thus, in broadest terms, counter-transference is thought of as a manifestation of the therapist's reluctance to know and/or learn something about himself, as a reflection of his wish to remain oblivious of certain facets of himself, and to leave unresolved conflicts buried. Many authors suggest that these wishes move the therapist to hostile behavior against his patient. His hostility may be overt or covert, is expressed in acts of omission or acts of commission, in irrational "friendliness" or irrational annoyance or anger. On this most theoreticians agree. They differ once again in their theories of anxiety and therefore they disagree on what material will arouse counter-transference as well as the specific meaning of the counter-transference reaction. Freud's (1937) recommendation to analysts that they periodically undergo reanalysis themselves was, of course, motivated by his belief that the origins and functions of anxiety need constant re-examination so they do not trigger undue counter-transference reactions.

If this understanding of the counter-transference process is valid, some important consequences are logically unavoidable. These consequences and their implications have been neglected all too long in many circles. However, Tauber (1952, 1954) first in two articles and later Tauber and Green (1959) in their book have delineated the potential usefulness of counter-transference reactions for psychotherapeutic investigation. The analyst's counter-transference reactions, they suggested, have important message value and if carefully examined will shed important light on the patient's defenses and their dynamics. Their position implies that the therapist's basic road to intimate knowledge of his patient is careful and constant attention to and examination of his own reactions to the patient.[2] Thus the analyst's ability to examine carefully and undefensively his emotional and intellectual reactions to the patient and his thorough knowledge of the circumstances which produce particular reactive states within him—in brief, his self-understanding—lead also to profound insights into his

[2] The situation outlined here is analogous to the *modus operandi* of scientists working in the physical and biological disciplines. They too can gain understanding of their material only when they pay attention to phenomena under examination, which means paying keen attention to sensory impressions and personal reactions called forth by the material.

patient. If, for instance, a therapist were to experience a sudden upsurge of intense hostility during a patient's discussion of some conflict he had had with a colleague at work; and if the analyst knew intimately what circumstances happen to arouse this type of hostile reactivity in him, he would be in an excellent position to know the deeper meaning of the patient's behavior. Thus examined, counter-transference reactions are powerful indicators that something has been communicated by the patient to the therapist, that the communication has registered, has been recorded, and has been reacted to, albeit in an unconscious and as yet not quite understandable fashion. Tauber and Green suggested ingeniously that the exploration of the counter-transference reactions by analyst and patient will lead to new insights into the nature of the patient's interpersonal processes:

> The acting-out of the therapist appears to be an unconscious scanning response to the neurotic atmosphere communicated in subthreshold form to the analyst's receptive unconscious. We are purposely not regarding this acting-out as a counter-transference operation in the conventional sense of the word [1959, p. 144].

They insisted that certain reactions of the therapist, usually referred to as counter-transference, are not harmful to the therapeutic process, provided they are carefully examined and analyzed. Here is another important parallel between transference and counter-transference. Just as the patient's transference reactions are genuine aids in the patient's and therapist's quest for understanding, and just as transference is harmful to the therapeutic enterprise *only* when it remains unexamined and is permitted to lie fallow, so are counter-transference reactions powerful tools in exploration and potent instruments for uncovering inner states which are damaging *only* if they are brushed aside, ignored, or not taken seriously. Tauber and Green could conclude with logical and psychological justification:

> Historically, the fact that counter-transference reactions can be profitably utilized without causing undue distress

has gained broader recognition. But the issue is one that deserves scientific scrutiny[3] in the interest of more fruitful psychoanalytic procedures. Counter-transference can neither be disregarded because of its unfortunate derogatory connotations nor merely bravely faced in defense of one's own reactions. We suggest that these types of reaction need to be considered, not as an unwarranted and proscribed intrusion into the patient's field, but as a legitimate and valuable form of contact between therapist and patient through the prelogical mode of communication [p. 148].

This view of counter-transference is very much in line with Sullivan's (1954) understanding of the therapeutic process; he insisted that the therapist could not remain a detached bystander but had to be a "participant observer." Furthermore, it offers the patient a "respectable card of admission," as Tauber and Green call it (p. 146) to the analytic relationship because through his carefully examined counter-transference reactions the analyst reveals himself as the patient's fellow human being. This point of view, strange as it may seem, is even consistent with some of Freud's (1912b) admonitions, notably his suggestion referred to in Chapter 8 that the analyst pay careful attention to all his reactions as he listens to the patient; the evenly suspended attention Freud demanded is of course a type of attention which facilitates the development and analysis of the therapist's emotional reactions to the patient.

[3] The call for "scientific scrutiny" is well taken. Experimentation relevant to this area, starting with Pötzl's (1960) studies in Vienna and McGinnies' (1950) research in the United States were valiant beginnings. Attacks have been levied upon a host of studies subsequent to these which were usually referred to under the rubric of "perceptual defense," attacks which primarily focused on methodological issues in psychological research (Turkel, 1955). More recent work in the area of what is perhaps inappropriately referred to as "subliminal perception" has also met severe criticism (Eriksen, 1960). But some of this criticism melts away in the light of data collected with more refined and sophisticated designs and techniques as they were employed by recent investigators (Spence and Holland, 1960). These data lend themselves easily to the inference that information is received by humans and reacted to by them without their conscious knowledge that such data were transmitted and reacted to. Counter-transference as Tauber and Green (1959) saw it may well represent such reactivity to data collected without awareness that such a collection process has taken place. (Also see Chapter 2.)

The recognition that in any genuine process of exploration new data reveal themselves not only about material to be understood but also about the observer (Hutchinson, 1941) gains vitality in Tauber's formulation. The observation that in his diligent and conscientious examination of the patient's life the therapist is bound to learn something new about himself may well be responsible for the all-too-common resistance to a careful investigation of counter-transference reactions. If the therapist is loath to learn something new about himself and feels compelled to believe that he has complete insight and is fully knowledgeable about himself, he will avoid investigating his own reactions to the patient lest his own fond dreams be disturbed. The therapist's reasons for resisting further self-understanding and self-knowledge are theoretically identical with those held responsible for the patients' resistance. The foundations for this resistance have already been outlined in the two preceding chapters, and an integrated presentation will be offered in Chapter 13.

Startling, fresh, and new as Tauber's position may appear, it is really so new only in its succinct formulation. Insightful observers have frequently although indirectly referred to processes and procedures Tauber described forthrightly. Reik (1949), for instance, has reported numerous instances in which his seemingly irrational comments and associations led to fruitful understanding. When he reported that in response to a female patient's remark about a book being upside down on a shelf he spontaneously questioned why she had never mentioned to him that she had had an abortion (pp. 263–64), he described an instance of immediate, direct, and incidentally correct insight into a patient's unconscious thought processes.

If an analyst hearing a remark like the one made by Reik's patient were to remember suddenly that he wants to call a hospital where a friend of his is recovering from an operation to inquire about his friend's condition, the inference may all too readily be drawn by many that the analyst is bored or wants to get away from the work at hand. Only careful and frank investigation of the intruding thought could then lead to the understanding which the spontaneously insightful genius

of Reik was capable of gleaning immediately. Fromm-Reichmann (1954), too, has reported how the investigation of some
of her counter-transference fright reactions shed invaluable
light on important facets of a fright-producing patient. Indeed,
it may well be true that *all* important insights into another
person are ultimately brought about by carefully examined
personal reactions to the person. The disciplined courage to
investigate these personal reactions may eventually turn out to
be the core of the analytic process. That such a position is
somewhat in ascendence, though haltingly and tentatively, is
suggested by the increasing frequency of references in the
literature to the potential value of counter-transference reactions. Such instances are still relatively rare, but comments like
the following quotation from Bonime are not so unusual as
they used to be:

> The whole subject of the emotional response of the
> analyst to the patient is an important one that has been
> extensively dealt with since the beginnings of psycho-
> analysis under the designation of *counter-transference*.
> Even in instances where it is to some degree pathological,
> the analyst's response may relate to something quite de-
> finable in the patient's dream and the behavior surround-
> ing it. The significant point is that the therapist can find a
> valuable source of insight into his patient's dreams
> through the recognition of his own associations to these
> dreams [1962, p. 17].

Quoting from and speculating about some already published
clinical material will serve as a bridge to subsequent presentation of original clinical data. Tarachow reported the following
incident from his clinical practice:

> I had an experience with a patient which is worth telling
> because it bears not so much on the patient's ability to
> tolerate a transference, but the therapist's ability to toler-
> ate his own countertransference impulses.
> I had a depressed female patient, for whom I felt it
> would be very bad if she missed any appointments at all,

no matter what the provocation. I needed to cancel several days' appointments to attend a convention, so I cancelled everybody's appointments except this one patient's. I told this patient to come quite early in the morning instead of at her usual time. We could have the session and I would still be able to attend the convention sessions. I knew in advance that I would have to get up earlier than usual and have breakfast earlier in order to do this.

That morning I woke up at nine o'clock. I leisurely prepared to go to the convention with the smug feeling I had the day off. I stopped at my office about ten o'clock to pick up my mail only to learn that a frantic woman had been in the lobby early in the morning looking for me. I had completely forgotten the appointment.

I called her up to apologize, which didn't mend matters too much. The patient rightly scolded me. I then said something to the patient which I think was correct. . . .

I mentioned my good intentions and that I had really wanted to do something for her, but then I added, "But I guess there's a limit to the kindness any one person has to another, and I'm no exception"; that apparently in my promise to her to keep that early appointment, I had really promised more than I was able to do. I let my hair down and said that my intentions to be good were there, but I hadn't been quite capable of being that very good; it went off quite satisfactorily [1963, pp. 124–25].

Tarachow's behavior may indeed serve as a model of therapeutic integrity. From genuine and thorough respect for the patient grew his ability to speak to her honestly and without defensiveness, to "let my hair down." Yet one must wonder to what extent his "forgetting," his slip, was the outcome of a deep and profound insight into his patient. Careful and concerned analyst that Tarachow is, it seems at least possible that he had noticed something in the patient which made him reluctant to make up the session. Looking at the incident long-distance, the possibility suggests itself that the doctor might have sensed manipulative facets, tendencies toward exaggeration of distress, or similar aspects and that he had unconsciously decided not to give in to her demands. The apparent ease with which the patient accepted the therapist's confession bespeaks more ego strength than one might suspect in a patient who could not bear a canceled appointment.

Counter-transference behavior can be grouped into roughly three categories: reactions of irrational "kindness" and "concern"; reactions of irrational hostility toward the patient; and anxiety reactions by the therapist to his patient. All of them may occur in waking life or while dreaming. The following illustrations were selected because they present examples of each grouping and because they indicate how an understanding of the analyst's counter-transference reactions can shed light not only on certain aspects of his psychic life but also on the character structure of the patient.

□ A woman in her mid-twenties had entered analytic therapy with symptoms of severe depression, suicidal ruminations, difficulties in concentrating on her work, and similar debilitating feelings. She was a highly intelligent and educated person, but somehow she managed to spoil things and she felt that everything she undertook was doomed to failure. A barren marriage was in the process of being terminated and terrible loneliness had ensued. Several affairs, always with men who for a variety of reasons were unavailable, made her more and more despondent and what little sexual excitement and satisfaction she had derived from them was waning; her sexual activities had become highly mechanistic and unrewarding. Patient and slow investigation had led to some relief of the grosser aspects of her depression; she seemed able to work more adequately and seemed a bit more cheerful.

About a year after therapy had been started, the patient became involved in a flirtation with one of her colleagues, a young married man of whom she seemed fond and who seemed equally fond of her. They engaged in flirtatious banter, passed suggestive remarks, but remained physically distant from each other. One day the patient came to her session and remarked with a smile that seemed somewhat pained how much she suffered from seeing her colleague, that the flirtation and all the "sexy talk" aroused her so much that she felt like "crawling up the walls," and that the frustration was almost unbearable.

Somewhere toward the end of the hour the therapist remarked that he had a fairly good idea of what was going on, that it all sounded like the proverbial fun around the water cooler in an office and that he wondered why the patient was so eager to expose herself to such frustration, what need this type of masochistic behavior satisfied.

Immediately following this session the patient seemed to decline seriously; her depression became much more severe. With this development there grew in the therapist some vague discomfort about the interpretive comment he had made, although he had felt that it had been offered out of concern with the woman's distress and in the hope of helping her to rid herself of self-damaging behavior.

Energetic investigation of her reactions led to the patient's expression of fury and her growing awareness that she had left the hour with rage in her heart. It became apparent that the analyst had grossly misunderstood her. He had responded to her overt complaint of suffering, but he had overlooked what should have been obvious to him—that the woman was delighted by feeling capable of physical excitement and arousal even if they left her frustrated. After all, for months she had complained about feeling withdrawn, about her inability to feel stimulated sexually and about intellectual, emotional, and physical detachment from everybody and everything. Bringing her fury into the open, the therapist's admission of his shortcoming, and the investigation of its dynamics resulted in an abating of symptoms. ☐

Why had the analyst reacted the way he did? Why had he overlooked what had been in plain view? His overt concern had in reality been covert hostility, expressed in his failure to recognize the patient's satisfaction, minimal though it was. Of course, the patient had obscured her true feelings, but just the same they should have been apparent. It was reasonable to suspect that the analyst had experienced annoyance—a feeling he was to experience again and again later during the patient's frequent testing of his sincerity—with her inability to admit fully any satisfaction whatsoever. She always seemed to play down and belittle any pleasure she had in living, and the verbal reporting of her excitement had been couched in precisely such belittling terms.

While the therapist had failed consciously to recognize his annoyance with the patient for dissembling her feelings of satisfaction and had failed to see that this was what she was doing, it now became clear that he had unconsciously caught this dishonesty and had eventually retaliated by taking her statements at face value. He had reacted to the patient's hostile transference reactions with equally hostile though camouflaged counter-transference. The patient's transference behavior—her attempts to deny or at least obscure any and all satisfaction—was based on her deeply ingrained belief that everybody would begrudge her even minimal pleasures, and that she would be envied for any success just as she had been envied by important figures in her past for any accomplishment. She viewed the analyst in similar terms: as a mean old miser who could not stand anybody's success or satisfactions in daily living.

This dynamic had been responsible for her continuous downgrading of herself, for her presenting herself as totally inadequate, and for her frequently acting as if she were grossly incompetent. It was to this facet in her make-up and the implied derogation of the analyst that the latter had responded with his silly and "misunderstanding" remark. Only when the therapist recalled that he had learned in his youth to deal incisively and successfully with the lamentations of a significant person, designed to make him feel guilty about the pursuit of his pleasures, by taking them at face value—only then could he fully understand what he had reacted to in the patient. Only by examining his counter-transference reaction was he able to learn something meaningful about his patient. He had reacted to the hostility implied in feigned distress with the hostility of taking this feigned distress seriously and at face value. This investigation of the therapist's counter-transference failure thus led to significant insights for both patient and therapist.

Even some apparently totally irrelevant counter-transference reactions can lead to significant insights and subsequent therapeutic progress.

☐ A therapist reported noticing his irrational annoyance with a patient. It seemed at first vague and unrelated to anything, but suddenly he became extremely angry with the patient when he noticed grammatical errors in her verbalizations. The use of adjectives where adverbs were called for was especially irritating to him. Examining his displeasure, the therapist noticed that his immediate inner reaction was: "She should really know better, a woman of her education." Self-examination led to his growing conviction that the patient was conversant with correct grammatical usage and that she tried to present herself as mediocre in her ability to speak correctly.

The therapist, who was of foreign origin and spoke with a heavy accent, suddenly had the distinct impression that the woman's language usage was patronizing and designed to say to him: "Don't worry about your mistakes, I'll make some mistakes myself and that will make you feel better." Examination of his annoyance with the patient eventually led to a validation of the therapist's understanding of her "mistakes" and to fruitful exploration of the dynamics of her patronizing defensive behavior. ☐

A counter-transference reaction of much more open and direct hostility was reported by a female therapist.

☐ She had worked with a rather successful intellectual who was plagued by many symptoms which interfered with his effectiveness, productivity, and satisfaction in his daily life. The analyst reported that one day, immediately after she had offered some interpretive comment about an episode the patient had related, she was convulsed with what seemed to her and must certainly have seemed to him a hysterical fit of laughter. Her reaction became so intense that she had to leave the office, go into another room, and sit there for several minutes before she could return and resume her work with the patient. It took the psychiatrist considerable soul-searching before she was able to understand the roots and the meaning of her counter-transference reaction. She realized that she had learned in her youth to laugh off being ridiculed and not being taken seriously and that she had unconsciously braced herself against what she expected from the patient in response to her interpretation: derogation and contempt for being "so stupid." □

Although the patient had never expressed contempt openly and although it had never been obvious that his transference was characterized by a superior and dismissing attitude, something in his manner had communicated this orientation to the therapist and she had reacted in this defensive manner to the anticipated assault. Her counter-transference reaction and its analysis brought her face to face with an important insight about the patient: he was a man whose well-disguised haughtiness helped him avoid the impact another person could make upon him and who could wall himself off, could remain unmoved and isolated by employing intellectual sophistry. This fundamentally rejecting orientation, no matter how elegantly obscured, was basically responsible for his impaired professional and personal efficiency. The pervasiveness of this rejecting orientation had not been grasped by the analyst up to the moment of her dramatic counter-transference reaction.

Some may argue that it would have been better and more desirable had the therapist grasped this aspect of the patient's make-up directly and without her seemingly illogical outburst. Such a position has some validity, but it is also conceivable that the analyst's understanding of the depth of her patient's defensiveness was furthered by her overwhelming experience and anything less stark might have detracted from the full grasp of the patient's essential difficulties, would have made them appear pale and less obvious. Be this as it may, the unavoidable fact that her counter-transference reaction was an aid in understanding cannot be denied.

Careful examination of a therapist's anxiety reactions while he works with a patient can also provide insights not only into his make-up but also into the patient's difficulties.

☐ A relatively young and inexperienced therapist had been working with a woman in her early twenties who, although clearly psychotic, had a variety of compensatory devices at her disposal. Although the therapist was in supervision and had realized intellectually how grossly disturbed the patient was, he was also quite unaware of the profundity of her distress and its bases. During one session, while listening to the patient reporting in what seemed to him a rather aimless and slightly incoherent manner her day's activities, seemingly from nowhere a melody intruded itself upon his awareness. It came from an old motion picture he had seen years before. Startled, he tried to recall sequences from the picture and vividly remembered one scene. It was a scene in which a carnival puppeteer performed his act. Immediately upon this recall he became intensely anxious, perspired profusely, and had a good deal of difficulty completing the hour with the patient.

In exploring the incident with his supervisor it became clear to both that the therapist had finally noted the overwhelming dependence needs of the patient, how much she looked to the therapist for being moved, influenced, guided, and how much like a puppet she acted and wanted to be treated. The therapist for his own personal reasons had avoided full awareness of these aspects in the patient's emotional life and had recognized them up to then merely in intellectualized fashion. Now, finally coming face to face with and fully experiencing the woman's pathology, he was clearly frightened. ☐

It was through his counter-transference reaction that the therapist finally became intimately familiar with his patient's depth of helplessness and learned how terrifying it could be to others. It became clear to him that anxiety aroused in others by this helplessness and its demanding implications was to a large extent responsible for the massive difficulties the patient encountered in daily living, occasioned by many people's avoidance of her. And some of her intense rage reactions were brought on precisely by her sensing that others tried to stay away from her. The therapist's intense fright reaction was partially brought about by his sensing a desire to withdraw from this terribly dependent patient and his dim awareness that were he to act on this desire he would provoke her extreme rage. The therapist had also learned something about himself: that he could be terribly frightened by the dependence of others on him and that this was a problem he had to investigate.

Some of the most dramatic instances of counter-transference reactions laden with potential therapeutic and diagnostic value occur in therapists' dreams about their patients. Tauber and Green (1959) offered several examples of such dreams making extensive illustrations unnecessary here. The only case material to be reported is presented because insight developed was readily validated.

☐ A therapist had been working with a man who, although in many ways conducting his life adequately and successfully, was greatly troubled by persistent, dangerous, and potentially extremely self-destructive compulsions. Part of his self-damaging tendencies were embodied in a blustering "bull in the china shop" attitude which offended friends, employers, and colleagues. The analyst had thought that he had grasped the meaning of the patient's behavior and believed that he had understood just how the patient hoped to avoid certain anxiety-arousing situations through his behavior and actions. These beliefs seemed supported by a partial abatement of symptoms. But when they suddenly reappeared in full force the analyst was certain that something crucial had escaped him. He therefore asked the patient to contact a psychologist whose insights and experience with projective evaluations the therapist greatly respected.

The night before the patient was to see the diagnostician the therapist had a startling dream. In his dream he was sitting in his office listening to a man whom he could not identify. The man suddenly got up and walked toward the therapist with menacing gestures. The analyst was somewhat apprehensive in his dream but he remembered distinctly not being frightened. However, he recalled becoming decidedly terror-stricken when this figure while moving threateningly toward him suddenly collapsed like a punctured balloon, as if he had been filled with air which was now escaping. He even recalled hearing the *f f f ft* noise of rapidly escaping air. He woke up in terror.

A series of associations led the analyst to the knowledge that he had dreamed about this particular patient and to the under-standing of the condensation and displacement which had taken place in the dream. The man in the dream was indeed a conglomeration of the patient and somebody else, leading the therapist to realize of whom the patient had unconsciously reminded him. This was a person in his own life who had always conveyed the impression of sublime self-confidence and highest adequacy and yet had been a person who had also felt pathetically incompetent, had acted without any genuine con-victions, and had eventually admitted his belief that he had wasted his life. But he had up to then managed to obscure this inner sense from others.

The condensation in the dream forced the therapist into the full realization that this was precisely the situation of his pa-tient. This seemingly overpowering man clearly felt totally in-adequate and pathologically dependent and the therapist, eager not to be reminded of the striking similarity between the patient and this significant figure in his life, had carefully avoided seeing the obvious connection.

While the therapist was still struggling toward a full under-standing of these connections and the implications of his dream, the psychologist called to give him a brief oral résumé of what he thought about the patient's Rorschach productions. The most striking findings, the psychologist reported, were the patient's all-pervasive feelings of being a fraud; his well-devel-oped ways of pretending to himself and others that he was a man of convictions; his ability to impress himself and others with simulated thoughtfulness; his ability to impress others with his adequacy while feeling quite mediocre in his abilities; and his sense that resembling an empty shell was the only way of avoiding anxiety and achieving security—no matter how painful such a security operation proved to be. ☐

Here again a dramatic counter-transference reaction forced important knowledge on the therapist. Why did the analyst not recognize the patient's inner constellation without the benefit of counter-transference manifestations or psychological test data? This is an empty question. It rests on the belief that counter-transference is something other than a vehicle for communication, that it is primarily an irrational and undesirable attitude toward another person and therefore, as Fenichel (1945) among others had proposed, an orientation which must be eliminated or at least reduced. The point presented here, a position which closely follows Tauber and Green's (1959), is that counter-transference attitudes are deleterious to the process of therapy only to the extent to which they represent defensive and therefore unexamined attitudes and reactions. Yet all a therapist can and does learn about the patient stems from his personal observations and his examination of subsequent attitudes and reactions to the patient. And just as the patient cannot discuss anything meaningfully except his own attitudes and reactions in the hope that their examination will help him understand himself and others, so the therapist can do nothing but deal with his own attitudes and reactions as they are called forth by the patient's behavior and verbalizations. Only if they remain unexamined and not understood can their potentially irrational character persist; only then are they hindrances in therapy.

► *Summary* ◄

1. What emerges from an examination of various theoretical positions on the origins and functions of counter-transference is the observation that each theorist views counter-transference in terms highly analogous to those proposed by him in his theory of transference.

2. Consequently most authorities on the topic propose that counter-transference represents a manifestation of a defensive orientation of the therapist in his relation to the patient. This defensiveness, they claim, results from anxieties the patient triggers in the therapist.

3. An additional point of view has been presented: All of the therapist's reactions, if carefully examined, potentially further therapeutic progress because they represent subtle and what some authors call "prelogical" communicative modes capable of leading to enhanced understanding and insights.

The Concept of Insight

FROM HIS FIRST TENTATIVE ATTEMPTS TO UNDERSTAND THE PA-
tient's inner state by grasping the communicative implications
of his symptoms through investigations of resistance, dreams,
transference and counter-transference processes, the therapist
aims at developing profound insights into the patient's experiential life. He does so in the hope that this knowledge will
enable him to help the patient become aware of his own inner
life and motivations. Since the earliest days of contemporary
psychotherapy the persistent theme running through its literature suggests that the development of *insight* is the basic aim
of psychotherapy and that gaining self-knowledge is somewhat
synonymous with emotional well-being (see Chapters 3 and
9). This paradigm is found continuously in the psychoanalytic
literature and is reflected in many of Freud's comments. For
instance:

> An analysis is ended when the analyst and the patient
> cease to meet each other for the analytic session. This
> happens when two conditions have been approximately
> fulfilled: first, that the patient shall no longer be suffering
> from his symptoms and shall have overcome his anxieties
> and his inhibitions; and secondly, that the analyst shall
> judge that so much repressed material has been made
> conscious, so much that was unintelligible has been ex-

plained, and so much internal resistance conquered, that there is no need to fear a repetition of the pathological processes concerned [1937, p. 219].

His statement is crystal-clear: unearthing repressed material reduces and prevents future pathological processes. Hobbs grasped this central and crucial psychoanalytic tenet when he noted:

> One of the firmly rooted assumptions in psychothera-peutic practice is that the development of insight on the part of the client is both a major goal of the therapeutic endeavor, intrinsically worth promulgating, and a pri-mary means of achieving step by step in the therapeutic process, the overall objective of more effective function-ing [1962, p. 741].

Again one sees Freud's abiding respect for reason and his un-flagging insistence that intellectual honesty is a prerequisite for dignified human existence (see Chapter 9). Whatever the ori-gins of his orientation, whether rooted partially in Freud's Jew-ishness and the traditional emphasis of Judaism on reason and intellectual understanding and/or in some aspects of his per-sonality, the perpetual insistence on intellectual appreciation of weighty issues permeated Freud's life and writings.[1] This outlook and deeply ingrained way of life had important conse-quences for the development of the concept of insight.

The term *insight* is traditionally associated in contemporary American psychological theory with the contributions of au-

---

[1] Jones remarked in this connection:

The question of whether only a Jew could have contrived psychoan-alysis is obviously much harder to answer. . . . What we can say with considerable assurance is that being Jewish accorded well with Freud's personality and his work [1955, pp. 398–99].

Fromm seemed more certain than Jones that this Jewish background was at least partially responsible for the development of Freud's ration-alist orientation:

Freud's Jewish background, if anything added to his embrace of the enlightenment spirit. The Jewish tradition itself was one of reason and intellectual discipline, and, besides that, a somewhat despised minority had a strong emotional interest to defeat the powers of darkness, of irrationality, of superstition, which blocked the road to its own emanci-pation and progress [1959, p. 3].

thors writing on learning theory. The concept of insight is intricately interwoven with Gestalt theory and Lewinian field theory (also see Chapter 1). Wertheimer (1959) has frequently referred to the phenomenon of insight as "seeing the light," but he usually meant this in a strictly intellectual sense, and he advanced challenging ideas about circumstances which facilitate or retard insightful learning. Köhler's (1925) experiments and Koffka's (1924) studies in this area were largely influenced by Wertheimer's thinking and also dealt with presumably purely intellectual processes.

When Lewin (1942) discussed insightful learning he referred to changes in cognitive structure, emphasizing again changes in intellectual appreciation and in the person's perception of his environmental surroundings rather than to a changed perception of his inner world, although it may be presumed that such internal realignments are closely associated with altered cognition. Whenever Lewin referred to insight his primary focus was on a clear and in certain ways abstract understanding of the person's outer world. It is therefore not surprising to hear Lewin say: ". . . differentiations can be closely connected with cognitive processes, for instance with experience or with an act of insight" (1936, p. 155).

The old topic of cognitive styles has recently come under renewed scrutiny precisely because of the suggestion that an intricate relationship existed between inner states and inner changes on the one hand and the adoption or the abandoning of particular cognitive modes on the other (Gardner, Holzman, Klein, Linton & Spence, 1959). These efforts systematically to relate intellectual insight into outer circumstances to inner emotional states are, however, of relatively recent vintage. In many circles the concept of insight was and still is defined as an understanding of outer events.

Freud's concept of insight had a similar definition. He too was convinced that insight and intellectual understanding were synonymous, and even though his writings may suggest some changes in his thinking, this suggestion is unfortunately illusory. Freud was quite frank in discussing his "early" position:

It is true that in the early days of analytic technique we took an intellectualist view of the situation. We set a high value on the patient's knowledge of what he had forgotten, and in this we made hardly any distinction between our knowledge and his. We thought it a special piece of good luck if we were able to obtain information about the forgotten childhood trauma from other sources—for instance from parents or nurses or the seducer himself— as in some cases it was possible to do; and we hastened to convey the information and the proofs of its correctness to the patient, in the certain expectation of bringing the neurosis and the treatment to a rapid end. It was a severe disappointment when the expected success was not forthcoming. How could it be that the patient, who now knew about his traumatic experience, nevertheless still behaved as if he knew no more about it than before? [1913, p. 141].

After reading this passage one would have expected that Freud would outline some radical change in his approach to the problem and abandon his emphasis on intellectual understanding. But he merely changed his tactics and shifted from "informing" the patient about the traumas of his childhood to attempts at "informing" the patient about the reasons for his inability to recall such data willingly. This is, of course, what was meant by the "analysis of the resistance." Once the resistances were overcome by helping the patient see the reasons for their existence, intellectual knowledge of the original traumas would be accepted. The emotional attachment of the patient to the analyst, his transference, was the vehicle which was to make acceptance and intellectual appreciation more palatable (also see Chapters 10 and 11). Freud was once again outspoken on his thinking in this area when he commented:

Often enough the transference is able to remove the symptoms of the disease by itself, but only for a while— only for as long as it itself lasts. In this case the treatment is a treatment of suggestion, and not a psycho-analysis at all. It only deserves the latter name if the intensity of the transference has been utilized for the overcoming of resistances. . . .

Thus the new sources of strength for which the patient is indebted to his analyst are reducible to transference and *instruction* (*through the communications made to him*). The patient, however, only makes use of the *instruction* in so far as he is induced to do so by the transference; and it is for this reason that our first *communication* should be withheld until a strong transference has been established [1913, pp. 143–44; emphasis supplied—E.S.].

Thus Freud proposed that the road to intellectual insight was more difficult and tortuous than he had first thought, but the end station, the intellectual understanding of one's motivations, remained intact.

Despite patients' eventual acceptance of explanations offered to them, in all too many instances their neuroses did not disappear. Various explanations for these disturbing persistences were advanced, but they were invariably couched in terms which would not violate the basic maxim that the road to emotional well-being was intellectual understanding. Eventually, however, it occurred to some that a discarding of this formulation was called for. And so a gradual decline of the equation *insight is intellectual understanding* set in. Some authors proposed that insight ought to be understood as a process of integrating unconscious tendencies into the conscious mind rather than as a process of understanding. Assimilation started to take the place of understanding in this definition. Jung spoke on this issue:

Assimilation guards against the dangerous isolation which everyone feels when confronted by an incomprehensible and irrational aspect of his personality. Isolation leads to panic, and this is only too often the beginning of a psychosis. The wider the gap between conscious and unconscious, the nearer creeps the fatal splitting of the personality, which in neurotically disposed individuals leads to neurosis, and, in those with psychotic constitutions, to schizophrenia and fragmentation of personality. The aim of psychotherapy is therefore to narrow down and eventually abolish the dissociation by integrating the tendencies of the unconscious into the conscious mind [1956b, p. 442].

Jung's reference to constitutionally predisposing factors did not detract from his main theme: insight is somewhat analogous to self-acceptance in the sense of acknowledging what exists in the unconscious. Although the contribution cited was written originally in 1950, Jung's thoughts on this issue go back as far as 1911.

Changing conceptualizations of insight in psychotherapy were not restricted to Europe. Sullivan's (1947) formulations employing different terms were essentially similar to Jung's in this area. His key concept analogous to insight was awareness. Self-knowledge or insight into oneself was to Sullivan knowledge of the nature or the *what* of experience and only secondarily knowledge of its *whys*. Security operations seemed to him designed to restrict awareness of this *what*, and he proposed that one was definitely severely disturbed when the restricting security operations designed to reduce this knowledge of one's experiences seriously interfered with the process of living (pp. 70, 72).

Therefore Sullivan thought that the ability to stand this knowledge, to bear the knowledge of one's experience, was the definition of well-being, because then the patient could dispense with debilitating security maneuvers. Thus he was moved to define cure as:

> . . . an expanding of the self to such final effect that the patient as known to himself is much the same person as the patient behaving with others. This is psychiatric cure [1947, p. 117].

At another point he commented:

> Every constructive effort of the psychiatrist, today, is a strategy of interpersonal field operations which (1) seek to map the areas of disjunctive force that block the efficient collaboration of the patient and others, and (2) seek to expand the patient's awareness so that this unnecessary blockage can be brought to an end [1953, p. 376].

Nowhere are references stressing the importance of the patient's developing an intellectual appreciation of the whys of his behavior to be found. Tauber (1960), summarizing Sullivan's position on the theory of cure, stresses this aspect of Sullivan's thinking, his emphasis on growth into awareness.

Turn to Fromm-Reichmann and the shift of focus from self-actualization by self-understanding in the intellectual or abstract sense to growth by self-awareness becomes even more apparent:

> There may be some readers who may wonder why, so far, I have used only the terms "understanding" and "awareness" and not the word "insight" for the understanding which is accomplished by interpretive clarification. The reason is the following: I wish to convey, by this very choice of terminology, that the intellectual and rational grasp of interpretation of a single experience, as a rule, will be changed only by the process of "working through" into the type of integrated creative understanding which deserves to be termed "insight" [1950, pp. 141–42].

In an earlier contribution she defined creative understanding or insight:

> The aim of psychoanalytic therapy is to bring these rejected drives and wishes, together with the patient's individual and environmental moral standards, which are the instruments of his rejections, into consciousness and in this way place them at his free disposal [1941, p. 49].

Once again there is emphasis on awareness rather than on understanding, on the awareness of inner situations which have been dissociated in an attempt to deny them.

The search for this experiential insight is synonymous with the search for identity. In grasping his inner situation the person experiences his identity, learns who he is and what he is. Lynd has described in original and provocative terms how such insight can lead to feelings of shame. She maintained that awareness of who one is and what one has done brings in its wake the recognition of self-betrayal and disregard of the welfare of others. Her highlighting of this connection between shame and identity offers a valuable clue to understanding why the achievement of profound insight is so difficult to reach. Despite the development of shame in the search for identity through insightful awareness, its pursuit must not be abandoned because personal identity represents the foundation for man's ability to relate constructively to others. Any genuine relationship requires that the participants have self-knowledge and awareness lest all their contacts with each other become facsimiles of interaction, pretenses in which two or more somnambulant creatures simulate a meeting. Conversely, the meeting of two individuals aware of themselves and therefore aware of each other's essence will produce increased self-awareness and further a progressive evolution of personal identity. Lynd summarized her ideas:

> The ability to enter into relations of intimacy and mutuality opens the way to experiences in which the self expands beyond its own limitations in depth of feeling, understanding and insight. One's own identity may be, not weakened, but strengthened by the meaning one has for the others in one's group and by respect for these other persons as distinct individuals [1961, p. 159].

Rogers (1951) too believed that insight in psychotherapy had little to do with formal understanding but was defined by awareness of experience. Anything resembling interpretation or explanation was clearly anathema to him—on the contrary, he insisted that such procedures were inimical to the development of real growth in experiencing (also see Chapter 9). Rogers (1942) was quite explicit in his definition of insight: ". . . insight is essentially a new way of perceiving" (pp. 206–7). This new way of perceiving was, for Rogers, both the foundation and the result of new learning. But this learning had little to do with intellectual presentation. What promotes insight was, in Rogers' eyes, the employment of what he called "the primary technique":

> The primary technique which leads to insight on the part of the client is one which demands the utmost of self-restraint on the counselor's part, rather than the utmost of action. The primary technique is to encourage the expression of attitudes and feelings . . . until insightful understanding appears spontaneously. Insight is often

delayed, and sometimes made impossible, by efforts of the counselor to create it or to bring it about. It is probably not delayed, and certainly never made impossible, by those interviewing approaches which encourage full expression of attitudes [1942, p. 195].

Rogers modified somewhat his early militant position, but he did not change his assertion that insight is fundamentally the development of self-acceptance, of accepting one's attitudes, feelings, and experiences. This deep self-love, similar to the love for self of which Fromm (1956) spoke so eloquently, was to Rogers' mind the ultimate reflection of insight.

All this sounds quite different from the thoughts expressed by Dollard and Miller, even though they too spoke about insight:

Becoming clearly aware of the problem and of the unrealistic basis of the fear serves as a challenge to try new modes of adjustment. As these new modes of adjustment are tried, the fears responsible for inhibition are extinguished. When the new responses produce more satisfactory drive reduction, they are strongly reinforced. . . .

In addition to permissiveness, to skill in decoding conflict, and to the ability to aid the patient to label and discriminate, the therapist has skill in "dosing" anxiety. Others have tried to punish the symptoms or force the patient to perform the inhibited act. Both of these methods tend to increase the fear and the conflict. The therapist concentrates on reducing the fears and other drives motivating repression and inhibition, or in other words on analyzing "resistance." He tries to present the patient with a graded series of learning situations. He realizes that the patient must set his own pace and learn for himself; that it is the patient not the therapist who must achieve insight [1950, p. 231].

Here too the term *insight* is employed, but the meaning is totally different from the meaning of the term as Rogers employed it or as Fromm-Reichmann used it; different from Sullivan's implied definition, Jung's usage of the word, and even to some extent Freud's conceptions about insight, despite Dollard and Miller's attempt to stay within an orthodox psychoanalytic frame of reference. *Insight* as they used it is an understanding of the changing scene outside, while as others wrote about it, it is essentially experiencing with awareness and developing knowledge of the inner self.

The definition of insight as understanding learned from external sources is found prominently in psychoanalytic thinking. French remarked:

> In a standard psychoanalysis, *giving* the patient insight into the nature of his repressed conflicts is our most effective means of bringing about the necessary emotional readjustments. Standard psychoanalysis, however, is a suitable method only for patients who are willing to cooperate in such an attempt to *understand* their unconscious conflicts. Attempting to *give* a patient insight has therapeutic value only for a patient who is capable of tolerating such insight . . . [1946a, p. 127; emphasis supplied—E.S.].

French described a point of view, not shared by him, which suggests that insight is somehow learned from others, is information received, and is usually unpleasant news in that. It is as if some authors did not think of insight as a road which each man must travel awkwardly and yet with dignity. For them insight was simply news; to others insight was experience.

One more point of view must be discussed. This is a conceptualization which in some respects takes a somewhat middle position between the two approaches outlined so far by proposing that insight is both an intellectual and an experiential process. This seems at least implied by Pearce and Newton:

> The therapist should be willing and able to clarify his assumptions whenever this would facilitate an interpretation. It is often useful to give a patient a brief elaboration of such concepts as the stages of development, the significance of chumship, the role of promiscuity in the development of sexual adequacy. Such theorizing will not itself change the structuring of the self-system, but it can undercut some of the logical support of the structure which maintains the mechanisms of dissociation [1963, p. 428].

These two authors apparently thought that intellectual "enlightenment" can reduce or even remove some of the obstacles to the development of experiential insight. Pearce and Newton's whole presentation portrayed their firm belief that the therapist's intellectual and theoretical presentations and summaries, offered to the patient with genuine conviction, represent stimuli for a patient's potentially significant emotional experience. They suggested that such sincere and therefore consistent presentations enable the patient to become aware of his reactions to an individual who does express a consistent and nonhypocritical position and that this awareness will further the patient's insight. The authors saw insight in essentially experiential terms but proposed that intellectual presentations can often be focal points and points of departure for the development of emotional insight, awareness of self, and the experience of self.

It is in their insistence that the development of self-respect and self-esteem requires as its precondition a person's knowledge of himself that those authors who think of insight in experiential terms meet. But some of them have suggested that the very development of deep insights into himself is already an indication that self-respect has grown—otherwise the patient would not have bothered to learn something about himself. Furthermore, these authors maintained that any meaningful change is precluded if the patient is oblivious to those aspects of himself which are presumably in need of change. Human beings who are alienated from the core of their experiences and attitudes or aware of them only in an abstract and formalized intellectual manner are truly incapable of inner change because for them their emotional life is a mirage. The development of varied reactions requires first and foremost the patient's full knowledge of his reactive experiences and his intimate awareness of the stimuli he reacted to—requires that he have insight.

Some of the attacks on insight as a curative agent were triggered by the narrow intellectual definition of the term as it evolved from learning theory and Freud's theorizing. French's conception of insight as something "given to the patient" makes understandable why he did not see much gain in patients' developing insight; one wonders how he imagined that this kind of enlightening process was at all useful even in what he called "standard psychoanalysis." French made an all-important observation:

> . . . it is important to remember [it is the] emotional read-justment which may result from insight that is our real therapeutic goal, and not insight for its own sake. Indeed, not infrequently, the relationship between insight and emotional readjustment is just the opposite from the one we expect in a standard psychoanalysis. In many cases it is not a matter of insight stimulating or forcing the patient to an emotional reorientation, but rather one in which a very considerable preliminary emotional read-justment is necessary before insight is possible at all [1946a, p. 127].

If one defines insight as intellectual theorizing or the ability to follow psychoanalytic propositions, then insight is certainly useless in psychotherapy. But if insight denotes the self-awareness always implicit in conscious emotional experience, if the term describes a direct contact with one's feelings toward another human being, then insight is very important for the therapeutic enterprise. French's attack on insight is well taken but it is levied upon a narrow and meaningless definition of the term.

Hobbs' doubts about the usefulness of insight as a change-bringing agent rested on an equally narrow definitional understanding. This is surprising because Hobbs acknowledged in his paper that insight can be conceived of in two ways: as an intellectual or an experiential and emotional process. Yet when he proposed other—and to his mind at least equally important —forces making for change, he mentioned most prominently the patient's experience of his relationship with the doctor:

> The client has a sustained experience of intimacy with another human being without getting hurt. He has an experience of contact, of engagement, of commitment. He learns directly and immediately, by concrete experience, that it is possible to risk to be close to another, to be open and honest, to let things happen to his feelings in

the presence of another, and indeed, even go so far as to dare to include the therapist himself as an object of these feelings [1962, p. 743].

It is hard to tell what Hobbs was talking about other than insight of a profound and gripping order. Undoubtedly the patient's growing awareness of the range of human experience represents insight; it would therefore have been better had Hobbs abstained from expressing doubts about the value of insight, when he really had justified doubts about the value of intellectualizations.

Clinical illustrations will help to describe the nature of non-intellectualized insight.[2]

☐ A gifted woman had been troubled for most of her life by a remarkable propensity for almost spoiling all her achievements and thereby depriving herself of the fruits of her labors and ability. It was as if she could not bear any successes or satisfactions in living and insisted on denying any adequacy by fantastic spoiling operations. In one of her sessions she described how during a conversation with a colleague she had been conscious of an inner push to make some comments which would have marred the relationship between them. In reporting this event she conveyed the impression that she knew nothing about the nature of this push and knew only that it was present. But when she saw the therapist the following day she confessed with a great deal of anxiety that she had really sensed in some detail what she had felt in her dealings with this colleague: her fear of offending through adequacy had forced itself into her awareness. What was equally clear to her

---

[2] The reader will note that some aspects of the material which follows have a familiar ring and he will be reminded of data already presented and discussed. He will be reminded especially of those sections which dealt with the concepts of memory and recall (Chapter 8) and others which addressed themselves to the investigation of experience, interpretation, and confrontation (Chapter 9). Such repetition is unavoidable because of the close linkage between these processes. Interpretations and confrontations eventuate in immediate experience and bring in their wake recall and memories of emotional reactions. And such immediate experiences and their full recall constitute the instrumentalities which force awareness and insight on the patient.

and even more important was that she had been afraid to mention this awareness lest the therapist too be hurt and disappointed by her ability to realize something sharply on her own. She had had the distinct sense: "I don't want to hurt him, poor old man; what will he do if I do not need him any longer?" And shortly thereafter she reported that she had had the thought: "He will then feel unimportant and at best my equal rather than my superior." □

The patient's experience reflected deep understanding of her motivations and therefore constituted a successful attempt at becoming aware of her experiential life. Her ability to connect this type of reactivity with memories and the recall of how she had felt it was necessary not to offend a significant person in her past was merely a question of time. Sophisticated woman that she was, the patient had spent many hours discussing in abstract and stylized fashion identical material. She had shown remarkable intellectual understanding of the nature of this security operation and how it had developed in her childhood. But this type of "insightful" discussion and this type of recalling had proven singularly unproductive.

Emotional insight and the insightful grasp of experience often occur during prolonged periods of silence. Although silence often serves resistance, it is also clear that patients frequently struggle during such periods toward capturing the exact nature of their emotions.

□ The obvious and grossly rejecting behavior he had developed during his adolescence and adulthood had brought a patient in his early forties much harm and grief. In his sessions he had often used sullen silence as an expression of anger with the therapist. The therapist had occasionally commented that a good deal of the patient's overt anger and frequent condescension seemed to appear whenever he was eager to reach out for another person. The usual response to this had been a shrug of the shoulders or a disparaging comment to the effect that he guessed the therapist was right and that it made sense but that he really had no awareness of such feelings.

One day the patient arrived at his session quite late, announced that he had nothing to talk about and jokingly invited the therapist to "supply the wisdom today." The therapist responded with silence and simply looked at him for some time with slightly raised eyebrows. Slowly the patient's face contorted, he stared at the therapist, started to perspire profusely, and eventually broke into long and silent crying. He finally remarked: "I had the intense urge to grab your hand and then I became terrified and so ashamed. . . ." And after a while he added: "How often I have known this feeling." □

Confronting the patient with his dissociated attitudes promotes insight. But the moment of insight, of growing recognition of previously dissociated tendencies and the self-confrontation implied in this recognition can occur at any time or any place and is not necessarily restricted to the time when the interpretive confrontation takes place.

□ A woman in her mid-forties consulted an analyst about rather vague and obscure complaints. She explained that they had caused her to see three other analysts over a period of more than six years without benefiting from those consultations and that she had stopped believing that she could be helped. But she was desperate again, severely depressed, felt empty and forced to "give therapy another try." She was obviously bitter and angry, although she claimed that she did not feel any such emotions.

After listening to her for a while the analyst informed her that he was familiar with two of the three colleagues she had consulted and that he respected their ability highly. He wondered out loud what could be responsible for her having benefited so little and finally asked whether she did not spend a lot of time and energy in destroying the usefulness, the value, and the self-esteem of others. He puzzled about the possibility of this being an important activity for her.

The patient was shocked by the therapist's inquiry but said that she would have to think about it, that she could not deal with this question right then, and that her inability to concentrate on important questions was precisely one of the difficulties that had brought her to a therapist. Before leaving she also mentioned that she thought his fee was "outlandishly" high and asked the therapist if he could reduce it. When asked, she said that she could afford it but that payment of these fees would cause some inconveniences such as waiting a year before trading in her two-year-old car and deferring extensive redecoration of her home. The therapist indicated that he was not willing to reduce his fee but that he also was certain that she would have little difficulty finding another therapist whose fees would be lower.

The patient entered the next session like a hurricane. "Why are all you analysts so arrogant? What right do you have to set fees the way you do? Why do you think you can say things to people that are painful?" She continued in a similar vein, but then started to discuss some important events that had occurred since their last meeting. Most notable among them was her noticing during the evening following the initial consultation an intense desire to hurt severely the feelings of some members of her family. She had caught a feeling of glee within her when she observed one of the persons involved squirm under her lashing derogations and had been aware of the validity of the therapist's initial inquiry. She finally remarked that she was ready to go ahead with intensive analytic investigations. □

The analyst's usefulness in correctly sensing her desire to destroy the value of others aroused the patient's hostility toward him. Yet his usefulness had also helped her to develop insight and gain awareness of her destructive impulses, not in sterile intellectual but rather in experiential terms. No matter how overtly discomfiting the achievement of her insights was, it helped her to enhanced well-being by reducing somewhat her sense of fragmentation and by bringing her closer to her reality. This development was revealed by the patient's report that her depression had lifted somewhat the following day and that for the first time in many months she had again felt the desire to live. These feelings were the result of the patient's sensing correctly that only full awareness of who she was and what she felt held any hope for growth and redevelopment. The generalization suggests itself: The achievement of some emotional insight represents for a patient *prima facie* evidence that he can grow because he has grown already, be it ever so little. (Also see Chapters 8 and 9.)

The patient's recognition that every genuine insight is undeniable evidence of his potential to grow is, however, at the same time one of the prime forces which make the development of insight so often a painfully slow process. It has already been suggested that the achievement of self-awareness is made difficult by the sense of shame implied in the growth of identity and brought about by self-awareness. This is the shame for having failed to live up to some cherished self-ideal. Lynd's (1961) previously cited thoughts on this issue are not only ingenious and theoretically valid but are also supported by clinical evidence. Yet an additional and supplementary line of thinking must be considered.

In a series of papers, Hutchinson (1939, 1940, 1941) made the point that any genuine insight, intellectual or experiential, represents a creative act in the sense that it changes more or less significantly what is. Insights, he maintained, expand not only an area of knowledge but also expand him who has developed them. In his straining to gain meaningful knowledge, whether about himself or material outside himself, in the very process of straining and achieving new perceptions the perceiver inevitably becomes something new himself. Hutchinson made his point so well that it bears quoting directly:

> It is hardly necessary at such a place in our discussion to recall that intellectual discovery, though depending upon certain casual factors at this point in its history, *is in no sense an accident* in its fundamental mechanism. It must have background and substructure from which to start, the result of continuous storing of the mind and growing polarization of interest. Focal points of interest must have been established by hard, deliberate labor in technical preparation, abetted by an inveterate habit of ranging far afield in intervals of less serious effort. A blundering charwoman entering a restaurant in Paris does not

make an *Old Wives' Tale;* a mistake of an apprentice does not give a scientist the needed coordination of scattered data, nor does an orange produce a *Don Giovanni* unless somehow materials versatile in their application, and capable of almost any organization are pressing to be written, the scientific interest already oriented, the musical theme tentatively scored in mind. Erudition, however, is not enough; unrelieved industry is not enough; accuracy in the use and presentation of data is not enough; care in the use of inference and all the tools of art and science are not enough. There must be more; and that *more* has to do with the spontaneous reorganization of these acquired elements under the aegis of an event which is in reality not a mere addendum to, but rather an interpenetration of the levels of mental experience. And as a result one not only *creates* something; he *becomes something* as well [1939, p. 332].

Hutchinson's thoughts, somewhat paralleled by Allport's (1955) ideas, raise an important question: Under what circumstances are individuals reluctant to experience the transforming impact of insight? The answer to this question demands a short digression. In Chapter 11 the suggestion was offered that awareness of oneself as a separate and unique entity can come about only through juxtapositions, changes, and the person's acknowledgment of such internal and external modifications. But if feelings of separateness, of uniqueness, and in this sense feelings of being alone are experienced as dangerous and as frightening, then the individual will do all in his power to prevent that single event which enhances his awareness of himself and of his separate existence: he will strenuously oppose the development of insight. The sense of being "alone" is of course not inherently identical with the feeling of "loneliness." On the contrary, only he who can be alone and can bear the awareness of his separateness is capable of genuine communion with others, because a sense of self-consciousness, a sense of "I am" is the necessary precondition for any genuine meeting with other separate entities. The full recognition of his personal "aloneness" is the only meaningful foundation for man's heroic struggle to transcend isolation.

Meetings of individuals who cannot bear this sense of aloneness are illusions of union because they resemble the interactions of amoebas which get lost in each other rather than contacts between humans, who hopefully find themselves and each other in their encounters. Under such circumstances the ability to love in the widest sense of the term, as Fromm (1956) defined it so well, becomes minimal. More will be said on this issue in the concluding chapter when the circumstances which move the individual to an unhappy equating of "aloneness" with "loneliness" will be discussed.

These considerations lead to the conclusion that only those who dare to be alone and separate can dare to develop insights into themselves and their surroundings. But the distinction between profound knowledge of oneself and insight into one's surroundings is in itself illusory and an artificial distinction. For he who dares to pay attention to himself will in this process inevitably become aware of the changing realities of his environs (see Chapters 11 and 12) and the capacity to pay genuine attention to the surrounding realities implies the willingness—the eagerness—to experience the new within by experiencing the new around him. Therefore, only that inner state which Tillich (1952) called "the courage to be" furthers man's willingness to become aware of himself and to develop those insights which remind him forcefully of his separate and changing existence. These observations clarify comments offered in Chapters 11 and 12. In assiduously maintaining transference or counter-transference distortions the individual expresses his reluctance to become aware of himself and in his perpetuation of such distortions he eliminates the foundations for growing self-awareness. Through his distorting behavior the patient rejects indications of changed and changing relatedness and in doing so he stops himself from gaining insight.

The systematic pursuit of this line of reasoning leads to an at least partial reduction of the dichotomy between intellectual and emotional insight. Since the days when Binet's (1902) work became popularized professional psychologists and the public at large have employed the term "intelligence" too often indiscriminately. Psychologists developed definitions of intelligence, usually operational in nature, and used them as a basis for constructing tests and measurements designed to assess the extent to which what they had conceptually defined as intelligence was to be found in individuals. This development led to the well-deserved quip that "Intelligence is what intelligence tests measure." They most usually assay those qualities which human beings presumably need if they want to get along in this world, and to "act purposefully," as one eminent psychologist (Wechsler, 1944) put it. Yet rarely if ever does one hear anything about the goals of such purposeful activity. A thief can be purposeful, a scientist can be purposeful, a stock manipulator or speculator can be purposeful, and a poet can act purposefully. Consequently the notion developed that purposefulness can easily be divorced from its specific aims and that a thief can be just as intelligent as an astronomer, the simple difference being that they put their respective intellectual capacities (ability to act purposefully) to different uses. One may hear statements that "Göring was certainly a murderous beast but you cannot deny that he was intelligent." What people mean by such a statement is that he had a clever and cunning understanding of the world around him, regardless of the use to which he put this understanding and independent of his emotional and motivational life. But contemporary psychological investigations have shown that this type of separation is impossible.

The introduction of procedures originally referred to as "pattern analysis" of intellectual functioning (Rapaport, Gill, and Schafer, 1945), though quite deficient in their approach to the clinical diagnosis, alerted the psychological community to the fact that different personality and character constellations were mirrored in the performance on tasks which many had thought measured an independent quality, intelligence. Some personality variables are apparently capable of accentuating and others of retarding various dimensions measured by "intelligence" tests (Schafer, 1948). This makes excellent sense if one recalls that selective attention and selectivity of interests are functions of personal orientations and that such selective

factors must have subsequent bearing upon test perform-
ances.[3] If intelligent behavior and understanding of issues
require a person's capacity to listen attentively to his environ-
ing world so that he may form a rational and reasonable judgment, it is obvious that people incapable of attentive concentration will be seriously handicapped in their ability to gain an
intelligent appreciation of questions surrounding them. (Even
before pattern analysis appeared full-fledged on the scene,
Hunt and Cofer [1944] discussed it under the heading of "intellectual deficit.")

Similarly, if the subject of observation and attention with
the aim of full understanding is the person himself, those who
for whatever reason are incapable of such focused concentration will be seriously handicapped in their development of
insight into themselves. Some of the tasks presented in most
intelligence tests are referred to and are often said to be measures of the individual's ability to form concepts. Most frequently they demand that the person find a common characteristic for two or more seemingly unrelated objects. For instance,
in simplest form, the person is asked in which way an orange
and a banana can be thought of as being similar or alike.
Rapaport and his associates (1945) in their discussion of such
tests suggested that the person confronted with such a question is asked to find a unifying realm for different objects, in this
instance to find the realm described by the concept "fruit."

If one goes one step farther and speculates about the underlying personal properties necessary for the execution of these
processes which Rapaport *et al.* believed were involved in the
adequate solution of concept formation tasks, the conclusion is
that personal willingness to go out on a limb and a readiness to
leave familiar and obvious grounds are called for. Thus some
exercise of personal courage is essential because the examiner

[3] The shortcomings of pattern analysis in clinical diagnosis do not derive from the concept *per se;* much more do they stem from difficulties
in delineating significant variables for diagnostic formulations and the
construction of measuring devices which assess these significant variables
in pure form. Furthermore, even if such delineations and the pure assess-
ments of delineated dimensions were feasible, it would still be necessary
to be mindful of the possibility that different dynamic constellations may
in time result in identical phenotypical manifestations.

does not offer any clues or guidelines for this unification process. In effect, the person is on his own and must creatively develop and then carefully examine the realms which can reasonably be used in establishing communalities or generalizations. Of course, a question such as "In which way are an orange and a banana similar or alike?" lends itself easily to responding with a deeply ingrained "verbal stereotype" (Rapaport, Gill, and Schafer, 1945) by mechanically and associatively saying "fruits" without really developing a concept. But with more difficult items such as "In which way are a fly and a tree similar or alike?" stereotyped or mechanical responses are not readily available.[4] The degree of abstract reasoning an individual employs is determined on the one hand by his readiness to venture away from the familiar and on the other by the amount of comfort which the familiar offers him.

This capacity to leave familiar ground and to stand uncertainty is precisely a quality so frequently missing in individuals who may on first sight appear intelligent and capable of understanding but who, upon further investigation, reveal that whatever natural potential is at their disposal is put into the service of avoiding the new, the unexpected, and the unfamiliar. Their quest to avoid the new often requires of them outright distortions—falsifications of the outside world or of their inner experience. Some of the most destructive tyrants history has known revealed in their dogmatic outlook and fanatic insistence on preconceived notions that the new and unforeseen and data which challenged their tight little systems were anathema to them. Data have been reported suggesting that the rigid and dogmatic evasion of outer reality is closely associated with a similar evasion of inner realities (Kaplan and Singer, 1963).

[4] Even in the orange-banana item it would be possible to check whether or not the person had engaged in abstracting processes by inquiring just what he had meant when he had responded with "fruit." If he were then to say, "Well, something you eat" one would know that the realm he had found was really "food" and not "fruit" and one would be justified in concluding that although the respondent seemed to venture away from the familiar and obvious, in actuality he had done so only in his verbalization and that he had stayed much closer to a safe and obvious realm.

It becomes clear that intellectual and emotional insight go hand in hand and that true intellectual insight cannot develop without its essential emotional precondition: the courage to bear surprise. Insight cannot occur when the person is not ready to observe himself carefully and when he is unwilling to establish in the course of this self-investigation intimate familiarity with the full range of his experiences. What one observes in the face of such refusal is neither intelligence nor intellectual insight but only their cheap facsimiles: intellectualizations and rationalizations. This observation is in harmony with the already-implied thought that genuine intelligence and genuine intellectual insights are neither the preconditions nor the vehicles for psychotherapy and that they are instead indications that profound changes and reorientations have taken place (see Chapter 3).

Freud's daughter once remarked:

> The intellectualization of drive life, the attempt to master drive processes by connecting them to ideas which can be handled in consciousness, belong to the more general, earliest and most necessary achievements of the human ego. It is an indispensible constituent of the ego, rather than merely one of its activities [Freud, A., 1946, p. 178].

This is a rather limiting picture of the ego and of intelligence; indeed, it is just what she called it, the description of "intellectualizing," the result of avoidance of experience. The history of ideas and creative insights supplies ample testimony that seminal thought occurs precisely at those moments when the ego is not so busy with intellectualizing but allows the seemingly primitive primary processes to make themselves known and when they are not immediately evaded by the development of secondary processes (Hutchinson, 1939, 1940, 1941). Psychoanalytic therapy started with the promise that it would help man free himself of self-destructive, hostile, and regressive id impulses by strengthening his ego and furthering his intellectualized understanding of himself. Psychotherapy may well be in the process of changing direction away from this promise to offering man hope that he can free himself from a restricting and restrictive culturally determined ego development so that he can once again hear his inner voices and put them to creative use. Although he wrote from a theoretical vantage point totally at variance with the position presented here, Kris came to essentially similar conclusions:

> This relationship between creativity and passivity exemplifies once more one of the leading theses of this presentation: the integrative functions of the ego include self-regulated regression and permit a combination of the most daring intellectual activity with the experience of passive receptiveness [1952, p. 318].

Barzun, one of the most articulate critics of the contemporary intellectual scene, writing within a still different frame of reference, commented:

> These considerations make only more imperative the safeguard of the master virtues of Intellect. They are, once again: *concentration,* continuity, articulate precision, and *self-awareness* [1959, p. 261; emphasis supplied—E.S.].

These safeguards can develop only in him who is conscious of his experience, in him who can allow consciousness of his separate existence to come upon him through the awareness of his inner experiences. *Cogito—my* thinking requires *my* presence. Therefore *sum* is the precondition for any meaningful *cogito.* Consequently in many psychological and psychotherapeutic circles insight has come to mean the full and multifaceted awareness of *sum* and the sharp consciousness of experience making eventually for intelligent thought.

► *Summary* ◄

1. In Freudian psychoanalytic theory and in learning theory the term *insight* described a process of perceiving and understanding connections in an essentially intellectualized fashion.

In psychoanalytic therapy it referred to a rational appreciation of one's behavior and its motivational mainsprings. Many psychoanalysts maintained that such an understanding had significant effects in bringing about modification of behavior.

2. Disappointing results in psychotherapeutic efforts which were based on such premises led to a search for new conceptualizations of insight and to the insistence that insight should be defined as an experiential process. Some authors proposed that only emotional insight and full awareness of personal experience could lead to any genuine change and modification of behavior.

3. A careful examination of the conditions necessary for the breakthrough of experience into consciousness leads to the reduction of the dichotomy between intellectual and emotional insight. Such a reconciliation rests on the recognition that the personal qualities necessary for true intellectual insight and emotional insight are identical. Intellectualization, on the other hand, is the antithesis of both intellectual and emotional insight.

CHAPTER FOURTEEN

The Concept of Termination and the Achievement of Identity

IN CHAPTERS 10 AND 11 AN ATTEMPT WAS MADE TO SHOW HOW some of the processes observable in the course of psychotherapeutic work serve the patient in a dual function: (1) they prevent him from gaining awareness of his nature and maintain dissociated what he desires to keep buried; (2) at the same time the patient's behavior forces him to reveal himself to the therapist, as if asking to be understood, that his human dilemma be grasped so that he in turn may reach higher levels of self-understanding. The patient's cry for help proceeds almost in spite of him and despite his simultaneous desire to remain oblivious. The essential ambivalence in the emotionally disturbed person who seeks help because he has some faint idea that life is not necessarily the way he sees it through his distortions was outlined. Incidents which reveal these obscuring yet self-revealing processes and developments constitute the day-to-day content of the psychotherapeutic encounter and exchange. Their full exploration ultimately results in the growth of insight which represents the essence of psychological well-being, replacing pathological states of repression and dissociation.

At what point is the therapeutic relationship to halt; when is termination to take place? The answer is deceptively simple—when the therapeutic goals have been achieved. This answer is *deceptively* simple and *deceptively* obvious because, as pointed out in Chapter 3, the definition of well-being is a very complex problem and the meaningful assessment of well-being is even more difficult. Therefore the aims and goals of psychotherapy must be restated briefly, making an inquiry into the operational reflections of their achievement possible. But before the indications for the termination of successful psychotherapy can be outlined, some consideration must be given to the problem of precipitous termination and the dangers attendant on undue prolongation of psychotherapy.

Premature termination of therapeutic contacts by the patient is not likely to occur if some genuinely curative exchange has been established. Once the patient has experienced any meaningful expansion of his horizons, his resistances and the despair they reflect will diminish and simultaneously curiosity and courage to be inquisitive will grow. The patient will be at least somewhat eager to pursue self-investigation to reach further insights, increased self-awareness, and increased self-actualization. Of course, it would be highly unrealistic to expect that on the basis of fruitful beginnings all resistance will disappear. At any point in the therapeutic progress at which new vistas open up, new resistances must be expected because each advance represents a simultaneous loss of familiar security and is therefore fraught with new anxieties. This increased discomfort is experienced by patients when new insights force themselves on them, heightening their temptation to leave therapy. Divergent theorists have ascribed this development to different factors, most of which have been discussed in Chapter 10.

There is another characterological force responsible for premature termination. One frequently meets patients who cannot bear the sense that anybody is useful to them. This inability is often caused by their intense feelings of dependence, which make them feel that the slightest degree of actual need for the analyst will result in their becoming putty in his hands and that their cravings for satisfaction of dependent needs will cause them to lose any outline and definition. In other instances unwillingness to permit the therapist to be helpful is occasioned by another factor. When in his development the patient has felt forced to identify with a highly depriving person, he frequently manifests an eagerness to perpetuate a tradition as if he tried to honor his teacher in deprivation by becoming equally depriving toward others, including the therapist, and he often does this by denying him the satisfaction of being useful and of service. Only patient and persistent analytic investigation of this urgency to perpetuate familial behavior plus constant interpretive and confrontational comments around this issue will lead to insight into this outlook, which seems life-sustaining to the patient. Unfortunately, the inner rage operating simultaneously in such patients often provokes the therapist's anxiety and countertransference reactions. Triggering these reactions may well lead to the therapist's unwitting and unconscious rejection of the patient. Then the patient feels doubly "hurt," and unless the therapist is willing and able to analyze his counter-transference reaction with the patient and by so doing help him see how he invites being hurt, precipitous termination is in the offing. The following example illustrates such an incident:

☐ An artist in her late thirties had been in analytic therapy for about a year. Her character orientation was highly depriving; she was extremely cynical and furious with all other artists, gallery owners, and the world at large. Despite all this she was quite successful and supported herself well in a field notorious for economic hardship. Of course her angry deprecation had also been vented continuously on the therapist.

One day she announced with a good deal of satisfaction and pride that she was to have a one-man show in a prominent gallery, and she invited the analyst to the private opening of her exhibition. She remarked sarcastically that she knew that he would not come anyhow because this was against the rules laid down by "St. Sigmund," but since she was to say whatever she thought or felt she thought she'd better mention it. Furthermore, she believed "it might do you some good to see serious art and perhaps you could learn something about me by seeing my work."

The opening was to be the next day and the analyst inquired with surprise how long she had been planning her show, only to be informed that negotiations and preparations had been going on for months even though the patient had not mentioned a word of it. The therapist remarked on this, and knowing that he was free at the time of the opening he decided to see for himself some of the patient's work and to accept the invitation.

The following day, however, he became involved in all kinds of activities connected with other professional commitments and finally arrived at the gallery a few minutes before closing time. During her next session, the patient became even more sarcastic and derogatory with the therapist, and instead of focusing on his own annoyance with her and his unconscious desire to punish her, the therapist started to analyze the patient's "infantile demandingness." Not long thereafter the patient left therapy. □

The therapist had not addressed himself to what really mattered. He had not helped the patient gain knowledge of her self-defeating ways, and in failing to do this he had failed her. Her resistance and its unpleasant manifestations were originally heightened by increased feelings of dependence and then increased further by her conviction that she had evidence that any efforts to seek contact led to fewer rather than more satisfactions in living. Only when the therapist's active interpretations help the patient see that satisfactions in living follow the progressive diminution of withdrawal tendencies will resistances decrease in intensity.

A patient's desire to perpetuate therapy even though the therapist can see no good reason for continuation must also be taken seriously and cannot be dismissed readily as an expression of what is commonly called separation anxiety (Rank, 1945). Not infrequently one meets patients who seem addicted to psychotherapy and yet do not grow significantly, almost as if they tried to avoid termination. This type of addiction, like any other, must be thought of as reflecting an inner state of emotional disturbance and therefore needs investigation and "working through" in its own right. It expresses itself in an extreme reluctance to terminate therapeutic contacts, but it must not be confused with the patient's and the therapist's realistic hesitance to end a relationship which was deeply meaningful to both. There is inevitably a sense of sadness in the parting of two people who have gained and shared knowledge—and the therapist–patient relationship should be one of profound gaining and sharing. This sadness is tempered— provided the relationship has been rational and constructive— by their gratifying knowledge that new and productive experiences lie ahead for both. But just as the child will be reluctant to do what he must do—leave the parents—if he has the silent conviction that they will be lost and will not know what to do with themselves once he is gone, so will the patient hesitate in leaving the therapist if he suspects that a sense of bewilderment about his own future well-being will overcome the therapist once the patient has left.

The patient's suspicions, whether conscious or out of awareness, may of course stem from transference distortions—or they may be realistic perceptions of a problem in the therapist's life, may represent a correct appreciation of counter-transference problems. A combination of transference distortions and realistic gleaning of counter-transference difficulties may occur, making for a stubborn prolongation of the therapeutic relationship to which both patient and therapist contribute for their own neurotic ends. Only when the therapist is capable of dealing with certain psychological problems easily triggered by termination can a fruitful dissolution of the relationship ensue. Because termination with a patient is often psychologically analogous to termination of parenthood, it potentially forces upon the therapist some awareness of his own aging. Therefore his rational acceptance and realistic dealing with the problems aging inevitably brings—a tall order indeed—are demanded. This maturity will prevent or remove counter-transference difficulties which often lead to undue prolongation. Only such maturity will prove to the patient that this "bind" is truly fictitious and a reflection of transference distortions which then are in need of being understood and dealt with as one would any other transference manifestations.

But dealing with the problem of one's aging is an extremely difficult undertaking for most human beings, including psychotherapists, and therefore troublesome and intricate combinations of transference—counter-transference binds produced by the problems outlined here are more frequent than one may think. The likelihood of their developing and making for prolongation of therapy is marked because the therapist's own extensive self-investigation usually occurred at a time in his life when aging was not an immediate problem for him and hence his reactions in this area were either not investigated at all or in only minimal and tangential fashion. Jung (1926b) has repeatedly suggested that the problems human beings face before forty revolve around issues markedly different from those of later years (and that therefore the focus of therapy before and after this admittedly arbitrary landmark cannot be the same). If this is true of all human beings, so much more is it true for the psychotherapist whose professional activity centers primarily on the preparation of others for future living while he has usually passed the prime of life. It is entirely possible that Freud (1937) had some such issues in mind when late in life he reiterated his conviction that the analyst must periodically re-enter analytic self-investigation.

Just as unduly prolonged therapy is a manifestation of unresolved counter-transference difficulties, so does the danger of therapy being terminated (by the therapist) before the therapeutic goals are achieved derive from similar sources. If therapy has been protracted and very slow in moving, the therapist may come to question his professional ability; in order to dispel his doubts and convince himself that he does a creditable job he may delude himself that important changes have taken place. Hopefully, the needs of the therapist will not demand the irrational satisfaction of being able to induce curative results faster than the patient is prepared to move. Hopefully, his self-esteem will rest on firmer grounds, but it must be admitted that under the best of circumstances these are potential human weaknesses in the most mature of therapists which he must reckon with and guard against (also see Chapter 5). Closely associated with his eagerness to insist that therapeutic results have been achieved when this is not so is of course the therapist's sense of guilt about perchance not having done as well as he might have had he been more attentive, and about having wasted his and the patient's time here and there. Burdened by such secret and perhaps even justified self-recriminations (conscious or unconscious), he is eager to stop his own wastefulness and at the same time convince himself that his work has been fully fruitful by terminating the relationship precipitously.

The therapist who has labored long and hard and with little results on behalf of a patient, and who experiences his self-esteem shaken by the slow progress, may come to resent the patient whose minuscule progress frustrates him. Such disappointments can lead to at least covert and unconscious hostility, overtly expressed in premature termination. When this happens it is not only an indication that the therapist has lost confidence in the patient's capacity to grow beyond an often rather minimal point and that he tries to convince himself that this is as far as the patient is capable of going, at least at this moment in his life, but it reflects more: rather than face his own disappointment and his "narcissistic injury" he turns against the patient and abandons him halfway with covert anger. There are instances when new personal growth cannot take place because the patient needs a period of consolidation and therefore a patient may need "time out," a period during which he can simply live with insights he has seen in dim outlines so that he may absorb and assimilate them. This is a period in which the patient can become more conversant with himself than he has been heretofore. It may well be that such periods demand a decrease in frequency of sessions or even a temporary interruption of therapy. This possibility must be faced by therapist and patient, but such a decrease or interruption of therapy represents an entirely different situation than outright premature termination.[1]

It is also possible that a therapist may come with his patient to the realistic conclusion that their collaboration has gone as

[1] Vacation periods are *de facto* limited terminations in therapy and lend themselves excellently for assessing how well the patient has integrated insights and to establish how much of the material he has investigated has remained within awareness.

far as it can go and that the interests of both would be served best were the patient to see another therapist for additional help. Such a transfer does not imply that the patient cannot go further; it clearly indicates that in the therapist's opinion the patient can progress. It simply represents recognition by the therapist that, for whatever reasons, *he* is incapable of helping the patient advance and that another therapist may yet render valuable service to the patient.

The general statement that suggests itself is obvious: premature termination and unduly prolonged therapy are essentially reflections of uninvestigated counter-transference difficulties which interfere with the therapist's effectiveness. To keep the number of such failures to a minimum, therapists who find it impossible to resolve their personal difficulties with some patients suggest to them that they work with other practitioners. While this step may strike the patient as a rejection, it is a course infinitely more desirable than a laborious prolongation of a relationship which brings both participants nothing but anguish, boredom, and disappointment.

Now let us turn to those indications which are genuinely convincing that the therapeutic relationship can be terminated. Obviously termination seems indicated when those symptoms which brought the patient to the therapist have disappeared. This conclusion appears reasonable enough, but the issue is actually more complicated. Even though the basic model of psychotherapeutic cure suggests that harmful and bothersome symptoms and the conflicts and anxieties underlying them disappear when genuine insight occurs, various authors have observed and reported on a phenomenon which is often referred to as "flight into health." The dynamics described by this somewhat awkward term were discussed by Alexander:

> . . . "flights into health" [are] sometimes observed in psychoanalyses when, because of some clear and successful reconstruction of repressed tendencies, the patient reacts by losing his symptoms in order to save himself from further unpleasant truths [1946b, p. 153].

Many analysts believe that some patients lose their symptoms in order to maintain their character pathology. (Alexander does not seem to share the orientation he describes.) Fundamental to postulating such a process is the notion that insight is noxious to human beings and that they don't "really" want to learn anything about themselves, though it might be more accurate to suggest that some patients have not bothered to become conversant with the expectations of certain psychoanalytic theoreticians. Why should one assume that "some clear and successful reconstruction of repressed tendencies," indications to the patient that he has been understood, move him to flight from his therapist, who in hearing him has rendered invaluable service? It is more reasonable to expect that after he has been heard and understood genuine relief will set in and the patient will grow without the dubious benefit of gaining familiarity with fanciful constructs. It is more likely that he has learned something real though in nonintellectualized terms.

French commented upon a related topic:

> The term "transference cure" was given . . . quick relief of symptoms to signify "apparent cure" as a result of the satisfaction the patient received from his emotional relationship to the therapist and not of any more permanent modification of his personality such as new insight would have brought. In the early days of psychoanalysis, we looked upon such "transference cures" as exceedingly superficial and felt it our duty to urge the patient, in spite of his relief, to face his more deepseated problems in order to achieve a more radical and "permanent" mastery of his difficulties.
>
> Sometimes, however, "transference cures" become permanent. Such a permanent improvement is usually to be explained by the fact that the relief the patient gets from unburdening his difficulties to the therapist makes possible a better adjustment in his real life situation; this, in turn, so improves the situation that the patient may, after a time, find he no longer needs the support of the therapist [1946b, p. 133].

Although French's willingness to consider the value of therapeutic procedures which were once frowned upon reflects a significant departure from traditional psychoanalytic thinking, he may have underestimated the profound transformation that can occur in patients even after relatively few contacts if the therapist's work is genuinely incisive. There is really nothing wrong with "supportive therapy" if "supportive" means taking the other person seriously and addressing oneself fully to the core of the patient's life situation and inner experience. Analysis to be fruitful must always be "supportive" in this sense of the term. On the basis of some such therapeutic contact the patient may gain enormous insight and can develop the deep knowledge of himself which is best summed up in the song title "It Ain't Necessarily So. . . ."[2]

This growth often influences the patient to engage in a more far-reaching reappraisal of his life and the basic assumptions which govern his relations with his fellow men. He may even proceed to a serious investigation of those historical circumstances in his life which moved him to adopt a reality-distorting outlook and orientation and address himself to a searching examination of the origins of his life style. It is difficult to understand why a serious search brought about by the patient's convincing sense that his premises for living are faulty is deemed "superficial" by some unless he also develops intellectual adherence to certain constructs.

Of course, it is true that some patients flee from therapy as if it were poison and in order to make this flight effective and yet reasonable they lose their symptoms, at least temporarily. But this usually happens when they have the uncomfortable suspicion that nobody is genuinely willing to understand their inner situation and/or that the therapist's intellectual appreciation of their emotional life will be used by him to their detriment. Unfortunately, such suspicions may be valid. Even the most able and empathic of therapists may not grasp the particular idiosyncratic expressions of a given patient's experience, and such failure results in termination leaving patient and therapist in a state once described by Sullivan (1953) as "mutual exhaustion" (p. 11). In other instances uninvestigated counter-

---

[2] Levenson and Kohn (1964) have recently described the impact of relatively short-term therapy upon a selected group of patients studied by them.

transference reactions give the patient the painful though accurate impression that he is confronted with hostility and rather than expose himself to more of the same he "reforms" —mends his ways and departs gracefully.

Finally, there are those moments in which the patient sees with terror that his whole world system is challenged fundamentally by the therapist's precise understanding and his own growing awareness of the nature of this system. This happens, indeed must happen, when the investigation of the transference premises is accurate. Then patients are tempted to leave but will actually terminate only when again some uninvestigated counter-transference difficulty prevents the analyst from a full and persistent investigation of the patient's belief that the analyst will not appreciate the agony caused by personal transformation and reorientation. This is of course what human beings dread most: that they will dare to institute basic changes and that they will be abandoned while engaged in this process because they will reveal something that they fear will revolt and terrify the other person; or because the analyst really "does not mean it"; or for some similar reasons.

They dread that then they will be left with nothing— without the identity (or rather the pseudo-identity) of their defensive world system and without any new sense of self. This deep fear of troubled human beings requires investigation in itself, this profound distrust and terrifying sense that one will be abandoned helpless and unprotected demands careful exploration in its own right. The more disturbed the patient, the more likely is his distrust to play a vital role in his life and it is well to recall that Erikson (1959) insisted that the development of trust is the first and most basic task in the growth of identity. "Flight into health" and "transference cures" truly reflecting avoidance of further and basic self-knowledge rather than the avoidance of intellectualized insight occur precisely at moments when the therapist for his own reasons fails to investigate the patient's basic feelings of distrust.

The reduction of troublesome and self-destructive symptomatology represents, then, the most obvious criterion for therapeutic termination. But it will be remembered that symptoms have been defined as merely overt and dramatic communications of inner states and orientations (see Chapter 4). Genuine disappearance of symptoms implies the resolution of underlying attitudes and the development of new orientations. To illustrate with obvious and familiar examples: when a patient with potency disturbances becomes genuinely potent with his partner, this represents not only the disappearance of a symptom but it also indicates that he has abandoned some of his orientation which underlies the impotence; if the compulsive patient stops his hand-washing rituals, this once again implies a changed outlook; and if a child starts to learn those basic skills which he seemed incapable of acquiring despite his biological and physiological ability to do so, this, too, reflects a reorientation and not just the disappearance of a symptom. Of course, questions about the nature of this reorientation immediately arise. Impotence can be exchanged for potency because the individual has grown into readiness to share with others, because he values life, experience, and generativity in general, and because it gives him joy to bring joy to his partner; or this exchange can be effected because the patient now feels that he has found a more effective way of hurting or humiliating his partner. Hand-washing rituals may be abandoned because the person does not feel as dirty inwardly as he used to; indeed, he may have reason to feel clean because in a meaningful sense of the word he is clean, or because he is less troubled about besmirching the surrounding world, is not frightened any longer of the consequences of his dirty work, is less afraid of being caught than he had been previously. Finally, a child may start to learn because the expansion of the universe is a joyous experience, because the flame of inherent or "epistemic" curiosity has been rekindled, and because he has grown convinced that his identity can be developed through self-expansion; or the youngster may start to learn because it has occurred to him that the learning of certain skills places him in a better position eventually to give vent to his hatred. The former possibilities reflect genuine changes from essential inactivity and/or pseudo-activity to genuine activity; the latter possibilities merely reflect the exchange of one form of inactivity or pseudo-activity for another. If the hegemony of pseudo-activity as the supreme value persists one cannot possibly talk of health or cure even though the symptom has disappeared. Only continued inquiry into the value system of the patient will reveal whether genuine transformation has taken place.

Even though most theorists—despite their divergent assumptions about the nature of man—agree that the patient's ability to engage in activity and to assume responsibility are the indicators that therapy can stop, the pertinent literature describes pathetically few specifics revealing that the patient has reached such a level of development. Freud offered a formulation describing the point at which therapy can be terminated with the knowledge that therapeutic goals have been achieved:

> The other meaning of the 'end' of an analysis is much more ambitious. In this sense of it, what we are asking is whether the analyst has had such a far-reaching influence on the patient that no further change could be expected to take place in him if his analysis were continued. It is as though it were possible by means of analysis to attain to a level of absolute psychical normality—a level, moreover, which we could feel confident would be able to remain stable, as though, perhaps, we had succeeded in resolving every one of the patient's repressions and in filling in all the gaps in his memory [1937, pp. 219–20].

Even if one were to agree with Freud's definition of well-being, and regardless of one's belief whether its attainment is possible—something apparently doubted by Freud himself—it is clear that he did not offer any criteria which make the analyst reasonably certain that these goals have been reached, either fully or at least approximately.

Turning to Nunberg, one of Freud's devoted and respected students, one finds that specificity is no more prominent than in the writings of his teacher:

> The ego becomes stronger since it does not have to expend its energy for defenses; it controls the instincts and acquires the ability to *master* and *tame* them. "Fantastic" thinking, subject to the primary process, is now replaced

by realist thinking, subject to the secondary process. The ego is enriched through the assimilation of repressed material. The severity of the superego is mitigated; it tolerates the repressed instinctual strivings better. The chaotic, disorderly neurotic ego, so full of contradictions, is replaced by an orderly, unifying, and mediating ego. In other words, the ego regains its synthetic function, its capacity to mediate between superego and id, as well as between id and external world [1955, p. 359].

The ideas are clear; the operational referents are missing.

The writings of a whole array of theorists and practitioners in psychotherapy reveal a similar paucity of specifics indicating cure. Adler (1927), for instance, gave the impression that the disappearance of what he called "disjunctive affects" such as anger, disgust, fear, and anxiety and their replacement by "conjunctive affects" such as joy and sympathy, to his mind reflections of social feelings, were his therapeutic goals (pp. 265–78). The patient's ability to engage in genuine cooperative interrelatedness indicated to him that therapy was to be terminated. How he assessed the attainment of this state he did not say. And in accordance with his own theoretical formulations Jung (1933) suggested that termination was indicated when therapy had progressed to the point where the patient was able to enjoy the benefits of his unconscious, its wisdom, and its creative powers. But here too specifics are sorely lacking.

Because Sullivan (1947) was most eager to define a state of well-being in strictly operational terms, he was also much more specific in outlining the criteria for termination than other, less operational theoreticians. When he defined mental health by saying "One achieves mental health to the extent to which one becomes aware of one's interpersonal relations . . ." (p. 102), he established bases for defining the conditions for termination more succinctly and directly than most other authors. Imbued with the spirit of logical positivism (*logical empiricism* would be more correct), a fact highlighted by Tauber (1960), Sullivan was prepared to spell out what he meant by mental health and in doing this he avoided postulating inner reorientations:

. . . insight into the actual fact of illusory, parataxic distortions as a factor that complicates the patient's interpersonal relations . . . constitutes the first therapeutic milestone . . . [1947, p. 116].

Thus Sullivan came quite close to a basic concern with overt and symptomatic aspects of the patient's life, and in doing so he sidestepped cumbersome constructs. If the patient exhibits behavior which reflects the achievement of satisfactions and securities and if this achievement is based on awareness of his relationships with others then, Sullivan insisted, one may assume that there operates within the patient whatever is necessary to make effective living possible. Of course, it is also evident that Sullivan, no matter how much he may have tried to take a pure positivistic stance, at least by implication suggested that this overt picture required a specific inner situation. He suggested that the absence of crippling anxiety was necessary, for he had always insisted that distortions were actually attempts to reduce the experience of anxiety (1953).

It would be belaboring an abundantly clear picture to proceed in further examination of the position of various authors on the question of termination. As already stated, they all considered the achievement of a state characterized by eagerness to engage in productive and creative activity in various spheres of living as the central criterion of well-being making termination of psychotherapy possible.[3] This generalization encompasses Sullivan's position, too, if those mental processes which bring about greater awareness of one's relationships with others are included in "creative and productive activity."

This formulation and generalization returns the discussion to the specific criteria offered in Chapter 3. It will be recalled that the attainment of a maturity characterized by childlikeness and reflected in man's willingness to become familiar with the new (within or without) was equated there with psychological well-being. This willingness and eagerness reflects itself in the way an individual listens to inner and outer voices, in his persistence in striving for deeper knowledge, and in his dissat-

---

[3] Zulliger (1963) has expressed a similar position in discussing the application of psychotherapeutic concepts to the study of education.

isfaction with stereotyped and schematized formulations. This leads to the obvious conclusion that the readiness to engage in a genuine search and to shoulder its burdens is the hallmark of therapeutic success and therefore the ultimate criterion for termination of therapy. Paradoxical as it may sound, the moment the patient enters therapy fully and genuinely, the therapeutic task has been fulfilled.

Psychotherapy is then primarily concerned with preparing the patient for searching and persistent self-investigation and self-awareness by removing those obstacles the patient employs in preventing his becoming his own therapist through reducing those encumbrances which interfere with the creative growth implied in self-investigation. With the development of the patient's intense desire to break the chains of self-alienation and its attending alienation from others and with the initiation of this self-expanding process, formal therapy may terminate. For at that moment the patient has arrived at a point where his individuality is not *overwhelmingly* frightening to him any longer, a point where he can endure the aloneness implied in individuality and where he can say with Shaw's (1951) Joan: ". . . I will dare, and dare, and dare, until I die" (p. 134).

The eventual outcome of psychotherapy, then, is not the achievement of ultimate insight and understanding of self but the willingness to engage in never-ending striving for such insight, a willingness characteristic of well-being and therapeutic success. It would be folly to believe that psychotherapy will activate the patient's total capacity to love and care and to use his powers fully and productively. All that one may hope for is that he will become engaged in a never-ending effort to love, to care, and to use his abilities fully and creatively. Belief in the perfectibility of man is not synonymous with belief in a perfect man. Perfectibility is rather defined as a capacity for continuous driving toward growth despite the full realization that the achievement of some absolute end state is a childish illusion.

The man struggling along this road to greater self-use and intimate relatedness to others, the man dedicated to this course, is already a man who has achieved a remarkable degree of well-being and perfectibility, provided his search is a genuine and serious dedication to effort and struggle. The illusions that blind him and prevent him from facing the road he must travel are the symptoms of pathological man and, as Fromm (1955, 1962) has pointed out so well, the symptoms of a pathological society. Psychotherapy is dedicated to a reduction of these "chains of illusion" in the individual and through him in the society in which he lives. This commitment, if it is a true one, cannot stop at some arbitrary point in life or in a formalized self-examination.

Focused a bit differently, one may say that formal therapy can terminate when the patient genuinely accepts his unique individuality and has become dedicated to a continuous refinement of his personal identity. But the growth of this identity cannot be achieved through identification, the basic instrumentality proposed by Freud (1914b, 1927a, 1933, 1951) as effecting maturity. Erikson (1950), even though he tried to reject the supreme value of identification, talked of individual identity as a "successful variant of a group identity" (p. 208), and in effect spoke of identification.

Nor can identity be achieved by stubborn negativism, a process somewhat akin to what Erikson (1962) called "negative identity." Much more does the development of genuine identity demand the capacity to say "No"—not in any isolating and oppositional terms but as an expression of the realization "I am I and not you; I am separate," a development well described by Spitz (1957). Only from this positive "No," the "No" of identity and the ultimate assertive "No" of Joyce's heroine, can the "Yes" of meaningful human solidarity arise. For only if one recognizes and accepts his separateness and aloneness can he possibly reach others and unite with them. Thus neither negativism and isolation nor self-destroying identification represent the road to well-being and the outcomes of the psychotherapeutic process but such outcomes are expressed in continuous heightening of identity and the interminable growth of human solidarity.

In 1937, with the specter of horrible events to come clearly in view, Freud wrote *Analysis Terminable and Interminable.*

There he indicated that he did not think that analysis was a terminable process. Two years before his death, a year before his forced exile, Freud returned again to an examination of Thanatos and a reassertion of what he believed was a justification for postulating this tendency in human beings. He took delight in making reference to the thinking of Empedocles and his system of thought which suggested the never-ceasing alternation between love and strife (Freud, 1937, pp. 347–50). Two and a half millennia ago a leading mind had outlined a world picture similar to his own biopsychical thinking, Freud exclaimed. And should not this constantly ongoing conflict between love and strife be held responsible for so much of the resistances observable in the analyst's work with his patients?

Freud enumerated several examples typifying large groups of patients with whom analysts' work seemed in vain, patients who constantly returned to neurotic patterns or showed a total unwillingness to abandon old roads even though "new paths are pointed out for the instinctual impulses":

> At this point, however, we must guard against a misconception. I am not intending to assert that analysis is altogether an endless business. Whatever one's theoretical attitude to the question may be, the termination of an analysis is, I think a practical matter. Every experienced analyst will be able to recall a number of cases in which he has bidden his patient a permanent farewell *rebus bene gestis* [1937, pp. 249–50].

He then proceeded to outline a type of "minimal program" for analytic work:

> Our aim will not be to rub off every peculiarity of human character for the sake of a schematic 'normality', nor yet to demand that the person who has been 'thoroughly analysed' shall feel no passion and develop no internal conflicts. The business of the analysis is to secure the best possible psychological conditions for the functions of the ego; with that it has discharged its task [1937, p. 250].

But these words were in strange contradiction to the thought Freud had expressed in the same paper immediately preceding the paragraph just quoted:

So not only the patient's analysis but that of the analyst himself has ceased to be terminable and become an interminable task [p. 250].

These contradictory thoughts can be reconciled only by defining "the best possible psychological conditions for the functioning of the ego" as tendencies which further and encourage interminable analysis—perpetual self-examination. But this view does not require postulating Thanatos or any other force which ceaselessly exerts regressive pulls and requires constant vigilant counteraction. In its stead this position requires the acknowledgment of man's finiteness and incompleteness and at the same time his inherent tendency to expansion. There is ample evidence supporting the assertion that such a tendency exists (see Chapter 2). And the acknowledgment of finiteness and incompleteness, the condition for expansive efforts, also brings about the sense of individuality, uniqueness, and separateness: the feeling of aloneness and responsibility. Once again it must be realized that, paradoxically, man's awareness and acceptance of aloneness is his ultimate guarantee against loneliness.

It would be foolish to insist that man's behavior in general and the reactions of neurotics in particular do not suggest directions proposed by Freud. Freud's "nihilism and pessimism," to use Burchard's (1958) phrase, seem justified to many. But, contrary to Burchard's assertion, these qualities in Freud's thinking derive not from his "very high level of therapeutic aspiration" (1958, p. 356) but from Freud's general orientation to life, which was characterized by a deeply ingrained and grim conservatism only slightly tempered by a benevolent paternalistic attitude. He had to see regressive tendencies as inherent in human nature rather than as man's reactions to and within a restrictive social and economic order. This conservatism and reluctance to examine the social and economic setting in which his patients lived and to notice its destructiveness is amply illustrated by a revealing comment made by Freud. At a time when the bankruptcy of the order in which Freud had grown up was only all too apparent; when the once-powerful Austrian Empire had collapsed and Europe in general and

Germany and Austria in particular were in ferment looking for new ways of social and economic organization; when men no matter how ineffectually and often for selfish motives advanced bold dreams to help humanity to its feet; at that moment in September 1918 Freud mused:

> We shall probably discover that the poor are even less ready to part with their neuroses than the rich, because the hard life that awaits them if they recover offers them no attraction, and illness gives them one more claim to social help. Often, perhaps, we may only be able to achieve anything by combining mental assistance with some material support in the manner of the Emperor Joseph [1919, p. 167].

The picture is devastating. "Claim to social help" is essentially what Freud envisioned as the inherently infantile and regressive striving in man. As Freud saw it, the inherent drive is not toward dignity, identity, and genuine independence, it is much more toward the "Küss die Hand, gnäh Herr"[4] of the Viennese mendicant. Freud could not let himself see that there are other forces operating in man and that as Fromm (1955) has put it, "Destructiveness is a secondary potentiality . . . ," that there exists also a "primary potentiality for love and reason . . ." (p. 37).

The "terminable" task of psychotherapy is to help man get on his way in search of this "primary potentiality"; the "interminable" aspect of psychotherapy is man's pursuit of this road and his everlasting quest for ways of making the journey meaningful.

► *Summary* ◄

1. Concepts such as "flight into health," "transference cure," and "supportive therapy" are employed to explain premature termination. Failures in therapy are to be understood as out-

---

[4] "I kiss your hand, merciful sir."

comes of unexamined counter-transference reactions and not as manifestations of the patient's inherent opposition to change.

2. Unduly prolonged therapy reflects the analyst's reluctance to examine the patient's transference beliefs; this reluctance is the result of the analyst's unexamined counter-transference difficulties.

3. Various conditions can be considered indices for fruitful termination of the therapist–patient relationship.

4. The formal aspects of therapy are terminable but strenuous self-examination is a life-long process and hence "interminable."

REFERENCES

ADLER, A. (1919). *The neurotic constitution.* New York: Moffatt, Yard and Company.

———. (1927). *Understanding human nature.* New York: Greenberg Publishers.

———. (1939). *Social interest.* New York: G. P. Putnam's Sons.

ALEXANDER, F. (1946a). The development of psychoanalytic therapy. In F. Alexander and T. M. French (Eds.), *Psychoanalytic therapy.* New York: The Ronald Press Company, 13–24.

———. (1946b). Efficacy of brief contact. In F. Alexander and T. M. French (Eds.), *Psychoanalytic therapy.* New York: The Ronald Press Company, 145–55.

———. (1946c). The principle of corrective emotional experience. In F. Alexander and T. M. French (Eds.), *Psychoanalytic therapy.* New York: The Ronald Press Company, 66–70.

———, and FRENCH, T. M. (Eds.) (1946). *Psychoanalytic therapy.* New York: The Ronald Press Company.

ALLEN, F. H. (1942) *Psychotherapy with children.* New York: W. W. Norton and Company.

ALLPORT, G. W. (1937a). *Personality: A psychological interpretation.* New York: Henry Holt and Company.

———. (1937b). The functional autonomy of motives. *Amer. J. Psychol.,* 50: 141–56.

———. (1955). *Becoming.* New Haven: Yale University Press.

———. (1961). *Pattern and growth in personality.* New York: Holt, Rinehart and Winston.

ARIETI, S. (1955). *Interpretation of schizophrenia.* New York: Robert Brunner.

AUSUBEL, D. P. (1961). Personality disorder *is* disease. *Amer. Psychol.,* 16: 69–74.

[360] References

AXLINE, V. M. (1947). *Play therapy.* Boston: Houghton Mifflin.

BACH, S., and KLEIN, G. S. (1957). The effects of prolonged subliminal exposure of words. *Amer. Psychol., 12:* 357–66.

BARRON, F. (1958). The needs for order and for disorder as motives in creative activity. In C. W. Taylor (Principal Investigator), *The second research conference on the identification of creative scientific talent.* Salt Lake City: University of Utah Press, 119–28.

BARZUN, J. (1959). *The house of intellect.* New York: Harper & Brothers.

BEN-AVI, A. H. (1959). The role of immediate experience for dynamic psychiatry. Zen Buddhism. In S. Arieti (Ed.), *American handbook of psychiatry.* New York: Basic Books, 1816–20.

BENEDEK, TH. (1946). Control of the transference relationship. In F. Alexander and T. M. French (Eds.), *Psychoanalytic therapy.* New York: The Ronald Press Company, 173–206.

BERGSON, H. (1912). *An introduction to metaphysics.* London: G. P. Putnam.

BERLYNE, D. E. (1950). Novelty and curiosity as determinants of exploratory behavior. *Brit. J. Psychol., 41:* 68–80.

———. (1955). The arousal and satiation of perceptual curiosity in the rat. *J. comp. physiol. Psychol., 48:* 238–46.

———. (1960). *Conflict, arousal, and curiosity.* New York: McGraw-Hill Book Company.

BETTELHEIM, B. (1950). *Love is not enough.* Glencoe, Ill.: Free Press.

BINET, A. (1902). *L'étude experimentale de l'intelligence.* Paris: Alfred Costes.

BLANCHARD, PH. (1946). Psychoanalytic contributions to the problem of reading disabilities. *The psychoanalytic study of the child, 2:* 163–86.

BONDEL, G. (1958). An investigation into the relationship between the Rorschach Test and the first dream in therapy. Unpublished dissertation, New York University.

BONIME, W. (1962). *The clinical use of dreams.* New York: Basic Books.

BOORSTIN, D. J. (1962). *The image.* New York: Atheneum.

BOSS, M. (1963). *Psychoanalysis and Daseinsanalysis.* New York: Basic Books.

BREUER, J., and FREUD, S. (1957). *Studies on hysteria.* New York: Basic Books.

BRIDGEWATER, W., and SHERWOOD, E. J. (Eds.) (1950). *The Columbia encyclopedia.* (2nd ed.) New York: Columbia University Press.

BRUNER, J. S. (1957). Freud and the image of man. In B. Nelson (Ed.), *Freud and the 20th century.* New York: Meridian Books, 277–85.

BUBER, M. (1926). Education. In M. Buber, *Between man and man.* London: Routledge and Kegan Paul, 1954, 83–103.

———. (1957). Guilt and guilt feelings. *Psychiatry, 20:* 114–29.

BUGENTHAL, J. F. T. (1964). The person who is the psychotherapist. *J. consult. Psychol., 28:* 272–77.

BÜHLER, K. (1922). *Die geistige Entwicklung des Kindes.* Jena: Verlag von Gustav Fischer.

BURCHARD, E. M. L. (1958). The evolution of psychoanalytic tasks and goals. *Psychiatry, 21:* 341–57.

BUTLER, R. A. (1953). Discrimination learning by rhesus monkeys to visual-exploration motivation. *J. comp. physiol. Psychol., 46:* 95–98.

———. (1958). Exploration and related behavior. *J. Individ. Psychol., 14:* 111–20.

———, and HARLOW, H. F. (1954). Persistence of visual exploration in monkeys. *J. comp. physiol. Psychol., 47:* 258–63.

CASSIRER, E. (1955). *The myth of the state.* Garden City: Doubleday and Company (Anchor Book).

———. (1956). *An essay on man.* Garden City: Doubleday and Company (Anchor Book).

CHEIN, I. (1962). The image of man. *J. soc. issues, 18:* 1–35.

COFER, C. N. (1959). Motivation. *Ann. rev. Psychol., 10:* 173–202.

COHN, M. (1930). Selbstmord. In *Jüdisches Lexikon, 4,* Berlin: Jüdischer Verlag, 350–51.

CONANT, J. C. (1950). *The overthrow of the phlogiston theory.* Cambridge: Harvard University Press.

DEUTSCH, H. (1925). The psychology of women in relation to the functions of reproduction. In R. Fliess (Ed.), *The psychoanalytic reader I.* New York: International Universities Press, 1948, 193–206.

———. (1930). The significance of masochism in the mental life of women. In R. Fliess (Ed.), *The psychoanalytic reader I.* New York: International Universities Press, 1948, 223–36.

———. (1932). On female homosexuality. In R. Fliess (Ed.), *The Psychoanalytic reader I.* New York: International Universities Press, 1948, 237–60.

DOLLARD, J., and MILLER, N. A. (1950). *Personality and psychotherapy.* New York: McGraw-Hill Book Company.

DUNBAR, H. F. (1954). *Emotions and bodily changes.* New York: Columbia University Press.

EAGLE, M. (1959). The effects of subliminal stimuli of aggressive content upon conscious cognition. *J. Personal., 27:* 578–600.

———. (1962). Personality correlates of sensitivity to subliminal stimuli. *J. nerv. ment. Dis., 134:* 1–17.

EDWARDS, N. (1962). The earliest memory and its relationship to activity as a personality variable. Unpublished M.A. thesis, School of Education, City College of the City University of New York.

EIMER, E. (1963). Relegation of unnecessary stimuli as a factor in concept formation. Unpublished research paper, School of Education, City College of the City University of New York.

———. (1964). Perception and concept formation: Variables of independence and identification. Unpublished M.A. thesis, School of Education, City College of the City University of New York.

ERIKSEN, C. W. (1960). Discrimination and learning without awareness: A methodological survey and evaluation. *Psychol. rev.*, 67: 279–300.

ERIKSON, E. H. (1950). *Childhood and society.* New York: W. W. Norton and Company.

———. (1953). On the sense of inner identity. In R. P. Knight (Ed.), *Psychoanalytic psychiatry and psychology.* New York: International Universities Press, 1954, 351–64.

———. (1954). The dream specimen of psychoanalysis. In R. P. Knight (Ed.), *Psychoanalytic psychiatry and psychology.* New York: International Universities Press, 1954, 131–70.

———. (1959). Identity and the life cycle. *Psychol. issues, 1(1):* 5–164.

———. (1962). *Young man Luther.* New York: W. W. Norton and Company.

Ethical standards of psychologists (1953). Washington, D.C.: The American Psychological Association.

FAGOTHEY, A. (1963). *Right and reason.* St. Louis: C. V. Mosby Company.

FEIGL, H. (1955). Philosophical embarrassments of psychology. *Amer. Psychol., 14:* 115–28.

FENICHEL, O. (1945). *The psychoanalytic theory of neurosis.* New York: W. W. Norton and Company.

FERENCZI, S. (1909). Introjection and transference. In S. Ferenczi, *Sex in psychoanalysis.* New York: Basic Books, 1950, 35–93.

———. (1913). The ontogenesis of symbols. In S. Ferenczi, *Sex in psychoanalysis.* New York: Basic Books, 1950, 276–81.

FRENCH, T. M. (1946a). Planning psychotherapy. In F. Alexander and T. M. French (Eds.), *Psychoanalytic therapy.* New York: The Ronald Press Company, 107–31.

———. (1946b). The dynamics of the therapeutic process. In F. Alexander and T. M. French (Eds.), *Psychoanalytic therapy.* New York: The Ronald Press Company, 132–44.

FRENKEL-BRUNSWIK, E. (1949). Intolerance of ambiguity as an emotional and perceptual personality variable. *J. personal., 18:* 108–43.

FREUD, A. (1928). *Introduction to the technique of child analysis.* New York: Nervous and Mental Disease Publishing Company.

————. (1946). *The ego and the mechanisms of defence.* New York: International Universities Press.

FREUD, S. (1894). On the grounds for detaching a particular syndrome from neurasthenia under the description 'anxiety neurosis.' In S. Freud, *Standard edition.* London: The Hogarth Press, 1953, *3:* 87–117.

————. (1900). The interpretation of dreams. In A. A. Brill (Ed.), *The basic writings of Sigmund Freud.* New York: The Modern Library, 1938, 179–549.

————. (1904a). Psychopathology of everyday life. In A. A. Brill (Ed.), *The basic writings of Sigmund Freud.* New York: The Modern Library, 1938, 33–178.

————. (1904b). On psychotherapy. In S. Freud, *Standard edition.* London: The Hogarth Press, 1953, *7:* 257–68.

————. (1904c). Freud's psycho-analytic procedure. In S. Freud, *Standard edition.* London: The Hogarth Press, 1953, *7:* 249–54.

————. (1905a). Fragments of an analysis of a case of hysteria. In S. Freud, *Standard edition.* London: The Hogarth Press, 1953, *7:* 7–122.

————. (1905b). Three contributions to the theory of sex. In A. A. Brill (Ed.), *The basic writings of Sigmund Freud.* New York: The Modern Library, 1938, 553–629.

————. (1909). Analysis of a phobia in a five-year-old boy. In S. Freud, *Standard edition.* London: The Hogarth Press, 1953, *10:* 5–147.

————. (1910). 'Wild' psycho-analysis. In S. Freud, *Standard edition.* London: The Hogarth Press, 1953, *11:* 221–27.

————. (1911). Psycho-analytic notes on an autobiographical account of a case of paranoia. In S. Freud, *Standard edition.* London: The Hogarth Press, 1953, *12:* 9–82.

————. (1912a). The dynamics of transference. In S. Freud, *Standard edition.* London: The Hogarth Press, 1953, *12:* 99–108.

————. (1912b). Recommendations to physicians practising psycho-analysis. In S. Freud, *Standard edition.* London: The Hogarth Press, 1953, *12:* 111–20.

————. (1913). On beginning the treatment. (Further recommendations on the technique of psycho-analysis I.) In S. Freud, *Standard edition.* London: The Hogarth Press, 1953, *12:* 123–44.

————. (1914a). Remembering, repeating, and working-through. (Further recommendations on the technique of psycho-analysis II.) In S. Freud, *Standard edition.* London: The Hogarth Press, 1953, *12:* 147–56.

————. (1914b). On narcissism: An introduction. In S. Freud, *Standard edition.* London: The Hogarth Press, 1953, *14:* 73–102.

————. (1914c). On the history of the psycho-analytic movement. In

S. Freud, *Standard edition*. London: The Hogarth Press, 1953, *14:* 7–66.

———. (1915a). Observations on transference love. (Further recommendations on the technique of psycho-analysis III.) In S. Freud, *Standard edition*. London: The Hogarth Press, 1953, *12:* 159–71.

———. (1915b). Repression. In S. Freud, *Standard edition*. London: The Hogarth Press, 1953, *14:* 146–58.

———. (1919). Lines of advance in psycho-analytic therapy. In S. Freud, *Standard edition*. London: The Hogarth Press, 1953, *17:* 159–68.

———. (1920). Totem and taboo. In A. A. Brill (Ed.), *The basic writings of Sigmund Freud.* New York: The Modern Library, 1938, 807–930.

———. (1922a). Two encyclopaedia articles. (A) Psycho-analysis. In S. Freud, *Standard edition*. London: The Hogarth Press, 1953, *18:* 235–54.

———. (1922b). Postscript. In S. Freud, *Standard edition*. London: The Hogarth Press, 1953, *10:* 148–49.

———. (1923). Remarks on the theory and practice of dream-interpretation. In S. Freud, *Standard edition*. London: The Hogarth Press, 1953, *19:* 109–21.

———. (1924a). The economic problem of masochism. In S. Freud, *Standard edition*. London: The Hogarth Press, 1953, *19:* 159–70.

———. (1924b). The dissolution of the Oedipus complex. In S. Freud, *Standard edition*. London: The Hogarth Press, 1953, *19:* 173–79.

———. (1925a). Some additional notes upon dream-interpretation as a whole. In S. Freud, *Standard edition*. London: The Hogarth Press, 1953, *19:* 127–38.

———. (1925b). The resistances to psycho-analysis. In S. Freud, *Standard edition*. London: The Hogarth Press, 1953, *19:* 213–22.

———. (1925c). Some psychical consequences of the anatomical distinction between the sexes. In S. Freud, *Standard edition*. London: The Hogarth Press, 1953, *19:* 248–58.

———. (1927a). *The ego and the id.* London: The Hogarth Press.

———. (1927b). Postscript. (The question of lay analysis.) In S. Freud, *Standard edition*. London: The Hogarth Press, 1953, *20:* 251–58.

———. (1933). *New introductory lectures on psycho-analysis.* New York: W. W. Norton and Company.

———. (1935). *A general introduction to psycho-analysis.* New York: Liveright Publishing Corporation.

———. (1936). *The problem of anxiety.* New York: W. W. Norton and Company.

———. (1937). Analysis terminable and interminable. In S. Freud, *Standard edition*. London: The Hogarth Press, 1953, *23:* 216–53.

———. (1938). Splitting the ego in the process of defence. In S. Freud, *Standard edition*. London: The Hogarth Press, 1953, *18:* 275–78.

———. (1942). *Beyond the pleasure principle.* London: The Hogarth Press.

———. (1945). *An outline of psychoanalysis.* New York: W. W. Norton and Company.

———. (1951). *Civilization and its discontents.* London: The Hogarth Press.

———. (1953). *The future of an illusion.* New York: Liveright Publishing Corporation.

FROMM, E. (1941). *Escape from freedom.* New York: Farrar and Rinehart.

———. (1947). *Man for himself.* New York: Rinehart and Company.

———. (1950). *Psychoanalysis and religion.* New Haven: Yale University Press.

———. (1951). *The forgotten language.* New York: Rinehart and Company.

———. (1955). *The sane society.* New York: Rinehart and Company.

———. (1956). *The art of loving.* New York: Harper & Brothers.

———. (1959). *Sigmund Freud's mission.* New York: Harper & Brothers.

———. (1961). *Marx's concept of man.* New York: Frederick Ungar Publishing Company.

———. (1962). *Beyond the chains of illusion.* New York: Simon and Schuster.

———, SUZUKI, D. T., and DE MARTINO, R. (1960). *Zen Buddhism and psychoanalysis.* New York: Harper & Brothers.

FROMM-REICHMANN, F. (1941). Recent advances in psychoanalytic therapy. In D. M. Bullard (Ed.), *Psychoanalysis and psychotherapy.* Chicago: University of Chicago Press, 1959, 49–54.

———. (1946). Remarks on the philosophy of mental disorder. In D. M. Bullard (Ed.), *Psychoanalysis and psychotherapy.* Chicago: The University of Chicago Press, 1959, 3–24.

———. (1949a). Recent advances in psychoanalysis. In D. M. Bullard (Ed.), *Psychoanalysis and psychotherapy.* Chicago: The University of Chicago Press, 1959, 88–99.

———. (1949b). Notes on the personal and professional requirements of a psychotherapist. In D. M. Bullard (Ed.), *Psychoanalysis and psychotherapy.* Chicago: The University of Chicago Press, 1959, 63–87.

———. (1950). *Principles of intensive psychotherapy.* Chicago: The University of Chicago Press.

———. (1952). Personality of the psychotherapist and the doctor-patient relationship. In D. M. Bullard (Ed.), *Psychoanalysis and psychotherapy.* Chicago: The University of Chicago Press, 1959, 100–4.

———. (1954). An intensive study of twelve cases of manic-depressive psychosis. In D. M. Bullard (Ed.), *Psychoanalysis and psychotherapy.* Chicago: The University of Chicago Press, 1959, 227–74.

———. (1956). Notes on the history and philosophy of psychotherapy. In D. M. Bullard (Ed.), *Psychoanalysis and psychotherapy.* Chicago: The University of Chicago Press, 1959, 25–46.

———. (1959). Loneliness. *Psychiatry,* 22: 1–15.

GARDNER, R. W., HOLZMAN, P. S., KLEIN, G. S., LINTON, H. B., and SPENCE, D. P. (1959). Cognitive control. *Psychol. issues.*, *1(4):* 1–185.

GETZELS, J. W., and JACKSON, P. W. (1962). *Creativity and intelligence.* London: John Wiley and Sons.

GILL, M., NEWMAN, R., and REDLICH, F. C. (1954). *The initial interview in psychiatric practice.* New York: International Universities Press.

GOETHE, J. W. VON (Part I, 1808, Part II, 1833). *Faust.* In W. Kaufmann (Ed.), *Goethe's Faust.* Garden City: Doubleday and Company (Anchor Book), 1962.

GOLDBERGER, L., and HOLT, R. R. (1958). Experimental inference with reality contact (perceptual isolation): Method and group results. *J. nerv. ment. dis.*, *127:* 99–112.

GOLDSTEIN, K. (1951). *Human nature in the light of psychopathology.* Cambridge: Harvard University Press.

GRODDECK, G. (1951). *The unknown self.* New York: Funk and Wagnalls.

GUTHEIL, E. A. (1951). *The handbook of dream analysis.* New York: Liveright Publishing Corporation.

HALL, C. S., and LINDZEY, G. (1957). *Theories of personality.* New York: John Wiley and Sons.

HARLOW, H. F. (1958). The nature of love. *Amer. Psychol.*, *13:* 673–85.

———, HARLOW, M. K., and MEYER, D. R. (1950). Learning motivated by a manipulation drive. *J. exp. Psychol.*, *40:* 228–34.

HARTMANN, H. (1939). Ego psychology and the problem of adaptation. In D. Rapaport (Ed.), *Organization and pathology of thought.* New York: Columbia University Press, 1951, 362–96.
———. (1964). *Essays on ego psychology.* New York: International Universities Press.

HEBB, D. O. (1955). Drives and the c. n. s. (conceptual nervous system). *Psychol. rev.*, *66:* 243–54.

HEIDEGGER, M. (1953). *Sein und Zeit.* Tübingen: Max Niemeyer Verlag.

HENDRICK, I. (1942). Instinct and the ego during infancy. *Psychoanal. quart.*, *11:* 33–58.

HERBERG, W. (1957). Freud, the revisionists, and social reality. In B. Nelson (Ed.), *Freud and the 20th century.* New York: Meridian Books, 143–63.

HILGARD, E. R. (1952). Experimental approaches to psychoanalysis.

In E. Pumpian-Mindlin (Ed.), *Psychoanalysis as a science*. Stanford: Stanford University Press.

———. (1956). *Theories of learning*. (2nd ed.) New York: Appleton-Century-Crofts.

HIRSCH, I. R., and SINGER, E. (1961). Adolescent dependence and rebelliousness. (Abstract.) *Amer. Psychol., 16:* 353.

HOBBS, N. (1962). Sources of gain in psychotherapy. *Amer. Psychol., 17:* 741–47.

HOLT, R. R. (1963). A report on subliminal studies at the Research Center for Mental Health, New York University. *The N.Y. State Psychol., 15(1):* 4–5.

HORNEY, K. (1945). *Our inner conflicts*. New York: W. W. Norton and Company.

HULL, C. L. (1943). *Principles of behavior*. New York: Appleton-Century-Crofts.

HUNT, J. McV. (1941). The effects of infant feeding-frustration upon adult hoarding behavior in the albino rat. *J. abnor. soc. Psychol., 36:* 338–60.

———, and COFER, C. N. (1944). Psychological deficit. In J. McV. Hunt (Ed.), *Personality and the behavior disorders*. (2 vols.) New York: The Ronald Press Company, 971–1032.

HUSSERL, E. (1928). *Vorlesungen zur Phänomenologie des Zeitbewusstseins*. Halle: Max Niemeyer Verlag.

HUTCHINSON, D. E. (1939). Varieties of insight in humans. *Psychiatry, 2:* 323–32.

———. (1940). The period of frustration in creative endeavor. *Psychiatry, 3:* 351–59.

———. (1941). The nature of insight. *Psychiatry, 4:* 31–43.

JOHNSON, A. M., FALSTEIN, E. I., SZUREK, S. A., and SVENDSEN, M. (1941). School phobia. *Amer. J. Orthopsychiat., 11:* 702–11.

JONES, E. (1955). *The life and work of Sigmund Freud*. (3 vols.) New York: Basic Books.

JUNG, C. G. (1929). *Das Unbewusste im normalen und kranken Seelenleben*. Zürich: Rascher und Cie.

———. (1933). *Modern man in search of a soul*. New York: Harcourt, Brace and Company.

———. (1939). *The integration of personality*. New York: Farrar and Rinehart.

———. (1946). Psychology of the transference. In C. G. Jung, *The practice of psychotherapy*. New York: Pantheon Books (Bollinger Series XX), *16*, 1954, 163–321.

————. (1953). *Psychology and alchemy.* New York: Pantheon Books.

————. (1956a). *Two essays on analytical psychology.* New York: Meridian Books.

————. (1956b). *Symbols of transformation.* (2 vols.) New York: Harper & Brothers.

KAISER, H. (1955). The problem of responsibility in psychotherapy. *Psychiatry, 18:* 205–12.

KAPLAN, M., and SINGER, E. (1963). Dogmatism and sensory alienation: An empirical investigation. *J. consult. Psychol., 27:* 486–91.

KAUFMANN, W. (1960). *From Shakespeare to existentialism.* Garden City: Doubleday and Company (Anchor Book).

KELLY, G. A. (1955). *The psychology of personal constructs.* (2 vols.) New York: W. W. Norton and Company.

KLEIN, G. S., SPENCE, D. P., HOLT, R. R., and GOUREVITCH, S. (1958). Cognition without awareness: Subliminal influences upon unconscious thought. *J. abnorm. soc. Psychol., 57:* 255–66.

KLEIN, M. (1960). *The psychoanalysis of children.* New York: Grove Press.

KOFFKA, K. (1924). *Growth of the mind.* New York: Harcourt, Brace and Company.

KÖHLER, W. (1925). *The mentality of apes.* New York: Harcourt, Brace and Company.

KRIS, E. (1952). *Psychoanalytic explorations in art.* New York: International Universities Press.

KUBZANSKY, P. E., and LEIDERMAN, P. H. (1961). Sensory deprivation: An overview. In P. Solomon *et al.* (Eds.), *Sensory deprivation.* Cambridge: Harvard University Press, 221–38.

LANGER, S. K. (1948). *Philosophy in a new key.* New York: The New American Library (Mentor Book).

LECKY, P. (1951). *Self-consistency: A theory of personality.* New York: Island Press Cooperative.

LEVENSON, E. A. (1961). "Jam tomorrow—jam yesterday": Cultural time perception and neurotic problem-solving. *A review of general semantics, 18:* 167–78.

————, and KOHN, M. (1964). A demonstration clinic for college dropouts. *College health, 12:* 382–91.

LEVY, D. M. (1934). Experiments on the sucking reflex and social behavior of dogs. *Amer. J. Orthopsych., 4:* 203–24.

LEWIN, K. (1936). *Principles of topological psychology.* New York: McGraw-Hill Book Company.

————. (1942). Field theory and learning. In *The psychology of learn-*

ing. (41st yearbook, Pt. II.) Chicago: National Society for the Study of Education, 215–42.

LINDNER, M. (1955). *The fifty minute hour.* New York: Rinehart and Company.

LITTMAN, R. A. (1961). Psychology: The socially indifferent science. *Amer. Psychol., 16:* 232–36.

LOEWENSTEIN, R. M. (1952). *Christians and Jews: A psychological study.* New York: International Universities Press.

LYND, H. M. (1961). *Shame and the search for identity.* New York: Science Editions.

MAIMONIDES, M. (1931). *Morgengebet.* Officina Serpentis. (Location not given.)

MANN, TH. (1948). *The permanent Goethe.* New York: The Dial Press.

MAY, R. (1950). *The meaning of anxiety.* New York: The Ronald Press Company.

———. (1953). *Man's search for himself.* New York: W. W. Norton and Company.

———, ANGEL, E., and ELLENBERGER, H. F. (1958) *Existence: A new dimension in psychiatry and psychology.* New York: Basic Books.

McGINNIES, E. (1950). Personal values as determinants of word association. *J. abnorm. soc. Psychol., 45:* 28–36.

MENNINGER, K. M. (1946). *The human mind.* New York: Alfred A. Knopf.

MONTAGU, A. (1951). *On being human.* New York: Henry Schuman.

MONTGOMERY, K. C. (1954). The role of the exploratory drive in learning. *J. comp. physiol. Psychol., 47:* 60–64.

MOWRER, O. H. (1960). "Sin," the lesser of two evils. *Amer. Psychol., 15:* 301–4.

MULLAHY, P. (1948). *Oedipus myth and complex.* New York: Grove Press.

MUNROE, R. L. (1955). *Schools of psychoanalytic thought.* New York: The Dryden Press.

MURPHY, G. (1958a). *Human potentialities.* New York: Basic Books.
———. (1958b). Trends in the study of extrasensory perception. *Amer. Psychol., 13:* 69–76.

NEISSER, U. (1963). The imitation of man by machine. *Science, 139:* 193–97.

NIETZSCHE, F. (1883, 1891). Thus spoke Zarathustra. In W. Kaufmann (Ed.), *The portable Nietzsche.* New York: The Viking Press, 1954, pp. 103–339.

NUNBERG, H. (1955). *Principles of psychoanalysis*. New York: International Universities Press.

OPPENHEIMER, J. R. (1953). *Science and the common understanding*. New York: Simon and Schuster.

PEARCE, J., and NEWTON, S. (1963). *The conditions of human growth*. New York: The Citadel Press.

PINE, F. (1960). Incidental stimulation: A study of preconscious transformation. *J. abnorm. soc. Psychol.*, 60: 68–75.

PINNEAU, S. R. (1955a). The infantile disorders of hospitalism and anaclitic depression. *Psychol. Bull.*, 52: 429–52.

———. (1955b). Reply to Dr. Spitz. *Psychol. Bull.*, 52: 459–62.

PLANK, N. E., and PLANK, R. (1954). Emotional components in arithmetic learning as seen through autobiographies. *The psychoanalytic study of the child*, 9: 274–93.

POSTMAN, L., BRUNER, J. S., and McGINNIES, E. (1948). Personal values as selective factors in perception. *J abnorm. soc. Psychol.*, 43: 142–54.

PÖTZL, O. (1960). The relationship between experimentally induced dream images and indirect vision. *Psychol. issues*, 3: 41–120.

PRATT, J. G., and WOODRUFF, J. L. (1939). Size of stimulus symbols in extrasensory perception. *J. Parapsychol.*, 3: 121–58.

RANK, O. (1945). *Will therapy* and *Truth and reality*. New York: Alfred A. Knopf.

———. (1959). *The myth of the birth of the hero and other writings*. New York: Vintage Books.

RAPAPORT, D. (1951). The autonomy of the ego. In R. P. Knight (Ed.), *Psychoanalytic psychiatry and psychology*. New York: International Universities Press, 1954, 248–54.

———. (1958). The theory of ego autonomy: A generalization. *Bull. Menninger Clin.*, 22: 13–35.

———, GILL, M., and SCHAFER, R. (1945). *Diagnostic psychological testing*. (2 vols.) Chicago: The Year Book Publishers.

REDL, F., and WINEMAN, D. (1951). *Children who hate*. Glencoe, Ill.: Free Press.

REICH, WM. (1928). On character analysis. In R. Fliess (Ed.), *The psychoanalytic reader I*. New York: International Universities Press, 1948. 129–47.

———. (1949). *Character analysis*. New York: Orgone Institute Press.

REIK, TH. (1949). *Listening with the third ear*. New York: Farrar, Straus and Company.

ROGERS, C. R. (1939). *The clinical treatment of the problem child*. Boston: Houghton Mifflin Company.

————. (1942). *Counseling and psychotherapy*. Boston: Houghton Mifflin Company.

————. (1951). *Client-centered therapy*. Boston: Houghton Mifflin Company.

————. (1961). Two divergent trends. In R. May (Ed.), *Existential psychology*. New York: Random House, 85–93.

ROKEACH, M. (1960). *The open and closed mind*. New York: Basic Books.

ROSEN, J. N. (1947). The treatment of schizophrenic psychosis by direct analytic therapy. *Psychiat. Quart.*, *21*: 3–37.

ROSWELL, F., and NATCHEZ, G. (1964). *Reading disability: Diagnosis and treatment*. New York: Basic Books.

ROYCE, JOSEPH R. (1965). Psychology at the crossroads between the sciences and the humanities. In Joseph R. Royce (Ed.), *Psychology and the symbol: An interdisciplinary symposium*. New York: Random House, 16.

RUBINFINE, D. L. (1961). Perception, reality testing, and symbolism. *The psychoanalytic study of the child*, *16*: 73–89.

RUESCH, J. (1961). *Therapeutic communication*. New York: W. W. Norton and Company.

SALTER, A. (1952). *The case against psychoanalysis*. New York: Henry Holt and Company.

SALZINGER, K. (1959). Experimental manipulation of verbal behavior: A review. *J. gen. Psychol.*, *61*: 65–94.

SARTRE, J. P. (1956). *Being and nothingness*. New York: The Philosophical Library.

————. (1957). *Existentialism and human emotions*. New York: The Philosophical Library.

SCHACHTEL, E. G. (1959). *Metamorphosis*. New York: Basic Books.

SCHAFER, R. (1948). *The clinical application of psychological tests*. New York: International Universities Press.

SCHERER, W. B. (1948). Spontaneity as a factor in ESP. *J. Parapsychol.*, *12*: 126–47.

SCHMEIDLER, G. R. (1960). *ESP in relation to Rorschach test evaluation*. New York: Parapsychology Foundation.

————. (1961). Are there two kinds of telepathy? *J. Amer. Soc. psychic. Res.*, *55*: 87–97.

————. (1962). ESP and tests of perception. *J. Amer. Soc. psychic. Res.*, *56*: 48–51.

SEARLES, H. F. (1955). The informational value of the supervisor's emotional experience. *Psychiatry*, *18*: 135–46.

SEARS, R. R. (1943). *Survey of objective studies of psychoanalytic concepts*. New York: Social Science Research Council.

SHAW, G. B. (1951). *Saint Joan.* Baltimore: Penguin Books.
————. (1962). *Major Barbara.* Baltimore: Penguin Books.

SINGER, E. (1951). An investigation of some aspects of empathic behavior. (Abstract.) *Amer. Psychol., 6:* 309–10.

————, and BERKOWITZ, M. L. (1958). Additional investigations of some aspects of empathic behavior. (Abstract.) *Amer. Psychol. 13:* 356.

SMITH, M. B. (1961). "Mental health" reconsidered: A special case of the problem of values in psychology. *Amer. Psychol., 16:* 299–306.

SOLOMON, P., KUBZANSKY, P. E., LEIDERMAN, P. H., MENDELSON, J. H., TRUMBULL, R., and WEXLER, D. (Eds.) (1961). *Sensory deprivation.* Cambridge: Harvard University Press.

SPENCE, D. P., and HOLLAND, B. (1962). The restricting effects of awareness: A paradox and an explanation. *J. abnorm. soc. Psychol., 64:* 163–74.

SPENCER, H. (1860). The social organism. *Westminster rev., 73:* 90–121.

SPITZ, R. A. (1945). Hospitalism: An inquiry into the genesis of psychiatric conditions in early childhood. *The psychoanalytic study of the child, 1:* 53–74.
————. (1946). Hospitalism: II. *The psychoanalytic study of the child, 2:* 113–17.
————. (1955). Reply to Dr. Pinneau. *Psychol. bull., 52:* 453–58.
————. (1957). *No and yes.* New York: International Universities Press.

SULLIVAN, H. S. (1947). *Conceptions of modern psychiatry.* Washington, D.C.: The William Alanson White Psychiatric Foundation.
————. (1949). Notes on investigation, therapy, and education in psychiatry and their relations to schizophrenia. In P. Mullahy (Ed.), *A study of interpersonal relations.* New York: Hermitage Press, 192–210.
————. (1953). *The interpersonal theory of psychiatry.* New York: W. W. Norton and Company.
————. (1954). *The psychiatric interview.* New York: W. W. Norton and Company.
————. (1956). *Clinical studies in psychiatry.* New York: W. W. Norton and Company.
————. (1962). *Schizophrenia as a human process.* New York: W. W. Norton and Company.

SZASZ, T. S. (1957). *Pain and pleasure: A study in bodily feelings.* New York: Basic Books.
————. (1958). Psychiatry, ethics and the criminal law. *Columbia law rev., 58:* 183–98.
————. (1960). The myth of mental illness. *Amer. Psychol., 15:* 113–18.

————. (1961). The use of naming and the origin of the myth of mental illness. *Amer. Psychol., 16:* 59–65.

TARACHOW, S. (1963). *An introduction to psychotherapy.* New York: International Universities Press.

TAUBER, E. S. (1952). Observations on counter-transference phenomena. *Samiksa, 6:* 220–28.

————. (1954). Exploring the therapeutic use of counter-transference data. *Psychiatry, 17:* 332–36.

————. (1960). Sullivan's conception of cure. *Amer. J. Psychotherapy, 14:* 666–76.

————, and GREEN, M. R. (1959). *Prelogical experience.* New York: Basic Books.

THOMPSON, C. (1949a). Cultural conflicts of women in our society. *Samiksa, 3:* 125–34.

————. (1949b). Cultural pressures in the psychology of women. In P. Mullahy (Ed.), *A study of interpersonal relations.* New York: Hermitage Press, 130–46.

————. (1949c). The role of women in this culture. In P. Mullahy (Ed.), *A study of interpersonal relations.* New York: Hermitage Press, 147–61.

————. (1950a). *Psychoanalysis: Evolution and development.* New York: Hermitage House.

————. (1950b). Some effects of the derogatory attitude towards female sexuality. *Psychiatry, 13:* 349–54.

————. (1952). Counter-transference. *Samiksa, 6:* 205–11.

TILLICH, P. (1952). *The courage to be.* New Haven: Yale University Press.

TRILLING, L. (1957). *The liberal imagination.* Garden City: Doubleday and Company (Anchor Book).

TURKEL, H. (1955). The generalized occurrence of perceptual defense to anxiety-provoking words: An experimental test of the concept under "alerting" and "non-alerting" conditions. Unpublished doctoral dissertation, New York University.

ULLMAN, M. (1958). Dreams and the therapeutic process. *Psychiatry, 21:* 123–31.

WALDFOGEL, S., COOLIDGE, J. C., and HAHN, P. B. (1959). The development, meaning, and management of school phobia. *Amer. J. Orthopsychiat., 27:* 754–80.

WECHSLER, D. (1944). *The measurement of adult intelligence.* Baltimore: The Williams and Wilkins Company.

WEIGERT, E. (1949). Existentialism and its relation to psychotherapy. *Psychiatry, 12:* 399–412.

————. (1961). The nature of sympathy in the art of psychotherapy. *Psychiatry, 24:* 187–96.

WERTHEIMER, M. (1959). *Productive thinking.* New York: Harper & Brothers.

WHEELIS, A. (1958). *The quest for identity.* New York: W. W. Norton and Company.

WHITE, M. J. (1952). Sullivan and treatment. In P. Mullahy (Ed.), *The contributions of Harry Stack Sullivan.* New York: Hermitage House, 117–50.

WHITE, R. W. (1959). Motivation reconsidered: The concept of competence. *Psychol. rev., 66:* 297–333.

WHYTE, W. H., JR. (1956). *The organization man.* New York: Simon and Schuster.

WILSON, C. (1956). *The outsider.* Boston: Houghton Mifflin Company.

WOLFE, J. B., and KAPLON, M. D. (1941). Effect of amount of reward and consummative activity on learning in chickens. *J. comp. Psychol., 31:* 353–61.

WOLPE, J. (1958). *Psychotherapy by reciprocal inhibition.* Palo Alto: Stanford University Press.

WOLSTEIN, B. (1954). *Transference: Its meaning and function in psychoanalytic therapy.* New York: Grune and Stratton.
————. (1959). *Countertransference.* New York: Grune and Stratton.
————. (1960). Transference: Historical roots and current concepts in psychoanalytic theory and practice. *Psychiatry, 23:* 159–72.

WYATT, F. (1963). The reconstruction of the individual and the collective past. In R. R. White (Ed.), *The study of lives: Essays on personality in honor of Henry A. Murray.* New York: Atherton Press, 304–20.

ZULLIGER, H. (1963). *Schwierige Kinder.* Bern: Verlag Hans Huber.

On the Limitation and Danger of Theory in Psychotherapy

IN 1896—QUITE EARLY IN HIS CAREER AS A PSYCHOANALYST—
Freud published a short, often overlooked, but nonetheless
highly significant paper, *Further Remarks on the Neuro-
Psychoses of Defense*. It is important not only because Freud
developed there for the first time the concept of projection
but also because he described in it his early ideas about psychoses in general and paranoia in particular. Furthermore,
the paper is noteworthy because it sounded quite optimistic
about the possibility that psychoanalysis could understand
them and eventually treat them. Freud wrote:

> For a considerable time I have harboured a suspicion
> that paranoia, too—or classes of cases which fall under
> the heading of paranoia—is a psychosis of defence; that
> is to say, that, like hysteria and obsessions, it proceeds
> from the repression of distressing memories and that its
> symptoms are determined in their form by the content of
> what has been repressed. Paranoia must, however, have a
> special method or mechanism of repression which is
> peculiar to it . . . [1896, pp. 174-75].

It was on the basis of these thoughts that Freud set out to

treat Mrs. P., and since repressed sexual impulses were to be the foundation of *all* disorders, psychoses, too, were, as far as he could see, amenable to psychoanalytic therapy.

But in 1937, forty-one years later, when Freud published *Analysis Terminable and Interminable,* his outlook concerning the therapeutic efficacy of psychoanalysis was rather gloomy. No longer did he think that psychotic states could be treated analytically, for he had concluded that a transference relationship, as he had defined it and considered by him the *sine qua non* of analytic therapy, could not be developed with a psychotic patient. (His reasons for this belief he had spelled out in other papers [1914b, 1924c, 1931, 1933].) The outlook vis-à-vis obsessions and compulsions seemed to him dim and even in hysteria he saw the prognosis for analytic success less promising than he had suggested earlier.

Why had Freud come to such depressing conclusions? The answer must be found in the theory he had developed about the nature of human resistance to consciousness. He had concluded that this resistance to consciousness was too powerful to allow for much insight and subsequent change to take place. These considerations led him to pen in 1937 the highly pessimistic comments quoted earlier.[1] What is obvious is that Freud's therapeutic expectations had diminished markedly while his metapsychology and his basic theory concerning the etiology of emotional disorders had remained intact.

That Freud was not likely to change his conceptions concerning the nature of man and the origins of his ills should have been obvious to thoughtful observers. Some modifications, to be sure of minor extent, could be expected, but clearly since 1905, when he had published *Three Contributions to the Theory of Sex* and developed the idea that the aim of all instincts was their at least temporary self-extinction, it became apparent that the theoretical structure he was in the process of evolving might be refined but would not be changed significantly. The publication of *Beyond the Pleasure Principle* was merely the culmination of a line of thought heralded much earlier. Freud's tendency to maintain vigorously a position

[1] See p. 194.

once he was committed to it—at least from 1905 on—is also illustrated by a characteristic comment he made in the course of his discussion of the case of little Hans. He said:

> Strictly speaking, I learnt nothing new from this analysis, nothing that I had not already been able to discover (though often less distinctly and more indirectly) from other patients analysed at a more advanced age [1909, p. 147].

This remarkable and progressively hardening insistence upon the validity of a theoretical structure even in the face of its failure when applied in therapeutic contexts is of course quite understandable when one remembers the virulent opposition Freud had encountered. And such insistence upon the validity of the theoretical structure was not restricted to Freud but also gripped many of his followers. This intensity of devotion to orthodox psychoanalytic theory led Eissler (1965), one of Freud's most faithful students, to outline a peculiar defense of the practice of psychoanalysis by non-medical personnel. His defense is grounded in the curious premise that psychoanalysis does *not* represent a therapeutic tool but instead is simply a method of research in personality theory. Therefore, Eissler argues, medicine cannot object to such research investigations when carried out by others. Thus Eissler, himself a physician, attempts to establish a strange demarcation between the practice of psychotherapy and the practice of psychoanalysis. And all this was said for the sake of keeping a theory of personality and a theory of psychopathology intact.

Let us turn to another eminent theorist. In 1912 Jung (1956b) published the first version of a manuscript known to the English-speaking world as *Symbols in Transformation* but more commonly referred to as the Miller papers. There Jung takes the psychotic break of a young American woman, Miss Miller, and her account of the episode as his point of departure to reflect on the nature of psychosis and its analytic treatment. In the epilogue to his book Jung mused:

> The aim of psychotherapy is therefore to narrow down and eventually abolish the dissociation by integrating the

tendencies of the unconscious into the conscious mind.
. . . If . . . there is already a tendency to dissociation,
perhaps dating back to youth, then every advance of the
unconscious only increases the gap between it and consciousness. . . . Had I treated Miss Miller I would have
had to tell her some of the things of which I have written
in this book, in order to help her build up her conscious
mind to the point where it could have understood the
contents of the collective unconscious. Without the help
of these "representations collectives," which have psychotherapeutic value even for the primitives, it is not possible to understand the archetypical associations of the
unconscious [p. 442].

Indeed, this sounds most hopeful. Clearly, Jung thought that
he could have helped Miss Miller psychotherapeutically; alas,
she had not consulted him. And the help he would have
offered her would have been a derivative of his particular
theoretical understanding of human experience and of his
understanding of the psychological foundations underlying
such experience.

But in 1958, forty-six years later, Jung wrote a paper, *Schizophrenia* (read the preceding year at the Second International
Congress for Psychiatry), and there he presented a much more
pessimistic picture. His remarks were full of references to
toxic agents, to the physiology and neuroanatomy of schizophrenic predisposition, and to brain localizations which presumably contribute significantly to psychotic manifestations.
Nothing had changed in his theory concerning the content and
the meaning of schizophrenia as he had outlined it in the Miller papers: the archaic forms of the collective unconscious rise
into consciousness and are strenuously opposed and dissociated. But while he thought that the neurotic responded to
the enlightenment offered by the therapist, the psychotic, he
concluded, did not respond. And this led him to comment:

If, therefore, archaic forms appear especially frequently
in schizophrenia, this points in my view to the fact that
the biological foundations of the psyche are affected to a

far greater extent in this disease than in neuroses [p. 262].

And he felt forced to conclude that therefore "fairly narrow limits . . . are set to the psychotherapy" (p. 265), at least in severe cases.

Just as Freud's refusal to change his theory was to be expected, so was Jung's reluctance to modify his conceptions even in the face of therapeutic failure not too surprising. As early as 1907, when he published his *The Psychology of Dementia Praecox,* he was preoccupied with archaic complexes which he said came to the fore and overwhelmed the patient, and in the very same book he wrote of the possibility that a toxin interfered with the psychotic's adequate management of these complexes. A theory had been launched and only minor alterations were to be instituted no matter what the empirical and therapeutic data might bring. His insistence upon the validity of his position once he had proposed it is highlighted by a well-known episode in Jung's life.[2] He reported a dream in which he felt compelled to kill *Siegfried.* In the dream he went out with a rifle and when Siegfried appeared on the crest of a mountain he killed him. Terrified and fearful of being discovered, he was saved by a heavy rain which washed away all traces of his crime. Upon awakening Jung felt that he would have to kill himself if he did not understand the dream and conveniently came to think that it meant that he had to kill his own wish to be a hero and that he had to develop more humility. The fact that the dream occurred just about the time when he finally broke with *Sigmund* Freud of course was overlooked, for Jung had to understand his dream within his own system of thought. By interpreting his dream in terms of his particular method of understanding human reactions, his own theories would gain greater validity. Freud had written of dreams as expressions of wish fulfillment; Jung had written about dreams as expressions of insight about one's true life line. To maintain his own theory

[2] For a penetrating discussion of this episode and certain of its implications see Fromm (1964), pp. 43–44.

all recognition of potential death wishes directed against Freud and the fulfillment of these wishes in his own dream had to be rejected.

Freud's interpretations of his own dreams of course also proceeded in accordance with the dream theory he had developed. And his adhering to his model of dream understanding, i.e., the wish-fulfillment hypothesis, also resulted in his missing potentially very useful insights about himself. One of the dreams Freud reports readily illustrates the point.

In his monumental book on the interpretation of dreams, Freud (1900) presents several of his own dreams. One of them, known as the Irma dream, contains sequences worthy of re-examination in the context of the present discussion. In this dream Freud meets a former patient, Irma, who had benefited only slightly from Freud's psychotherapeutic efforts, and now in his dream she is once again quite ill. Freud is alarmed and annoyed by this relapse and reproaches Irma by telling her: " 'If you still get pains, it's really only your fault' " (p. 107). In the course of the dream Freud becomes convinced that her present suffering is due to an infection brought about by the injection of a drug administered to Irma by his friend Otto, a medical procedure of which Freud thoroughly disapproved. He concludes his report of the dream by recalling that toward its end the thought had crossed his mind: *"Injections of that sort ought not to be made so thoughtlessly. . . . And probably the syringe had not been clean"* (p. 107). Freud is remarkably candid in commenting on the understanding of his dream although he does admit to omissions of important insights revealed by it to him when he says:

> But considerations which arise in the case of every dream of my own restrain me from pursuing my interpretive work. If anyone should feel tempted to express a hasty condemnation of my reticence, I would advise him to make the experiment of being franker than I am [p. 121].

But Freud also concludes that despite such justifiable omissions the message of the dream is readily understandable:

> The dream represents a particular state of affairs as I

should have wished it to be. *Thus its content was the fulfillment of a wish and its motive was a wish* [pp. 118–19].

Clearly Freud thought that the various symbols and metaphors employed in this dream depicted, though in *obscuring* fashion, two aspects of his emotional life: first, the desire to rid himself of the discomfort occasioned by his sense that Irma had derived very little benefit from seeing him; and, second, his eagerness to take revenge on his friend Otto by making him the guilty one, for Freud thought that Otto had been subtly but also all too persistently reminding him of his at least partial failure in working with Irma. The Irma dream he thought depicted a reality situation of professional backbiting, each participant being accurately represented and appearing in his own image and all that was implied was an all too human wish to be free of blame and to blame mishaps on others.

Yet, Freud is much more subtle and deft in his theoretical discussions of dream material when in a later section of his book he insists that dreams are always "completely egoistic" (p. 322) and that the "concealing" quality of a dream and its symbols can be removed most adequately when one keeps in mind this "egoistic" quality of the dream. He remarked specifically:

Whenever my own ego does not appear in the content of a dream, but only some extraneous person, I may safely assume that my own ego lies *concealed* [emphasis mine —E.S.] by identification, behind this other person; I can insert my own ego into the context. On other occasions when my own *ego* does appear in the dream, the situation in which it occurs may teach me that some other person lies *concealed* [emphasis mine—E.S.], by identification, behind my ego. In that case the dream should warn me to transfer myself, when I am interpreting the dream, the *concealed* [emphasis mine—E.S.] common element attached to this other person. There are also dreams in which my ego appears along with other people who, when the identification is resolved, are revealed once again as my ego [pp. 322–23].

Freud's emphasis upon concealment in dream symbolization is striking. But equally striking is Freud's reluctance to follow his own guidelines in interpreting the Irma dream. Were one to employ the suggestions embodied in the quotation cited above, one would be led to conclude that Otto represents part of Freud himself and that the dream depicts a grave self-accusation based on an insight and a serious suspicion: that the dreamer who had always prided himself on scientific meticulousness sensed an important scientific failing of his own, namely his propensity for using a dirty syringe, by definition a syringe that had been used with another patient earlier, a syringe now inappropriately employed with another person. Might it not be that Freud stated, as unequivocally as metaphor allows, the dim recognition of a dangerous tendency within himself: the inclination to apply indiscriminately insights developed in one setting to another, to use the same old tool inappropriately over and over again. If these inferences have merit then one would be justified in concluding that his symbolic representation of applying a dirty syringe reflects Freud's mechanistic tendencies in understanding human behavior, tendencies which made it difficult for Irma to recover fully. Thus, far from concealing or obscuring, Freud's symbolization outlines as graphically as possible the nature of his inner situation and the dreamer's recognition of this particular aspect of himself. Indeed, Freud's dream may well reflect an identity crisis in his life as Erikson (1954), in discussing the Irma dream, has suggested, though an identity crisis with implications and consequences different from those outlined in Erikson's paper.

The thought developed thus far, simply stated, suggests that immersion in theoretical formulations and concern with system building move seminal thinkers from their original therapeutic optimism to stark therapeutic pessimism. Freud and Jung are not alone in this sequence of development. Several other examples could be cited but the discussion will be restricted to but one more illustration. Even as flexible a thinker as Fromm became a pessimistic prisoner of his own theory, though clearly to a much lesser degree than Freud and Jung became enchained. His emphasis during the sixties upon what he calls necrophilia (1964), a defect which when severe makes therapeutic intervention, to his mind, most difficult if not impossible altogether, also represents an instance of growing pessimism engendered by increasing theoretical concerns.

Tracing Fromm's development of a personality theory one notes two persistent central themes: (1) man's urge to transcend himself, be this through acts of construction or acts of destruction; and (2) the problem of freedom of choice. These issues have been and remain Fromm's foci of interest from his earliest publications, some of them incorporated in his book *The Dogma of Christ and Other Essays on Religion, Psychology and Culture* (1963) through today. And throughout his writings there is, of course, his constant concern with the role social, economic, and cultural forces play in influencing the choices individuals make, in determining whether they chose productive or non-productive orientations, including all these terms denote in Fromm's theoretical constructions. To illustrate, in 1941 Fromm remarked:

> . . . [man] has no choice but to unite himself with the world in the spontaneity of love and productive work or else seek a kind of security by such ties with the world as destroy his freedom and the integrity of his individual self [p. 23].

Fromm left little doubt that he thought that given the proper environmental circumstances or that within the process of adequate therapy the former choice represented the genuine direction of the individual.

Similarly, in 1947 he concluded:

> If I repeat now the question raised in the beginning of the book, whether we have reason to be proud and hopeful, the answer is again in the affirmative, but with the one qualification which follows from what we have discussed throughout: neither the good nor the evil outcome is automatic or preordained. The decision rests with man. It rests upon his ability to take himself, his life and happiness seriously; on his willingness to face his and his

society's moral problems. It rests upon his courage to be himself and to be for himself [p. 250].

Again Fromm left little doubt of his conviction that everyone was capable of such a courageous effort given the proper therapeutic and/or environmental setting. This optimism moved him to remark a few years later—in 1951—that destructiveness "is only the alternative to creativeness" (p. 38) because he saw the former as a *secondary* potentiality in man and considered his ability to develop love and reason as the *primary* inclination (p. 37).

But as time progressed Fromm's outlook also grew less and less hopeful. This change is reflected in some comments he offered in 1964 and even more pointedly in the content of some of his lectures. Consider these remarks:

> Man is inclined to regress and to move forward. . . . If both inclinations are still in some balance he is free to choose. . . . If, however, his heart has hardened to such a degree that there is no longer a balance of inclinations he is no longer free to choose [1964, p. 149].

And later:

> Man's heart can harden; it can become inhuman. . . . We must become aware in order to choose the good— but no awareness will help us if we have lost the capacity to be moved by the distress of another human being, by the friendly gaze of another person, by the song of a bird, by the greenness of the grass. If man becomes indifferent to life there is no longer any hope that he can choose the good [p. 150].

If we translate Fromm's term "good" into psychological well-being and understand awareness as he does as the aim of psychotherapy, then it becomes apparent that he came to believe that there are pathologies—what he calls "hardening of the heart"—beyond hope of cure. While Fromm has so far refrained from spelling out in print the conditions bringing about this hardening, he has done so in his lectures: he proposes that early social and psychological experience *and* constitutional factors must be held responsible for the development of such a sorry state of affairs.

It becomes apparent once again that a theorist's basic conceptions have remained intact while his outlook has changed. Fromm's definition of health and his definition of pathology, his understanding of personality development and his ideas about therapy, all remain more or less unchanged. What is, however, once again markedly diminished, especially in Fromm's lectures, is his early therapeutic hopefulness. And so, despite the temperamental, philosophical, and theoretical differences which separate the three men discussed, they share the common road which leads from a therapeutic optimism to a more or less pronounced therapeutic pessimism.

The question arises: what makes for this growing pessimism in some of the greatest minds the discipline of psychoanalysis has produced? What makes for their return to or adoption of notions and assumptions about basic and irremediable defects, be they inherited or acquired? Certainly research findings cannot be held responsible. Although the search for the toxin Jung spoke about goes on in many places—and, incidentally, Freud also had some ideas about a basic psychopathogenic toxin—despite these efforts over the years nobody has presented data in any way convincing. Research investigating genetic factors associated with psychopathology has been equally disappointing. And Fromm's concept of an irreversible hardening of the heart and the possibility of man adopting an immutable necrophiliac attitude, while interesting, is at least at this point unverified and possibly altogether unverifiable.

Perhaps the aging process could be held responsible. Few men if any can look with equanimity at the decline of their lives, and so the idea arises that this therapeutic pessimism is potentially a reflection of a generalized attitude associated with advancing age. But as we shall see in a moment, other authors, notably Fromm-Reichman, have shown no such gloomy therapeutic tendency while aging. This brings to mind Erikson (1964), who, in one of his profound and thought-provoking essays, has suggested that despair in advanced age is the outcome of earlier and unresolved identity crises. I am inclined to believe that Erikson's thought has relevance to the present discussion, but in order to clarify my point I must first present additional observations.

The obvious thought suggests itself that disappointing therapeutic results led them to search for reasons which would make their failures understandable; and that they searched for explanations which did not demand of them the consideration of the very real possibility that personal investment in their respective theories at least contributed significantly to the miscarriage of some of their therapeutic efforts. Other prominent persons in the field of psychotherapy, though outstanding more for their contributions to the *clinical literature* than to *theory*, have also experienced failures, but their failures led them to modify their own theoretical understanding without giving way to pessimism concerning the efficacy of analytic therapy and the possibility of human growth.

Fromm-Reichman is an outstanding member of this group. She was quite candid in discussing her clinical work and the difficulties she encountered. What apparently characterized her work more than anything else, however, was an absence of any preconceived theoretical notions. Not that she was unfamiliar with theories, not that she was immune to being occasionally caught up in efforts to push a particular theoretical understanding, but she was apparently capable of dismissing her or anyone else's theory when it appeared worthless in truly understanding the patient. Hannah Green (1967), Fromm-Reichman's most famous psychotic patient, in accepting the Fromm-Reichman Memorial Award has ascribed her own recovery to a large extent to this willingness on the part of her therapist to dismiss preconceived notions. Specifically, Miss Green remarked about Fromm-Reichman:

> She had the endearing quality of not exploiting her patients to prove herself or her theories.

Throughout Searles' (1965) essentially clinical papers, there runs the same strain of willingness to abandon theory and *a priori* notions coupled with a remarkable willingness to hear what is to be heard and *not* to hear it through the hearing aid of a cherished metapsychological system. And Sullivan was always more interested in hearing and building theories on the basis of what he had heard than hearing and understanding his patients in terms of theories previously developed. As one examines the contributions of these authors, one finds them singularly devoid of the despair and pessimism concerning therapeutic efficacy which is so prominently associated with authors whose theories are metapsychologically oriented, especially when they discuss severe pathologies.

Sullivan, for instance, whom Tauber (1960), one of his most serious students, rightly described as a pragmatist, in one of his very last papers presented shortly before his untimely death, *Notes on the Investigation, Therapy, and Education in Psychiatry and Their Relations to Schizophrenia* (1960), was quite optimistic about the possibility of reaching and helping the psychotic psychotherapeutically. Typical of his thoughts concerning this possibility was the comment:

> The possibilities of therapeutic intervention in schizophrenic situations are, therefore, to an extraordinary extent a simple function of the psychiatrist's skill at avoiding incidental, unintentional collision with the patient's self-system. With the bitterest feeling about the human costs involved, I have to say that the testing ground of one's psychiatric skill lies in this area of disturbed interpersonal relations [p. 202].

This implicit optimism runs throughout all of Sullivan's contributions. Or consider Fromm-Reichman's comments in 1939:

> Schizophrenics are capable of developing workable relationships and transference reactions, but successful psychotherapy with schizophrenics depends upon whether the analyst understands the significance of these transference phenomena and meets them appropriately [p. 126].

Many years later, in 1957, when she published a paper on *Basic Problems in the Psychotherapy of Schizophrenics*, precisely the same ring of optimism prevailed even though or perhaps because in the course of the years certain of her basic

conceptions concerning the fundamental problems of schizophrenics had undergone significant modification. This openness to change, this willingness to abandon cherished propositions, and this readiness to let the data lead her, these qualities
are most pointedly illustrated by her starting on a new course
of investigation shortly before her death, although precursors
of this direction on which she was about to embark can be
found in several earlier papers. The draft of a paper, *On
Loneliness* (1959), posthumously published, pictures her as
ready to examine new dimensions and willing to abandon
anxiety in its usual sense as the cherished and central theme
of therapeutic investigation.

Similarly, Searles' freedom from preconceived theoretical
shackles makes it possible for him to remark in 1963:

> . . . it is my experience that even the most otherworldly,
> even the most "crazy" manifestations of schizophrenia
> come to reveal meaningfulness and reality-relatedness
> not only as transference reactions to the therapist, but,
> even beyond this, as delusional identifications with real
> aspects of the therapist's own personality. When we come
> to see such meaning in the schizophrenic individual's
> behavior, we come more and more to realize not only
> that he is now in the human fold but that, if only there
> had been someone all along wise and perceptive enough
> to know, and brave enough to acknowledge, he has never
> really been out of it [p. 716].

This refreshing simplicity of thought and the absence of
metapsychological constructs make Searles the astute listener
he is and consequently a superb non-despairing therapist.

These observations bring me to my basic point. I do not
know whether Jung was right or wrong; and the same ignorance holds true when it comes to my appreciation of Fromm's
insights. Future research and future conceptualizations may
prove one or the other correct in his particular understanding
of mental phenomena, though I have of course my personal
preferences and their nature has been all too apparent throughout the pages of this book. What strikes me as more important
than the question of the correctness or the shortcomings of a

particular theoretical position is the dangerous possibility that he who is the originator or the vociferous proponent of a given approach becomes the captive of his own creation and is in danger of subsequently not fully hearing his patient, for he may become wittingly or unwittingly more interested in proving himself right and in proving the value of his creation than in genuinely listening and hearing the other person. Here we see the great danger of the therapist's transference producing the patient's countertransference—the exact reverse of what is usually proposed as the likely though unfortunate sequence of events. The patient confronting a therapist who has a theoretical ax to grind must have the uncomfortable experience that once again the very same things which were experienced as most painful in his own life are being re-enacted: once again he is a pawn, a tool in the service of increasing someone else's self-esteem with the added and all too familiar bind that nobody is willing to acknowledge this, that everything is presumably said and done in his best interest. It is hard to escape the sense that Dora's unfortunate later development was in a large measure the outcome of Freud's intense eagerness to prove a point. For what other reason than to prove his point could Freud have overlooked the abysmal shabbiness with which Dora's father had treated not only his daughter, but also Freud himself, the doctor to whom he literally owed his life? Of course Freud knew and acknowledged the fact that Dora saw correctly what went on around her, but he was more interested in helping her uncover her presumably incestuous impulses than in helping her face her own reluctance to see the father fully for what he was and to recognize how this reluctance maintained a more profoundly incestuous attachment to him than mere physical desires imply.

Only when theory becomes secondary, only when theory construction becomes an *a posteriori* rather than an *a priori* endeavor, is there any chance of therapeutic hearing, any chance of therapeutic success, and any protection against the therapist's despair. Only when the practitioner is clear about his identity as a healer and can resolve and reject his urge to be at the same moment also a system builder, only then can he hear and only then can his patient hear him meaningfully. The early unresolved identity crisis from which so many in our discipline suffer and the identity crisis from which many of our greatest theorists have suffered is the confusion between our dual roles of scientists and practitioners. And so they and we unfortunately all too often long to be a system builder while sitting with the patient when all our client desires is our understanding him. Patients seem remarkably willing to forgive the inanities all too often thrown at them; they seem remarkably willing to understand that at best we know little; but they seem rightfully unwilling to forgive us our intentions of having them prove us right in our theoretical preconceptions. And indeed, a patient would be remarkably disturbed if he reached sanity simply to satisfy the therapist's vain investment in his theory.

Therefore it seems to me that all of us can take a leaf from what is reputed to be Maimonides' (1931) morning prayer referred to earlier. (See p. 9.) In it Maimon implores the deity not only to give him the strength necessary to do God's work so as to further growth and life; but he also spells out the specifics of this strength and among them he sees as essential the strength to listen to all his more learned and wiser colleagues have to say—but then he asks God to give him the courage to discard all he has heard if it makes no sense or seems inapplicable to the problem under consideration so that he may see clearly what is relevant and genuinely true.

I am not proposing to do away with theory. Far from it. Theory has its rightful place as a guide in the wilderness and as the potentially helpful summation of serious reflections carried out by our colleagues and teachers, reflections which they are willing to share with us. We must respectfully attend to them and we must make every effort to understand the intellectual and emotional struggles which go into all thoughtful theory. I am merely suggesting that the insight of this wise physician, Maimon's insight of skepticism, must also be considered seriously as a basic guideline for all creative understanding and for all curative efforts.

ADDITIONAL REFERENCES

EISSLER, K. R. (1965). *Medical orthodoxy and the future of psychoanalysis.* New York: International Universities Press.

ERIKSON, E. H. (1964). Identity and uprootedness in our time. In E. H. Erikson, *Insight and responsibility.* New York: W. W. Norton and Company, 81–107.

FREUD, S. (1896). Further remarks on the neuro-psychoses of defence. In S. Freud, *Standard edition.* London: The Hogarth Press, 1953, *3:* 159–85.

———. (1924c). Neurosis and psychosis. In S. Freud, *Standard edition.* London: The Hogarth Press, 1953, *19:* 149–53.

———. (1931). Libidinal types. In S. Freud, *Standard edition.* London: The Hogarth Press, 1953, *21:* 215–20.

FROMM, E. (1963). *The dogma of Christ and other essays on religion, psychology, and culture.* New York: Holt, Rinehart & Winston.

———. (1964). *The heart of man.* New York: Harper & Row.

FROMM-REICHMAN, F. (1939). Transference problems in schizophrenia. In D. M. Bullard (Ed.), *Psychoanalysis and psychotherapy.* Chicago: University of Chicago Press, 1959, 117–28.

———. (1957). Basic problems in the psychotherapy of schizophrenics. In D. M. Bullard (Ed.), *Psychoanalysis and psychotherapy.* Chicago: University of Chicago Press, 1959, 210–17.

GREEN, H. (1967). "In praise of my doctor"—Frieda Fromm-Reichman. *Contemporary Psychoanalysis, 4:* 73–77.

JUNG, C. G. (1907). The psychology of dementia praecox. In C. G. Jung, *The psychogenesis of mental disease.* New York: Pantheon Books (Bollinger Series XX), 1960, *3:* 3–151.

———. (1958). Schizophrenia. In C. G. Jung, *The psychogenesis of mental disease.* New York: Pantheon Books (Bollinger Series XX), 1960, *3:* 256–72.

SEARLES, H. F. (1963). Transference psychosis in the psychotherapy of schizophrenia. In H. F. Searles, *Collected papers on schizophrenia and related subjects.* New York: International Universities Press, 654–716.

SULLIVAN, H. S. (1950). Notes on the investigation, therapy, and education in psychiatry and their relations to schizophrenia. In P. Mullahy (Ed.), *A study of interpersonal relations*. New York: Hermitage House, 192–210.

INDEX